Peach Girl
Change of Heart

by Miwa Ueda

4

Los Angeles • Tokyo • London

ピーチガール

12

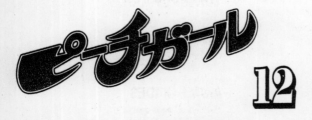

Translator - Ray Yoshimoto
English Adaptation - Jodi Bryson
Retouch and Lettering - Vivian Choi
Cover Layout - Anna Kernbaum
Graphic Designer - James Lee

Senior Editor - Julie Taylor
Managing Editor - Jill Freshney
Production Coordinator - Antonio DePietro
Production Manager - Jennifer Miller
Art Director - Matthew Alford
Director of Editorial - Jeremy Ross
VP of Production - Ron Klamert
President & C.O.O. - John Parker
Publisher & C.E.O. - Stuart Levy

Email: editor@TOKYOPOP.com
Come visit us online at www.TOKYOPOP.com

A  Manga

TOKYOPOP Inc.
5900 Wilshire Blvd. Suite 2000
Los Angeles, CA 90036

ISBN: 1-59182-197-5

First TOKYOPOP® printing: September 2003

10 9 8 7 6 5 4 3 2 1

Printed in the USA

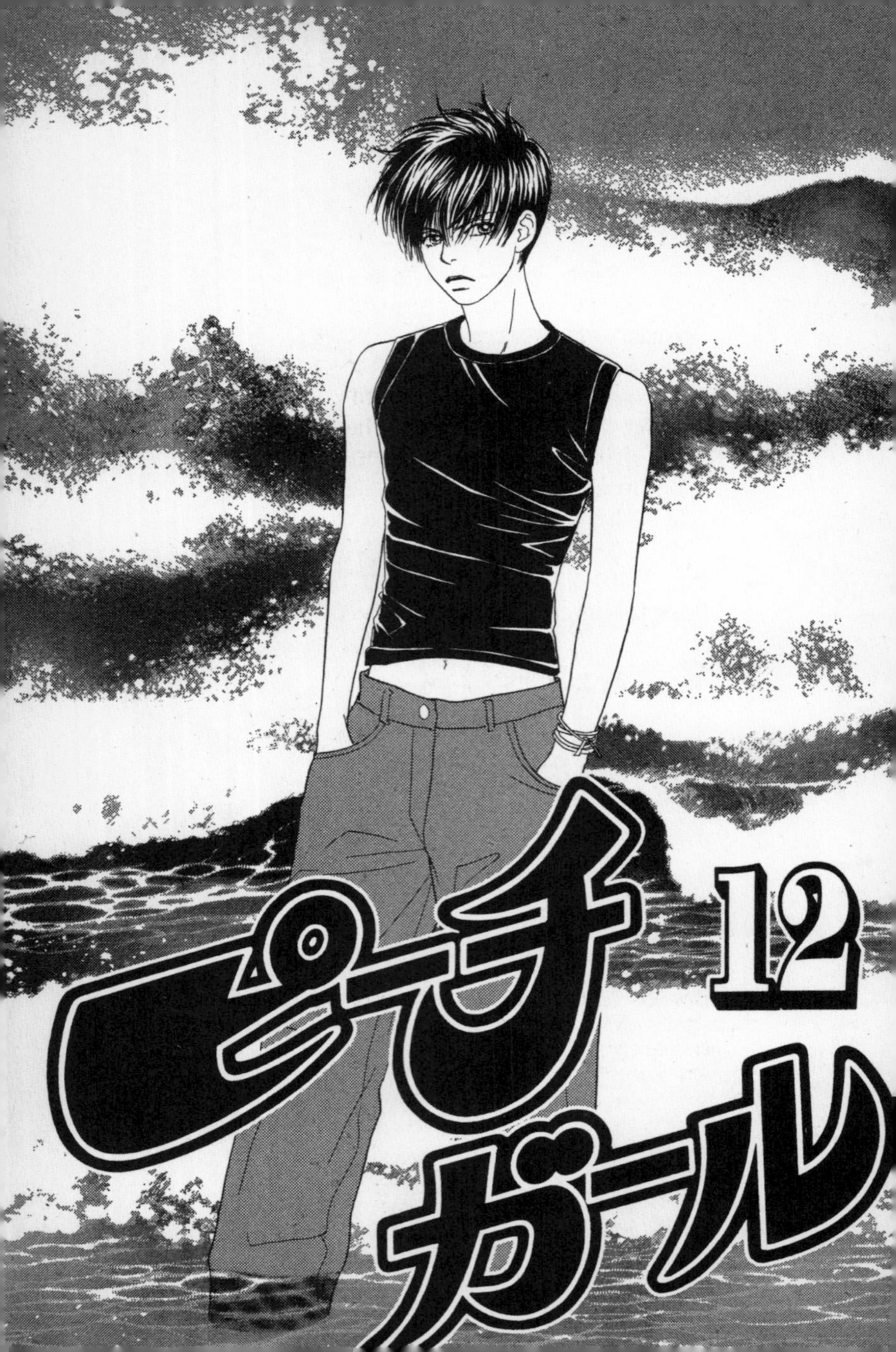
ピーチガール
12

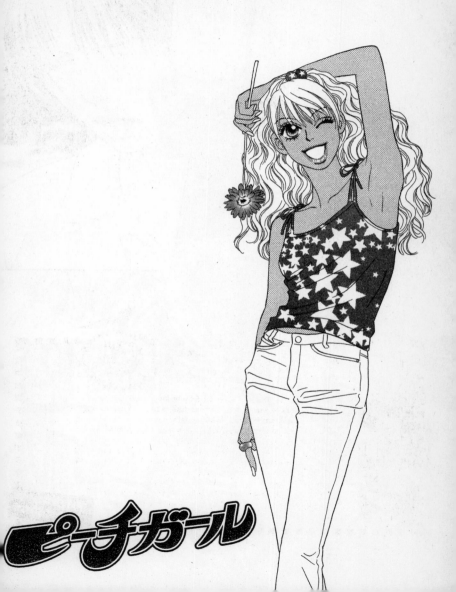

ピーチガール

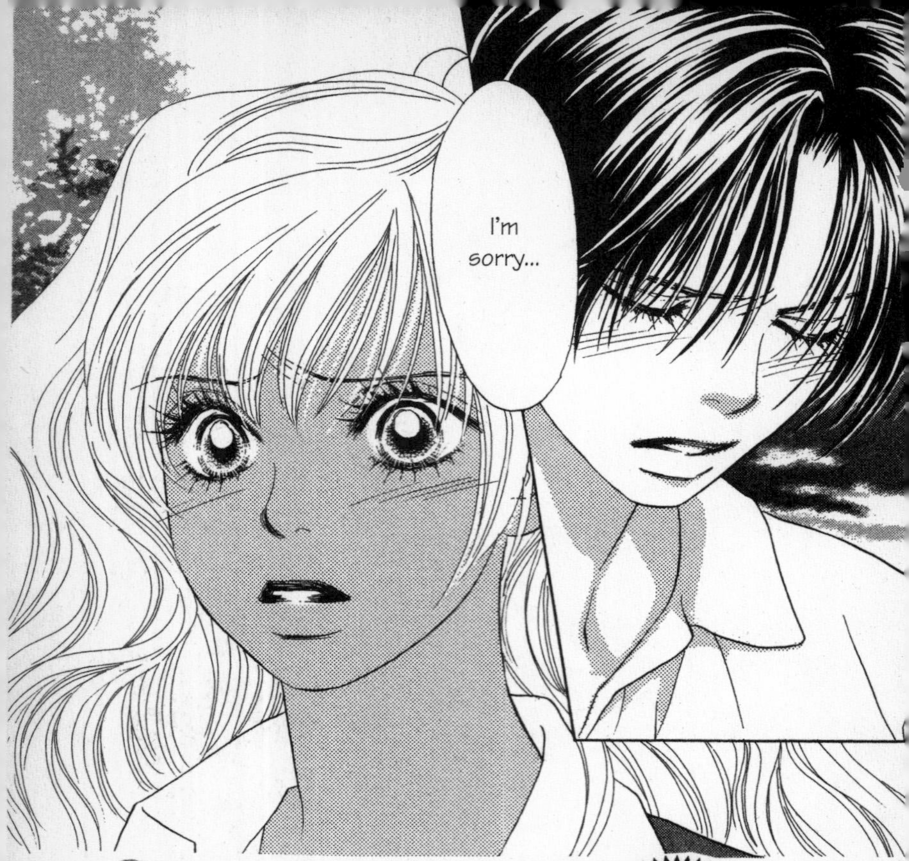
I'm sorry...

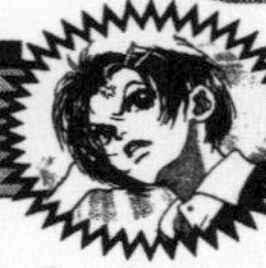

MOMO vs. SAE

Death match, the whole story!!

Momo and Toji were happily in love. But Sae, who always wants what Momo has, stole Toji away by blackmailing. Momo eventually gets over the breakup and begins dating Kiley. But into the picture comes Kiley's older brother, Ryo. Ryo puts the charms on Sae and begins to manipulate her. Then, Momo and Kiley are about to make love! But at the last minute, Kiley backs off. A confused Momo consults Misao, but discovers the same picture in Misao's photo album as the one Kiley's been carrying around in his student handbook. Momo stresses out that Kiley is still in love with Misao...

Everything you need to know.

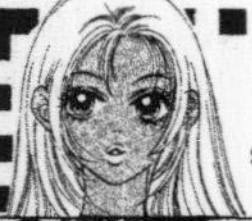

MOMO ADACHI
Currently dating Kiley. Shocked by his revelation!

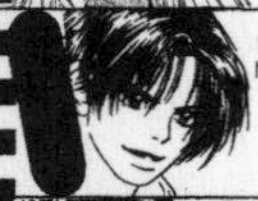

KILEY OKAYASU,
Momo's boyfriend. Happily dating Momo, but is Misao his true love?!

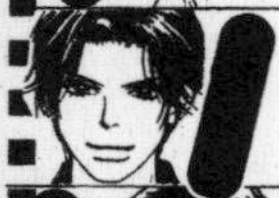

RYO
The male version of Sae. Kiley's older brother. Game designer. Can he conquer the evil Sae?

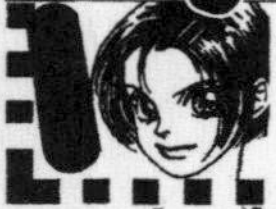

SAE KASHIWAGI
Momo's sworn enemy. Currently dating Toji, but now in love with Ryo.

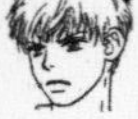

TOJI TOJIKAMORI
Momo's former boyfriend. Sae blackmailed him into dumping Momo for her.

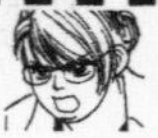

MISAO
The school nurse. Formerly Kiley's tutor, now in love with Ryo.

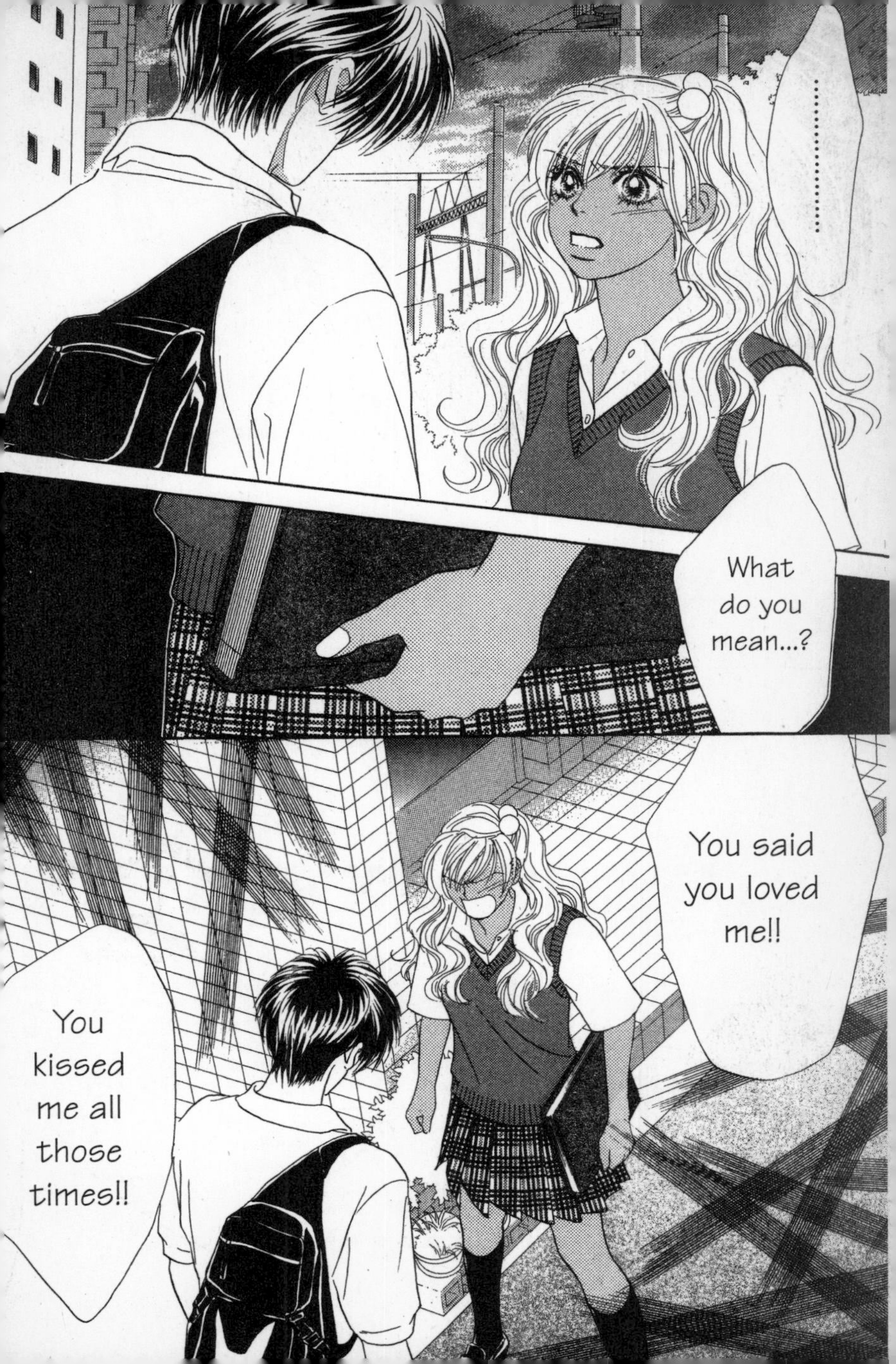
......
What do you mean...?
You said you loved me!!
You kissed me all those times!!

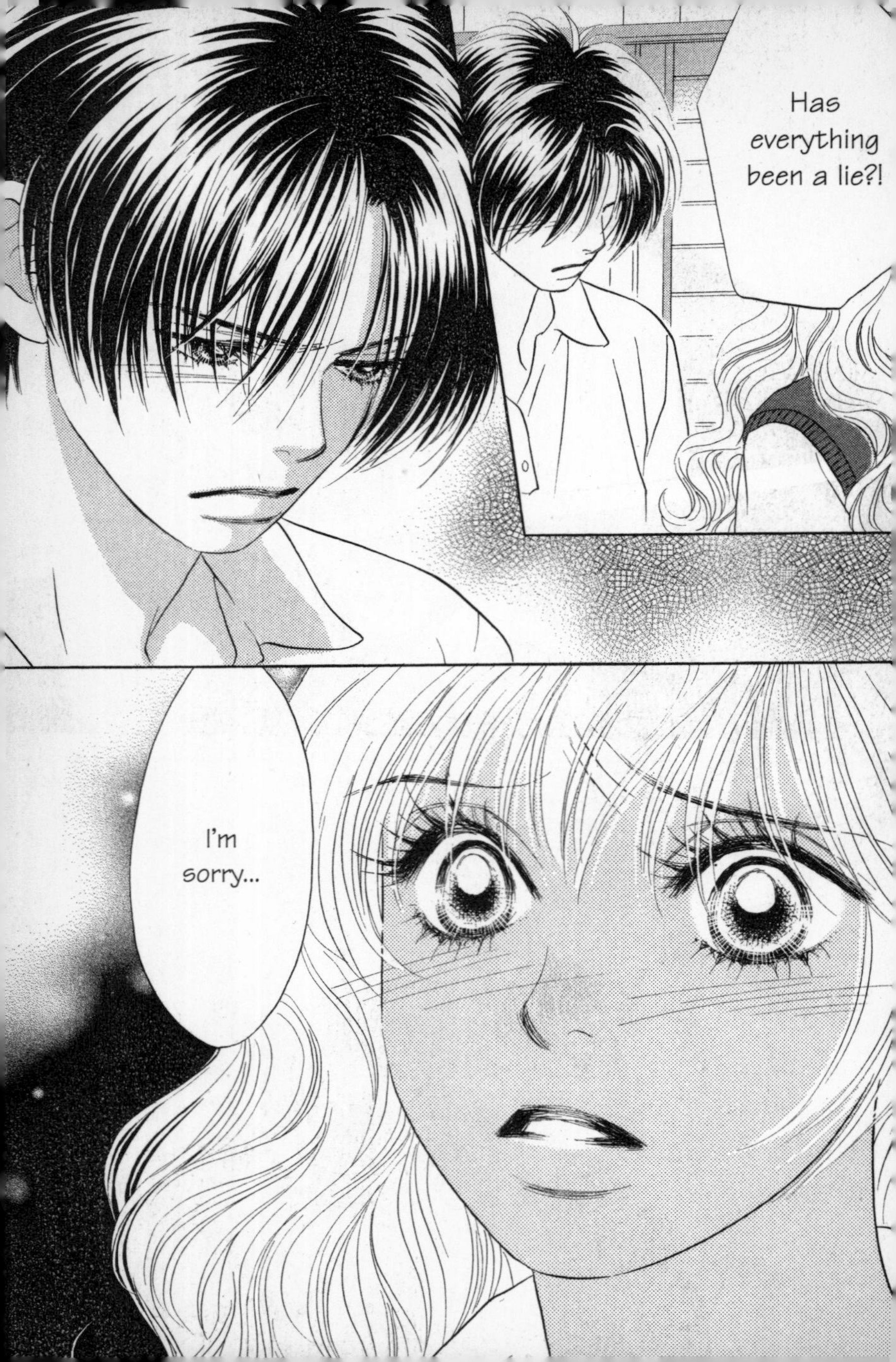
Has everything been a lie?!
I'm sorry...

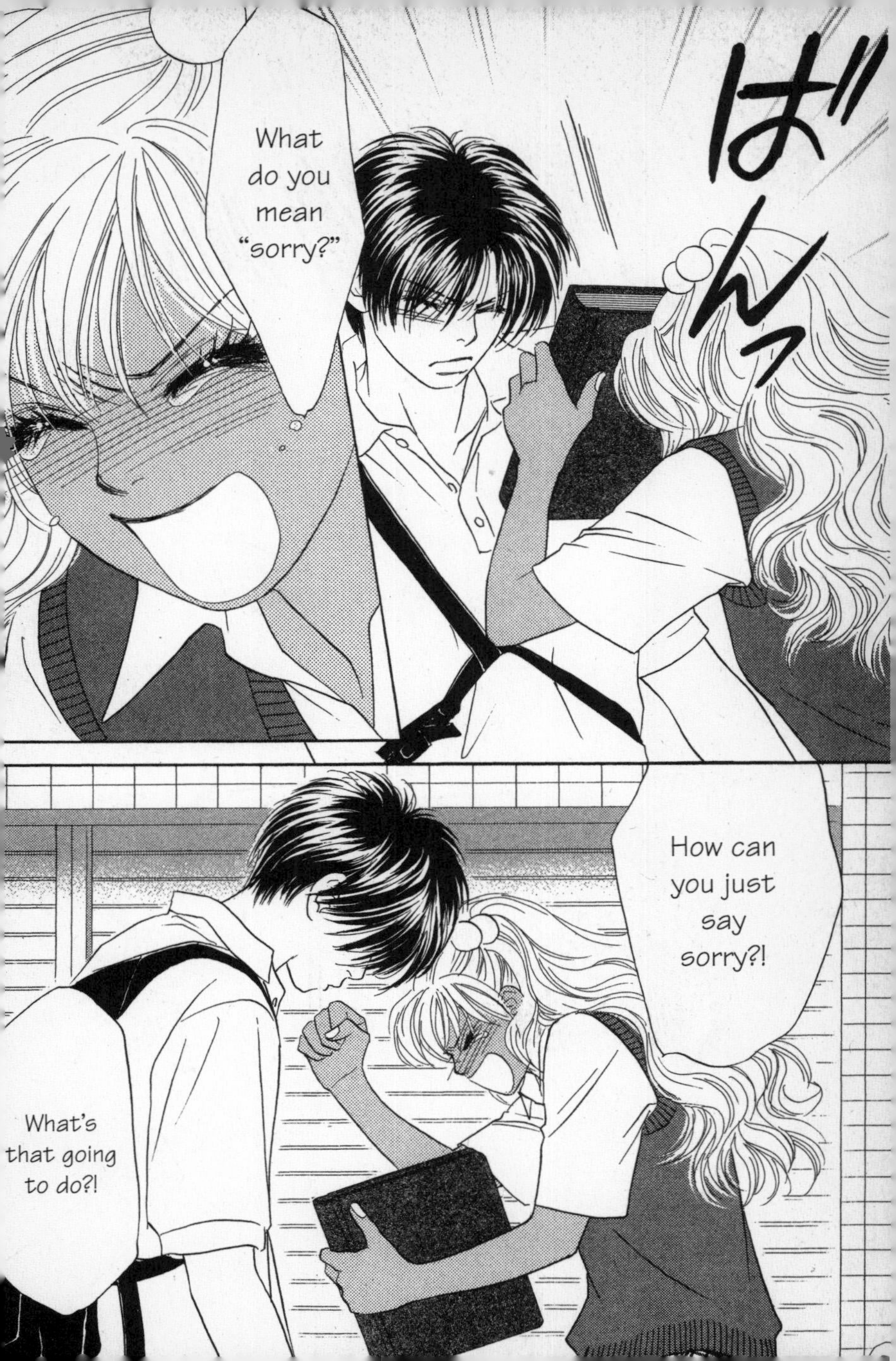
ばんっ
What do you mean "sorry?"
How can you just say sorry?!
What's that going to do?!

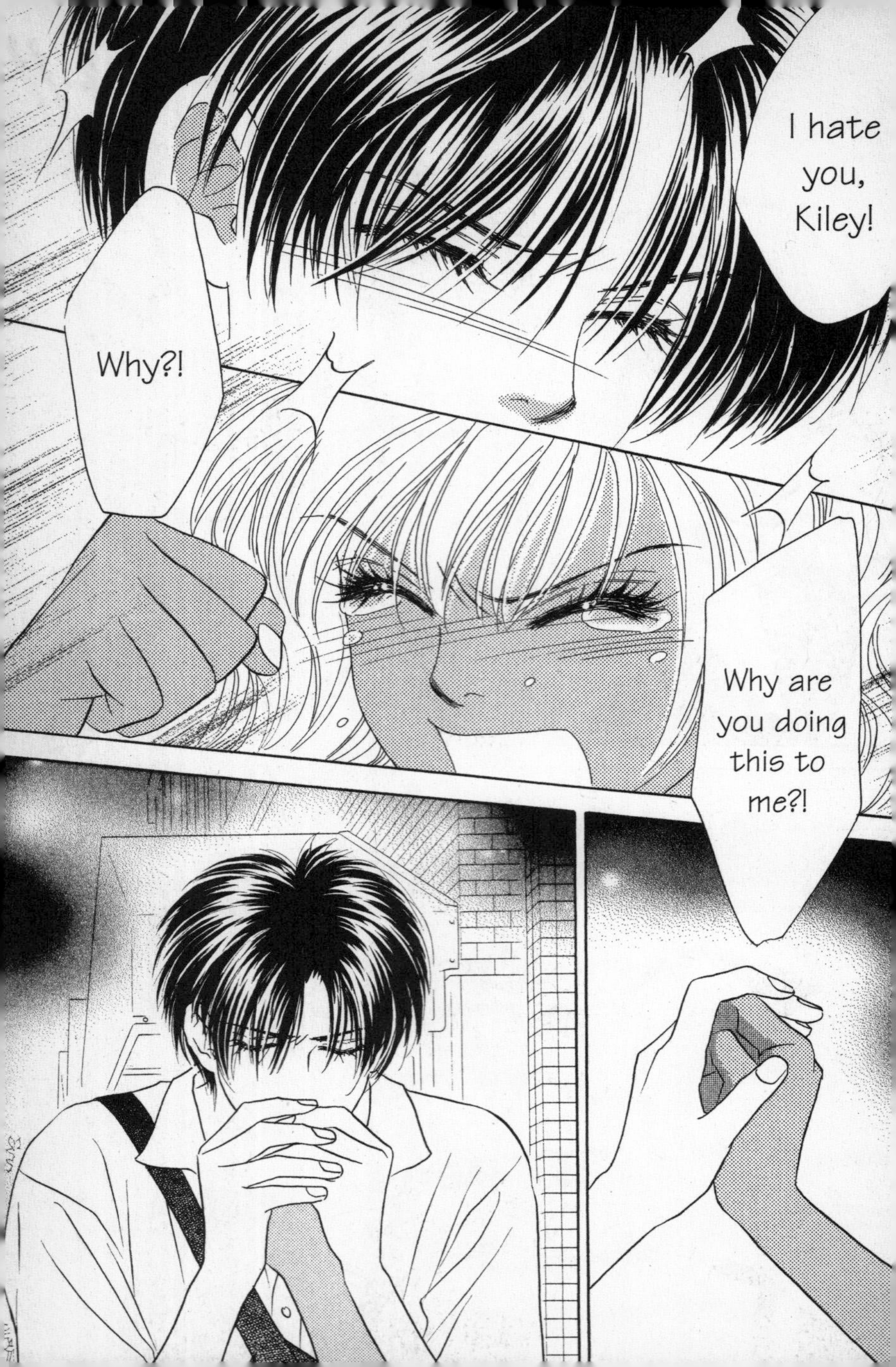
I hate you, Kiley!
Why?!
Why are you doing this to me?!

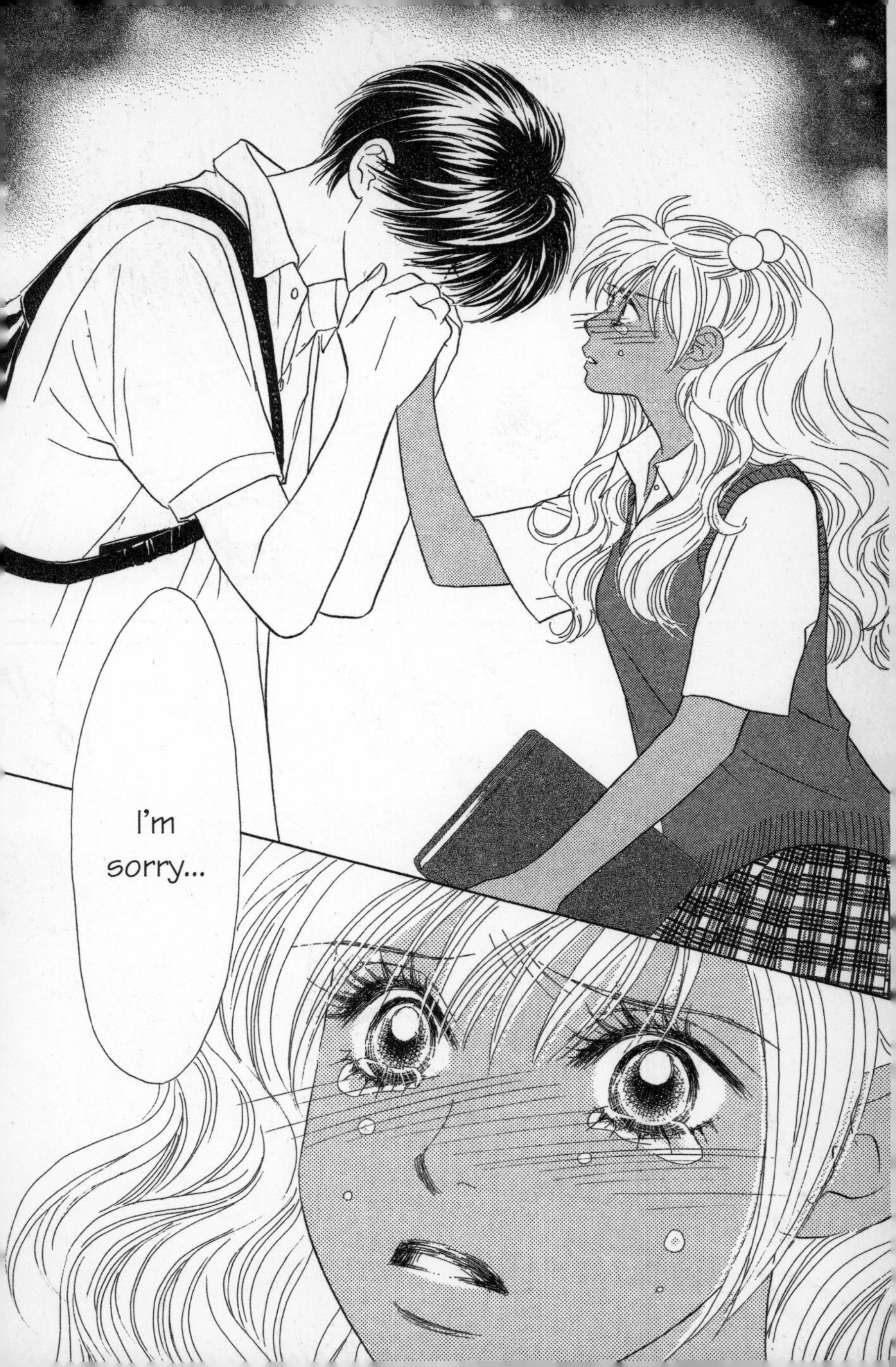
I'm sorry...

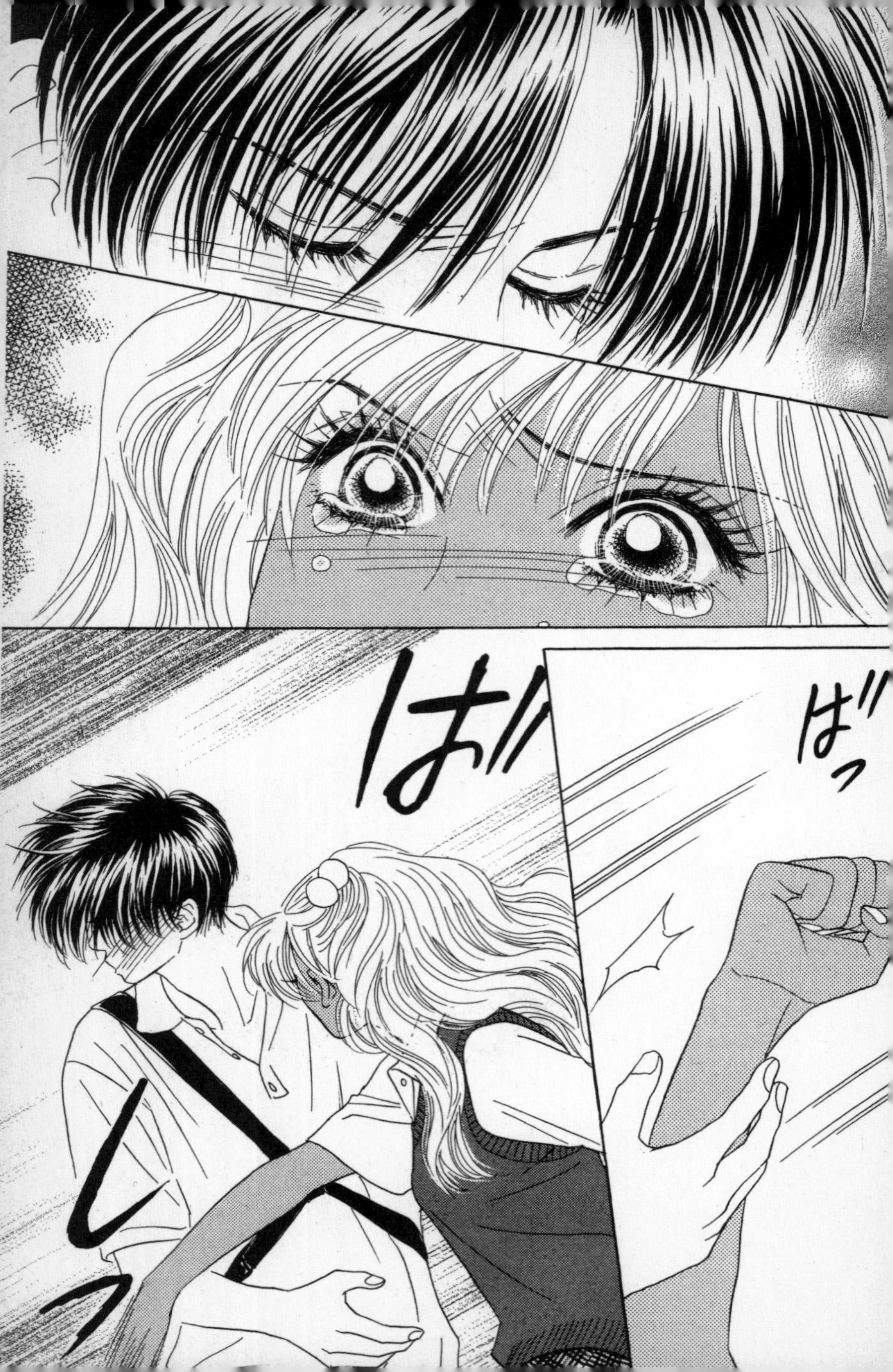
ばっ

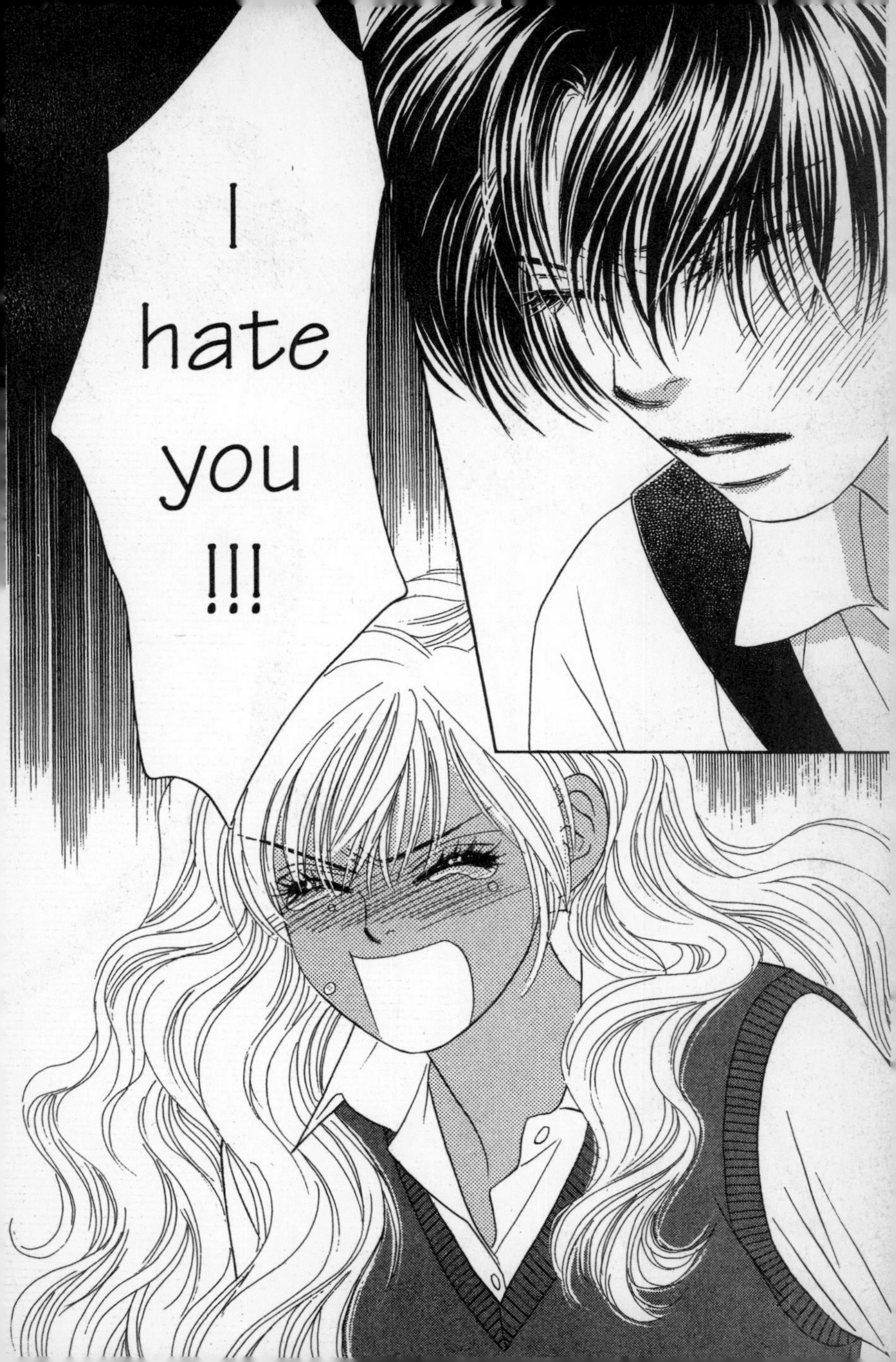
I hate you !!!

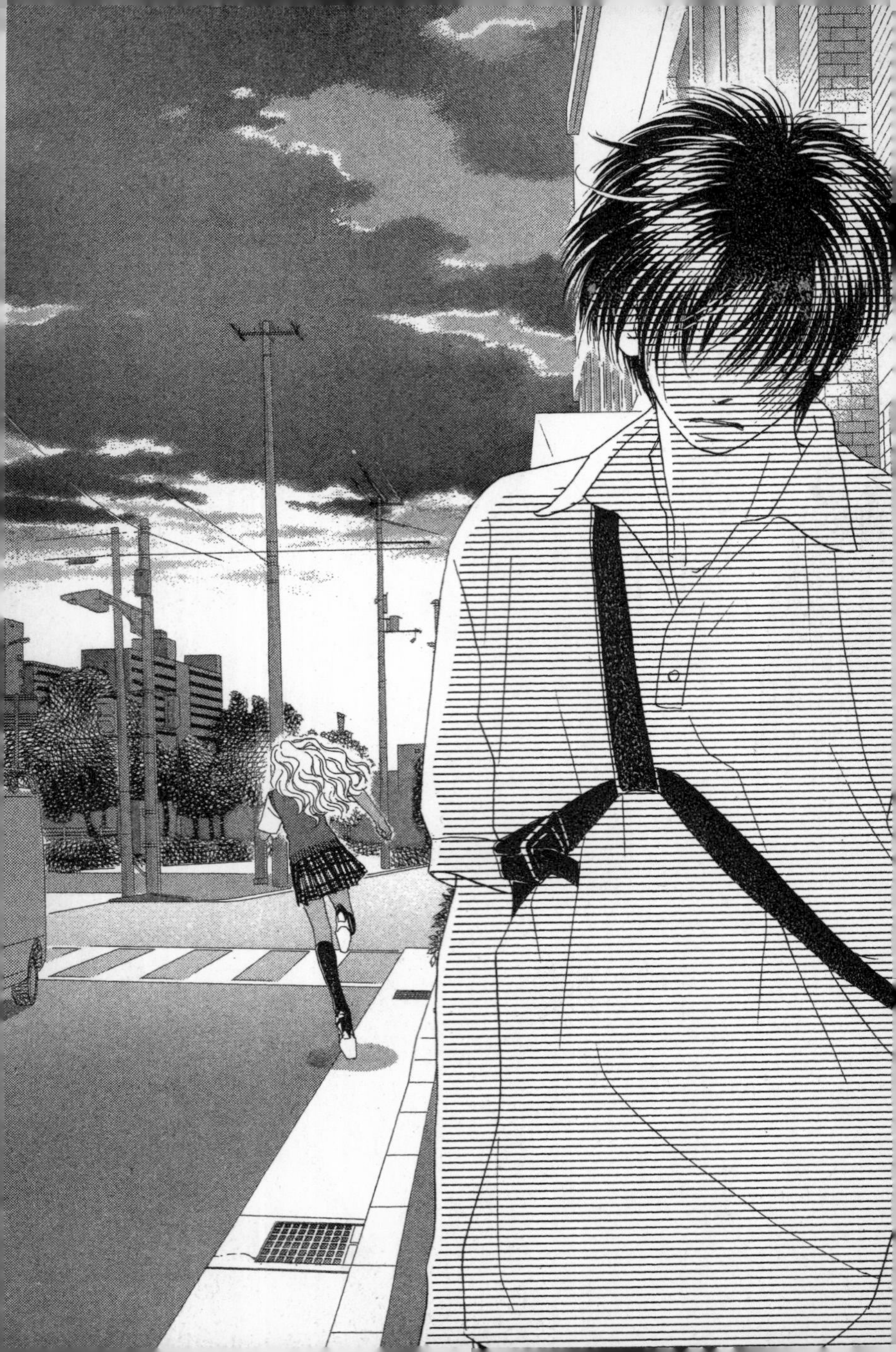

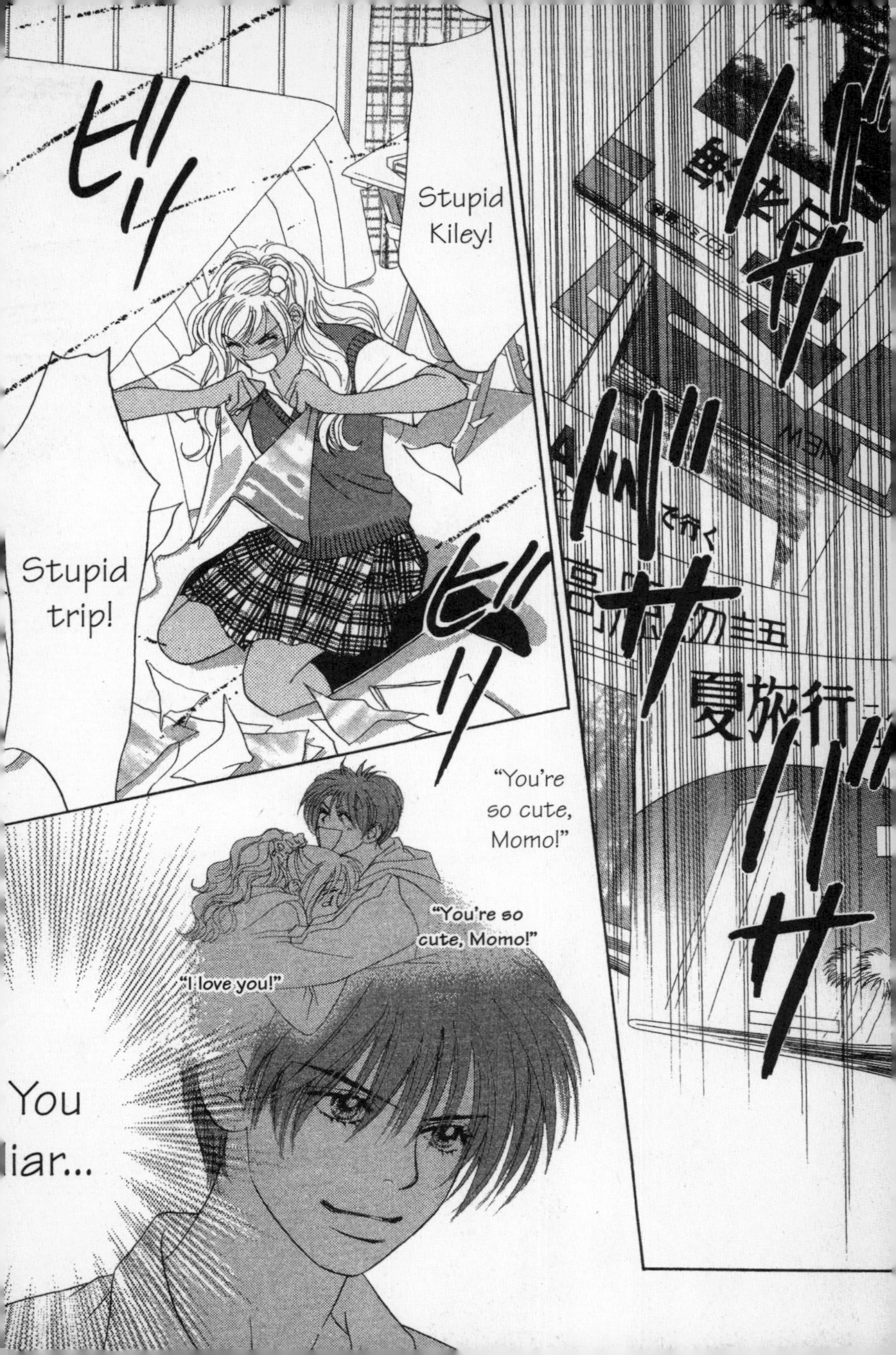
夏旅行
ビリ
Stupid Kiley!
Stupid trip!
ビリ
"You're so cute, Momo!"
"You're so cute, Momo!"
"I love you!"
You liar...

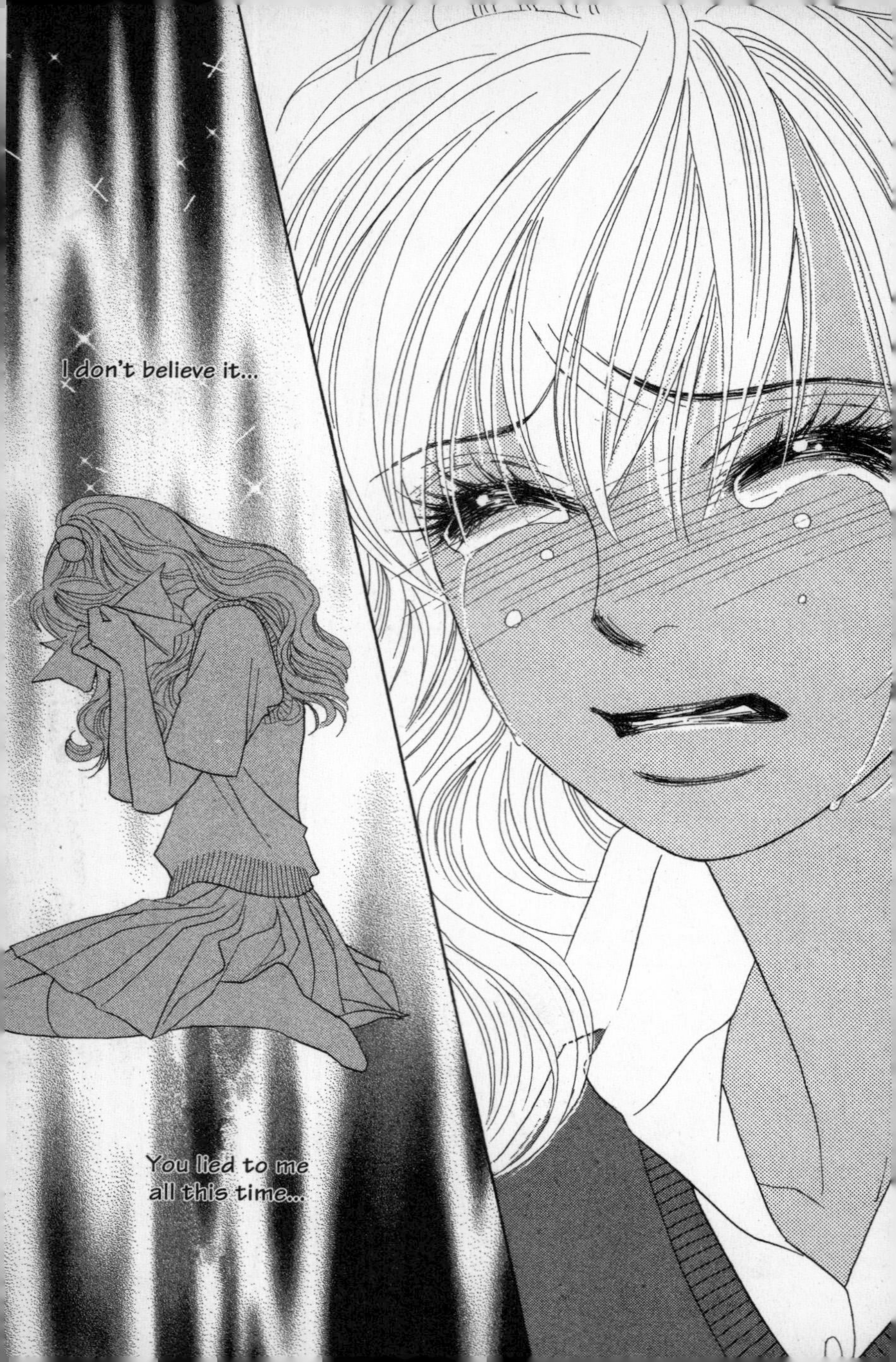
I don't believe it...
You lied to me all this time...

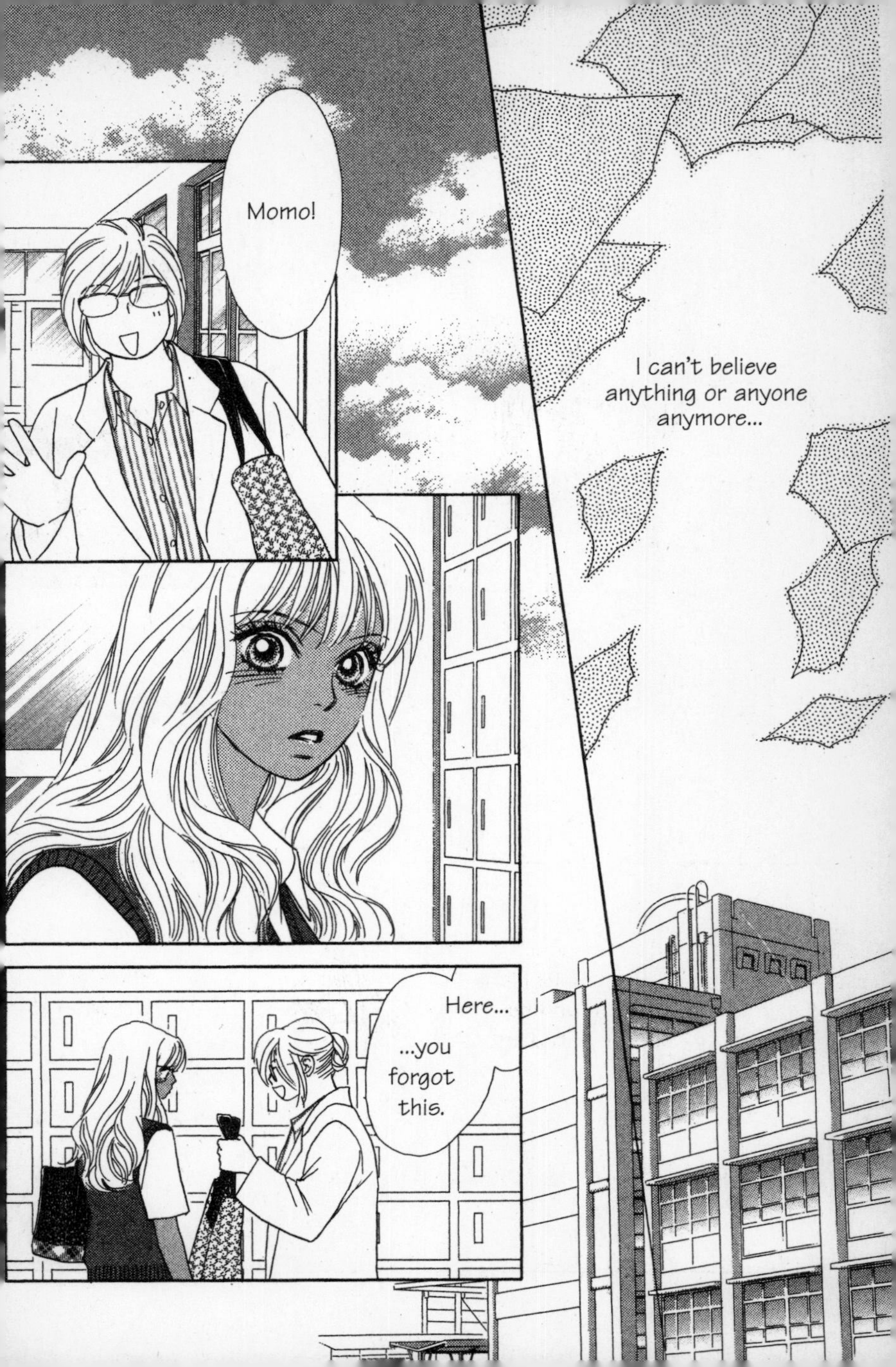
I can't believe anything or anyone anymore...
Momo!
Here...
...you forgot this.

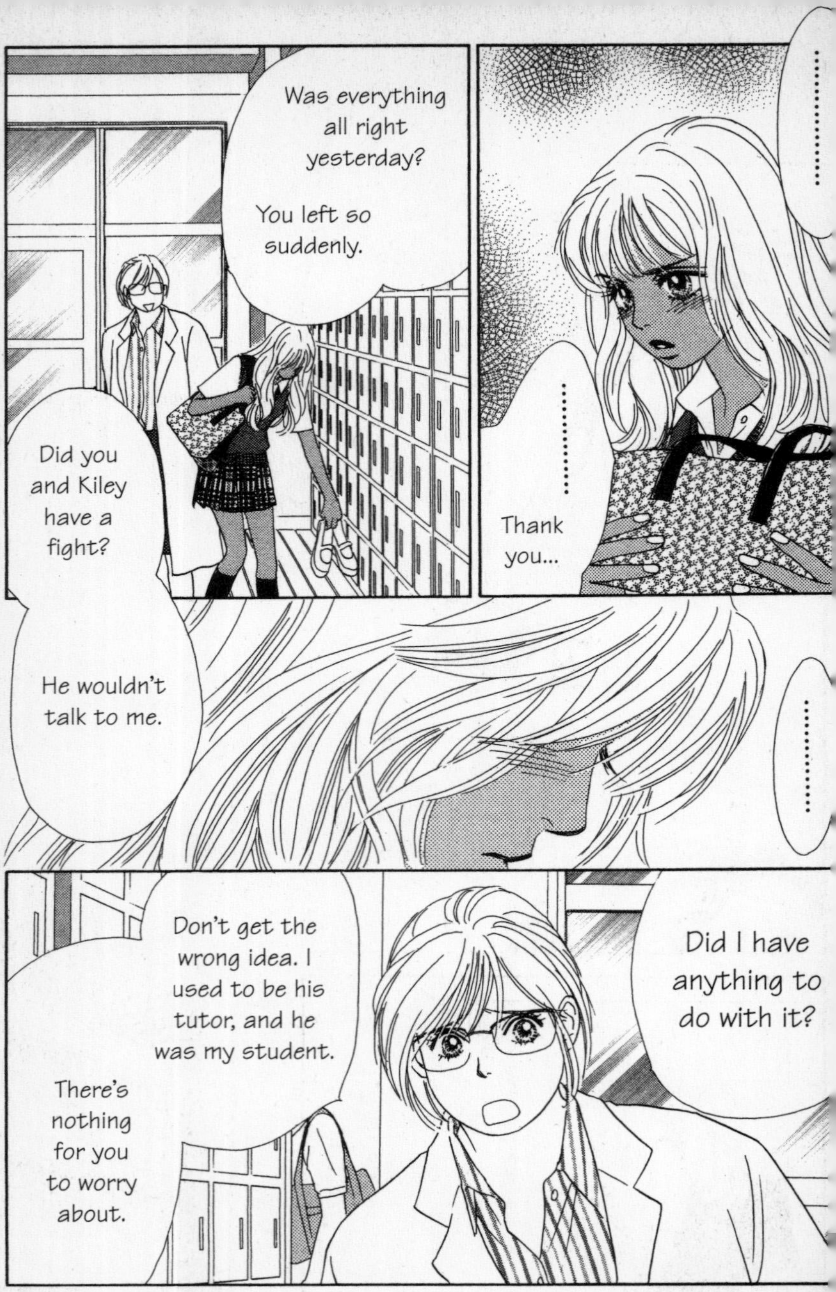
......
......
Thank you...
Was everything all right yesterday?
You left so suddenly.
Did you and Kiley have a fight?
......
He wouldn't talk to me.
Did I have anything to do with it?
Don't get the wrong idea. I used to be his tutor, and he was my student.
There's nothing for you to worry about.

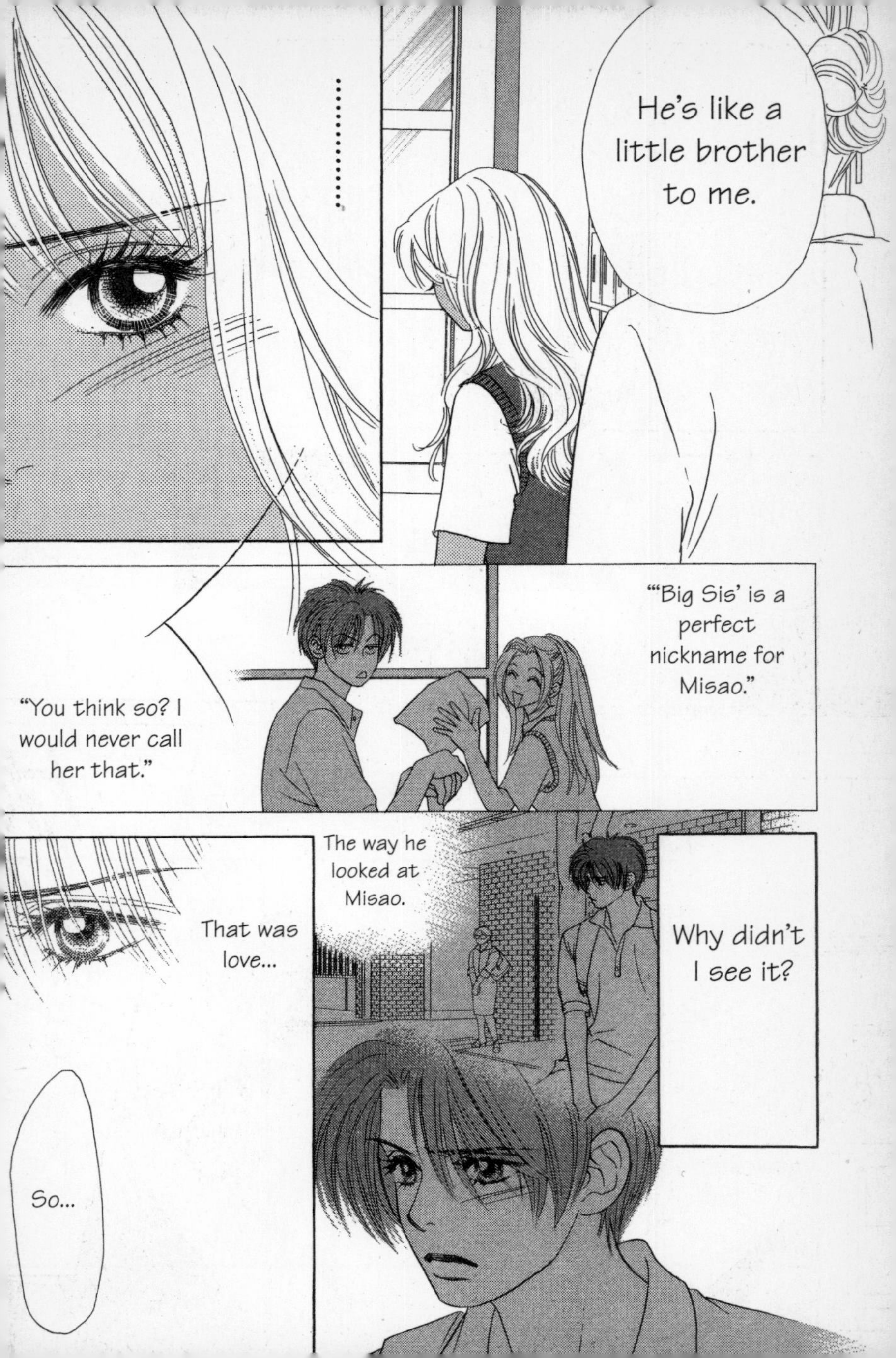

He's like a little brother to me.
……
"'Big Sis' is a perfect nickname for Misao."
"You think so? I would never call her that."
Why didn't I see it?
The way he looked at Misao.
That was love...
So...

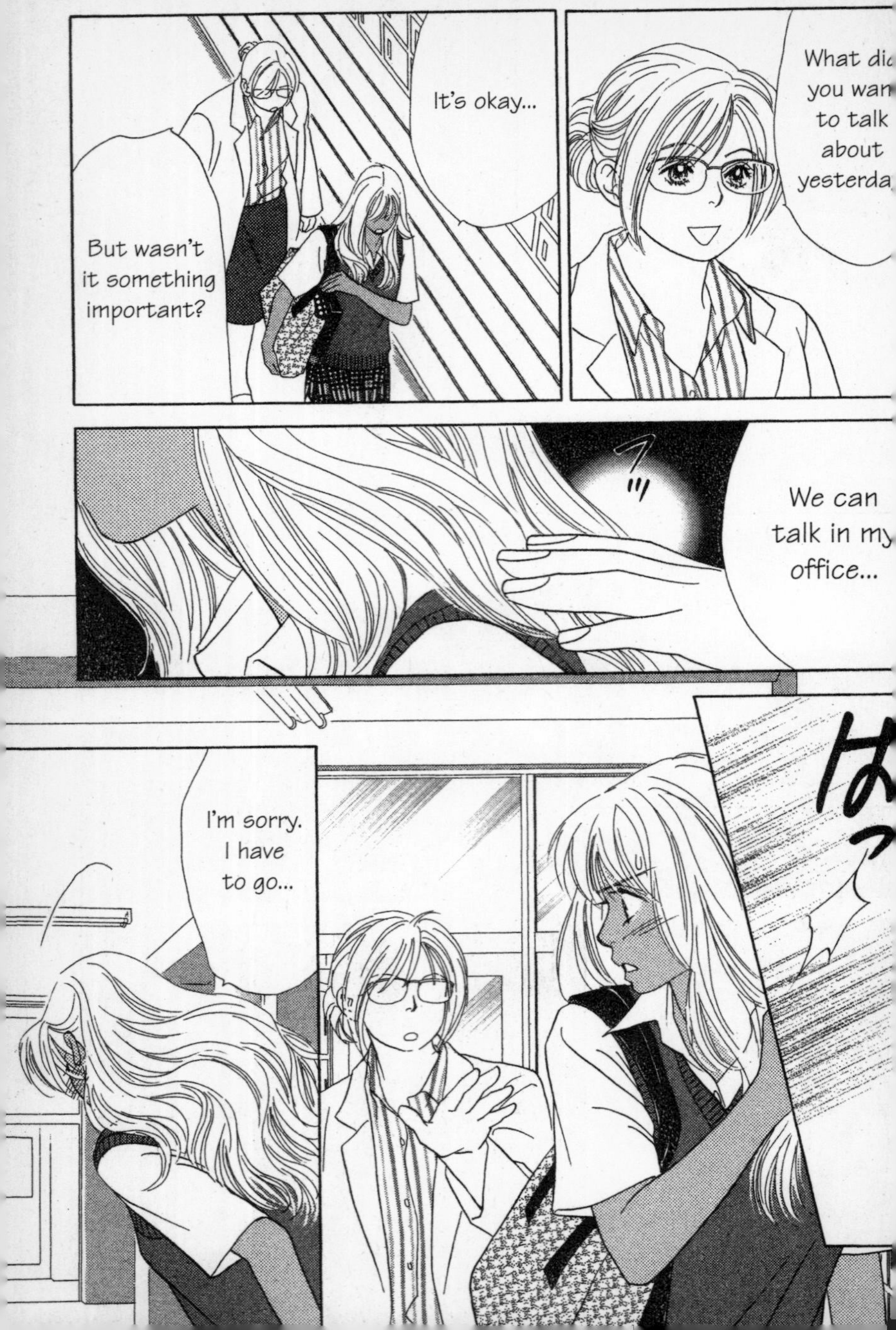
What di you wan to talk about yesterda
It's okay...
But wasn't it something important?
We can talk in my office...
は
I'm sorry. I have to go...

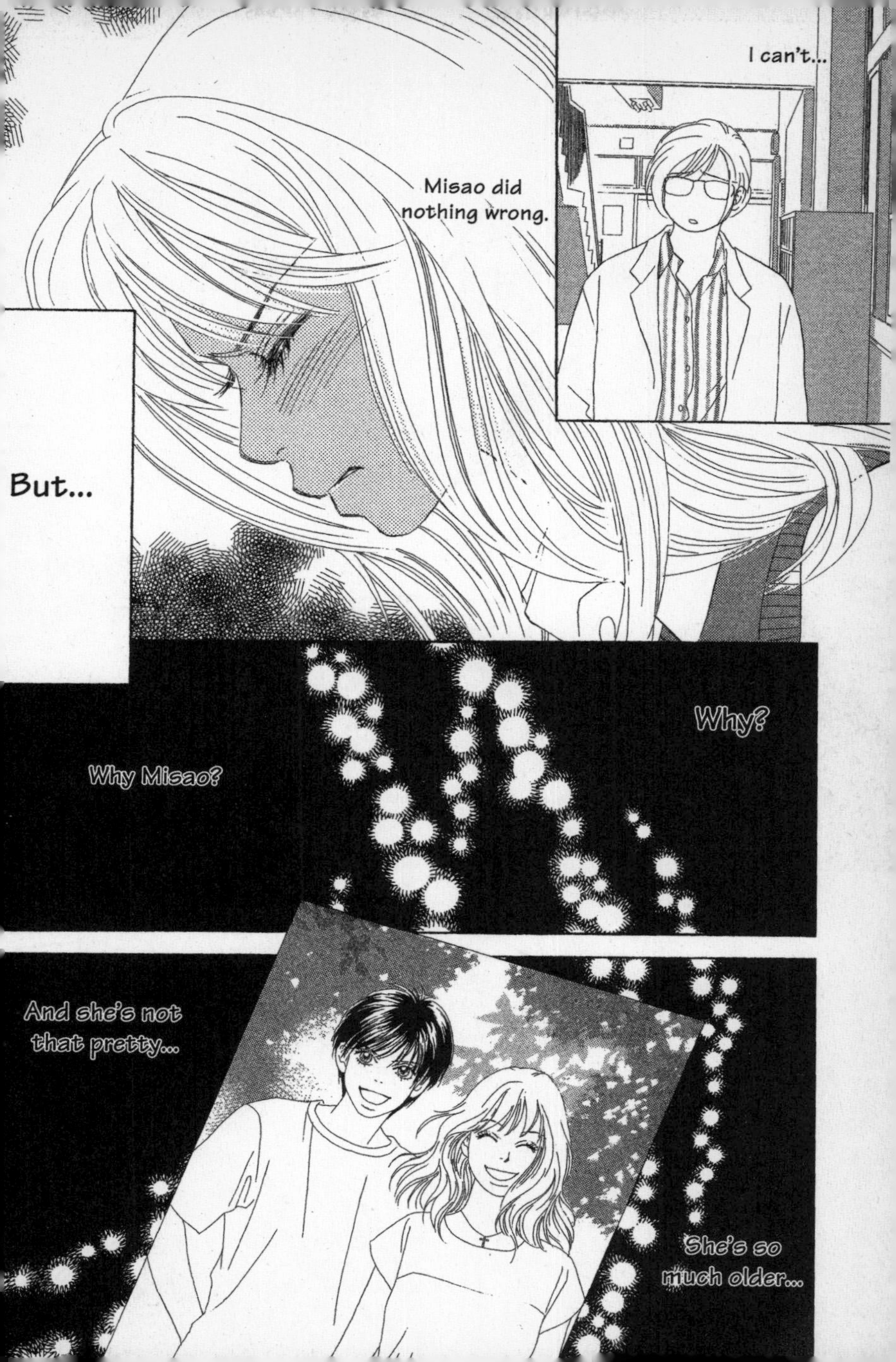
I can't...
Misao did nothing wrong.
But...
Why?
Why Misao?
She's so much older...
And she's not that pretty...

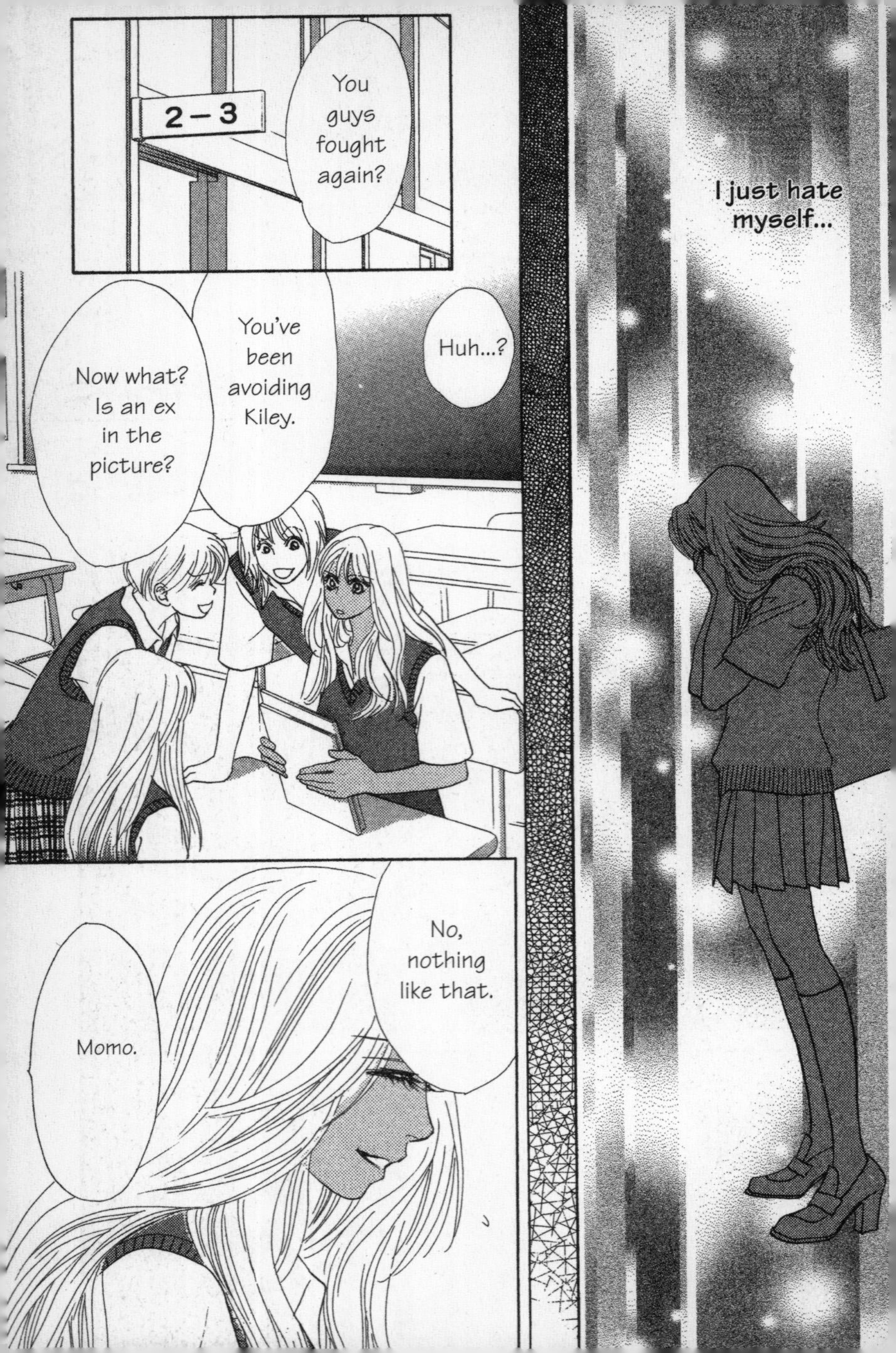
I just hate myself...
You guys fought again?
Huh...?
You've been avoiding Kiley.
Now what? Is an ex in the picture?
No, nothing like that.
Momo.

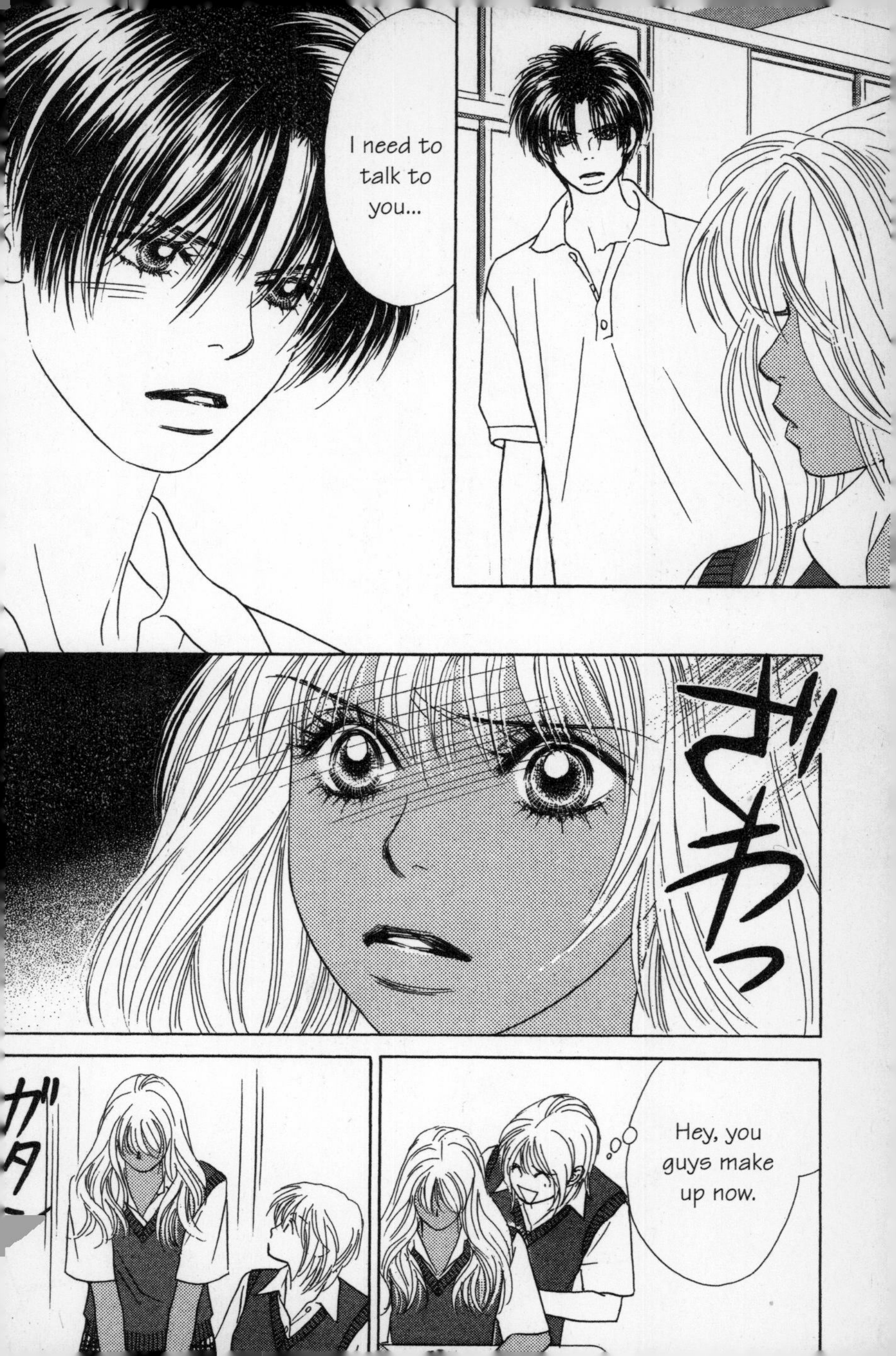

I need to talk to you...
ぎくっ
Hey, you guys make up now.
ガタ

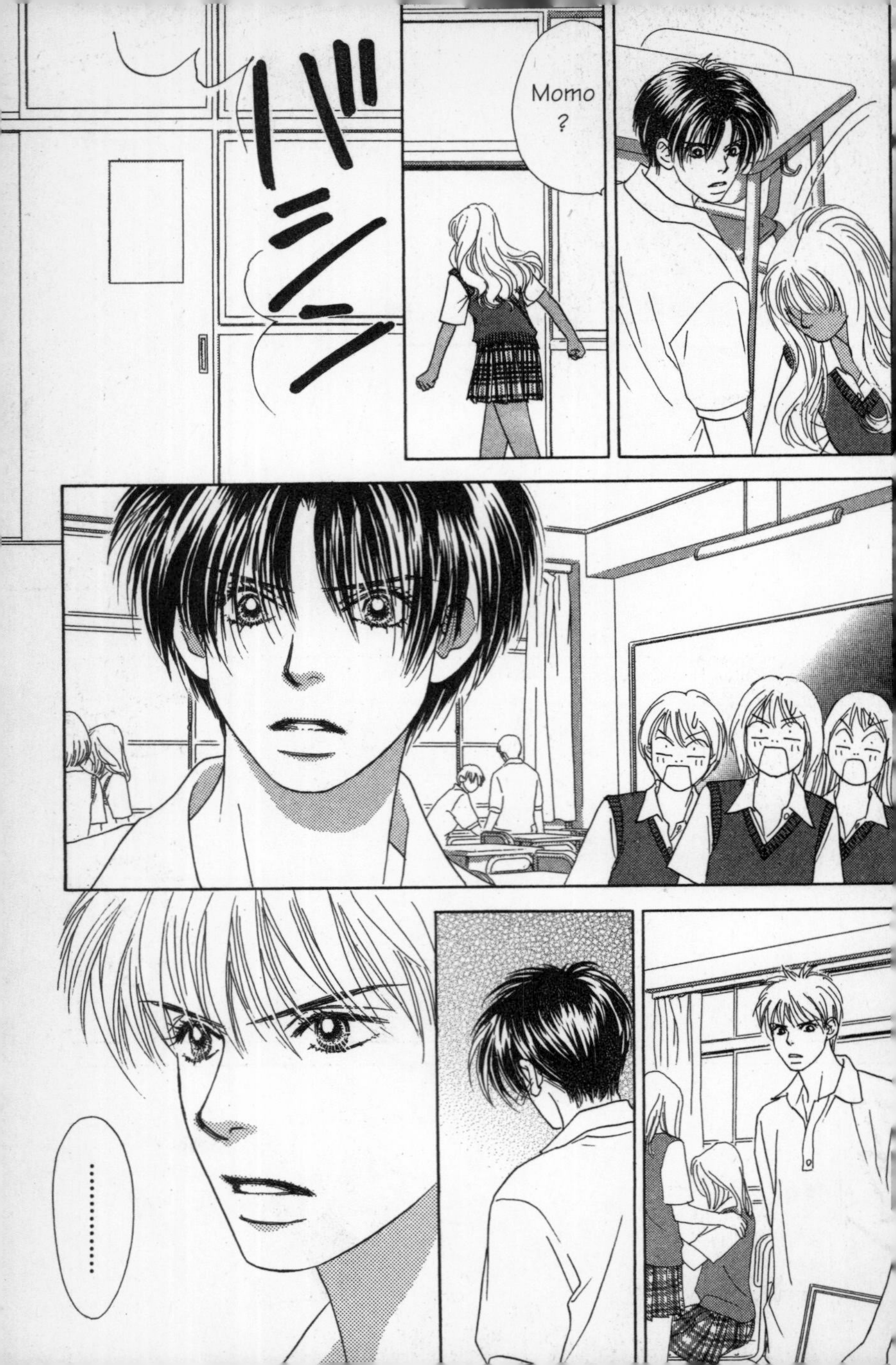
Momo ?
バシーン
....

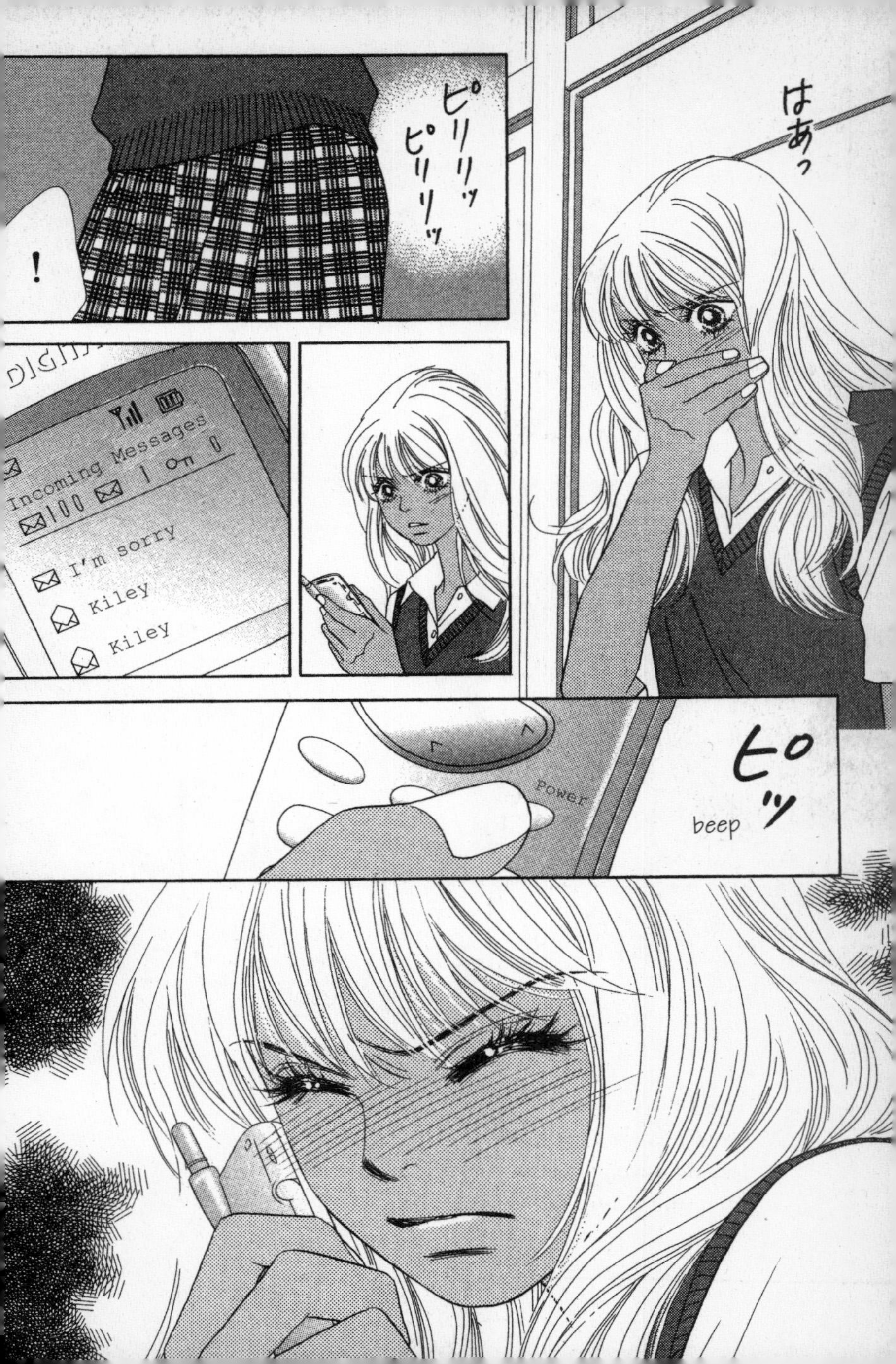
はあっ
ピリリッ
ピリリッ
!
Incoming Messages
100
1
0
I'm sorry
Kiley
Kiley
ピッ
beep
power

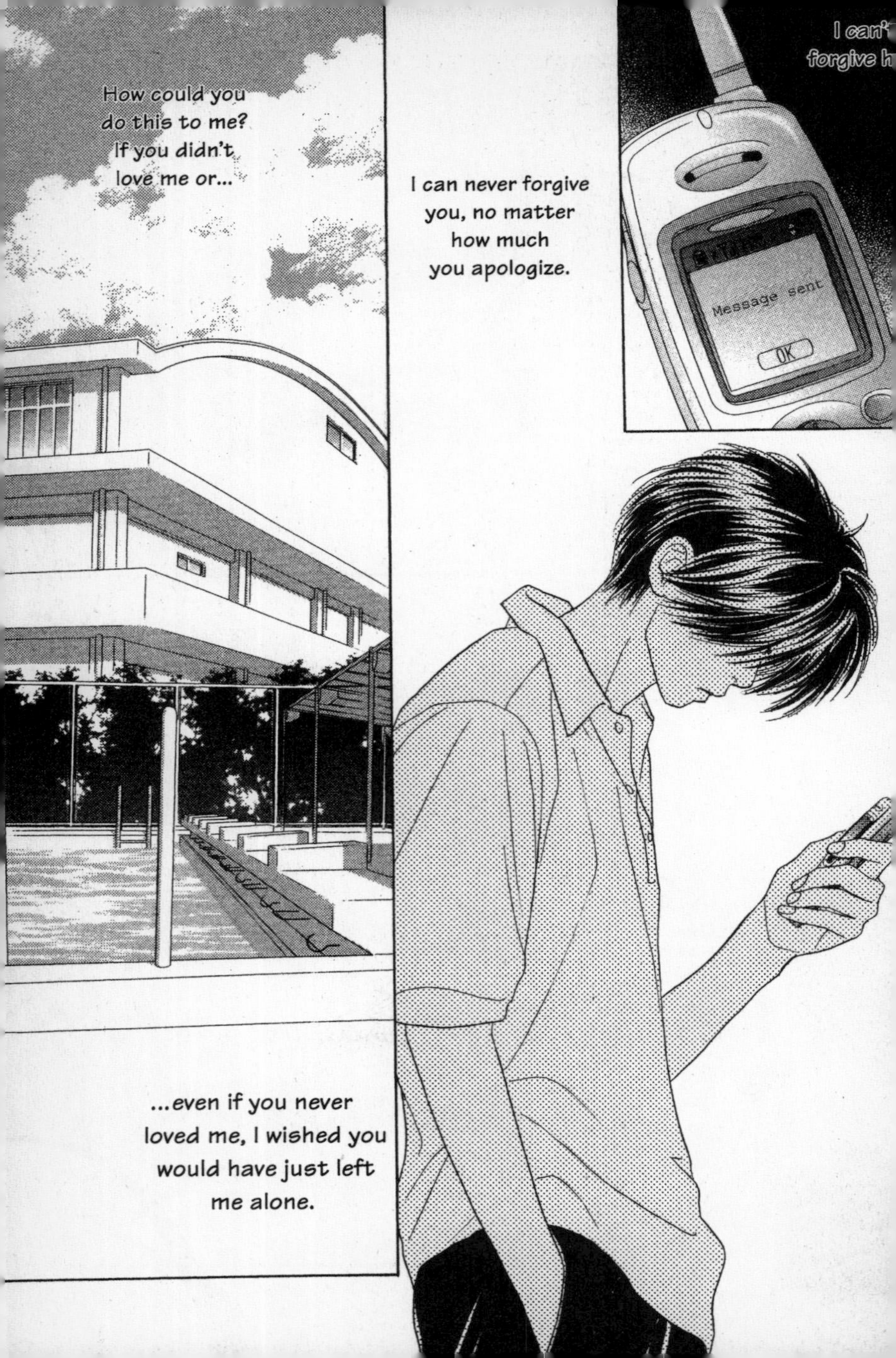
I can't forgive h
Message sent
OK
I can never forgive you, no matter how much you apologize.
How could you do this to me? If you didn't love me or...
...even if you never loved me, I wished you would have just left me alone.

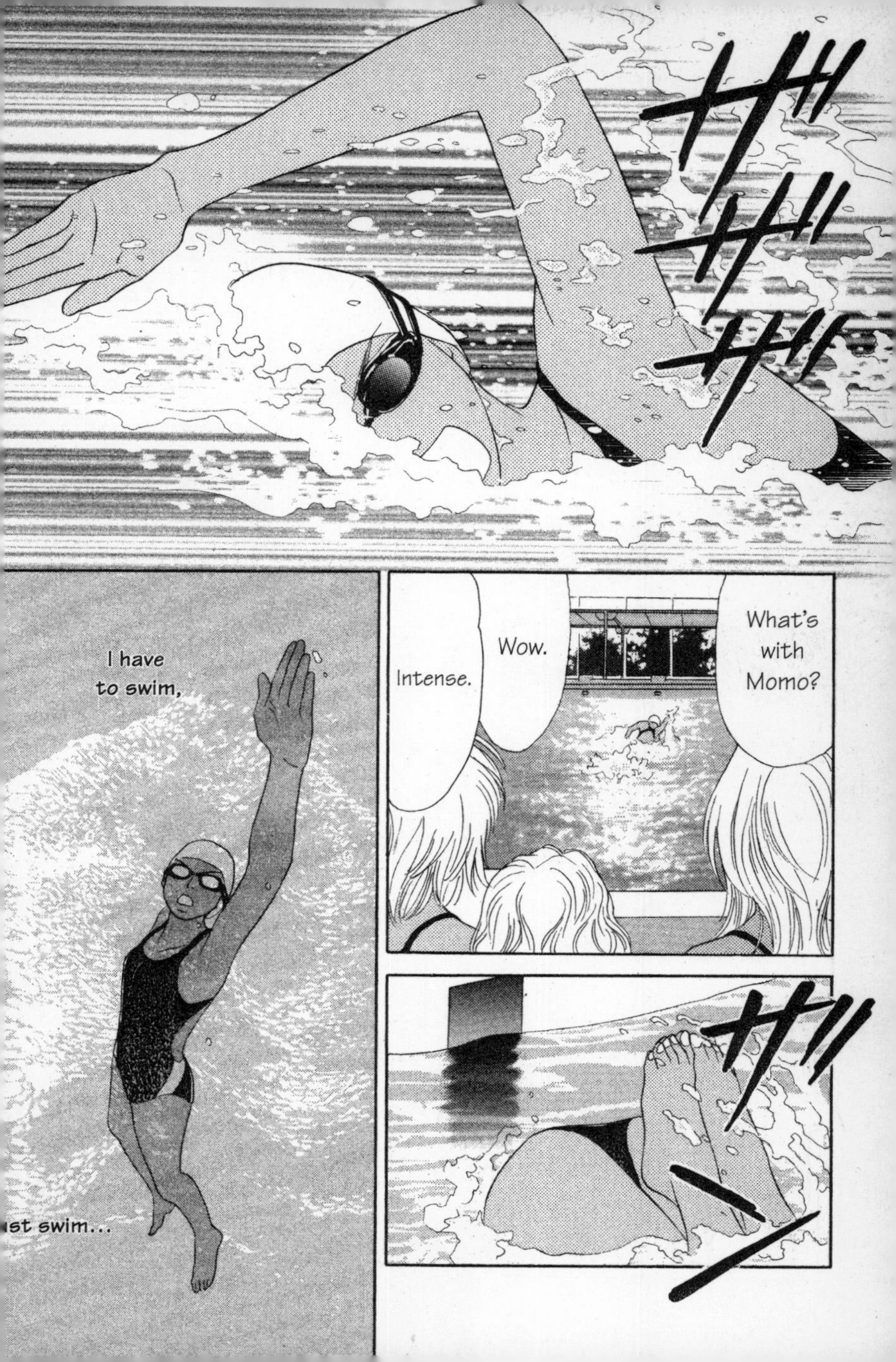
ザザザ
What's with Momo?
Wow.
Intense.
ザ
I have to swim,
st swim...

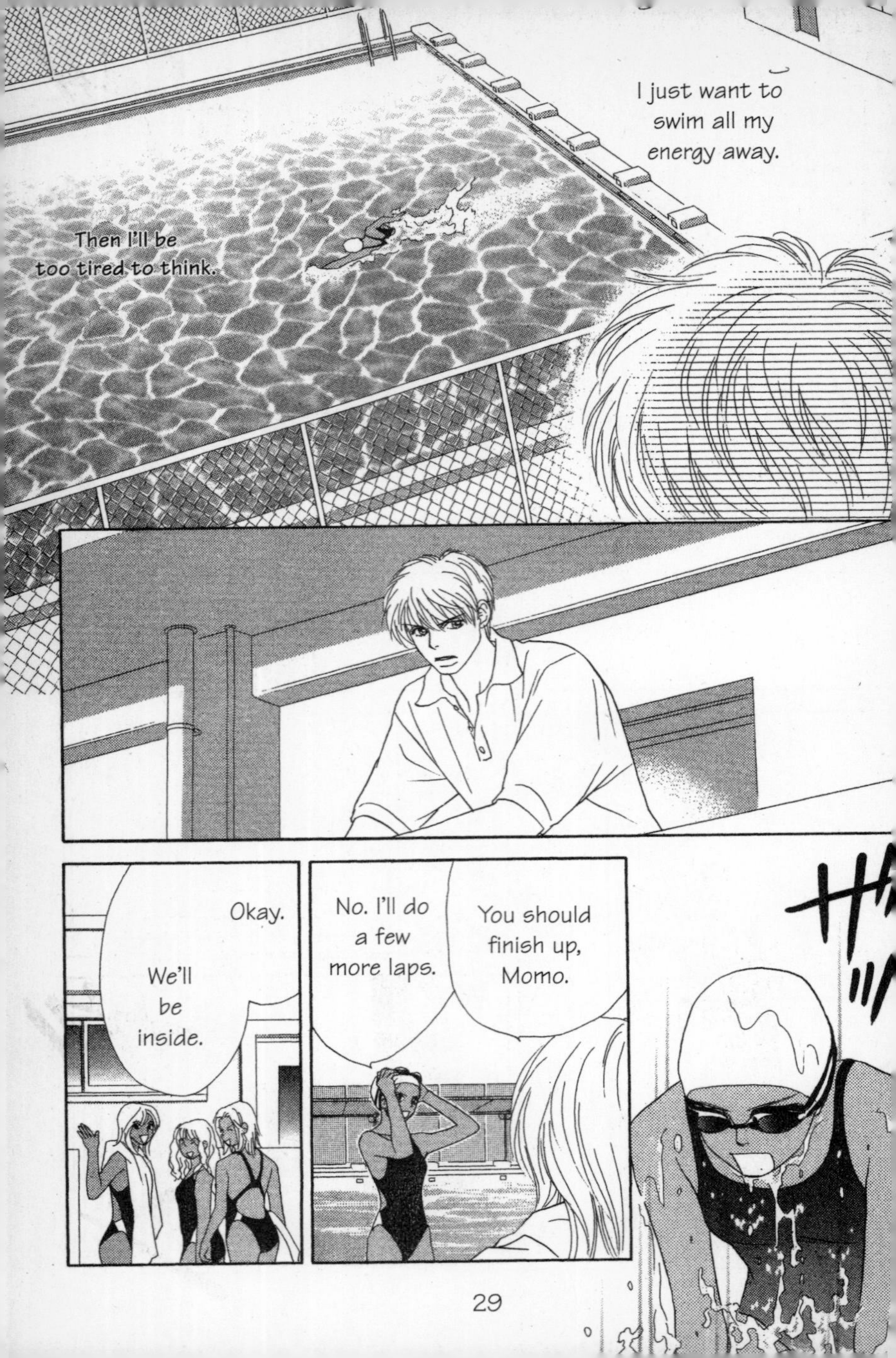
I just want to swim all my energy away.
Then I'll be too tired to think.
You should finish up, Momo.
No. I'll do a few more laps.
Okay.
We'll be inside.

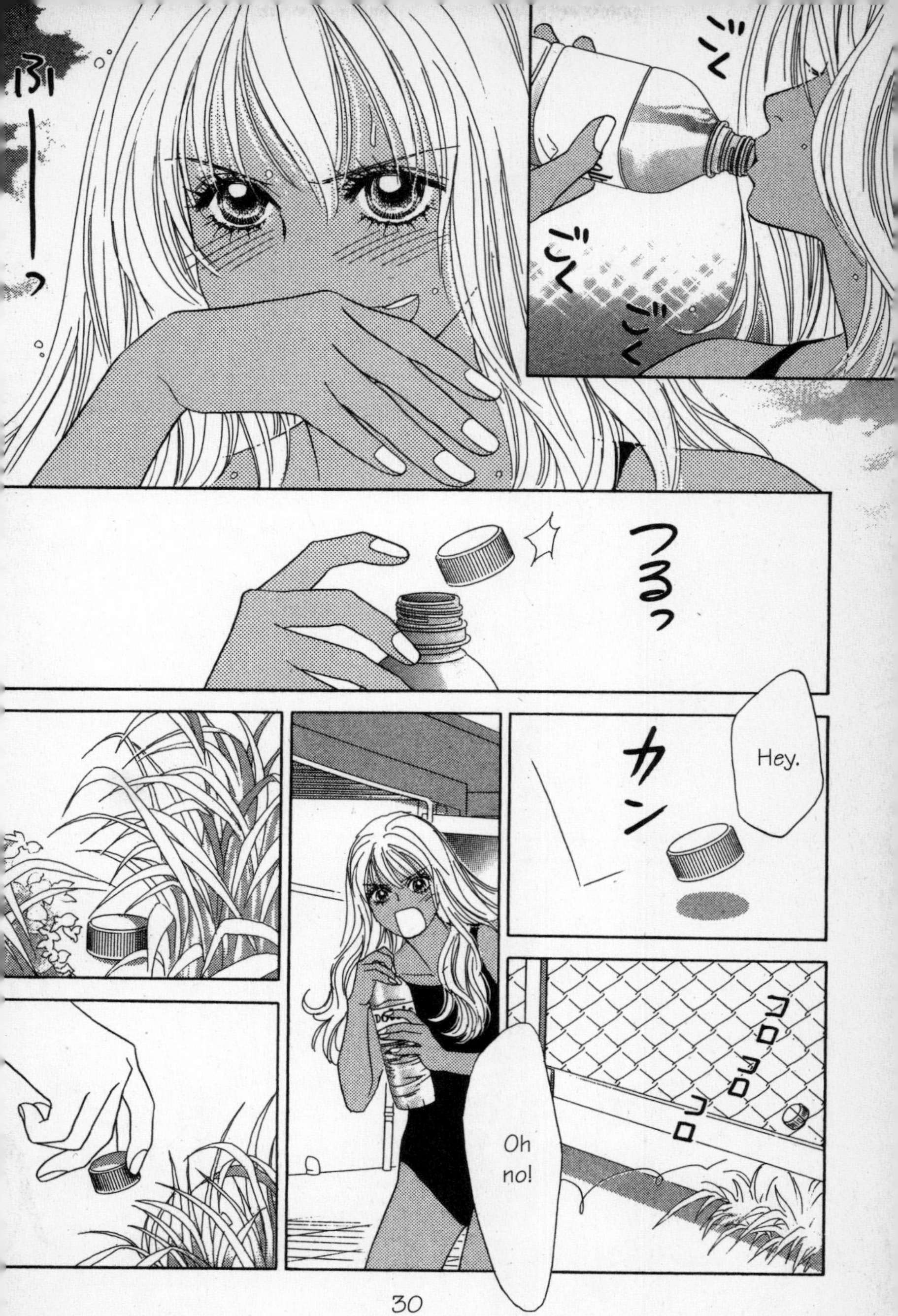
ごく
ごく
ごく
ごく
ふーーっ
つるっ
Hey.
カン
コロ
コロ
コロ
Oh no!

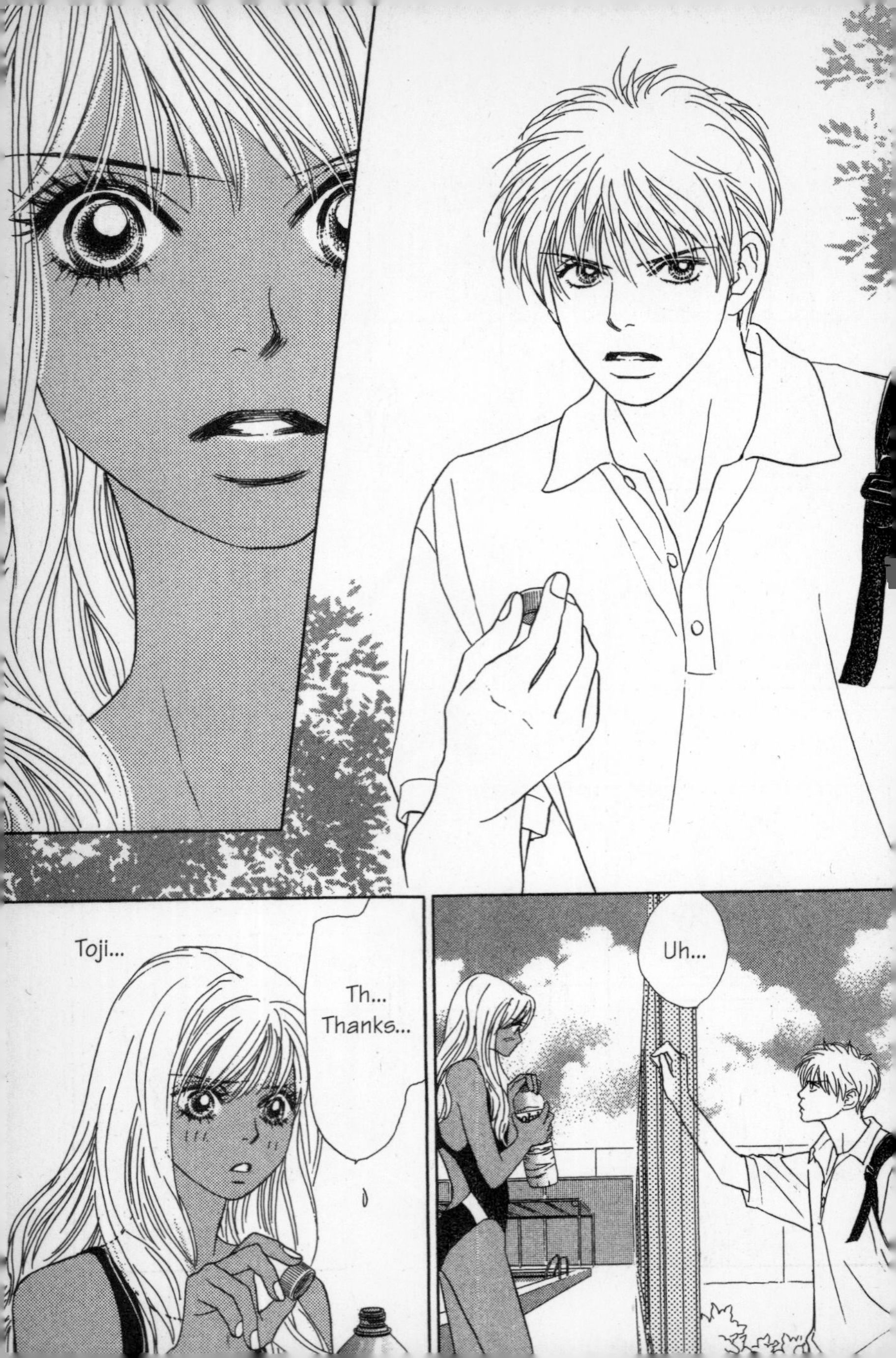
Uh...
Toji...
Th... Thanks...

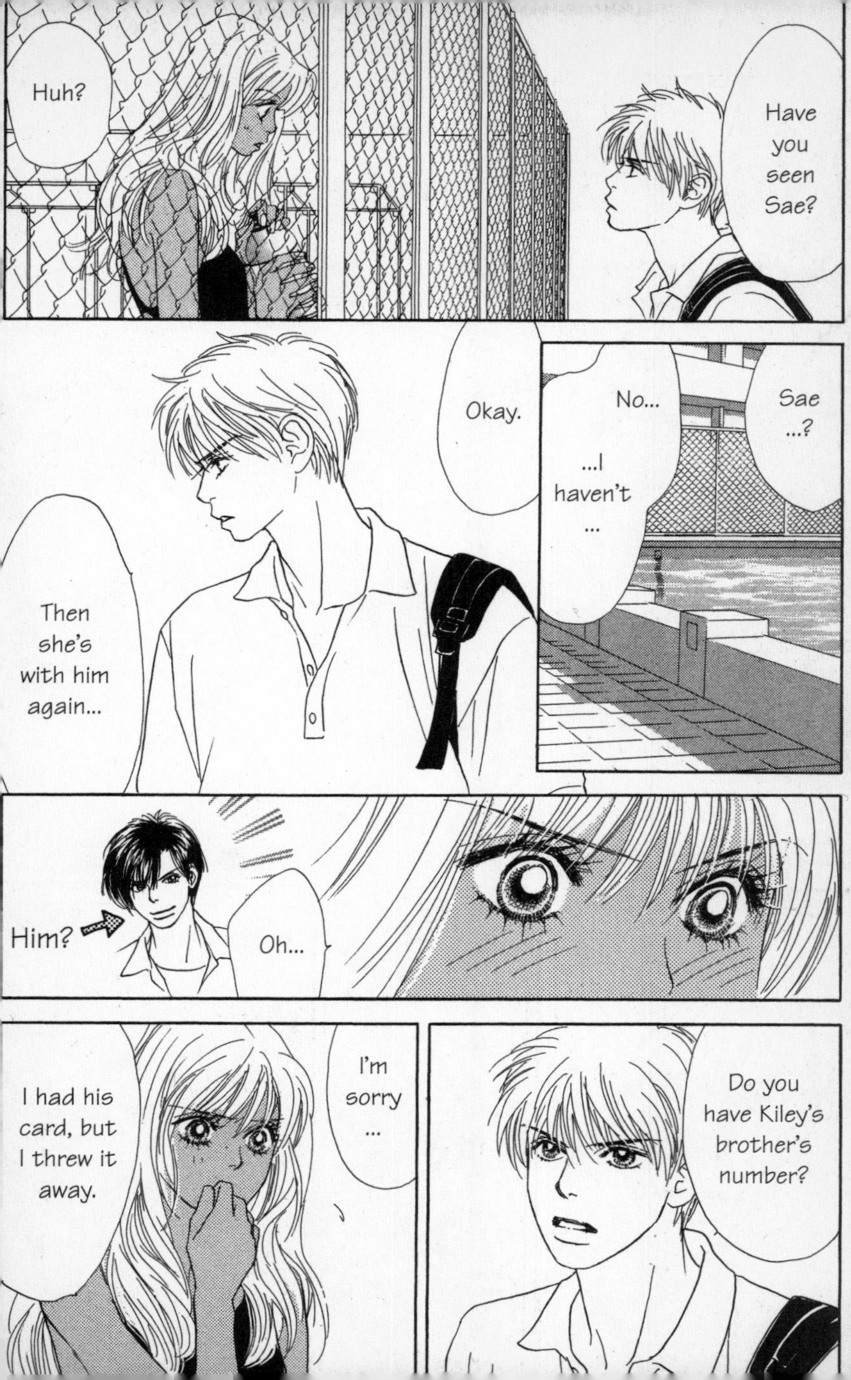
Have you seen Sae?
Huh?
Sae ...?
No... ...I haven't ...
Okay.
Then she's with him again...
Oh...
Him?
Do you have Kiley's brother's number?
I'm sorry ...
I had his card, but I threw it away.

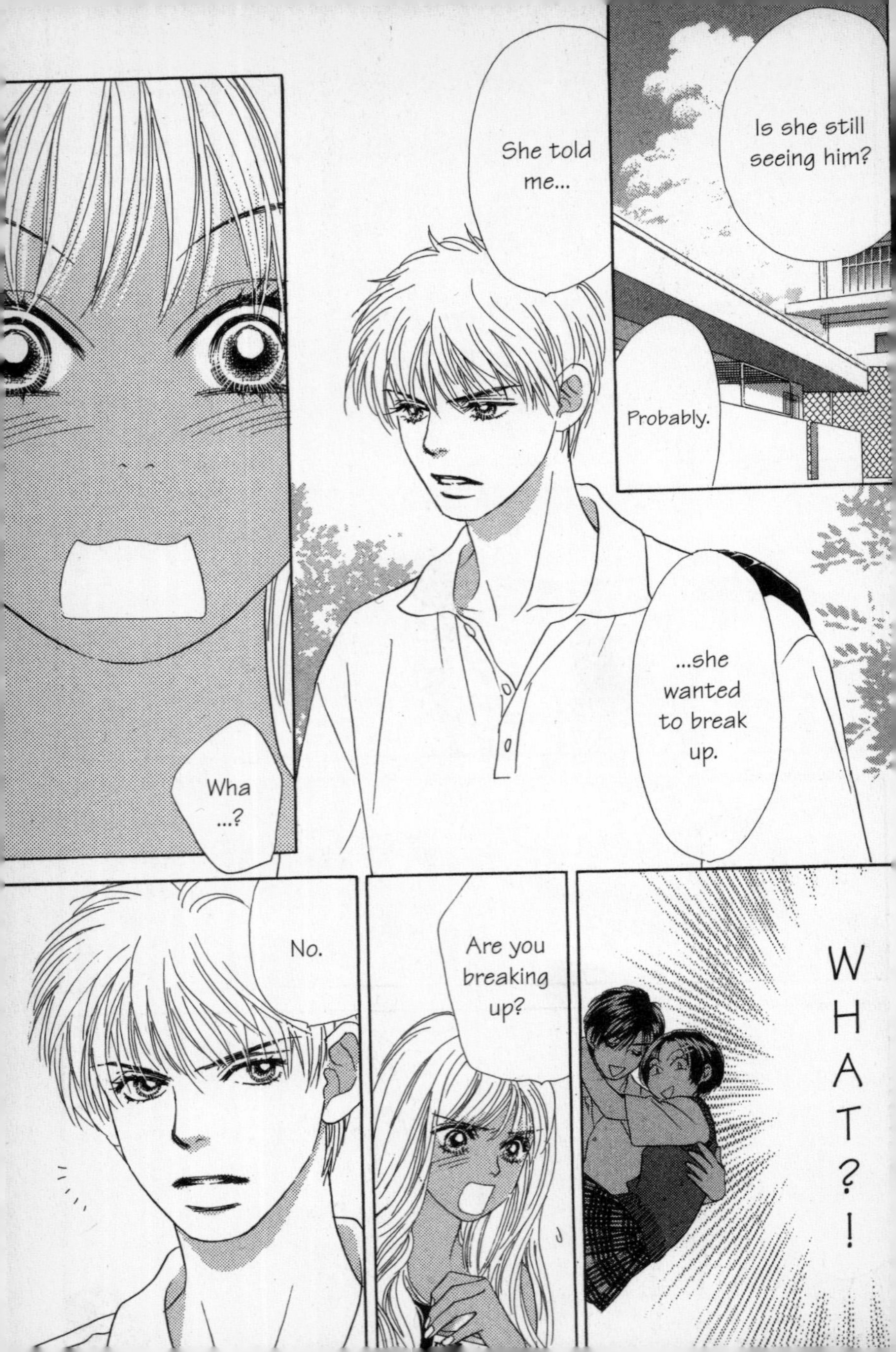
Is she still seeing him?
Probably.
She told me...
...she wanted to break up.
Wha ...?
WHAT?!
Are you breaking up?
No.

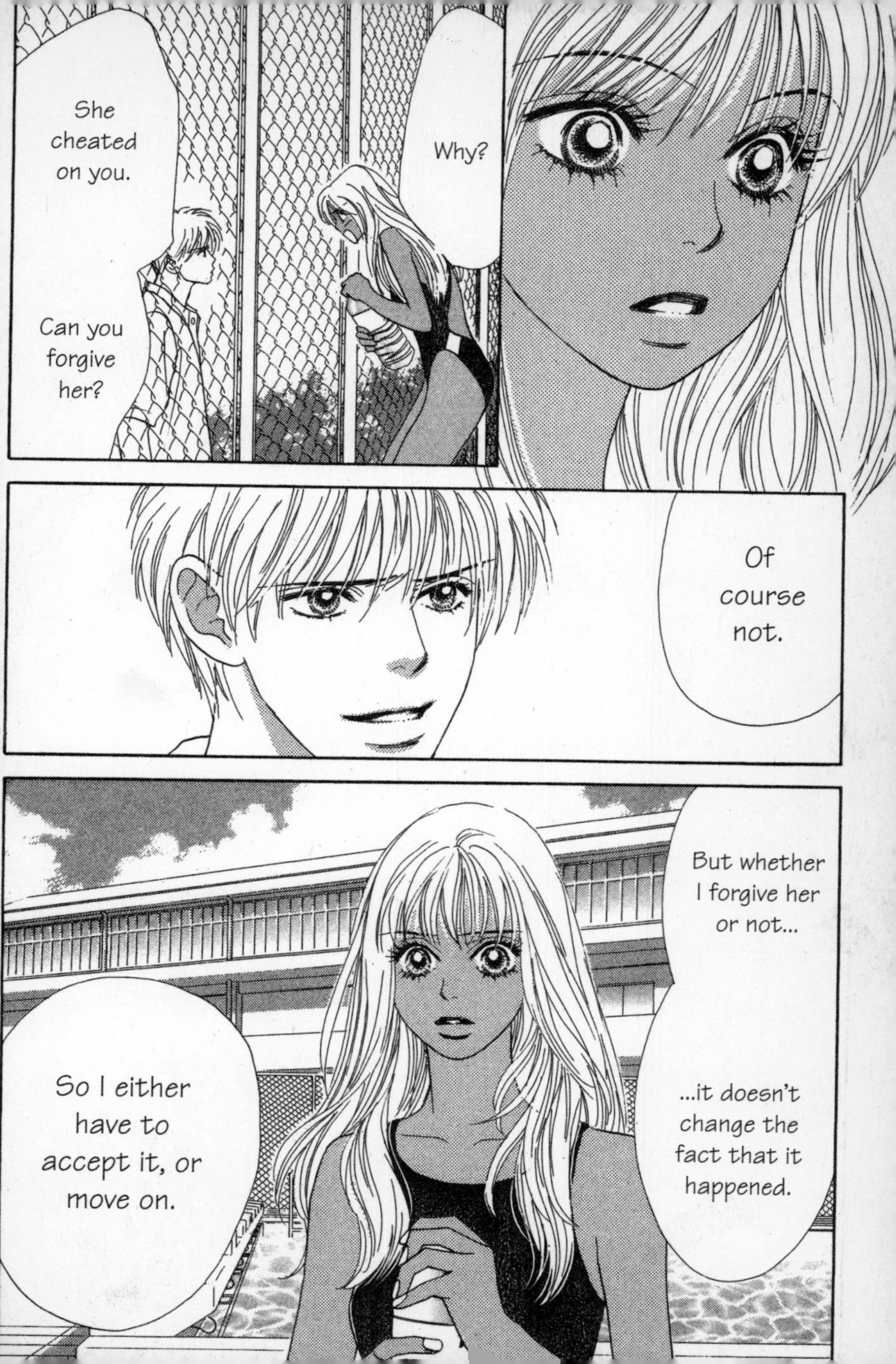
Why?
She cheated on you.
Can you forgive her?
Of course not.
But whether I forgive her or not...
...it doesn't change the fact that it happened.
So I either have to accept it, or move on.

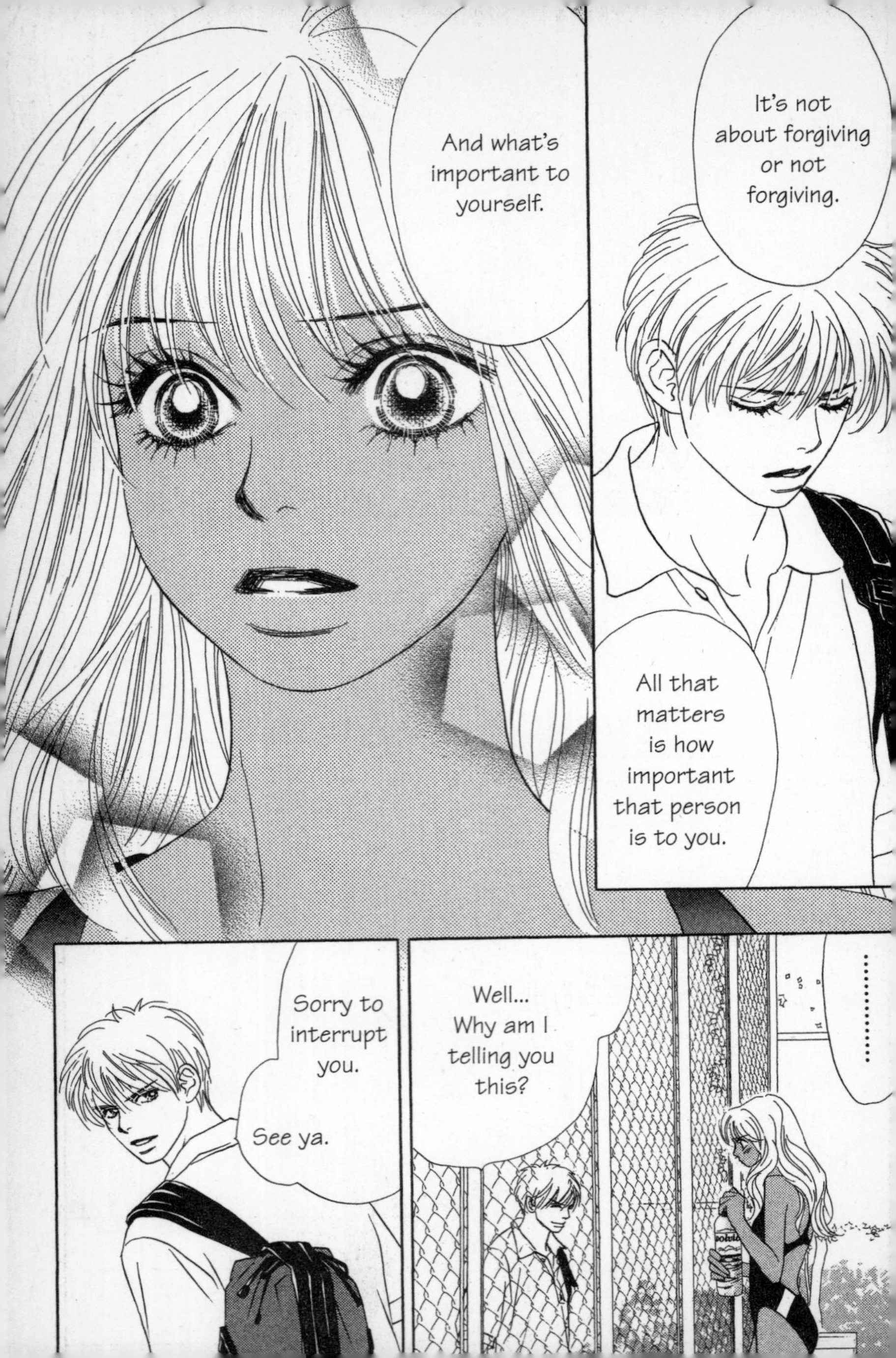

It's not about forgiving or not forgiving.
All that matters is how important that person is to you.
And what's important to yourself.
....
Well... Why am I telling you this?
Sorry to interrupt you.
See ya.

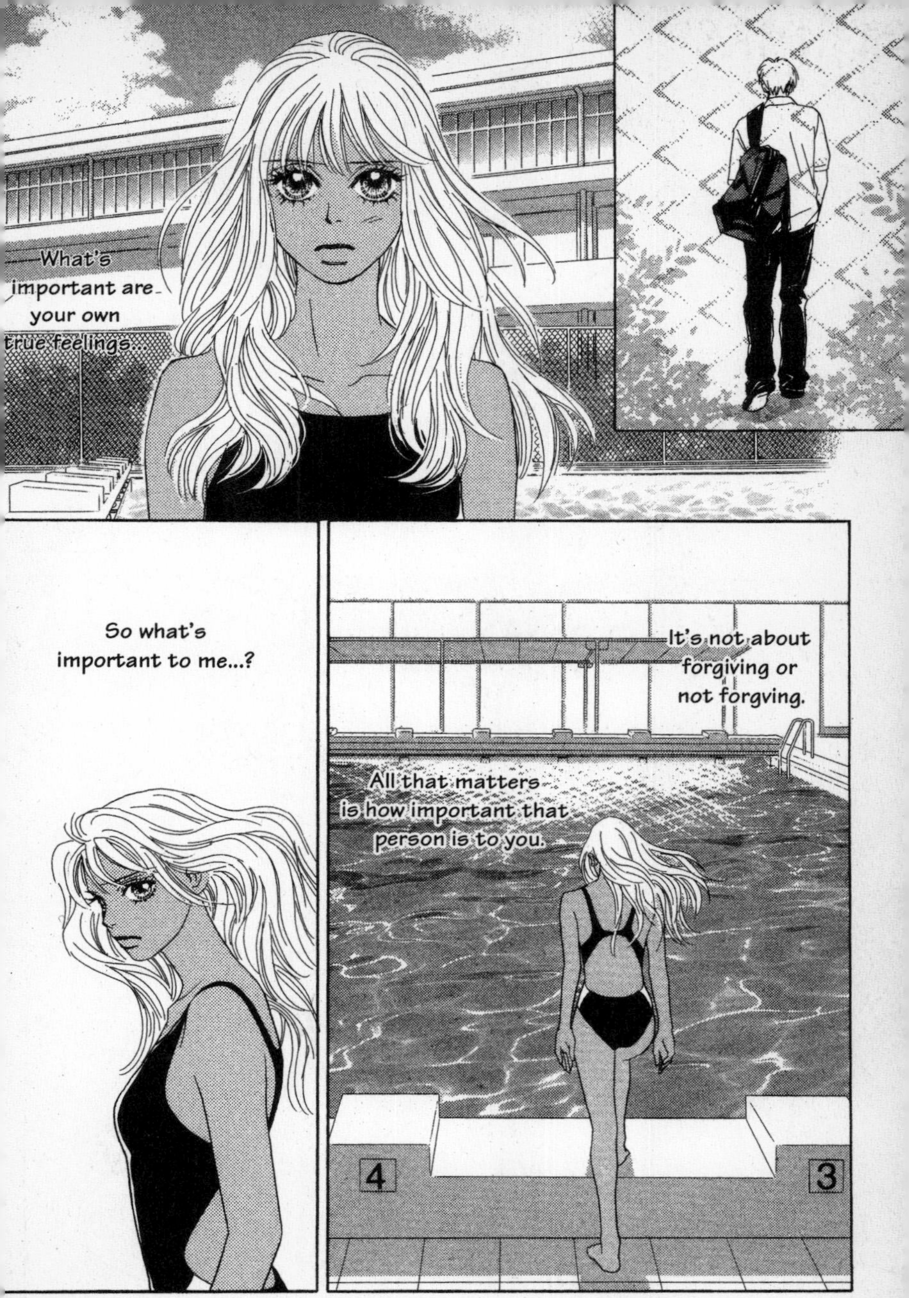

What's important are your own true feelings...
It's not about forgiving or not forgving.
All that matters is how important that person is to you.
So what's important to me...?

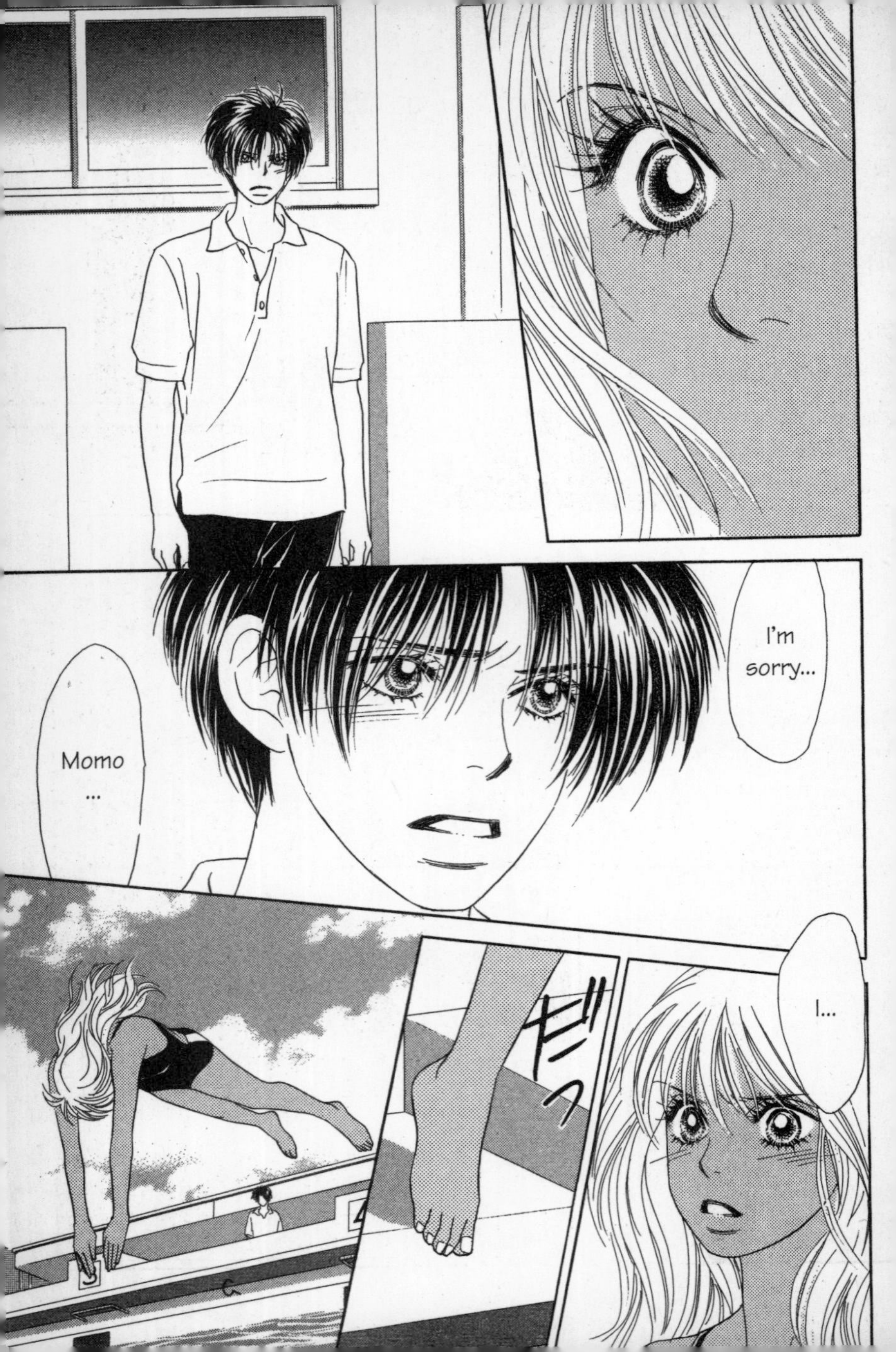
I'm sorry...
Momo ...
I...
ギっ

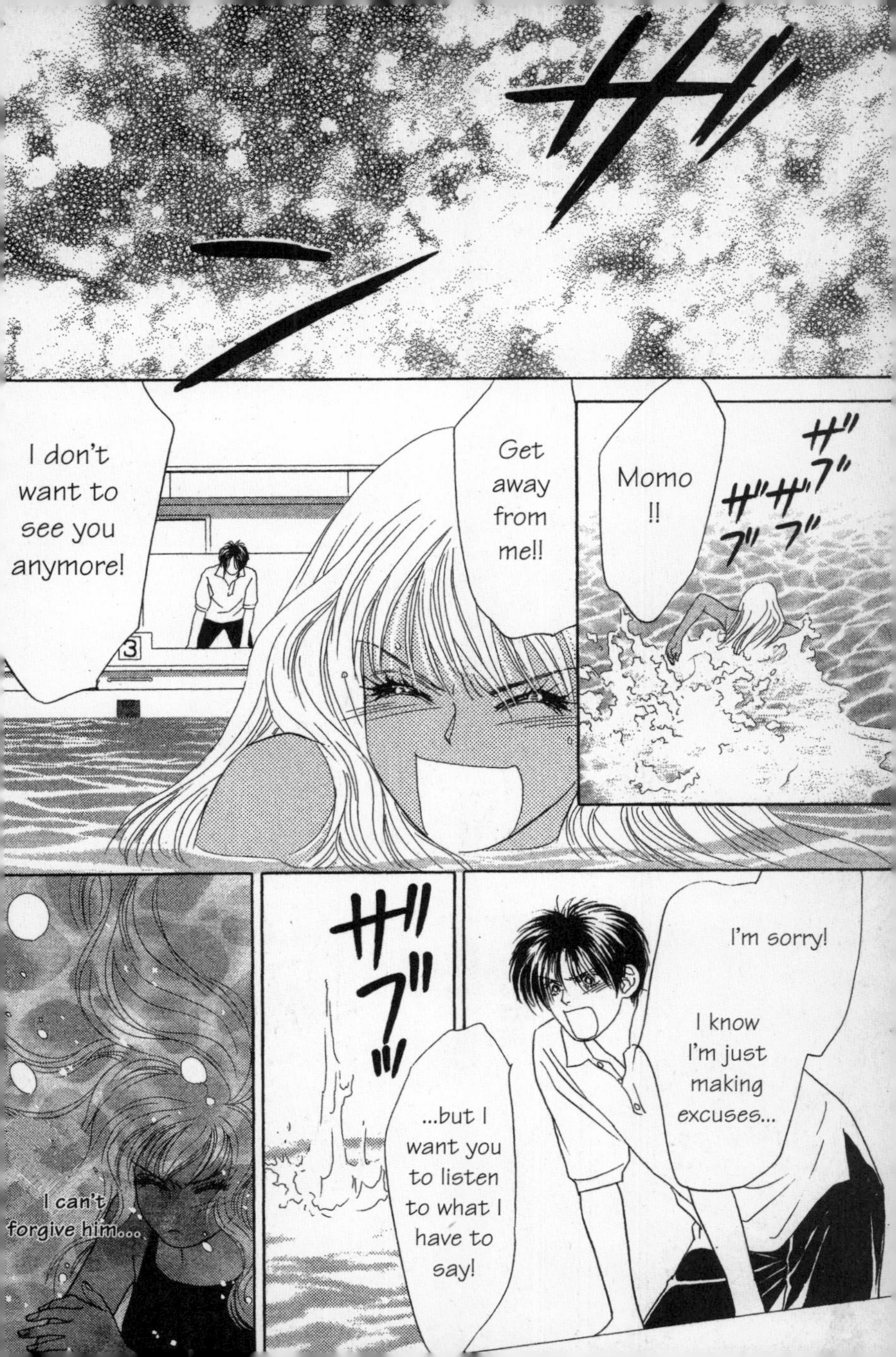
ザブ
ザブ
ザブ
Momo !!
Get away from me!!
I don't want to see you anymore!
I'm sorry!
I know I'm just making excuses...
...but I want you to listen to what I have to say!
ザブッ
I can't forgive him...

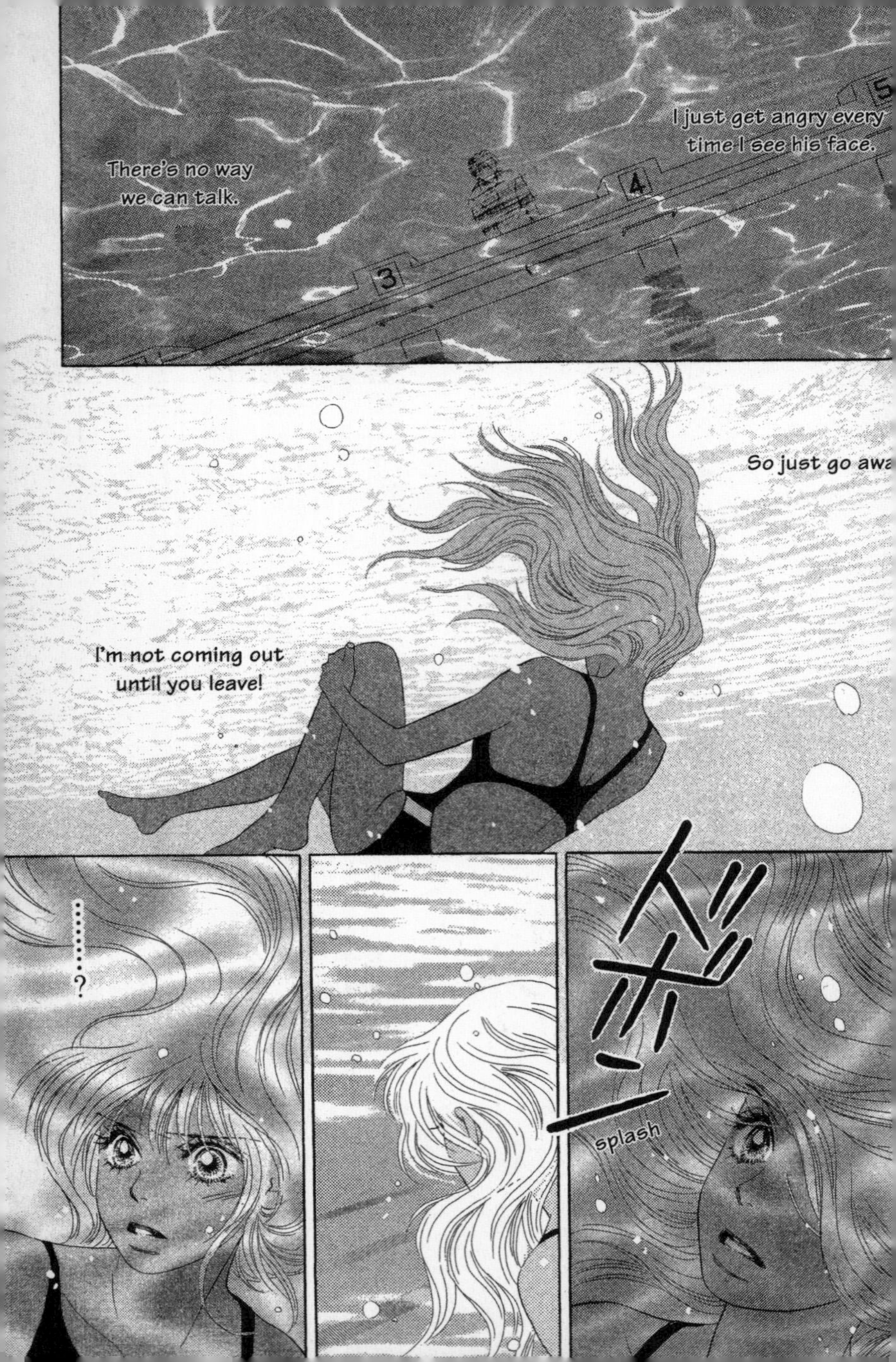
I just get angry every time I see his face.
There's no way we can talk.
So just go awa
I'm not coming out until you leave!
ドッボー
splash
......?

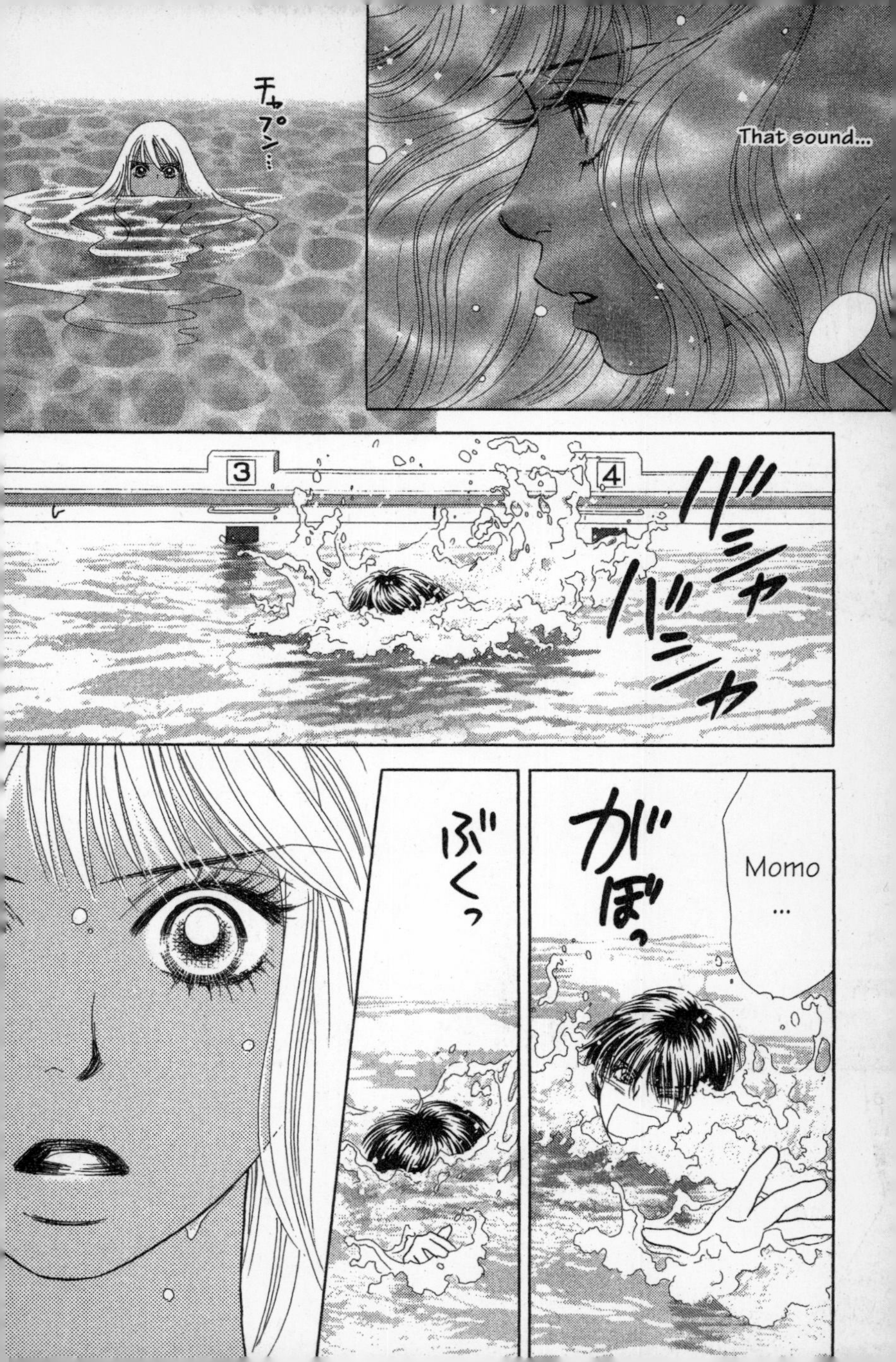
That sound...
チャプン…
ザシャ
バシャ
Momo
...
がぼっ
ぶくっ

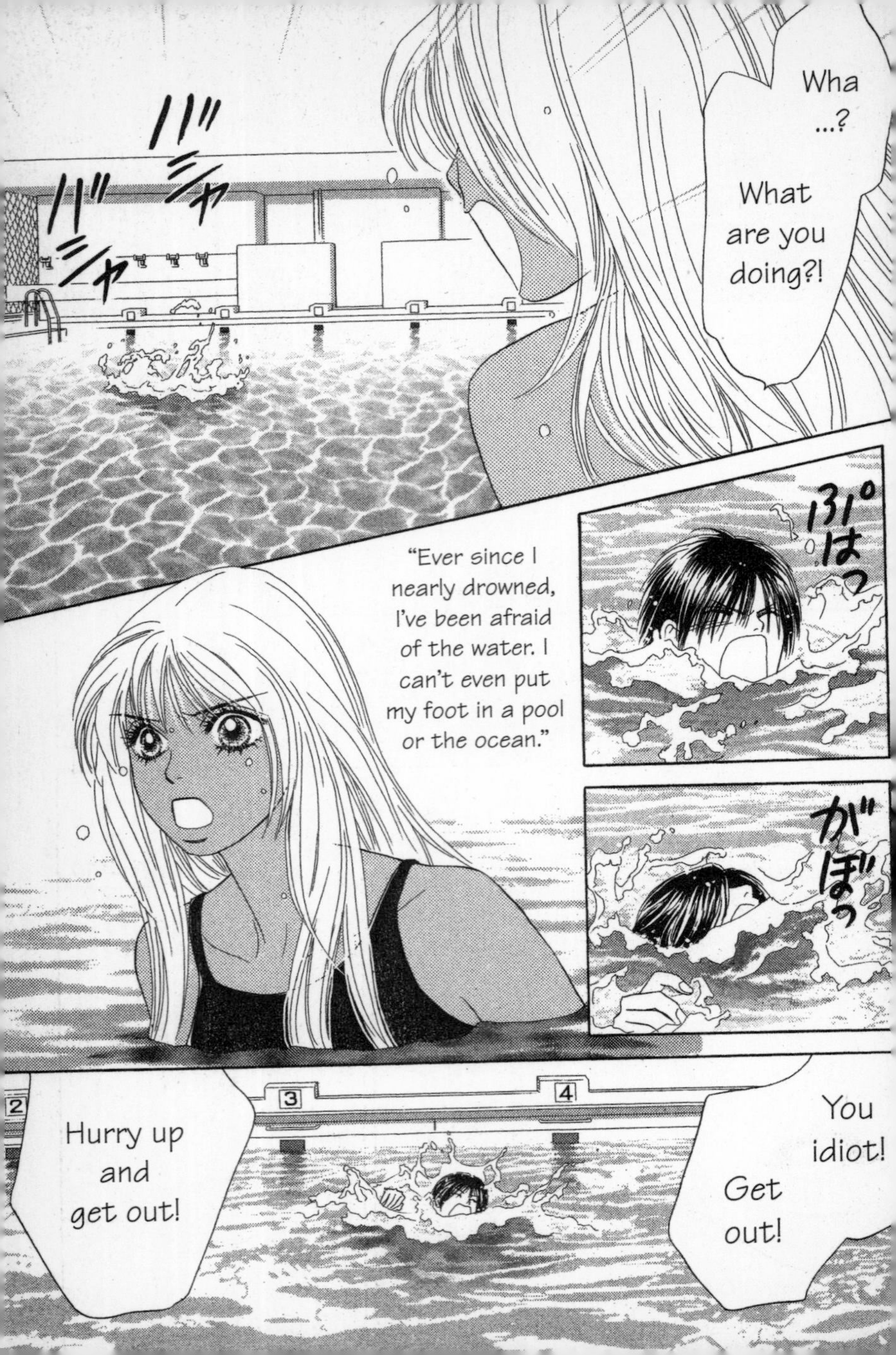
Wha...?
What are you doing?!
バシャ
バシャ
ぷはっ
がぼっ
"Ever since I nearly drowned, I've been afraid of the water. I can't even put my foot in a pool or the ocean."
You idiot!
Get out!
Hurry up and get out!

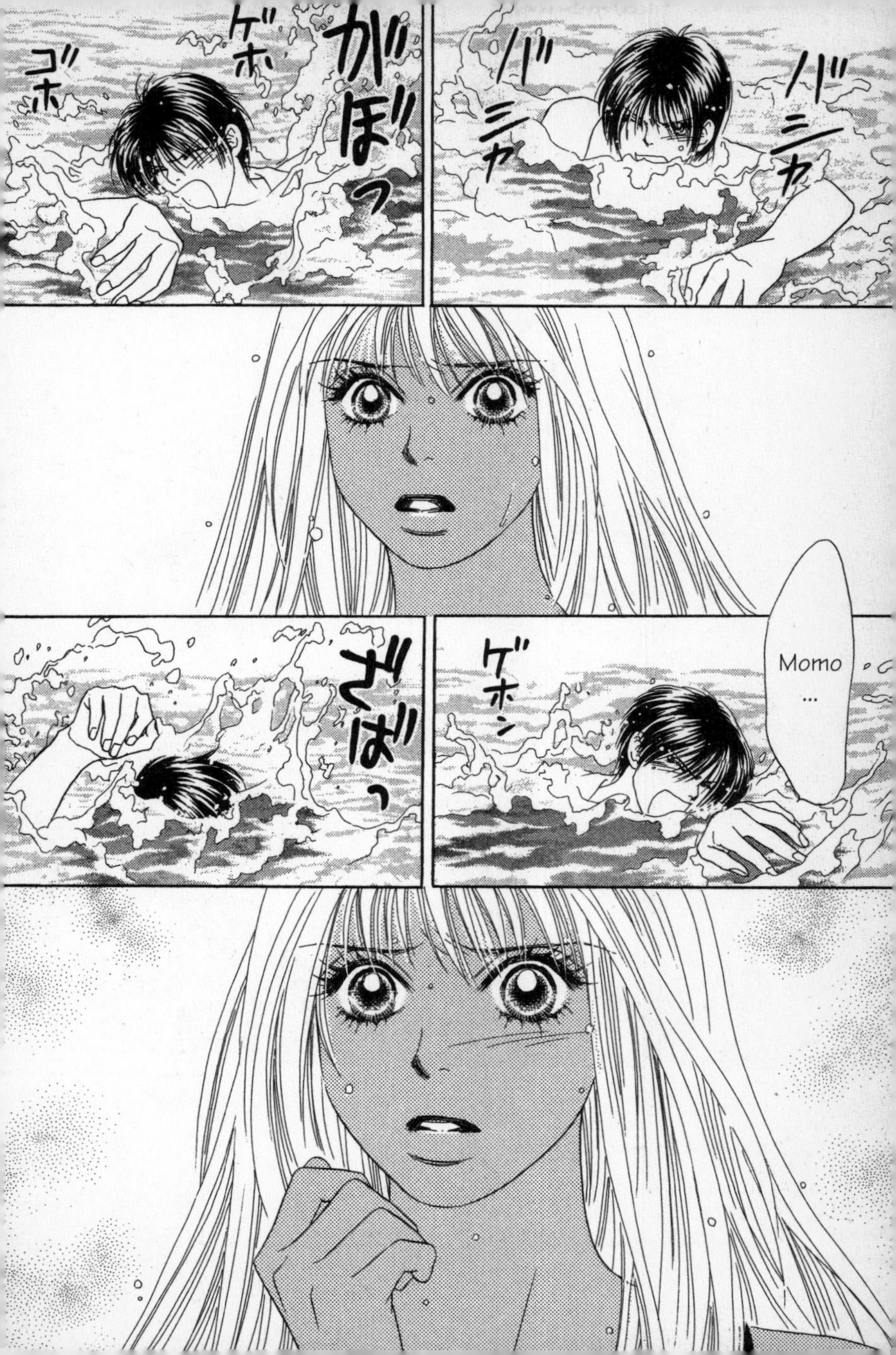

バシャ
バシャ
がぼっ
ゲホ
ゴホ
Momo ...
ゲホン
ざばっ

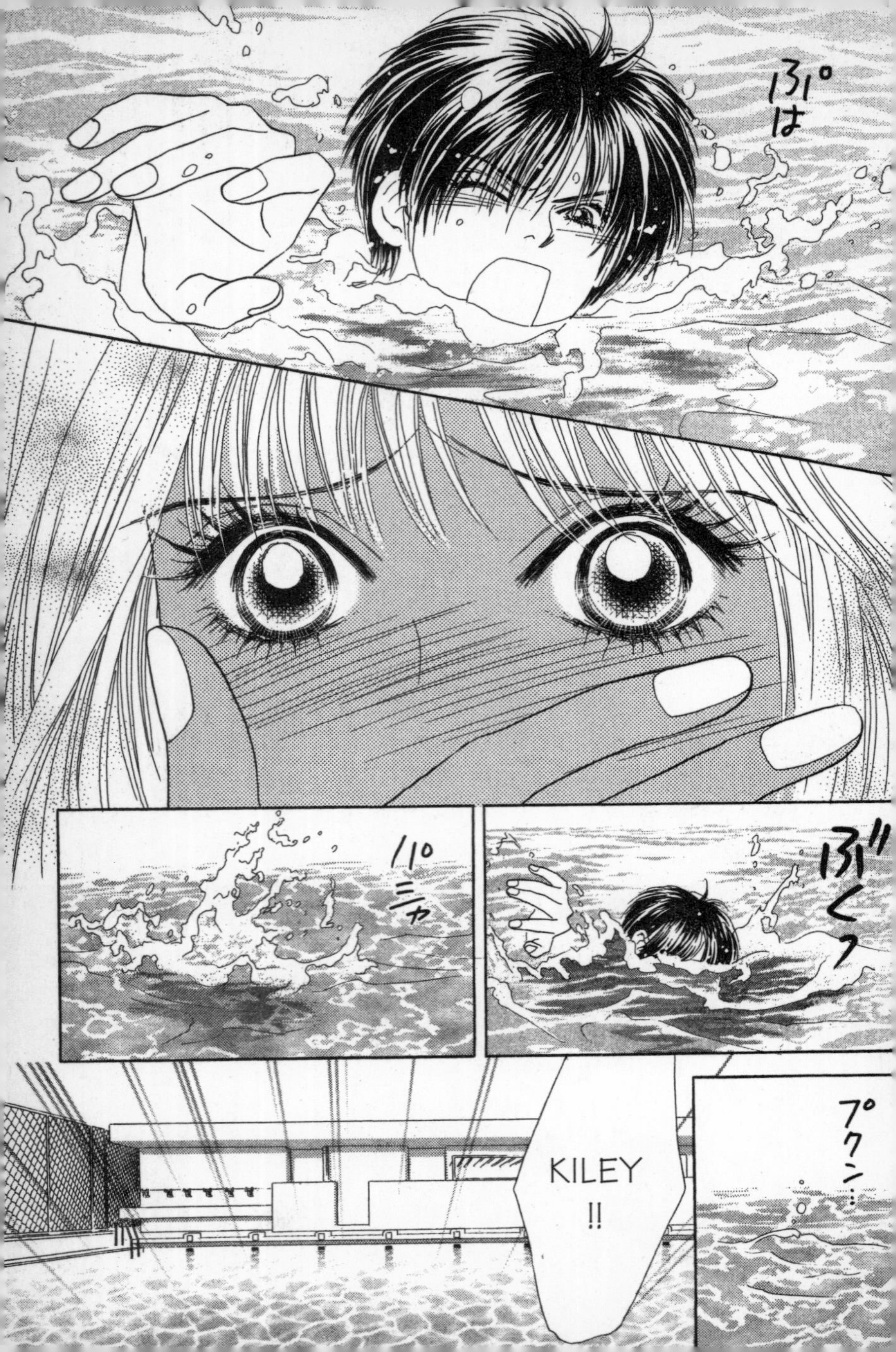
ぷは
ぶくっ
パシャ
プクン…
KILEY !!

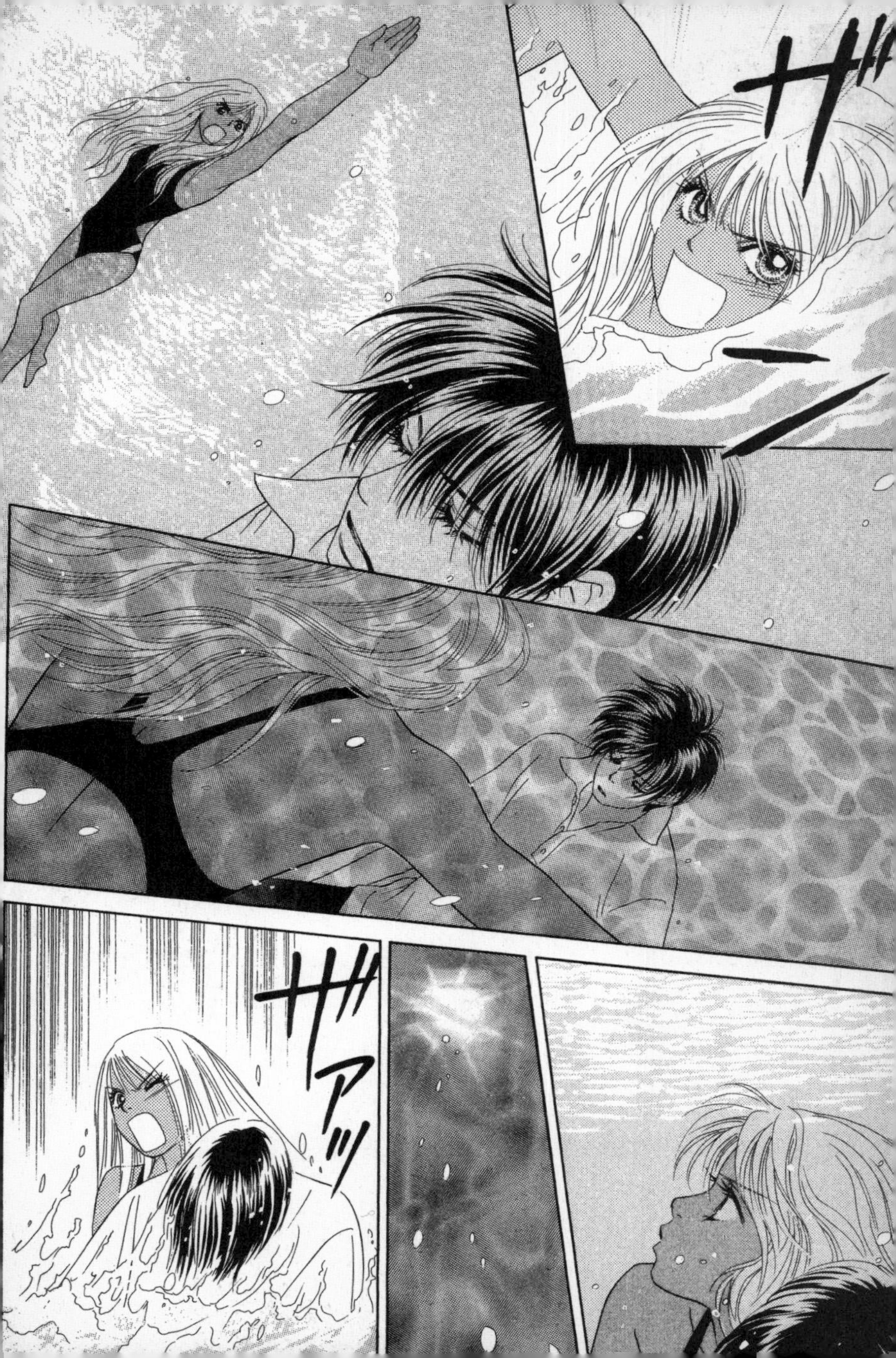
ザ
ザアッ

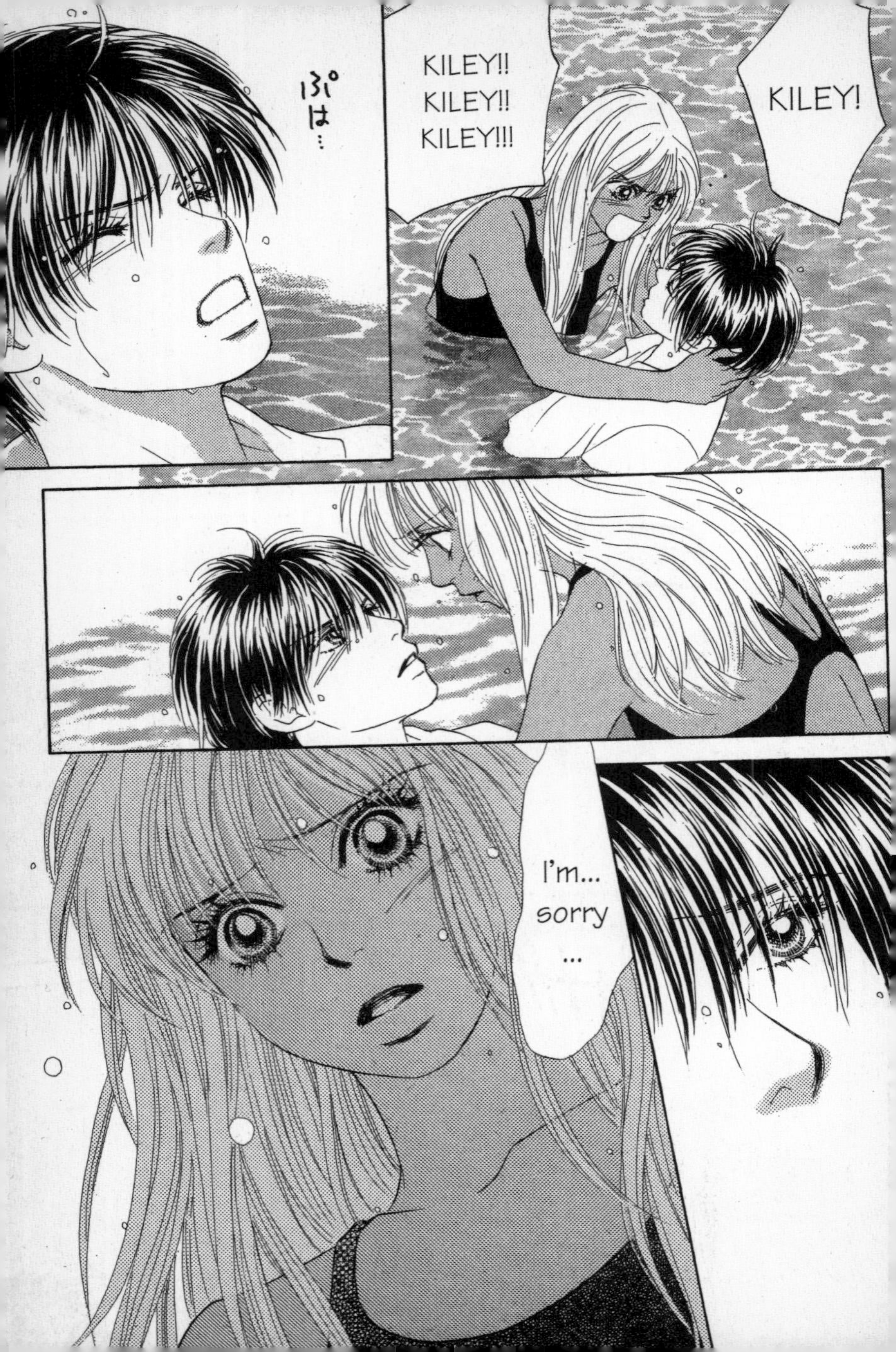
KILEY!
KILEY!! KILEY!! KILEY!!!
ぷは…
I'm... sorry ...

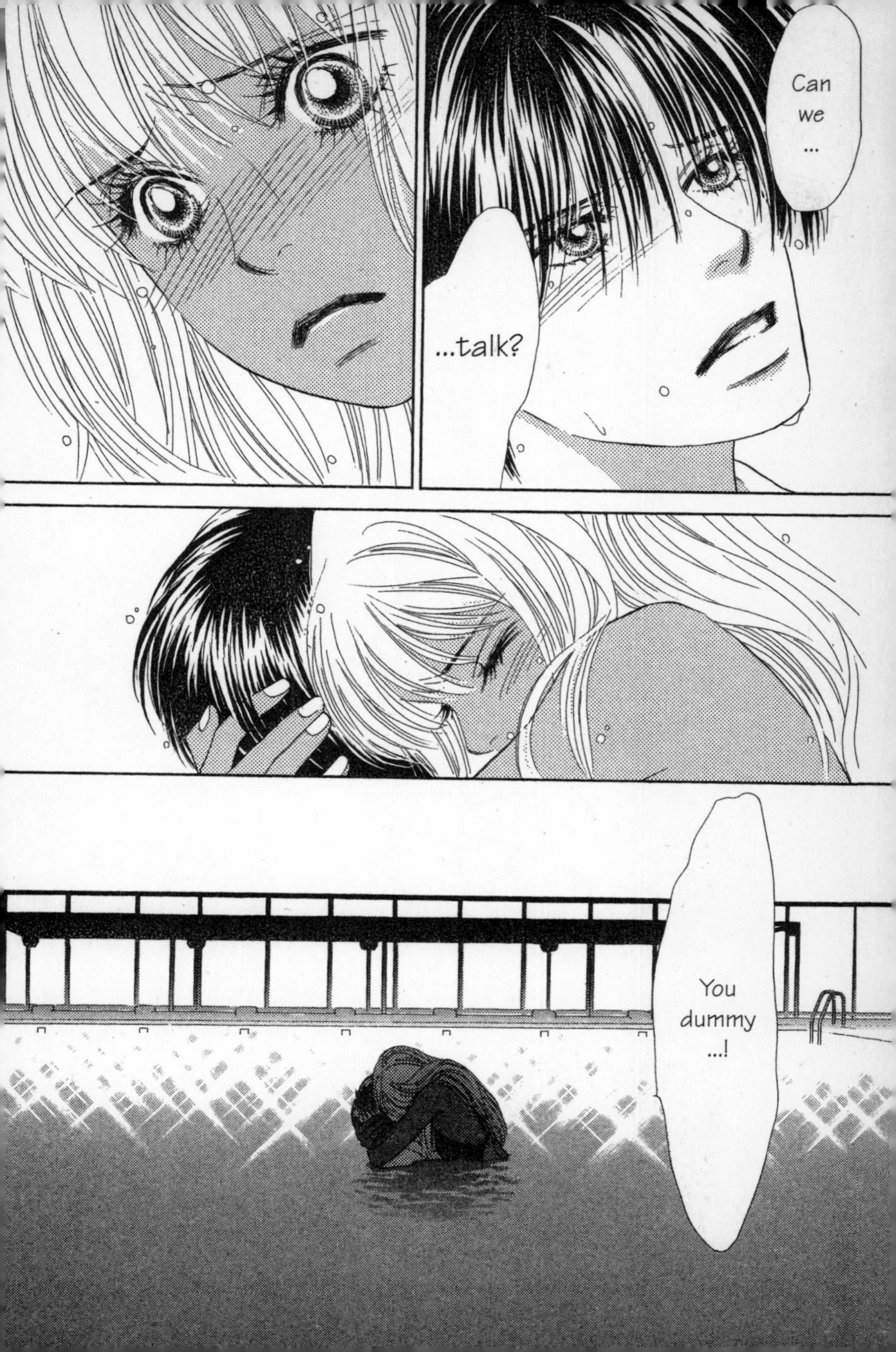
Can we ...
...talk?
You dummy ...!

ピーチガール

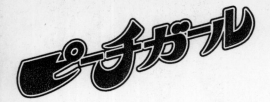

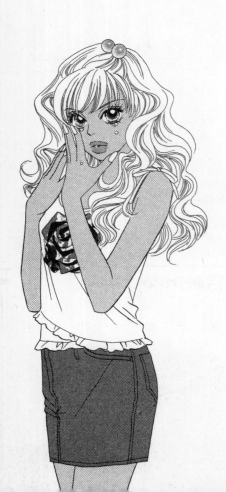

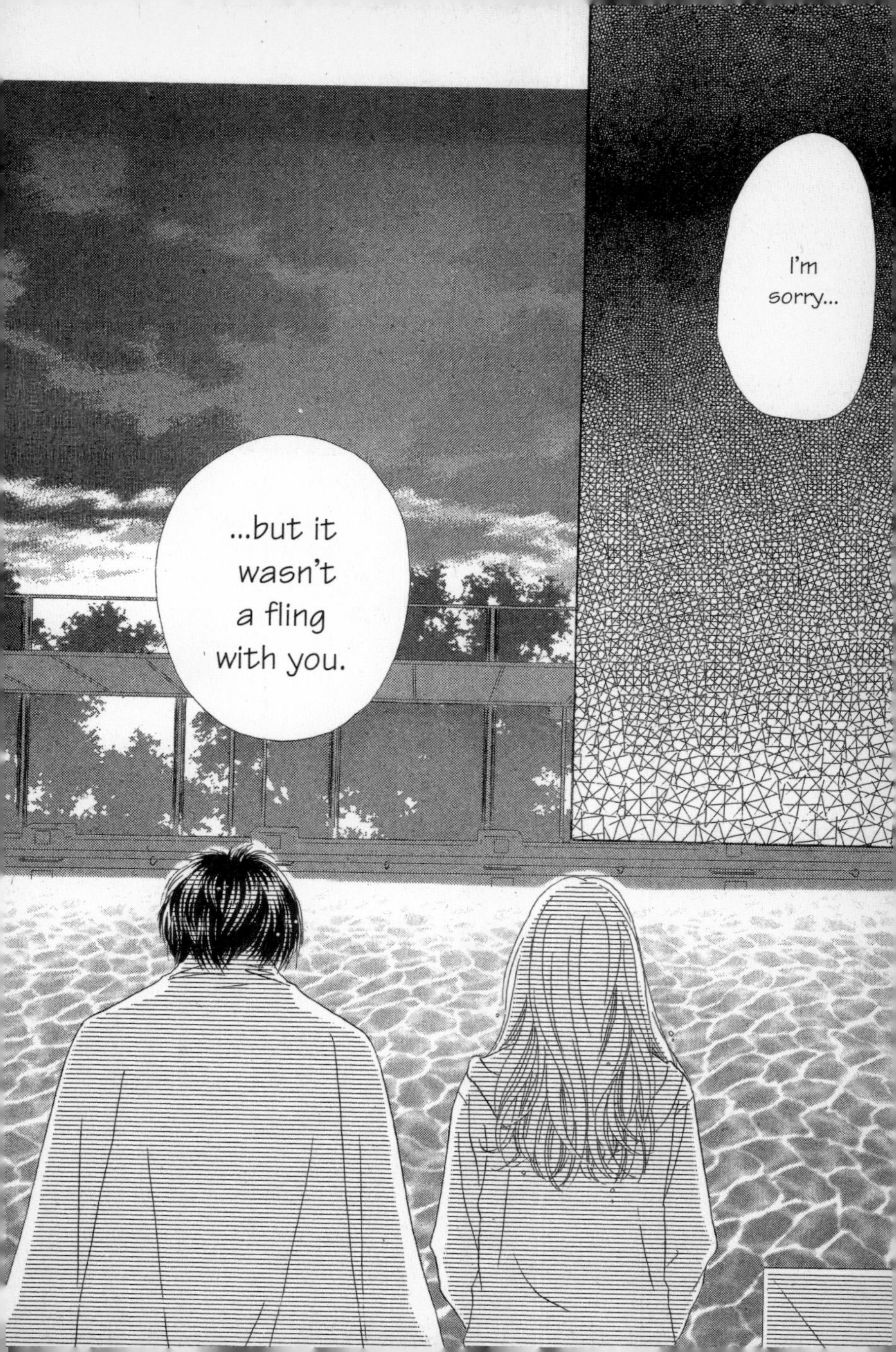
I'm sorry...
...but it wasn't a fling with you.

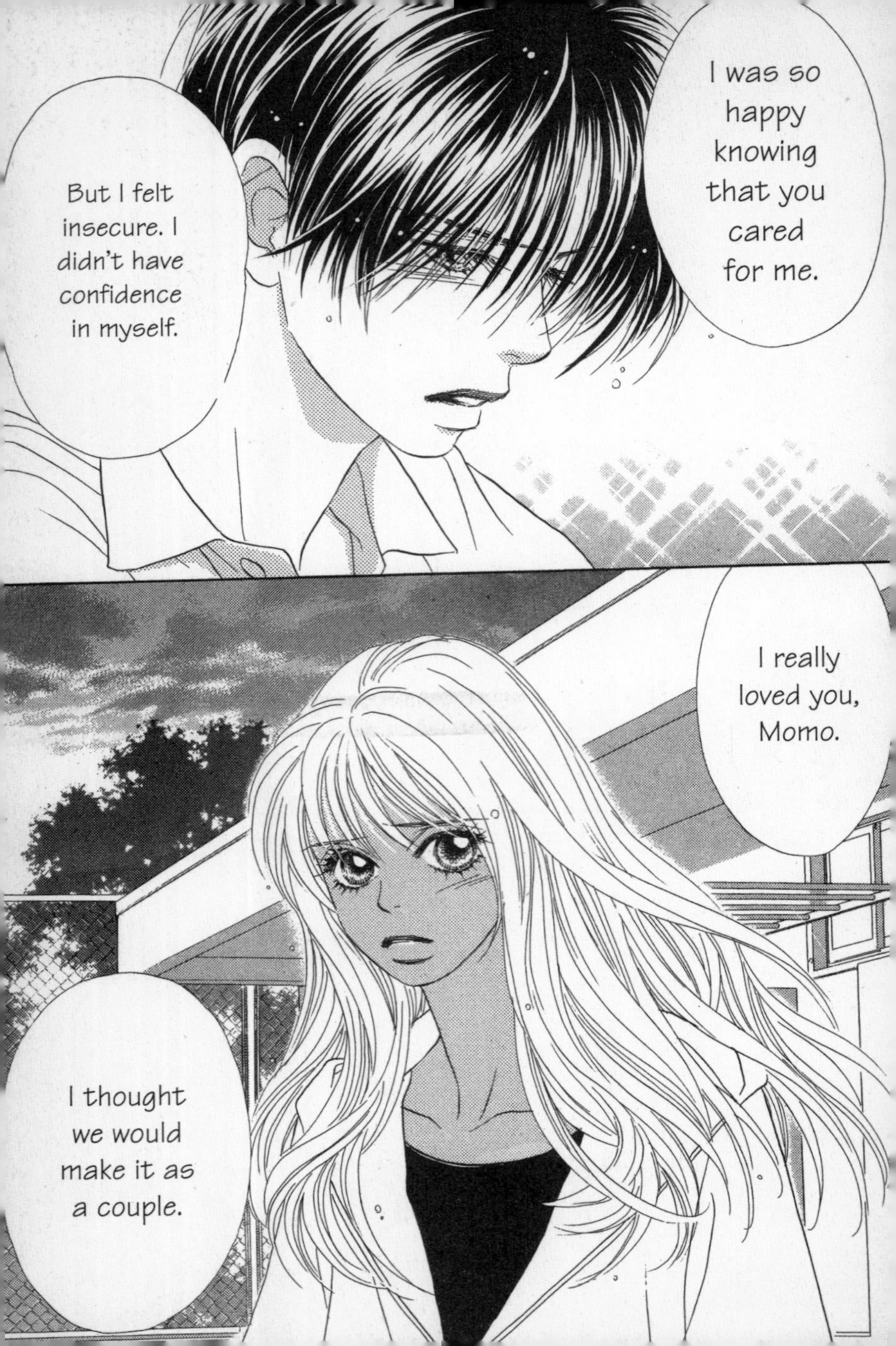
I was so happy knowing that you cared for me.
But I felt insecure. I didn't have confidence in myself.
I really loved you, Momo.
I thought we would make it as a couple.

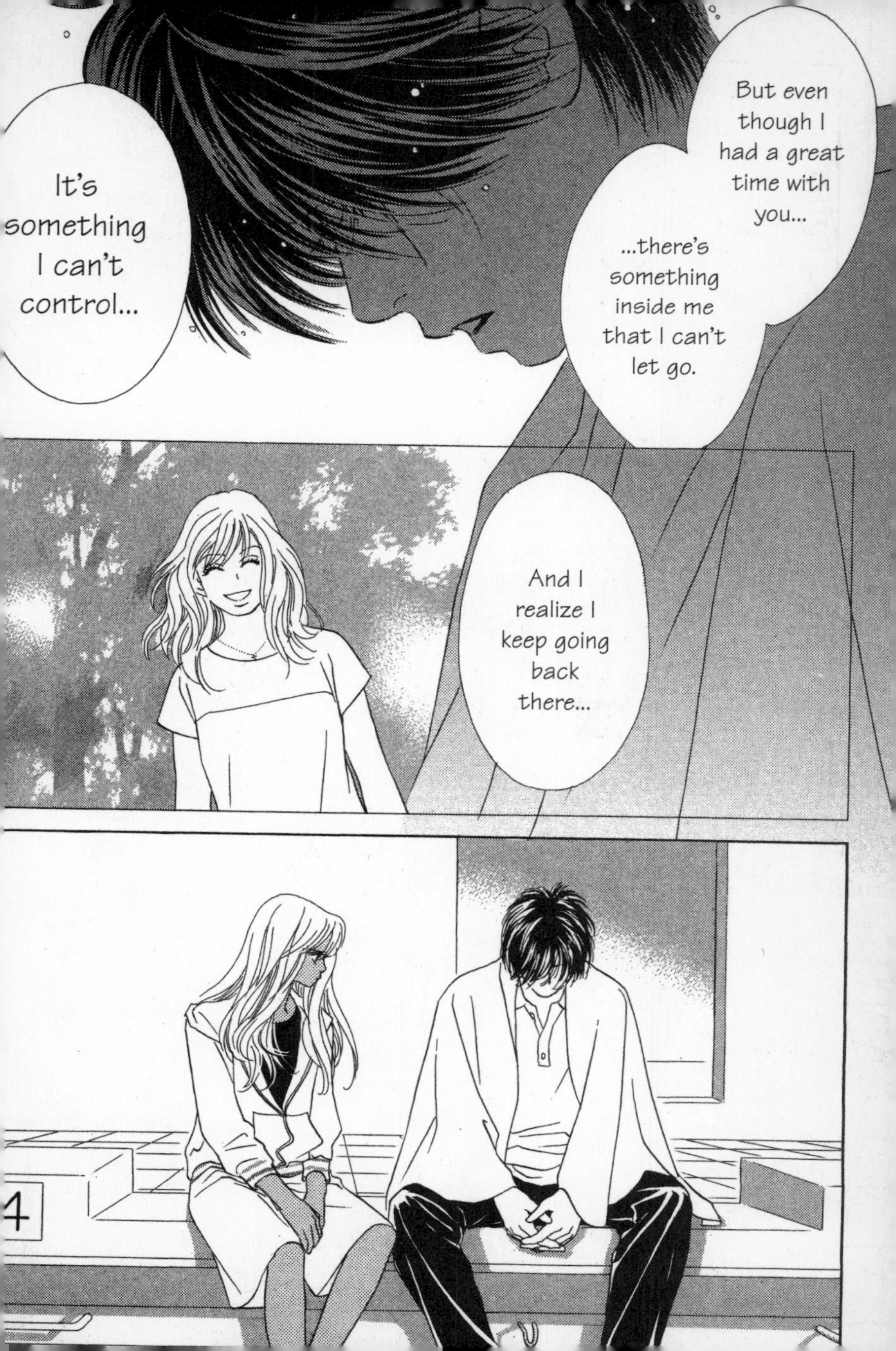
But even though I had a great time with you...
...there's something inside me that I can't let go.
It's something I can't control...
And I realize I keep going back there...
4

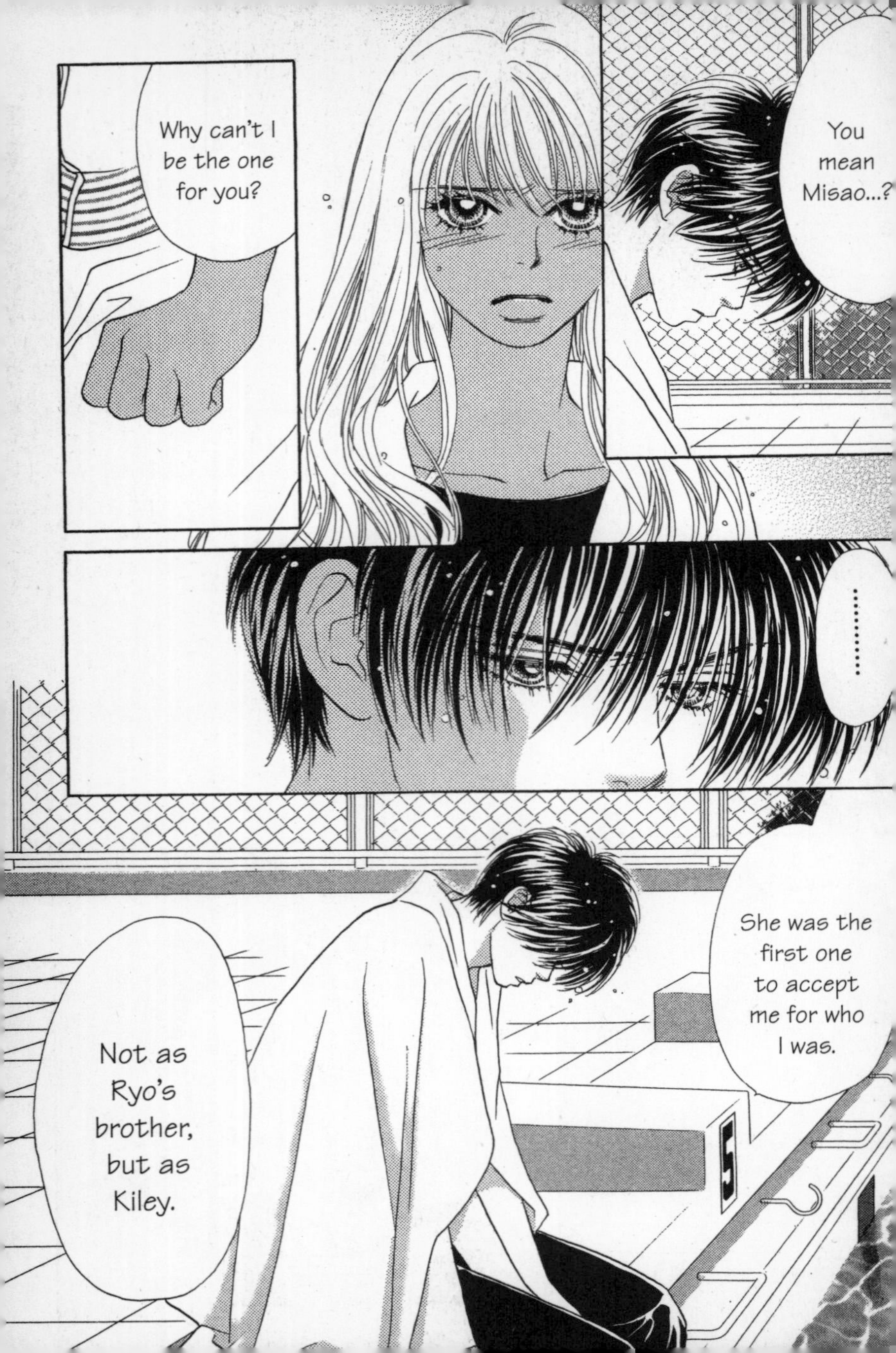
You mean Misao...?
Why can't I be the one for you?
......
She was the first one to accept me for who I was.
Not as Ryo's brother, but as Kiley.

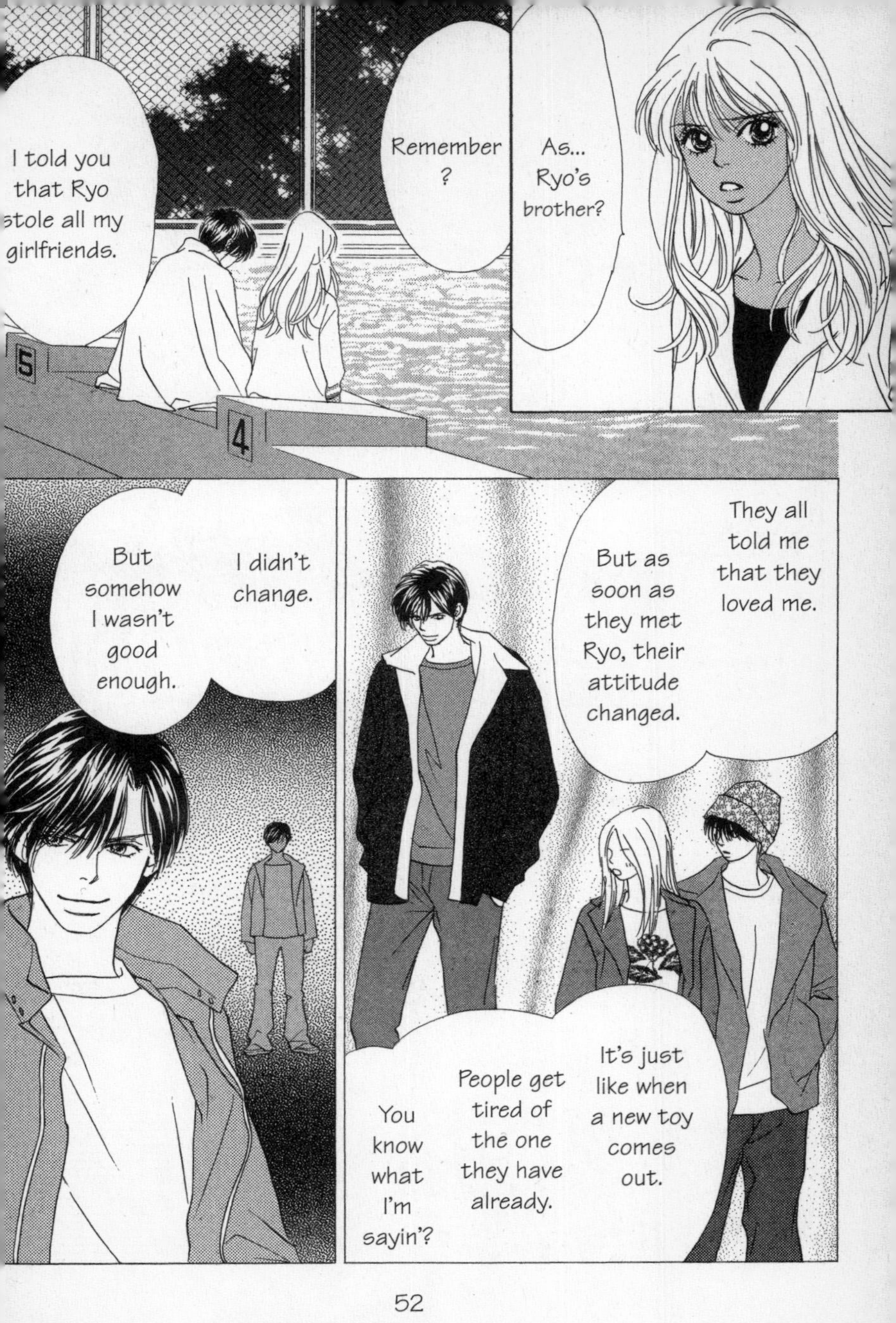
As... Ryo's brother?
Remember?
I told you that Ryo stole all my girlfriends.
They all told me that they loved me.
But as soon as they met Ryo, their attitude changed.
It's just like when a new toy comes out.
People get tired of the one they have already.
You know what I'm sayin'?
I didn't change.
But somehow I wasn't good enough.

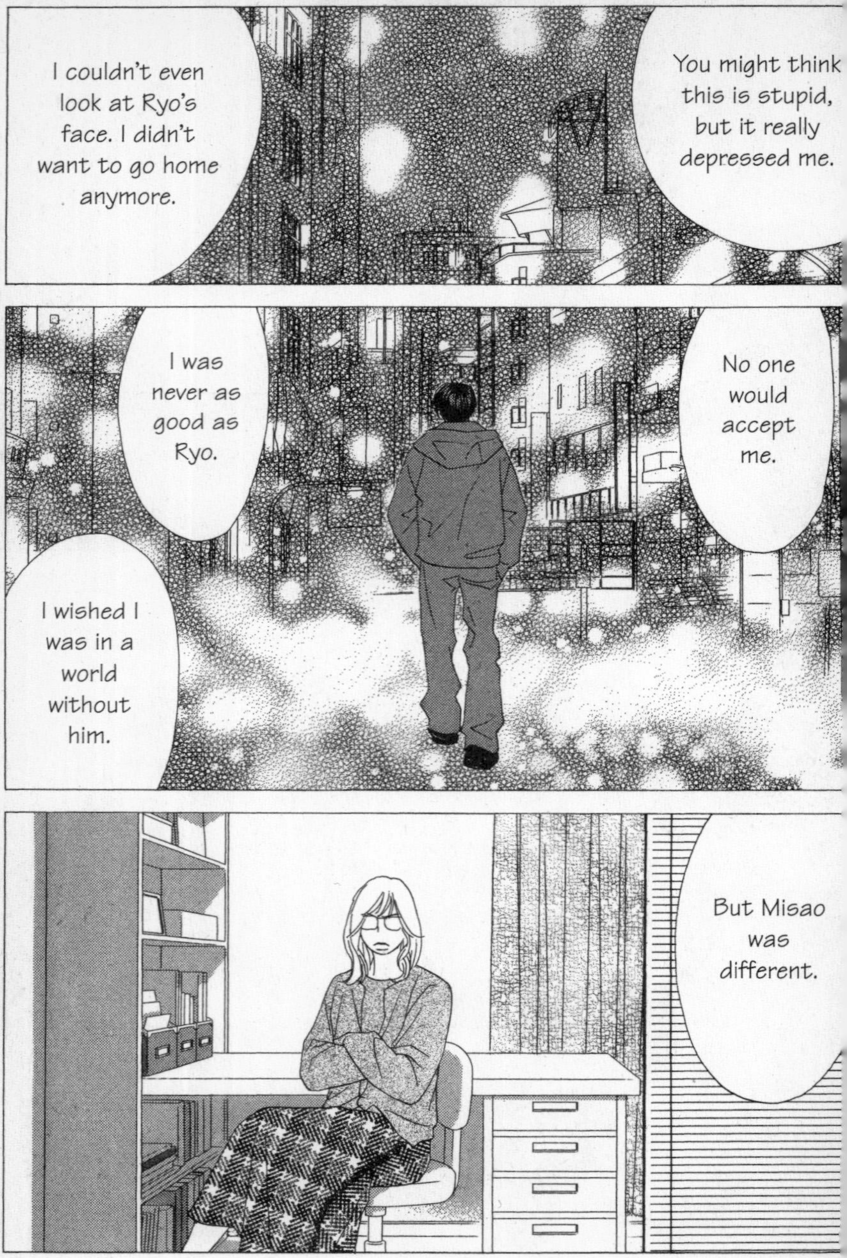
You might think this is stupid, but it really depressed me.
I couldn't even look at Ryo's face. I didn't want to go home anymore.
No one would accept me.
I was never as good as Ryo.
I wished I was in a world without him.
But Misao was different.

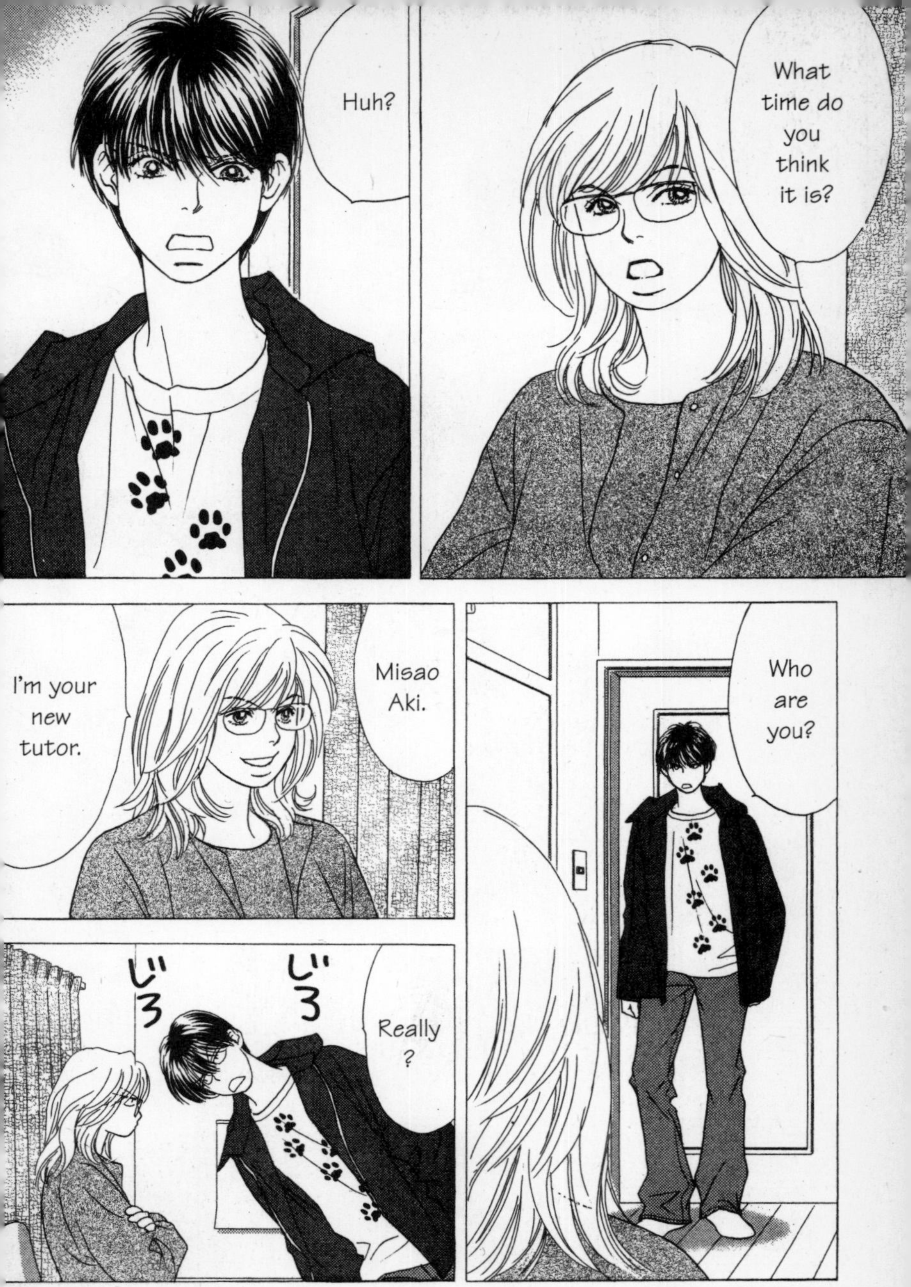
What time do you think it is?
Huh?
Who are you?
Misao Aki.
I'm your new tutor.
Really?
じろ
じろ

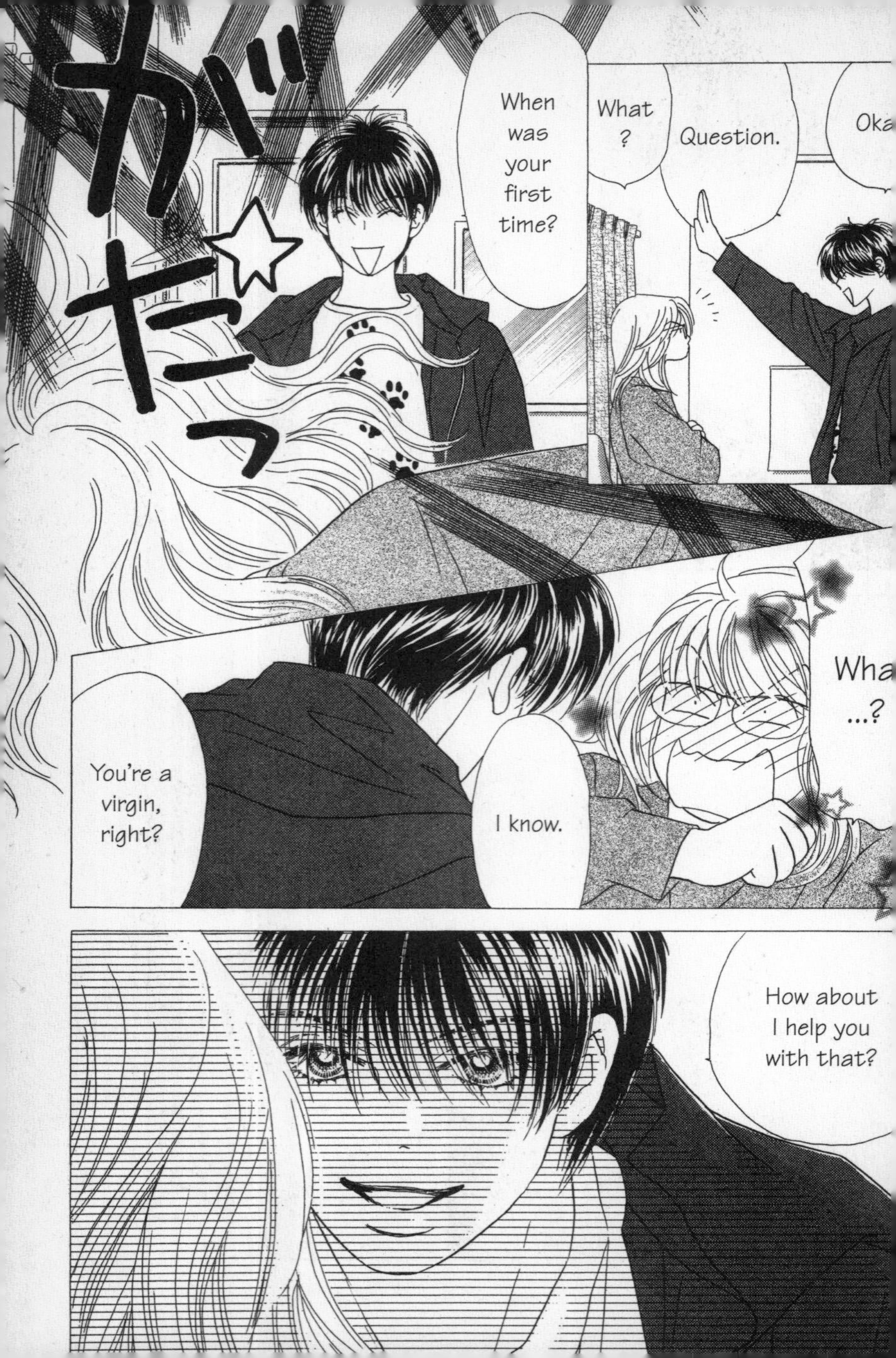

Oka
Question.
What?
When was your first time?
がたーっ
What...?
I know.
You're a virgin, right?
How about I help you with that?

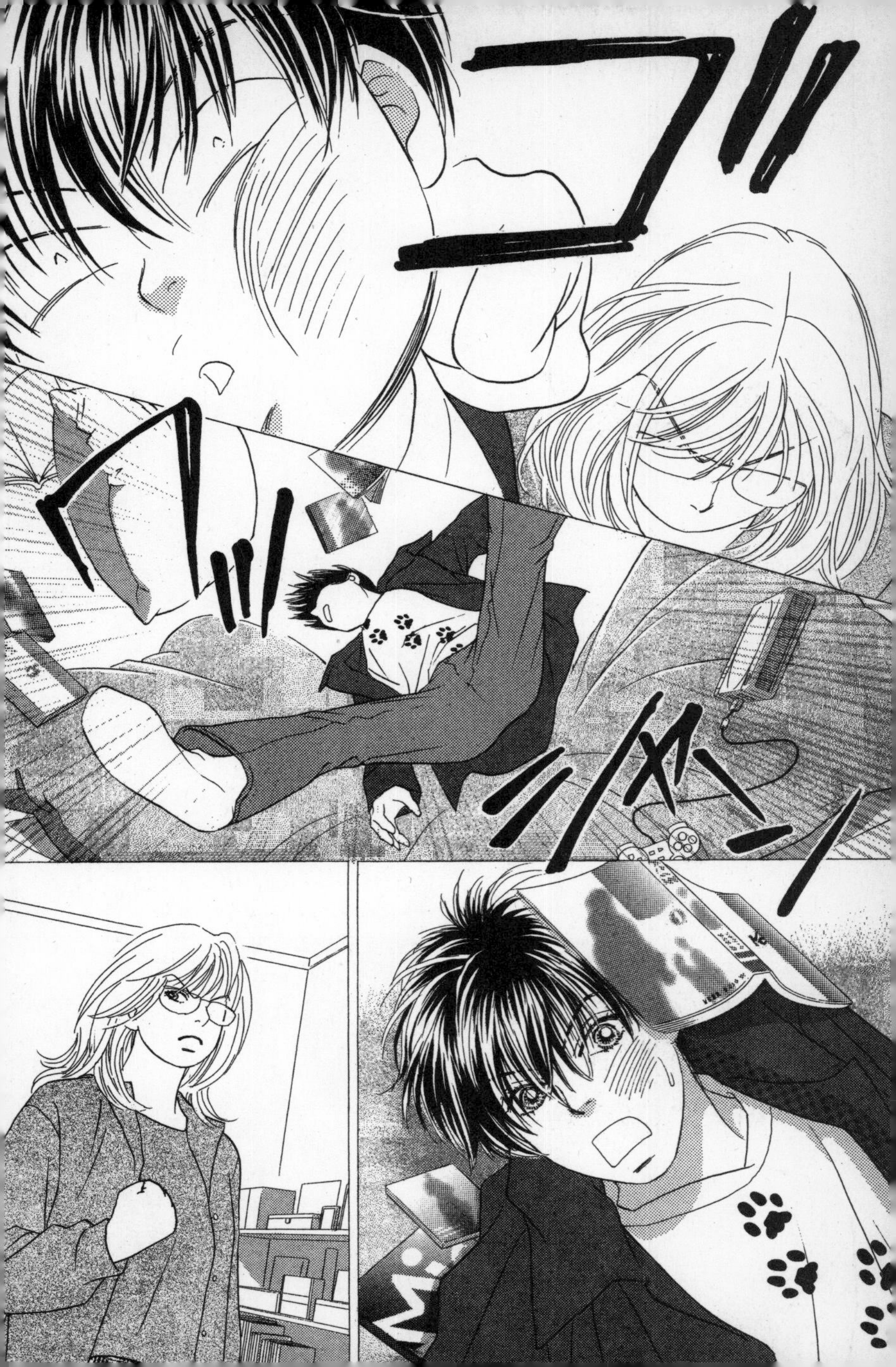

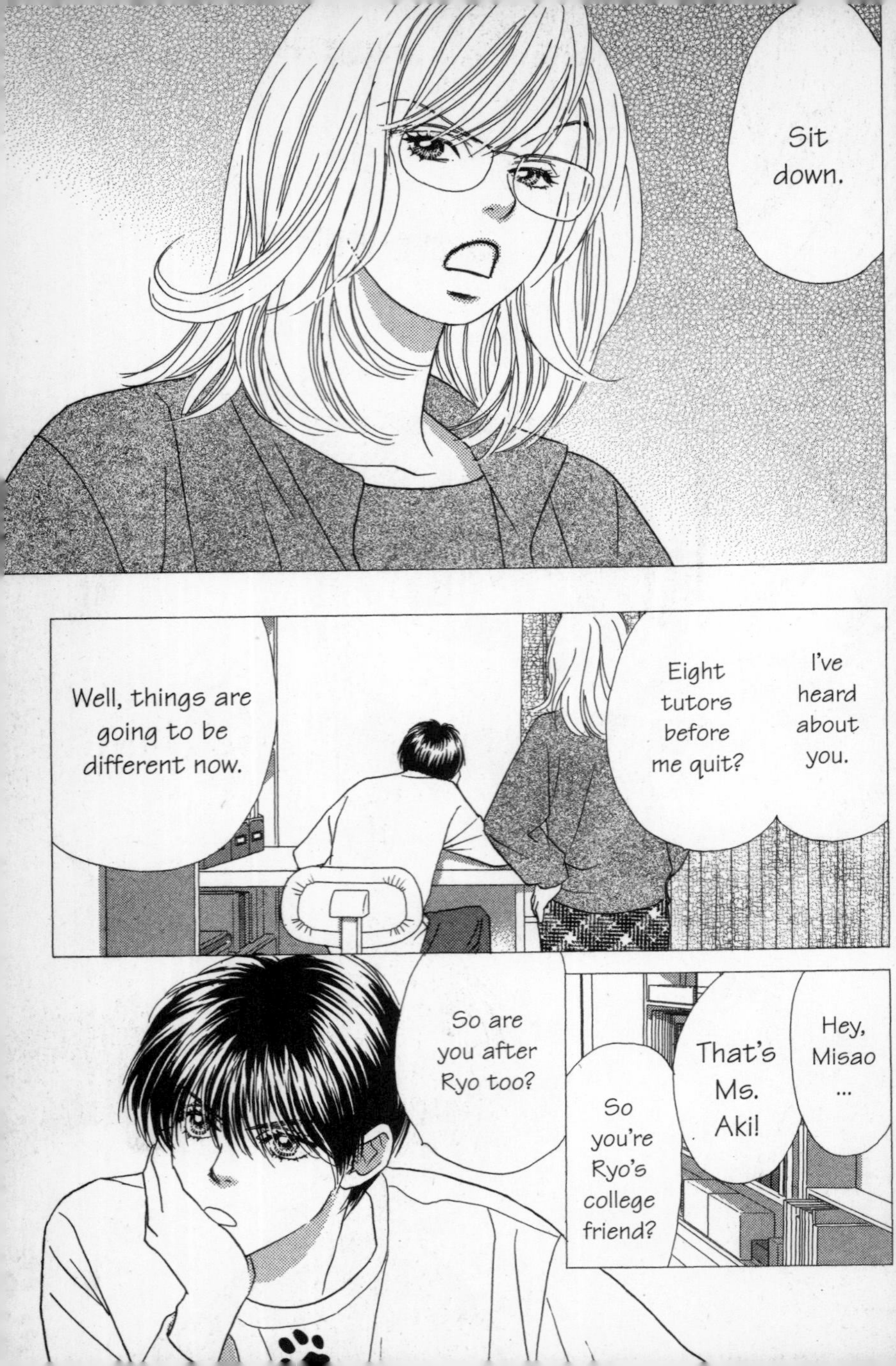
Sit down.
I've heard about you.
Eight tutors before me quit?
Well, things are going to be different now.
Hey, Misao ...
That's Ms. Aki!
So you're Ryo's college friend?
So are you after Ryo too?

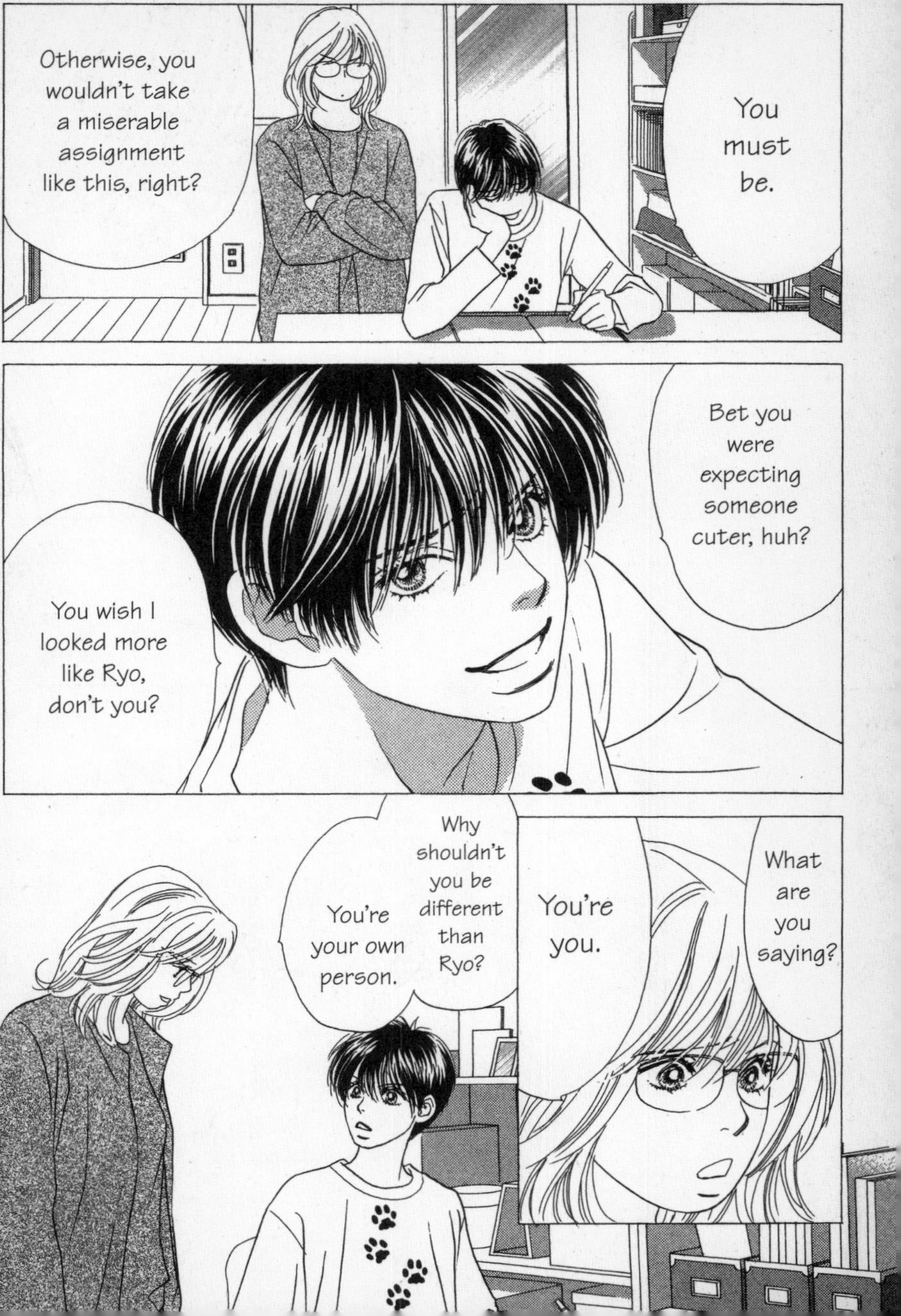
You must be.
Otherwise, you wouldn't take a miserable assignment like this, right?
Bet you were expecting someone cuter, huh?
You wish I looked more like Ryo, don't you?
What are you saying?
You're you.
Why shouldn't you be different than Ryo?
You're your own person.

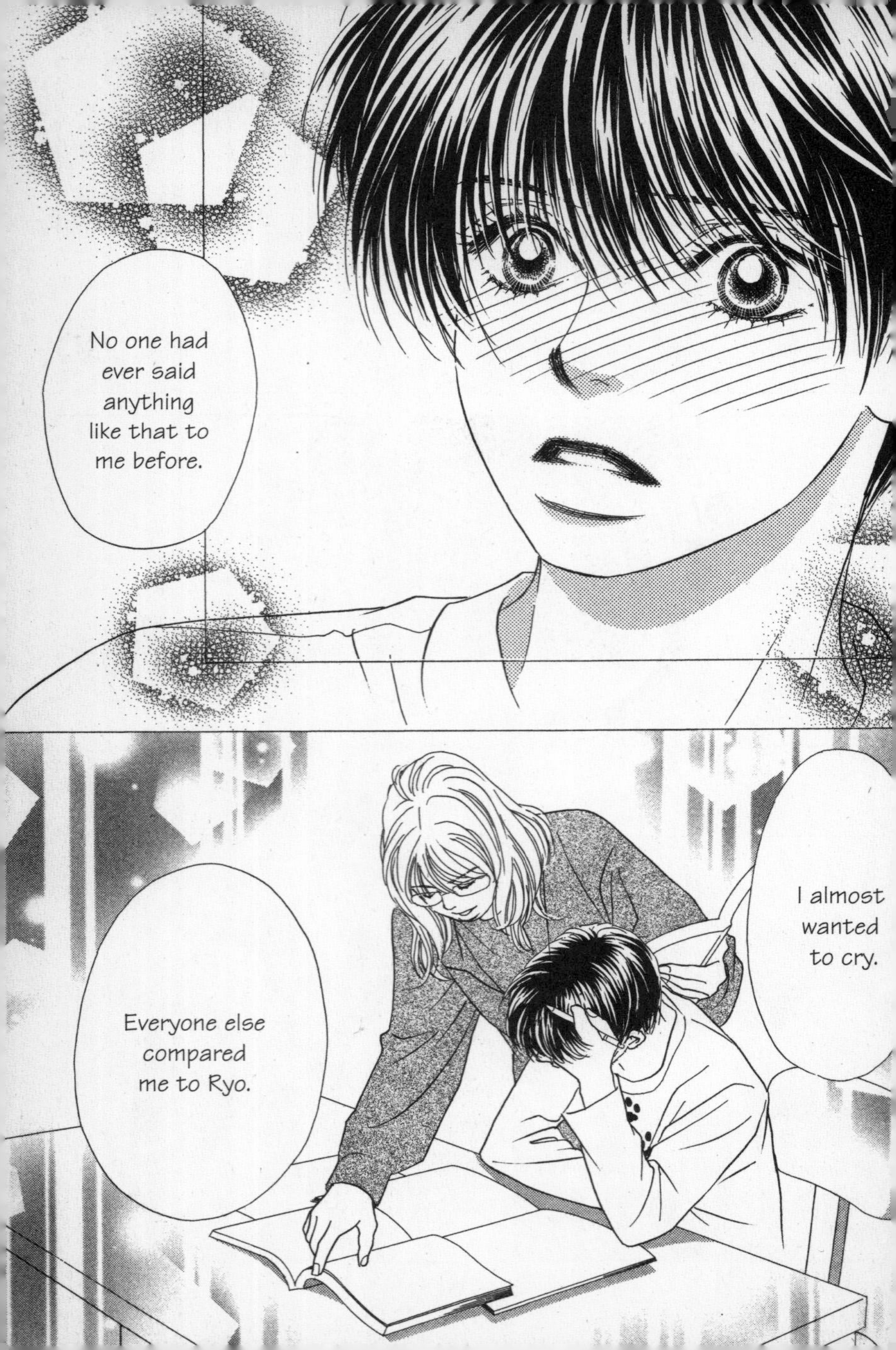
No one had ever said anything like that to me before.
I almost wanted to cry.
Everyone else compared me to Ryo.

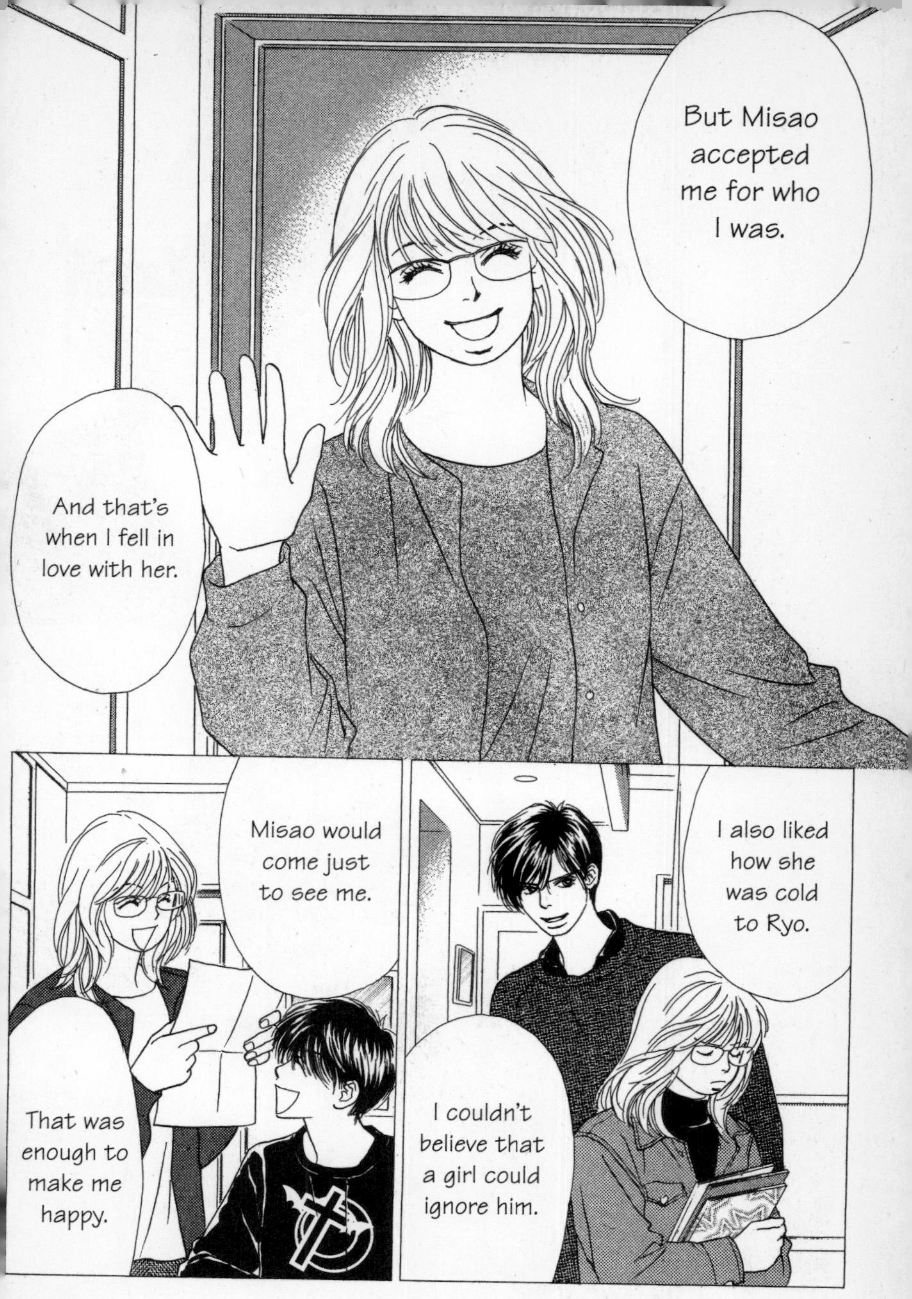
But Misao accepted me for who I was.
And that's when I fell in love with her.
I also liked how she was cold to Ryo.
I couldn't believe that a girl could ignore him.
Misao would come just to see me.
That was enough to make me happy.

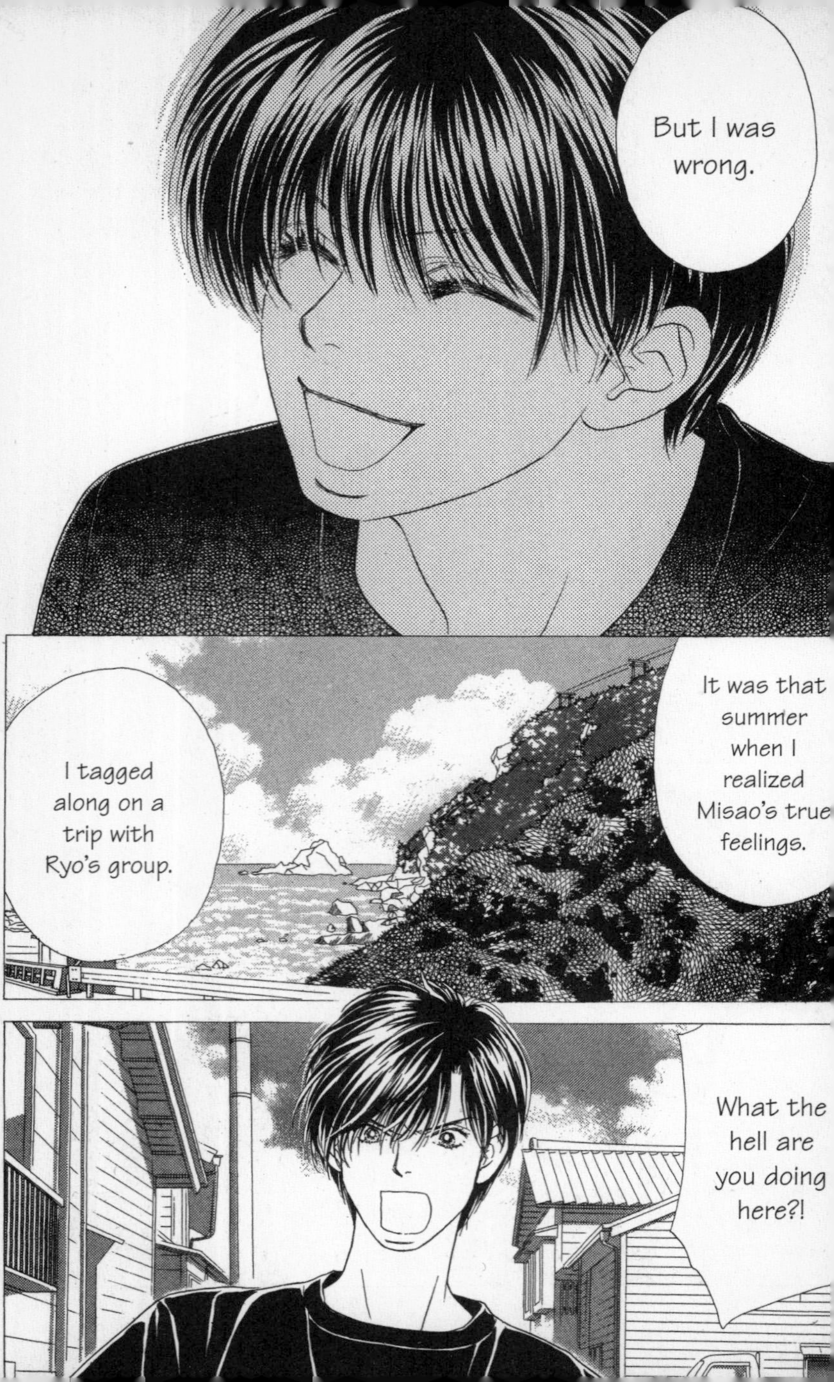
But I was wrong.
It was that summer when I realized Misao's true feelings.
I tagged along on a trip with Ryo's group.
What the hell are you doing here?!

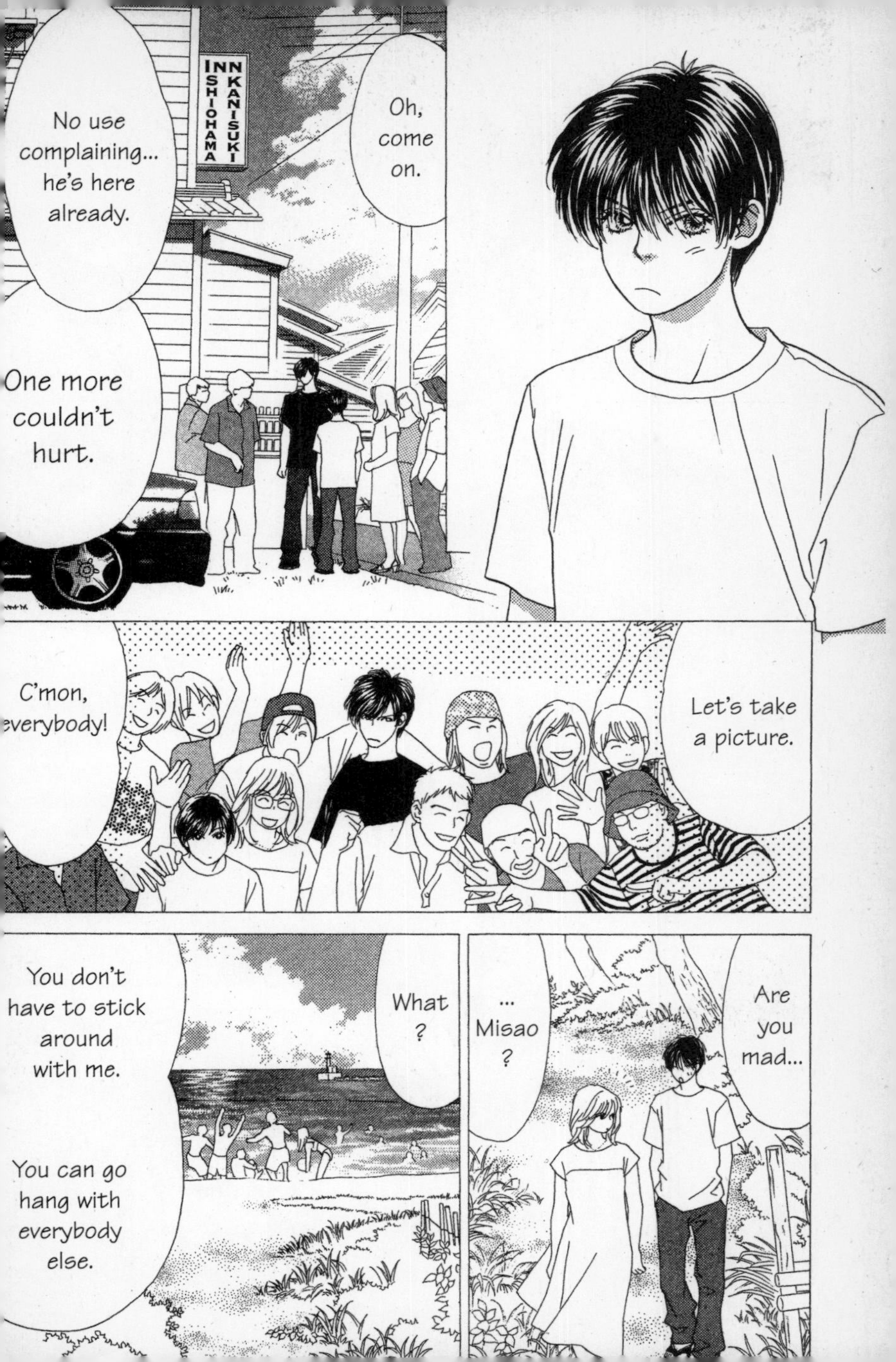
Oh, come on.
No use complaining... he's here already.
One more couldn't hurt.
Let's take a picture.
C'mon, everybody!
Are you mad...
...Misao?
What?
You don't have to stick around with me.
You can go hang with everybody else.

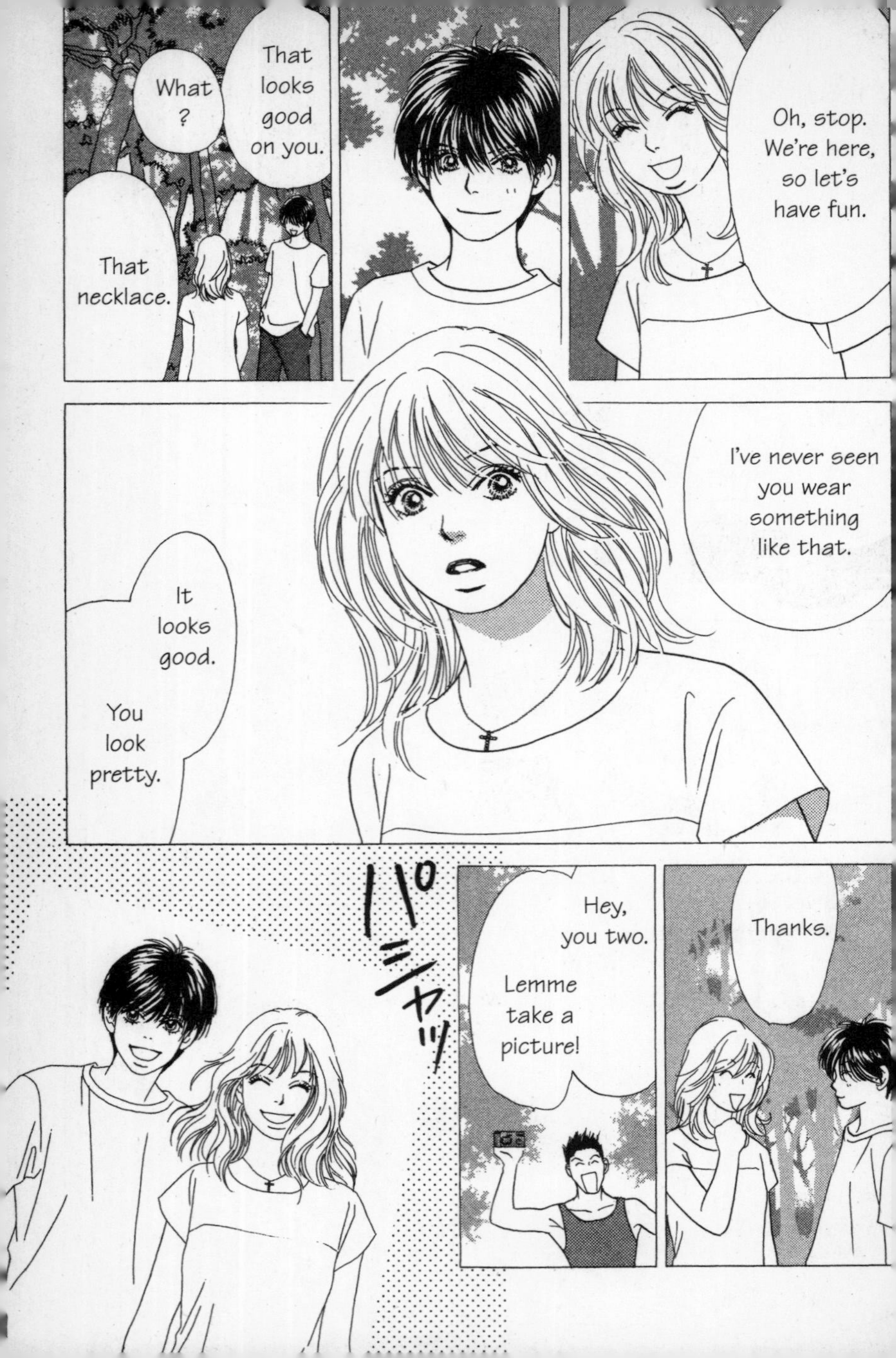
Oh, stop. We're here, so let's have fun.
That looks good on you.
What?
That necklace.
I've never seen you wear something like that.
It looks good.
You look pretty.
Thanks.
Hey, you two.
Lemme take a picture!
パシャッ

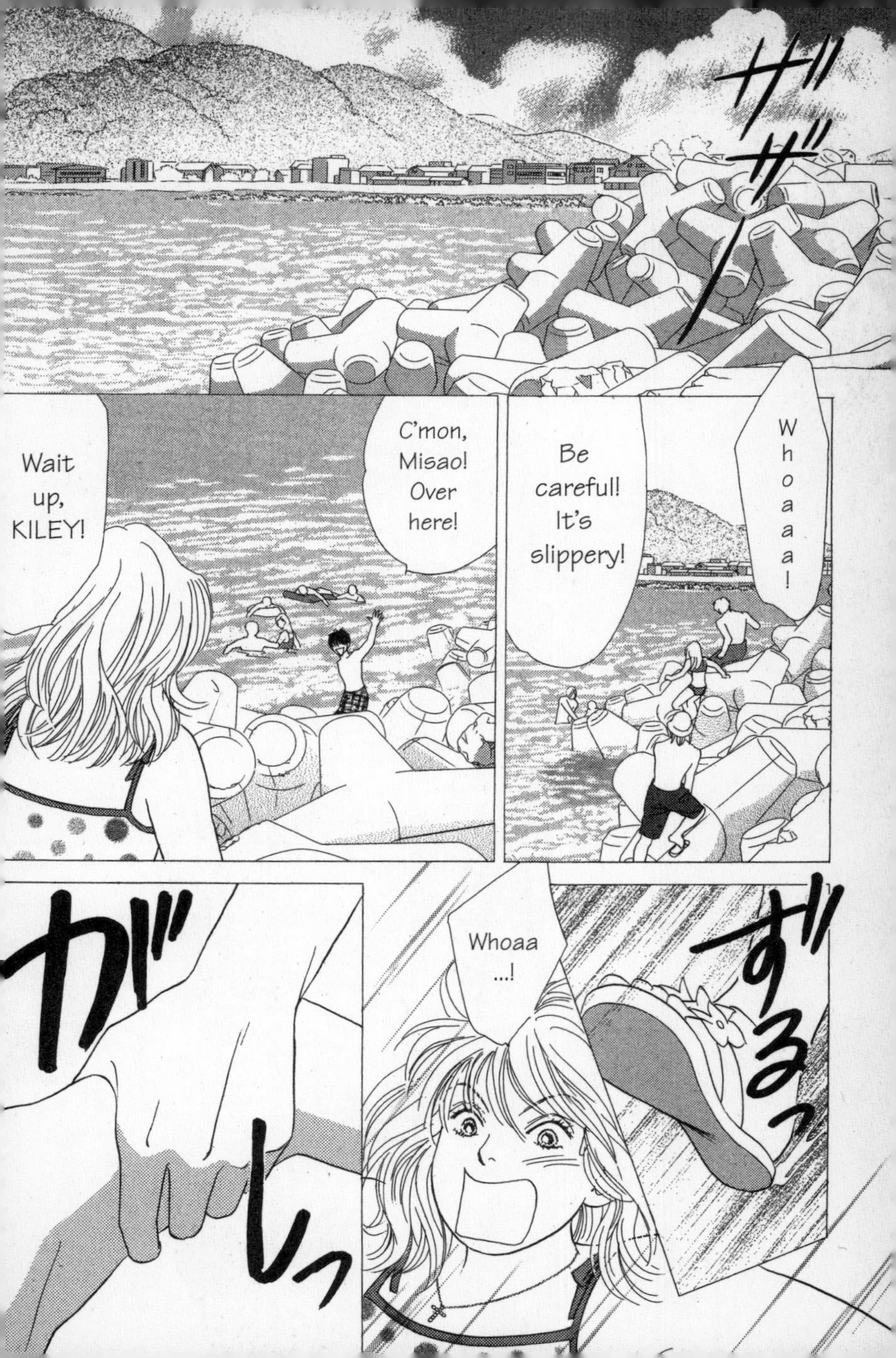
ザザ
Whoaaa!
Be careful! It's slippery!
C'mon, Misao! Over here!
Wait up, KILEY!
Whoaa ...!
ずるっ
ガしっ

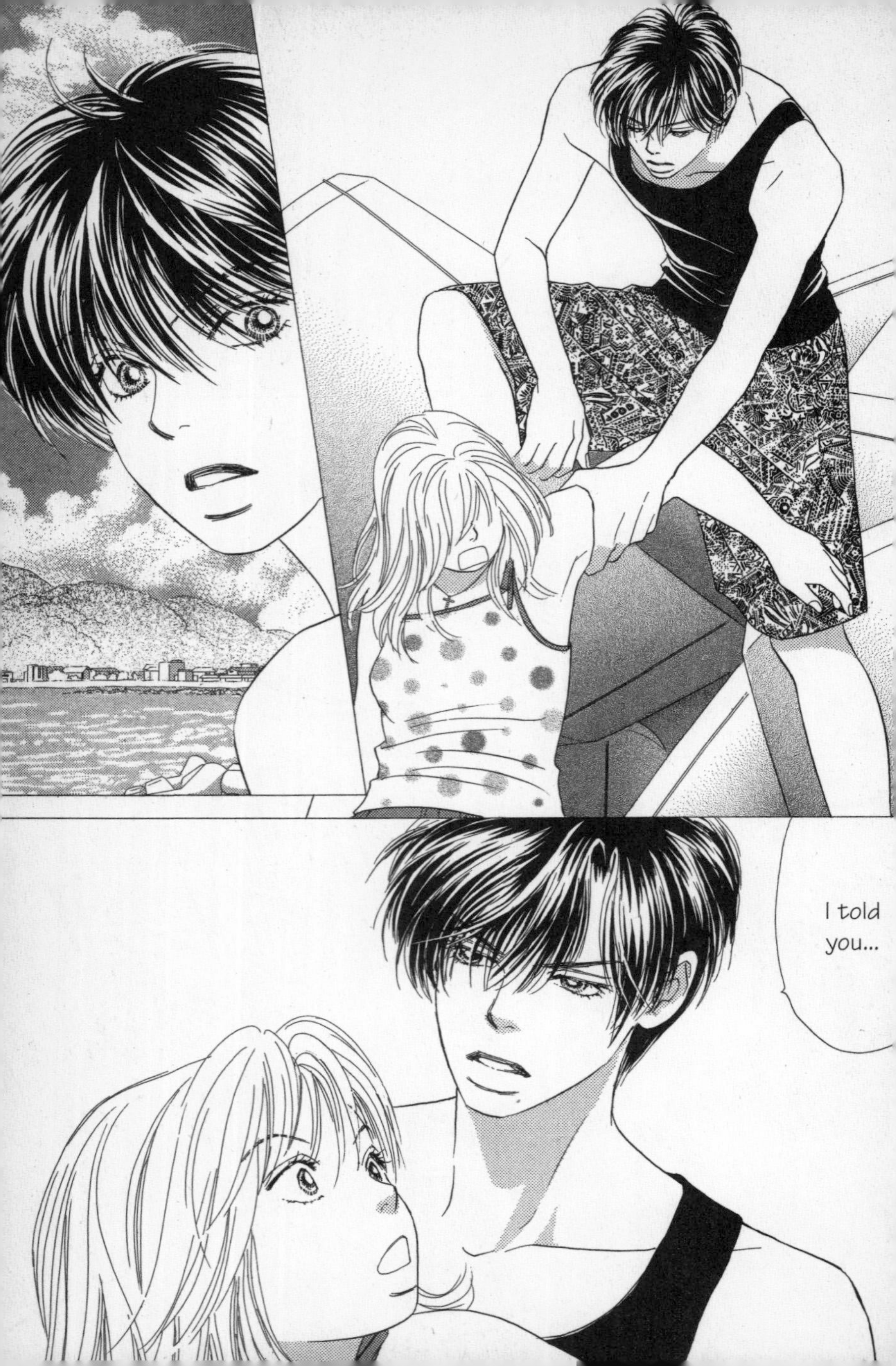
I told you...

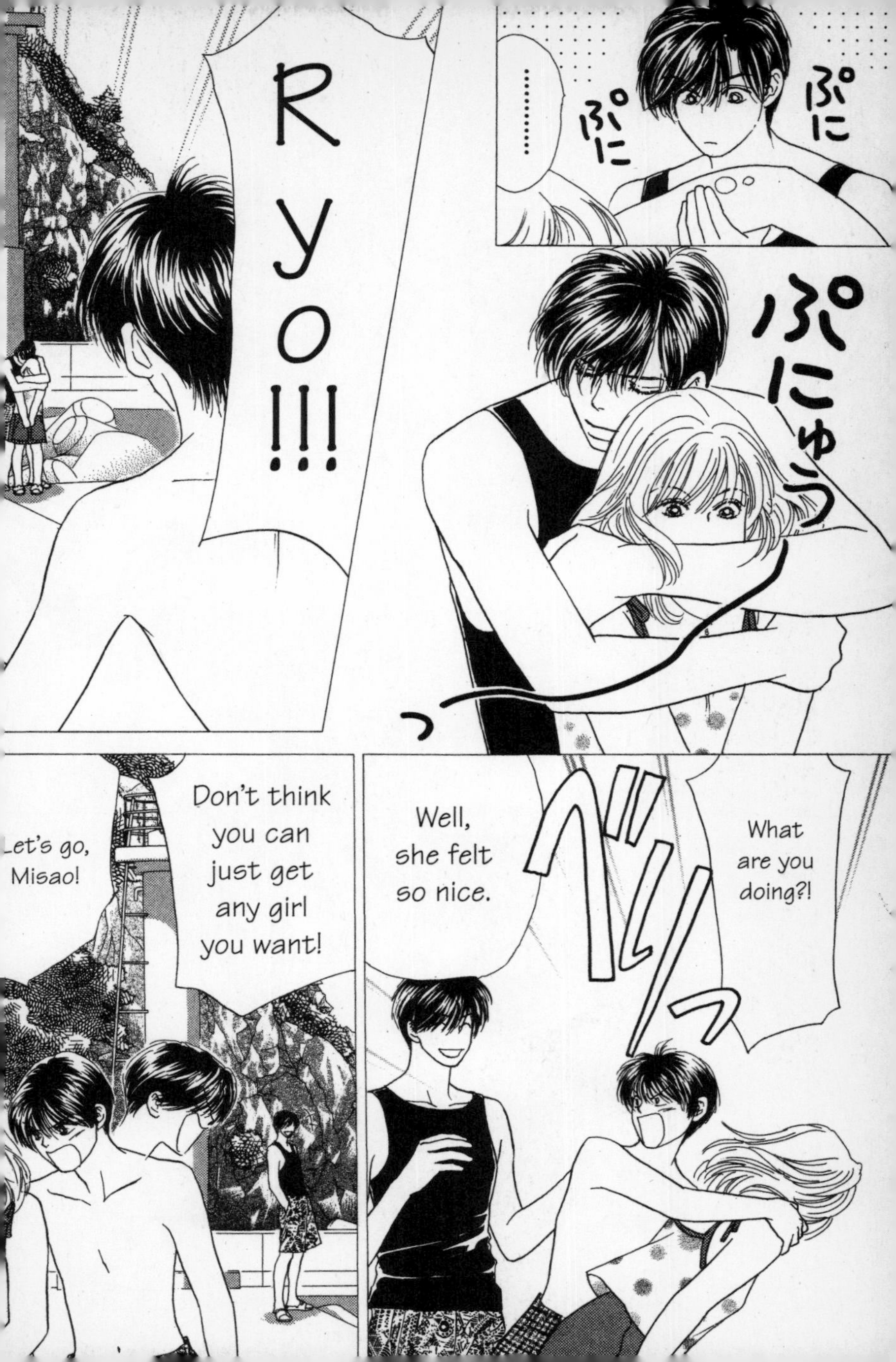

ぷに
ぷに
……
ぷにゅう
っ
Ryo!!!
What are you doing?!
ベリッ
Well, she felt so nice.
Don't think you can just get any girl you want!
Let's go, Misao!

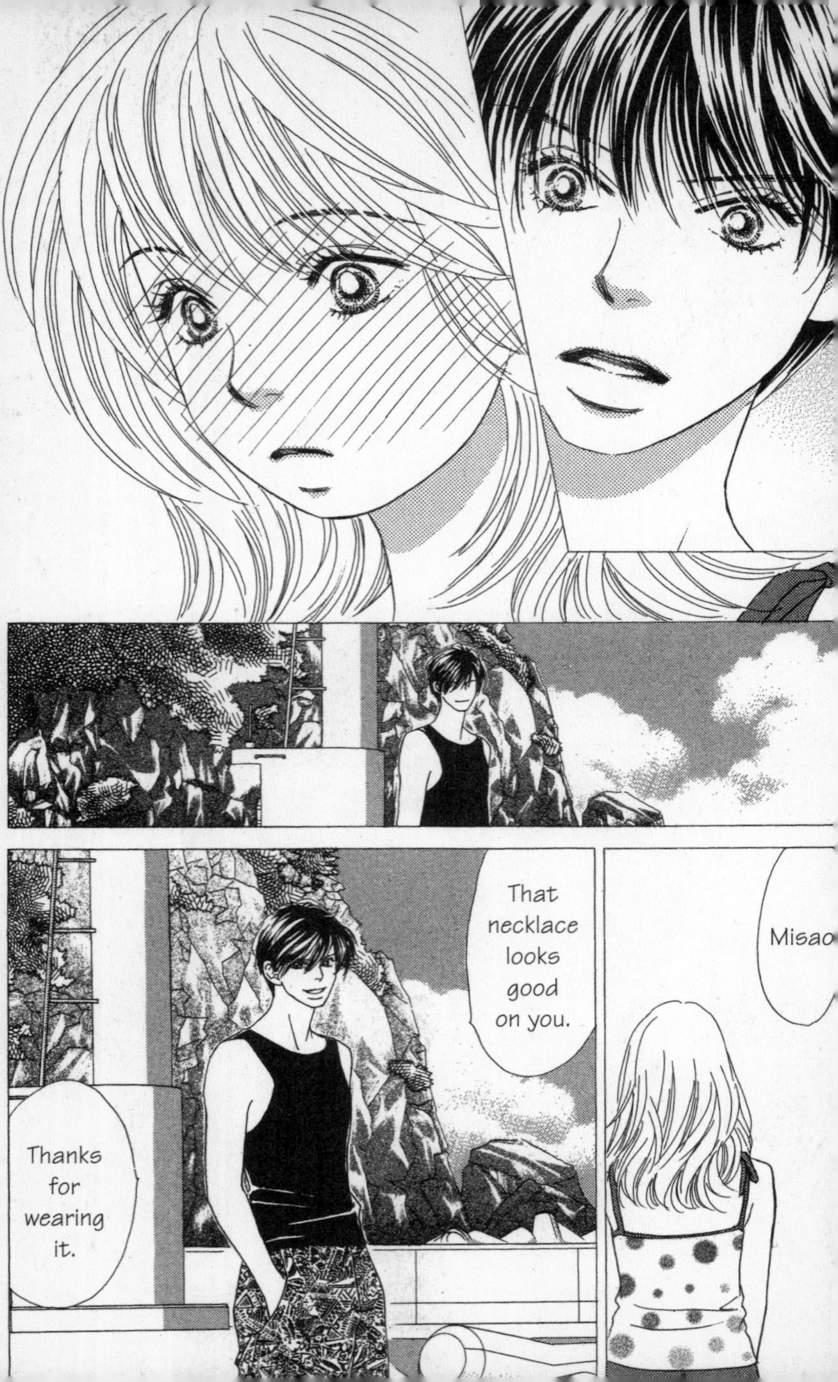
Misao
That necklace looks good on you.
Thanks for wearing it.

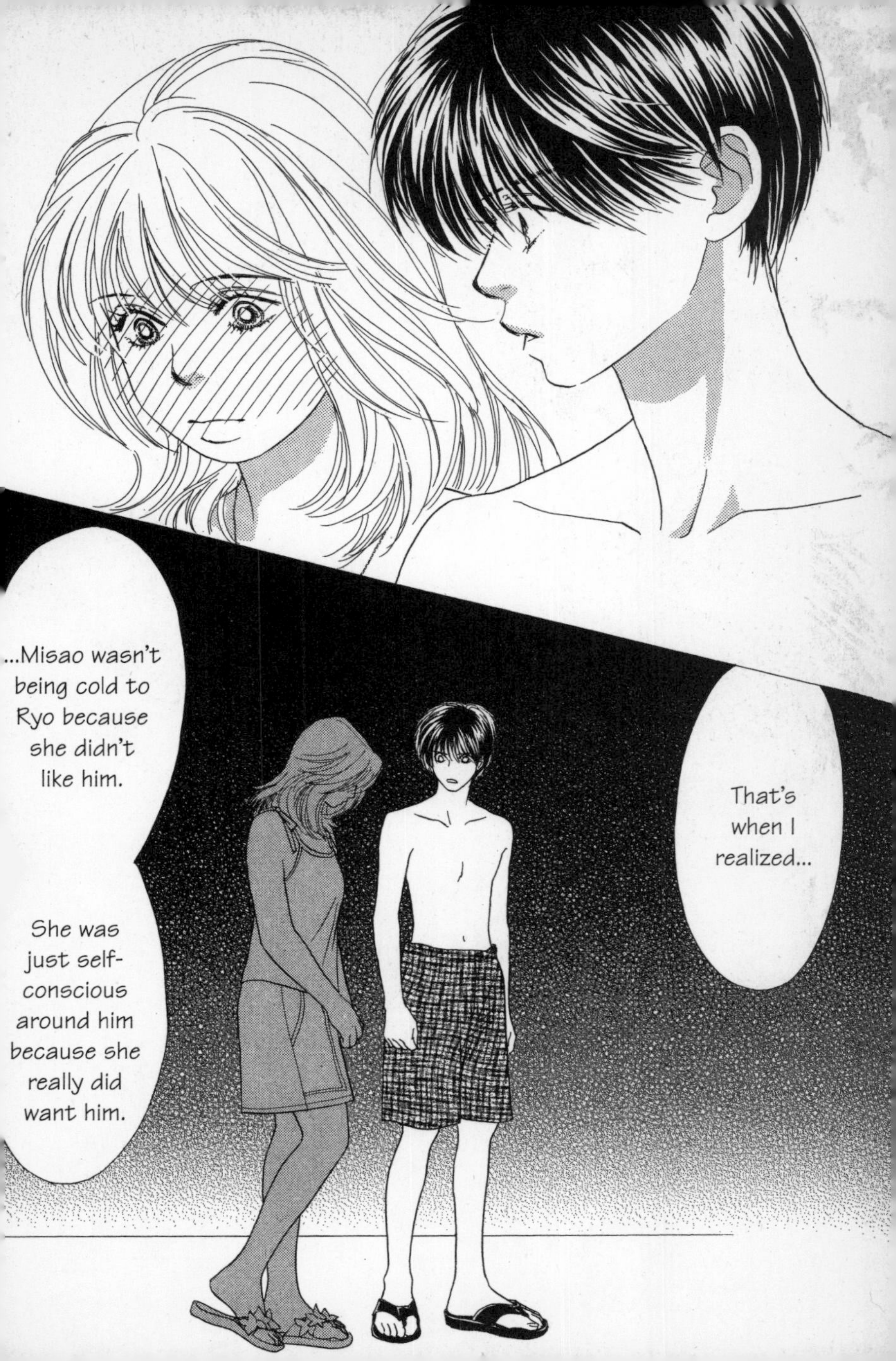
That's when I realized...
...Misao wasn't being cold to Ryo because she didn't like him.
She was just self-conscious around him because she really did want him.

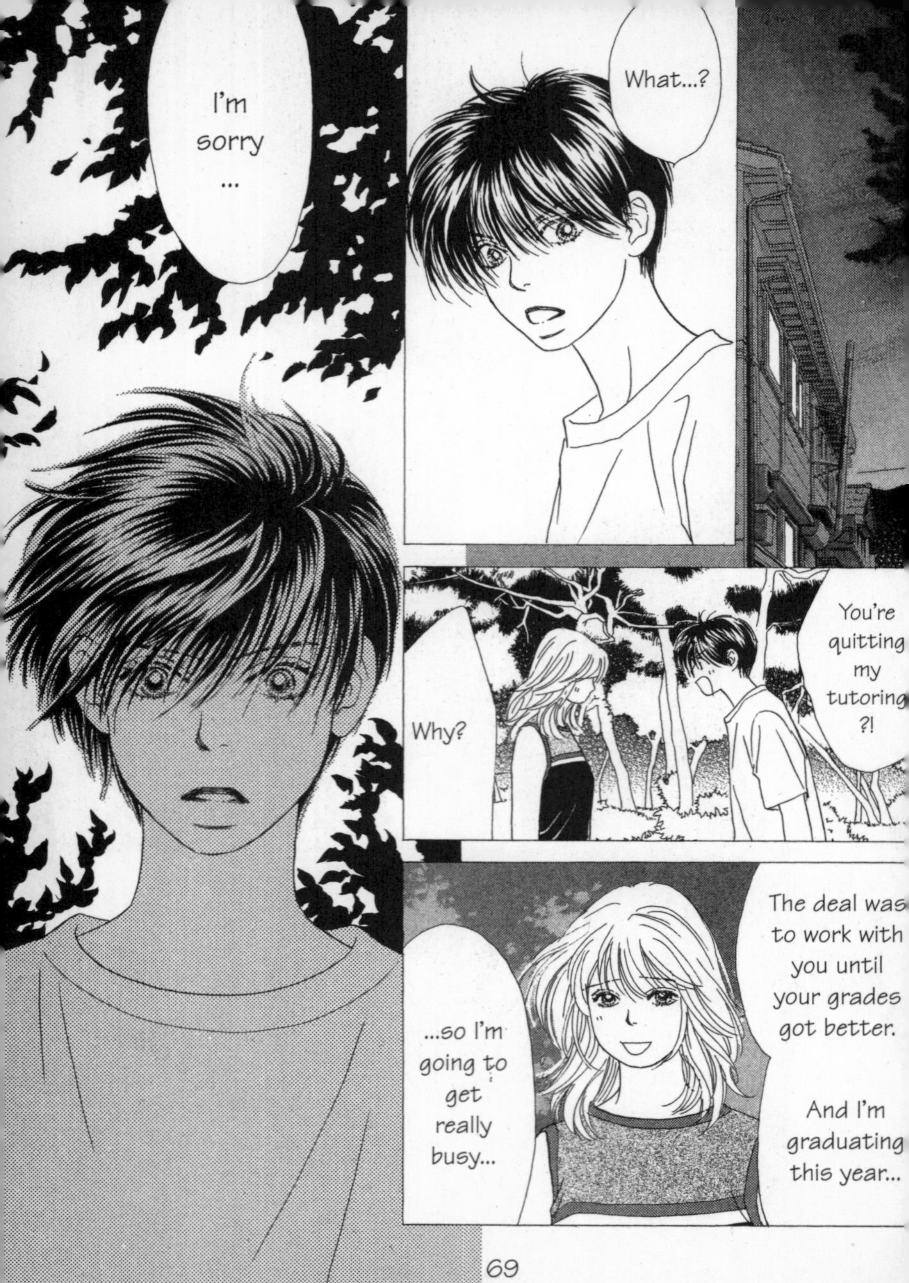
What...?
You're quitting my tutoring?!
Why?
The deal was to work with you until your grades got better.
And I'm graduating this year...
...so I'm going to get really busy...
I'm sorry ...

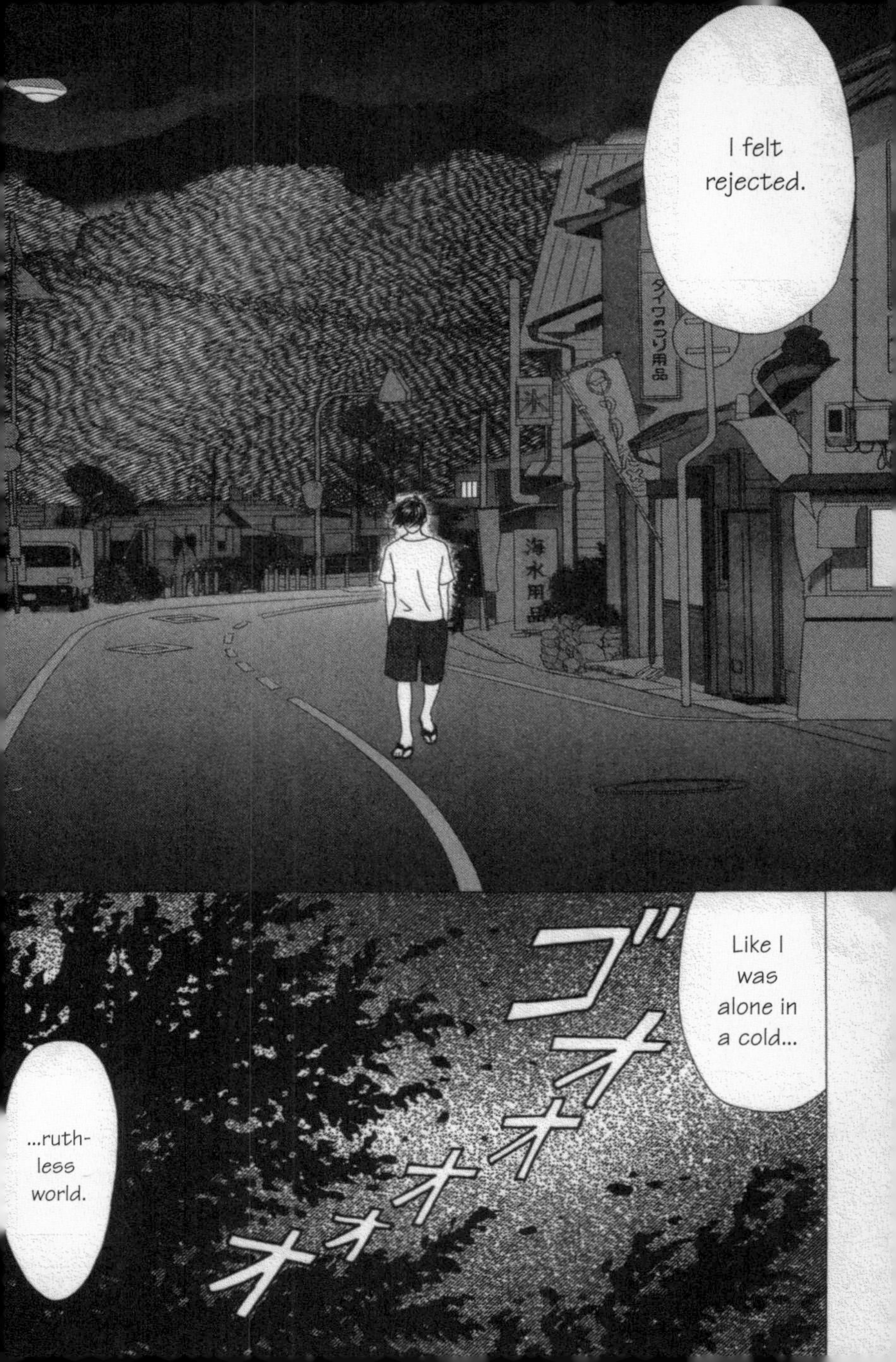
I felt rejected.
氷
海水用品
Like I was alone in a cold...
ゴオオォオ
...ruth-less world.

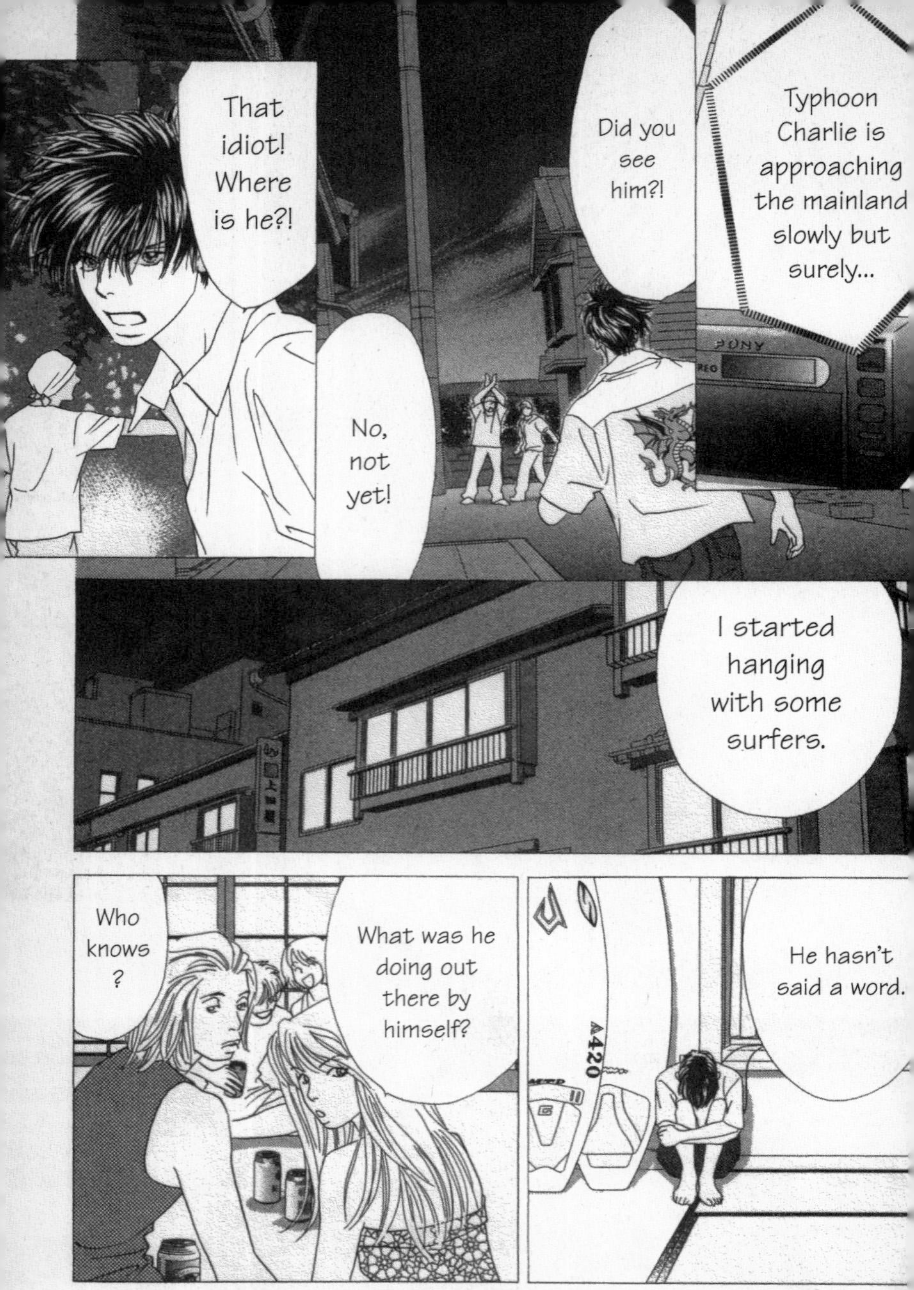
Typhoon Charlie is approaching the mainland slowly but surely...
Did you see him?!
No, not yet!
That idiot! Where is he?!
I started hanging with some surfers.
He hasn't said a word.
What was he doing out there by himself?
Who knows?

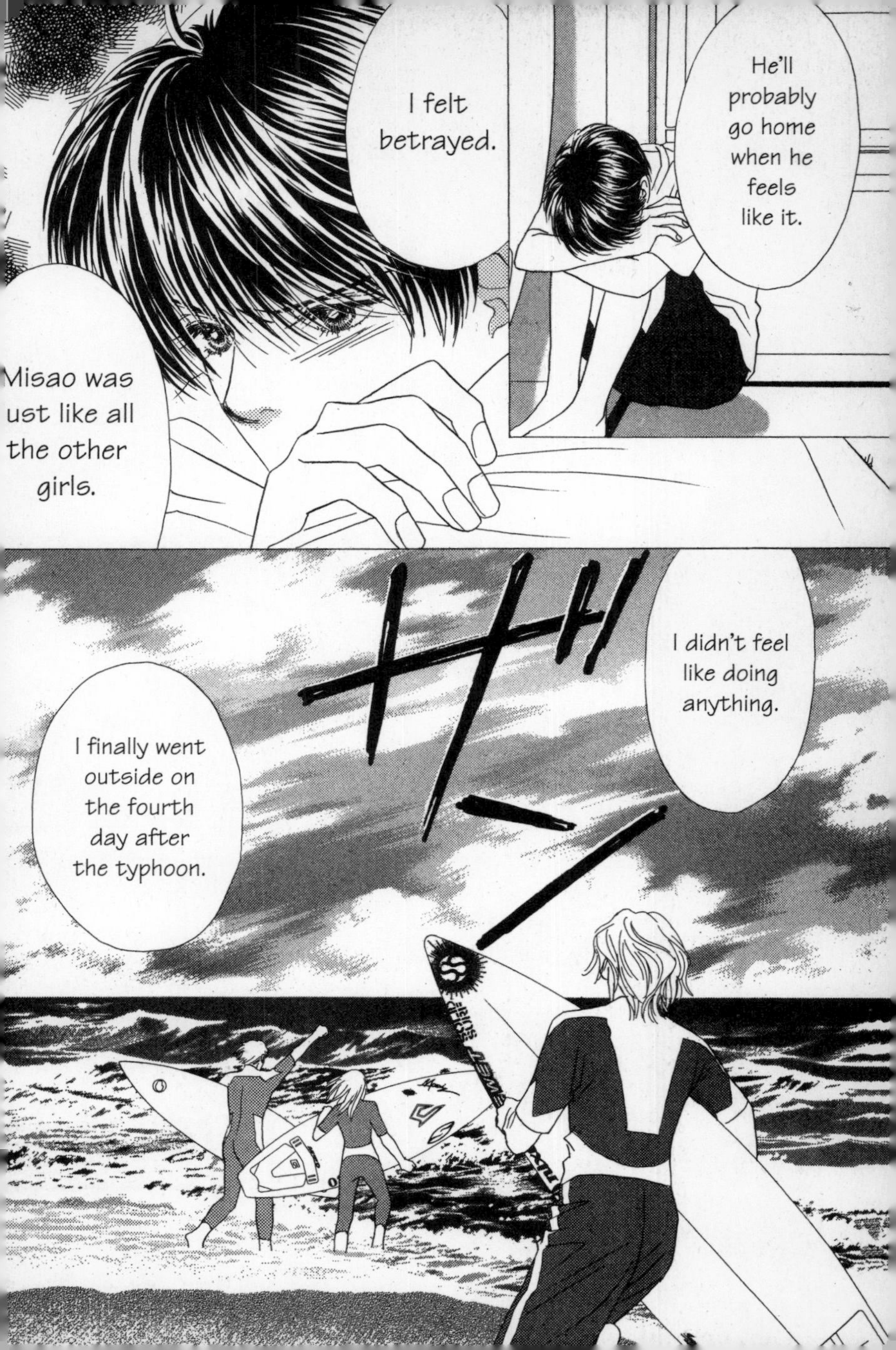

He'll probably go home when he feels like it.
I felt betrayed.
Misao was ust like all the other girls.
I didn't feel like doing anything.
I finally went outside on the fourth day after the typhoon.

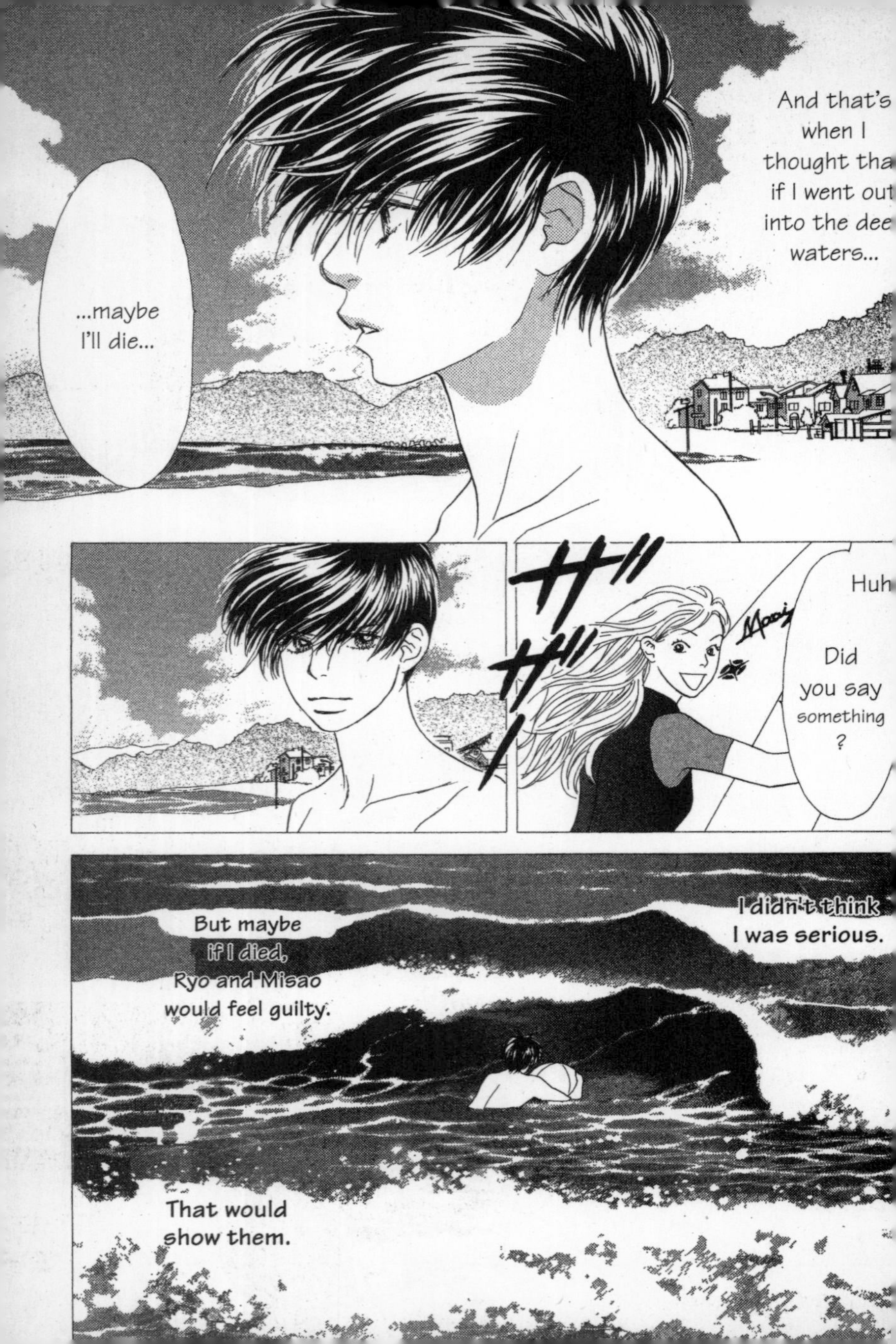
And that's when I thought tha if I went out into the dee waters...
...maybe I'll die...
ザザ
Huh
Did you say something ?
I didn't think I was serious.
But maybe if I died, Ryo and Misao would feel guilty.
That would show them.

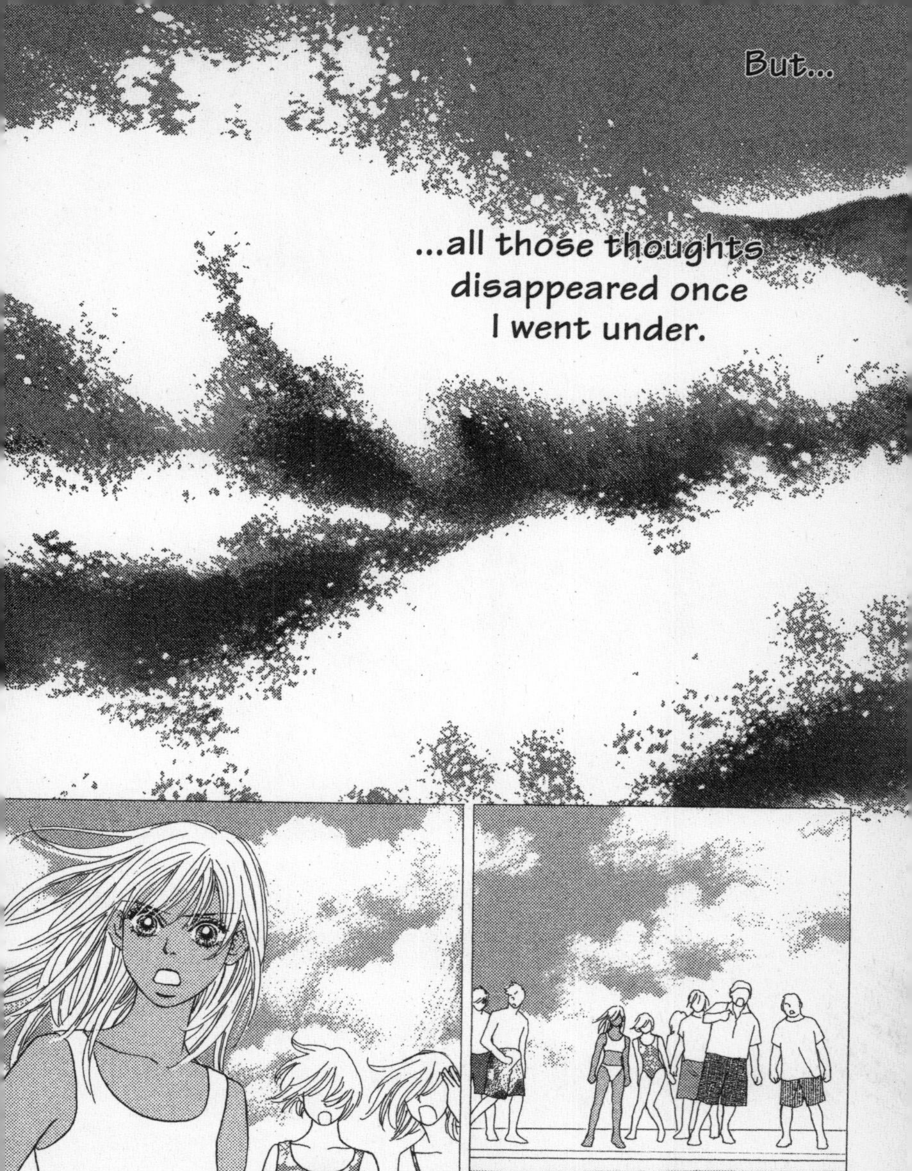
But...
...all those thoughts disappeared once I went under.

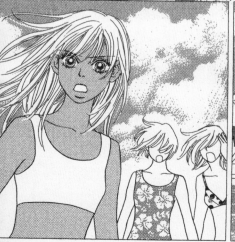

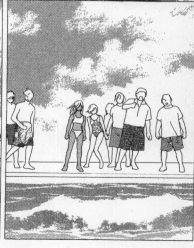

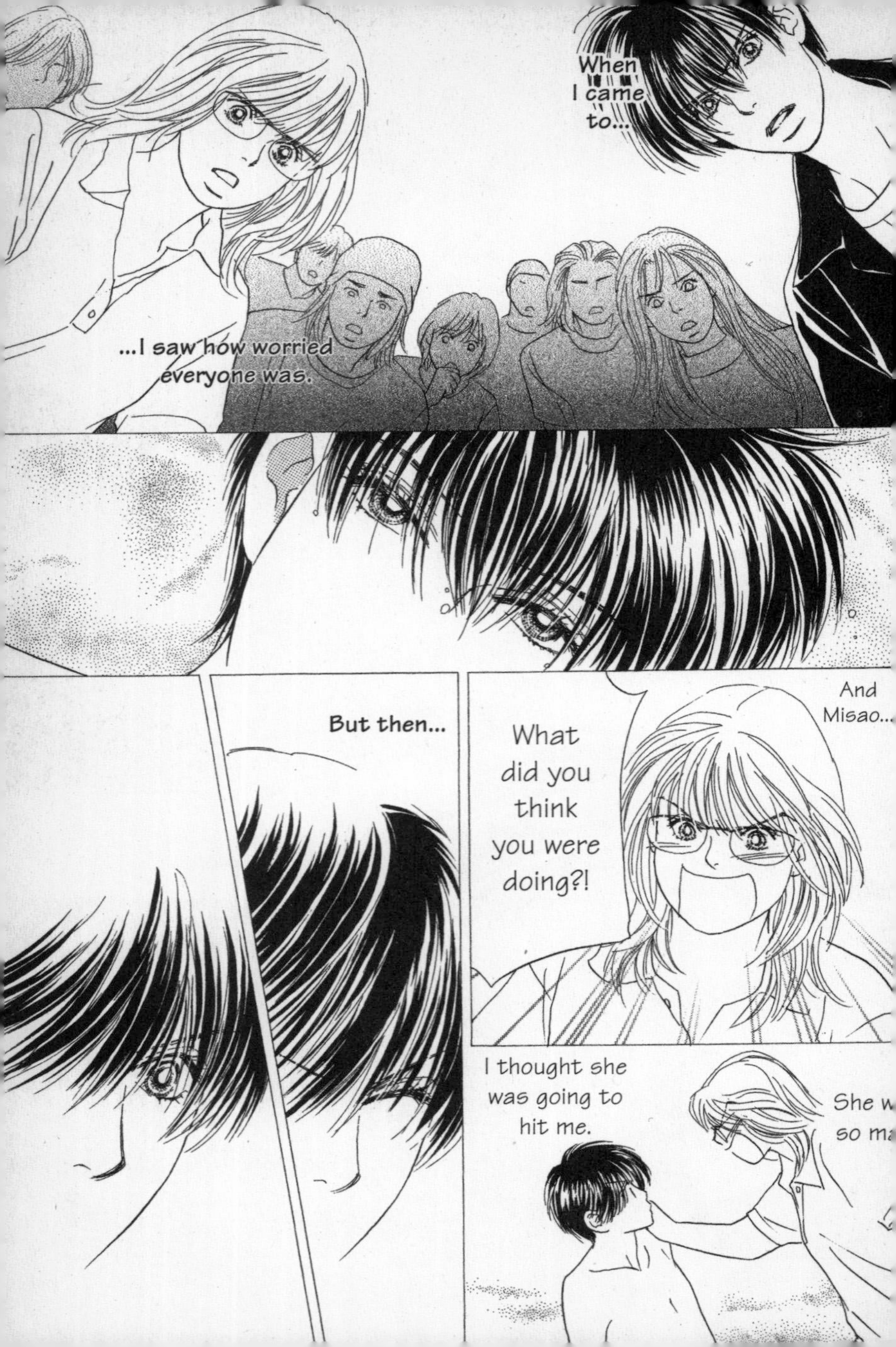
When I came to...
...I saw how worried everyone was.
And Misao...
What did you think you were doing?!
I thought she was going to hit me.
But then...

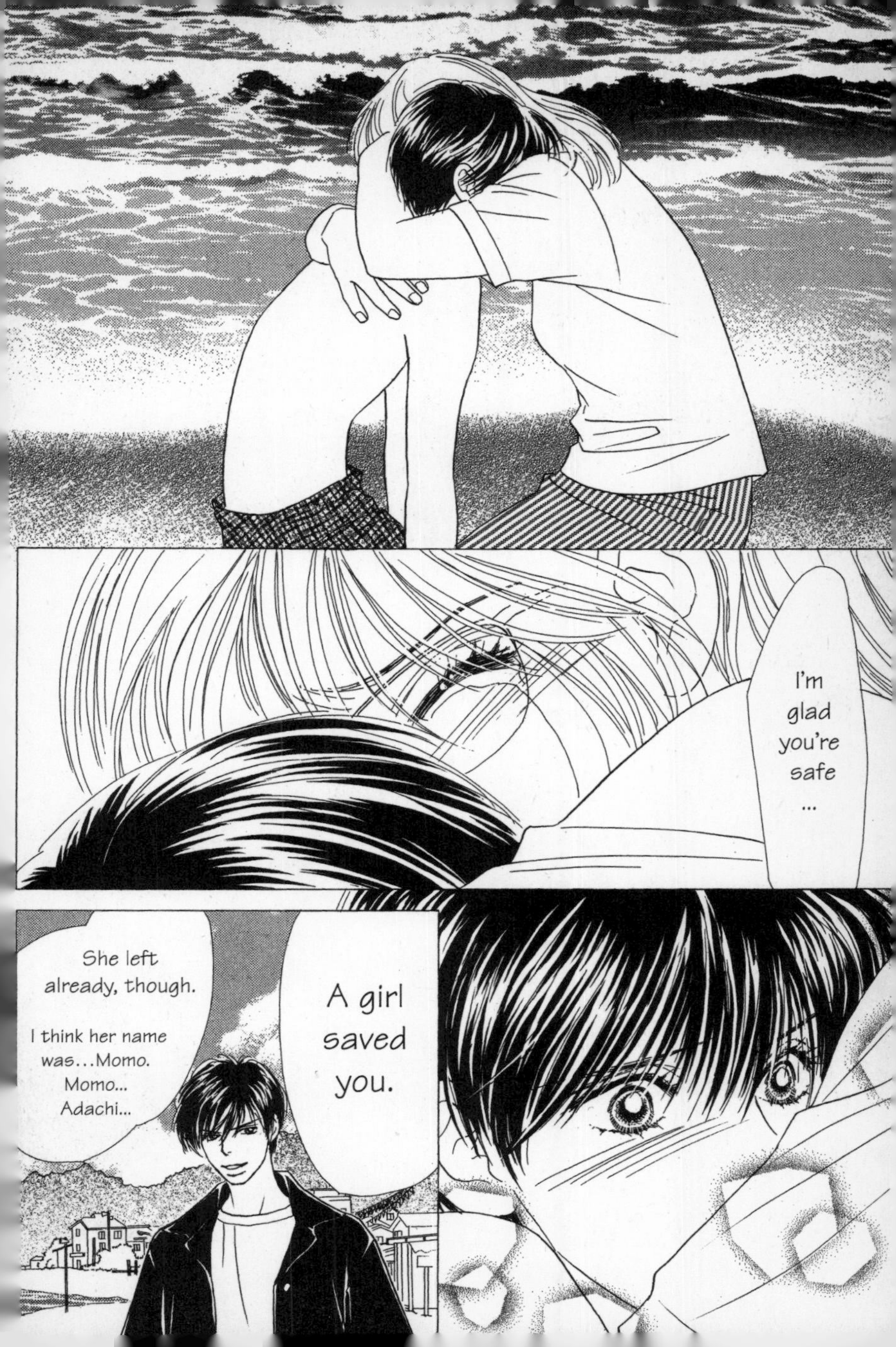
I'm glad you're safe...
A girl saved you.
She left already, though.
I think her name was…Momo. Momo... Adachi...

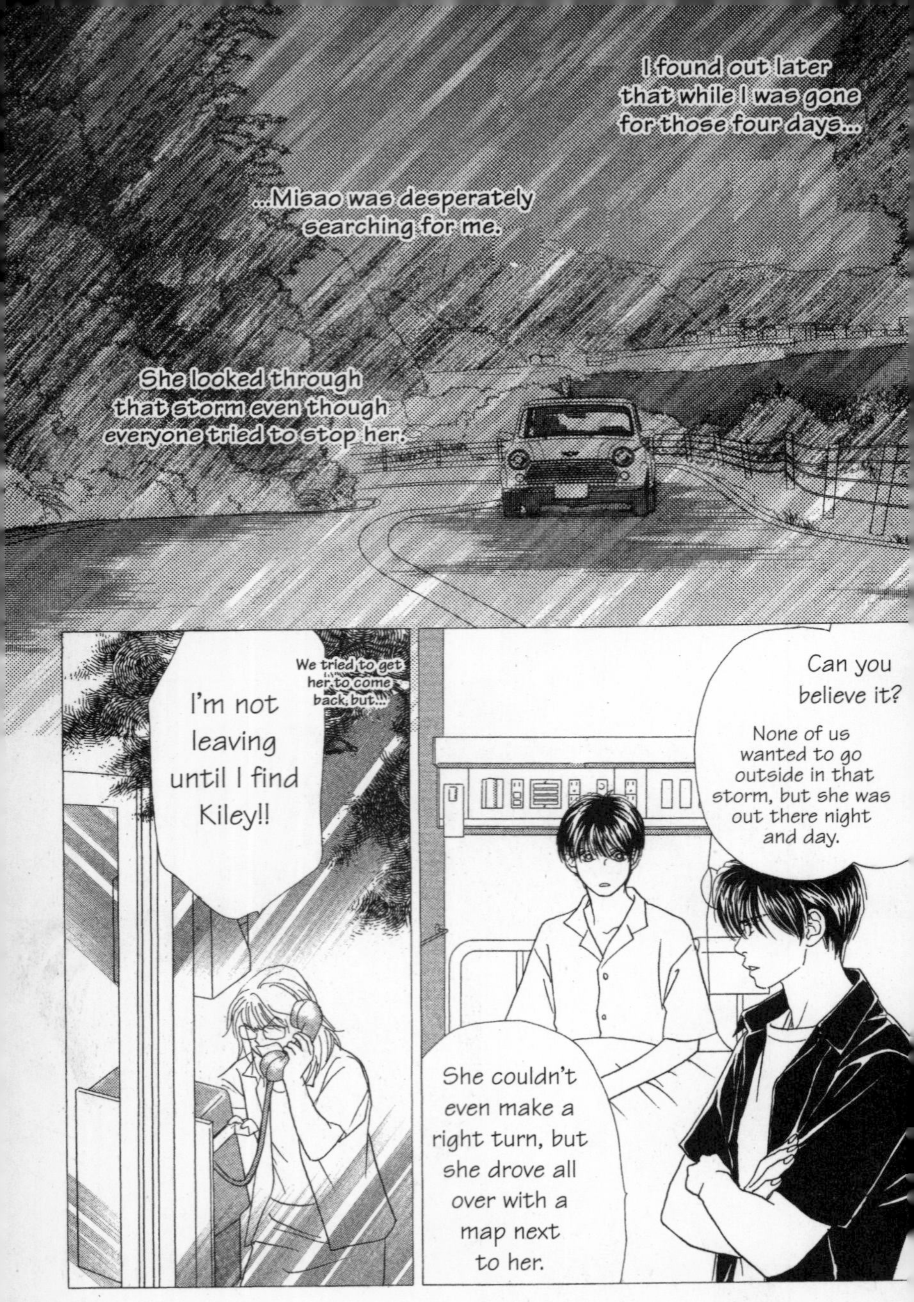

I found out later that while I was gone for those four days...
...Misao was desperately searching for me.
She looked through that storm even though everyone tried to stop her.
Can you believe it?
None of us wanted to go outside in that storm, but she was out there night and day.
She couldn't even make a right turn, but she drove all over with a map next to her.
We tried to get her to come back, but...
I'm not leaving until I find Kiley!!

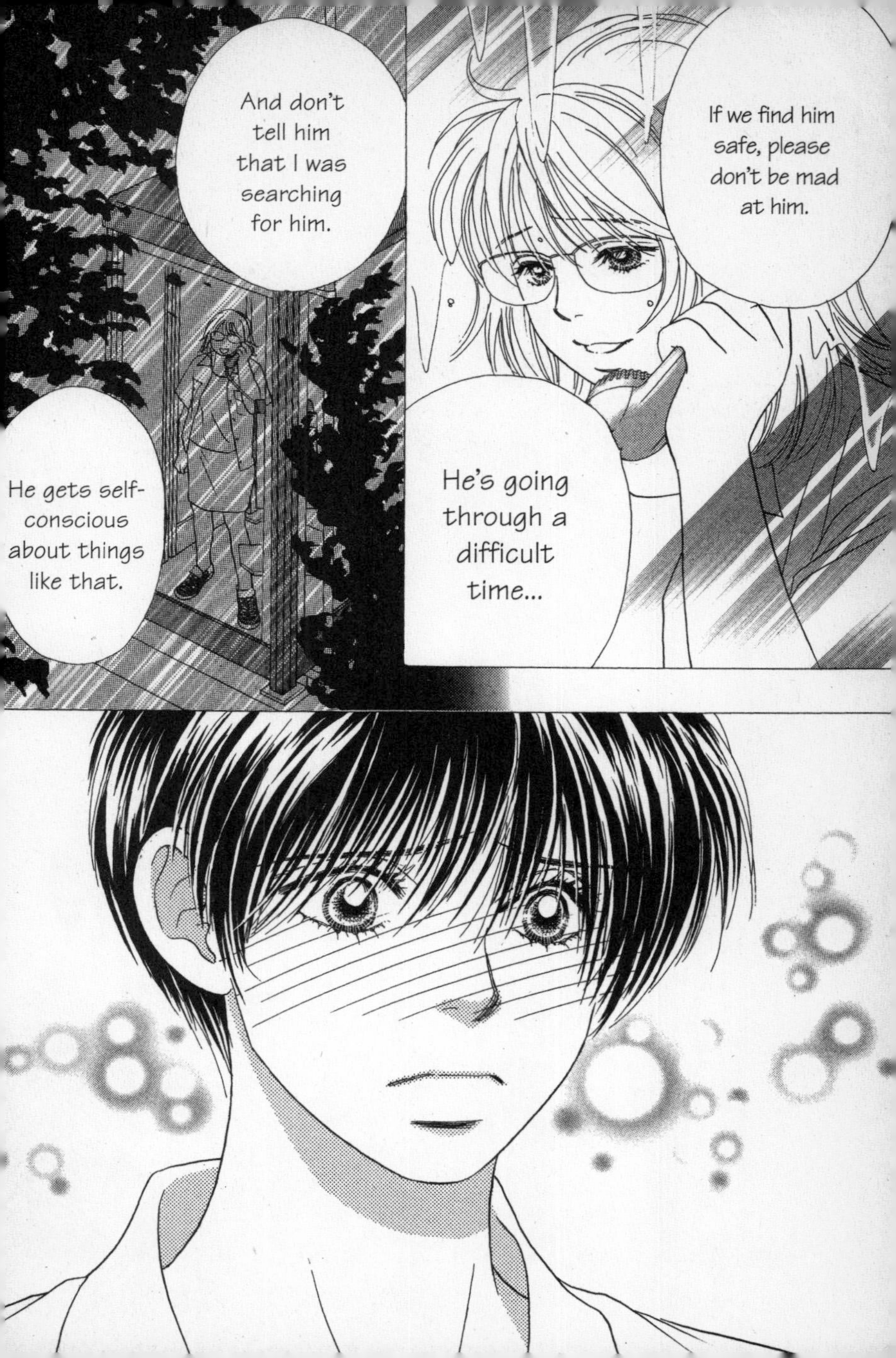
If we find him safe, please don't be mad at him.
He's going through a difficult time...
And don't tell him that I was searching for him.
He gets self-conscious about things like that.

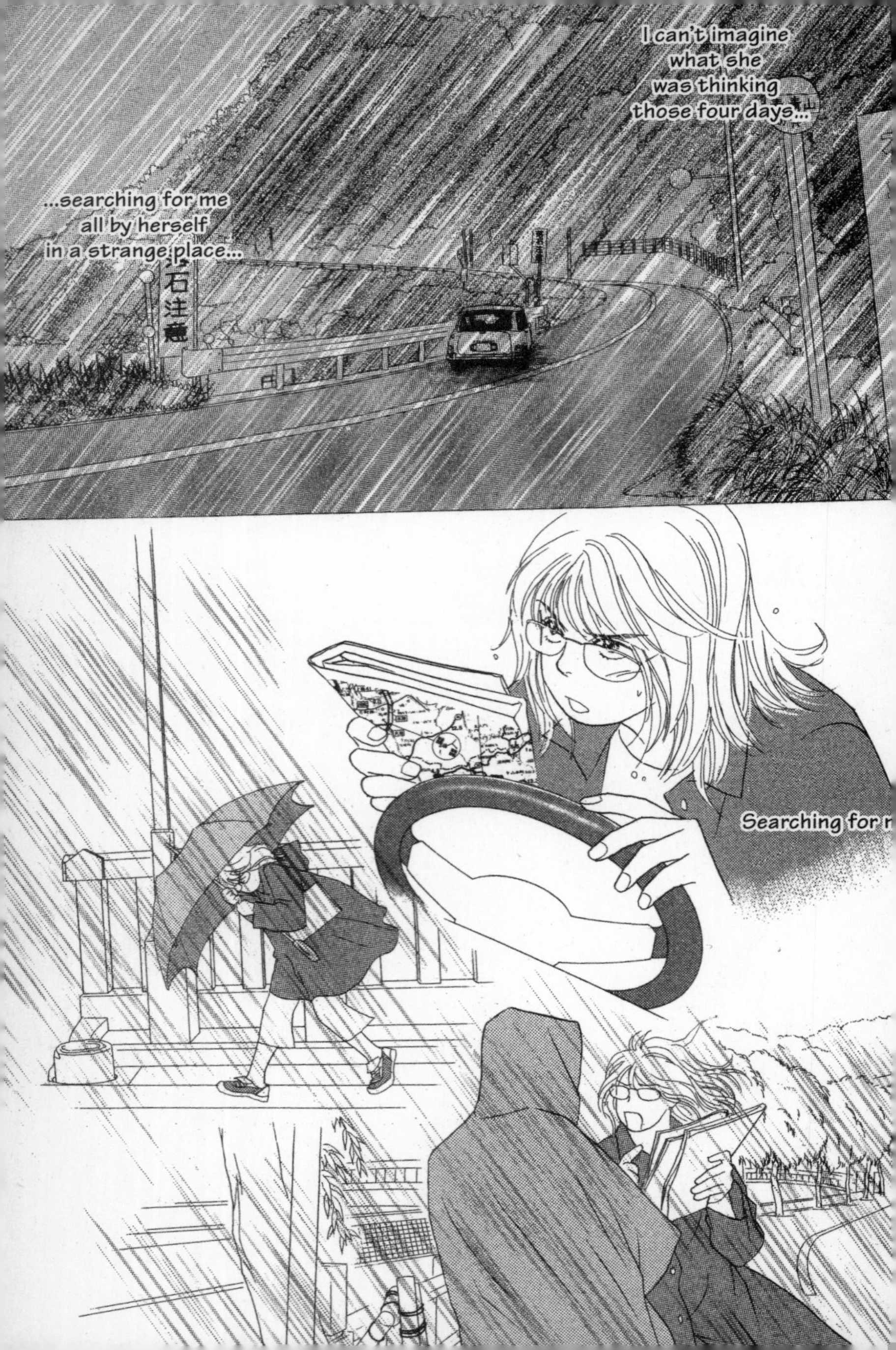
I can't imagine what she was thinking those four days...
...searching for me all by herself in a strange place...
Searching for m

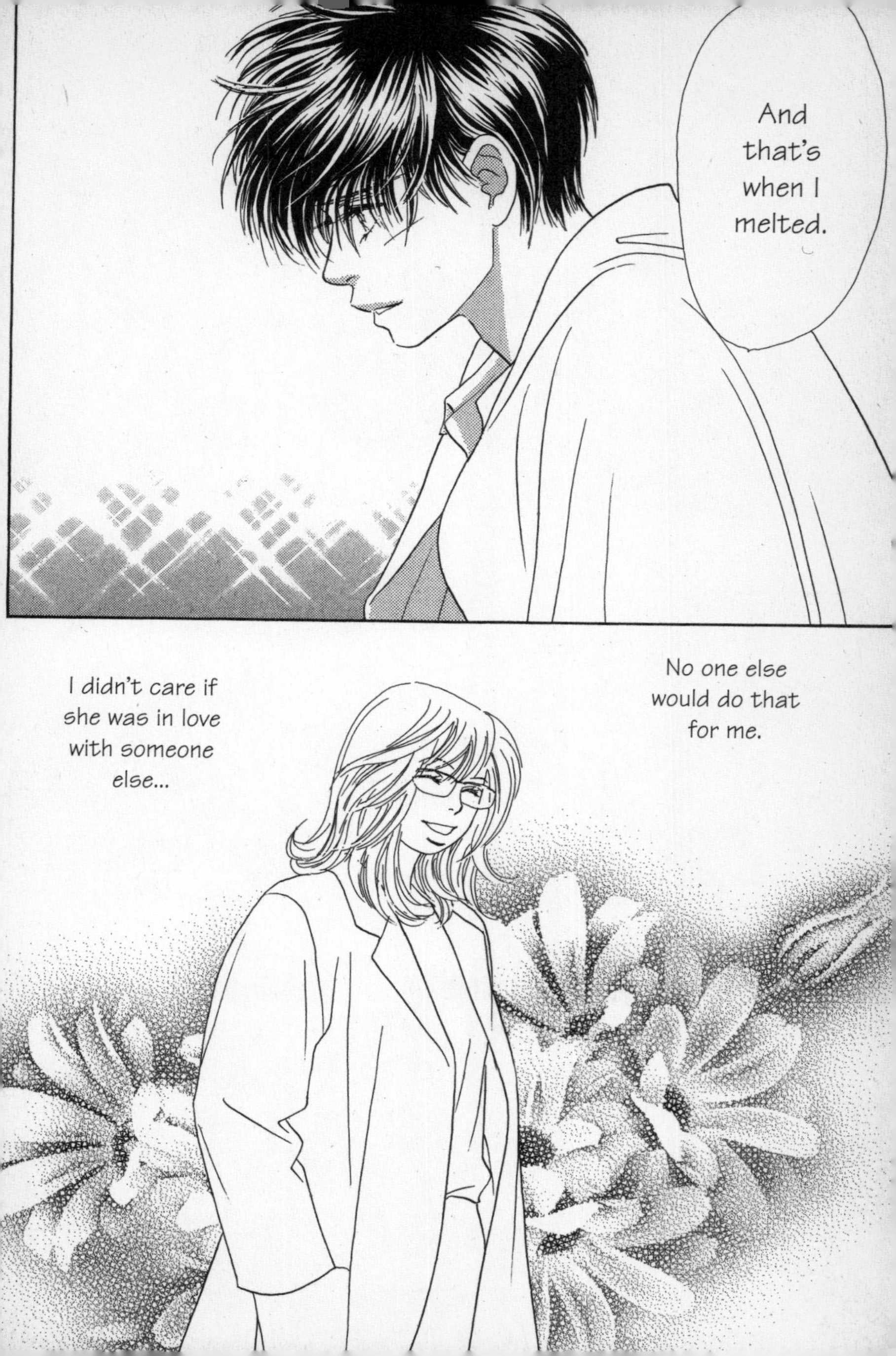
And that's when I melted.
No one else would do that for me.
I didn't care if she was in love with someone else...

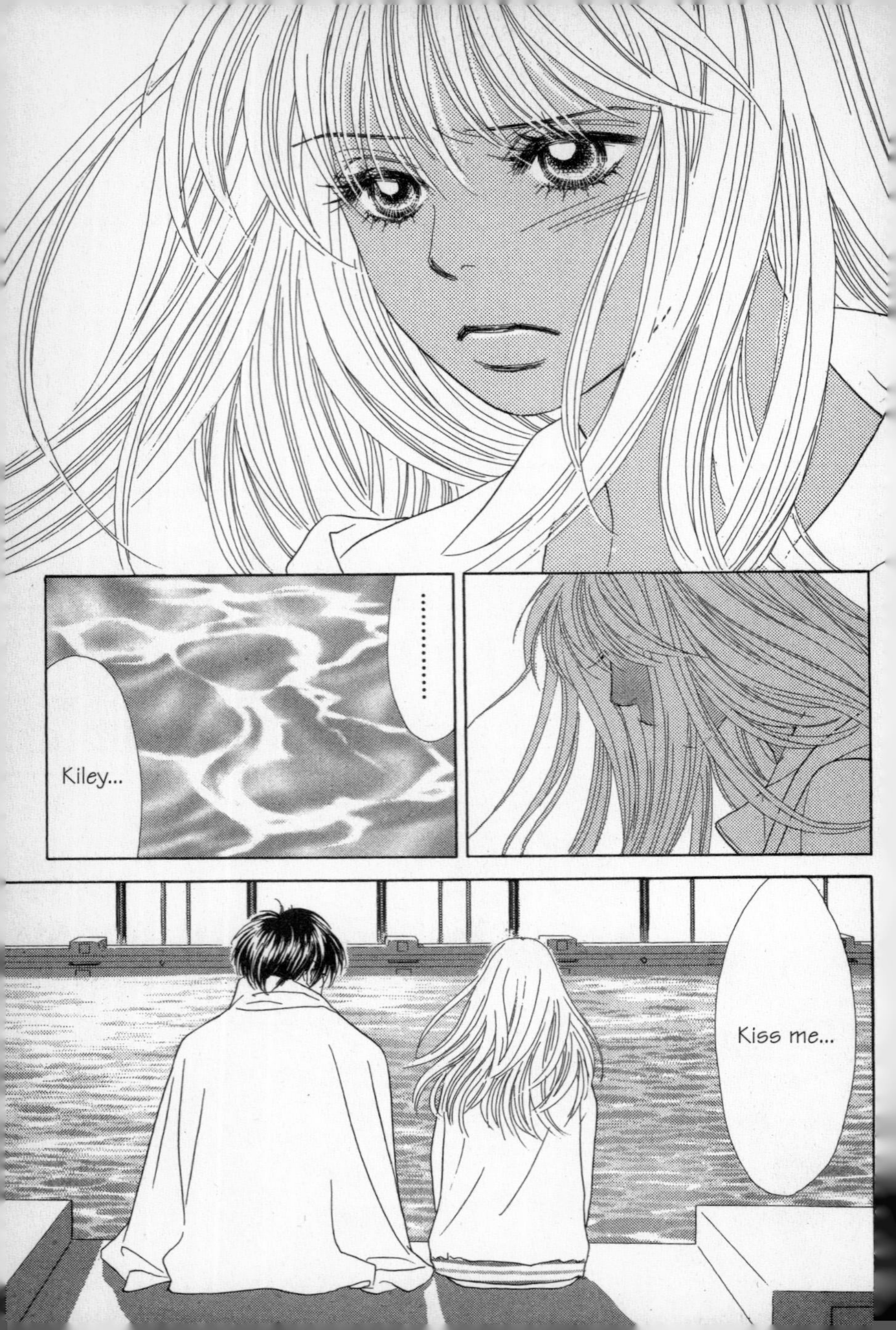
......
Kiley...
Kiss me...

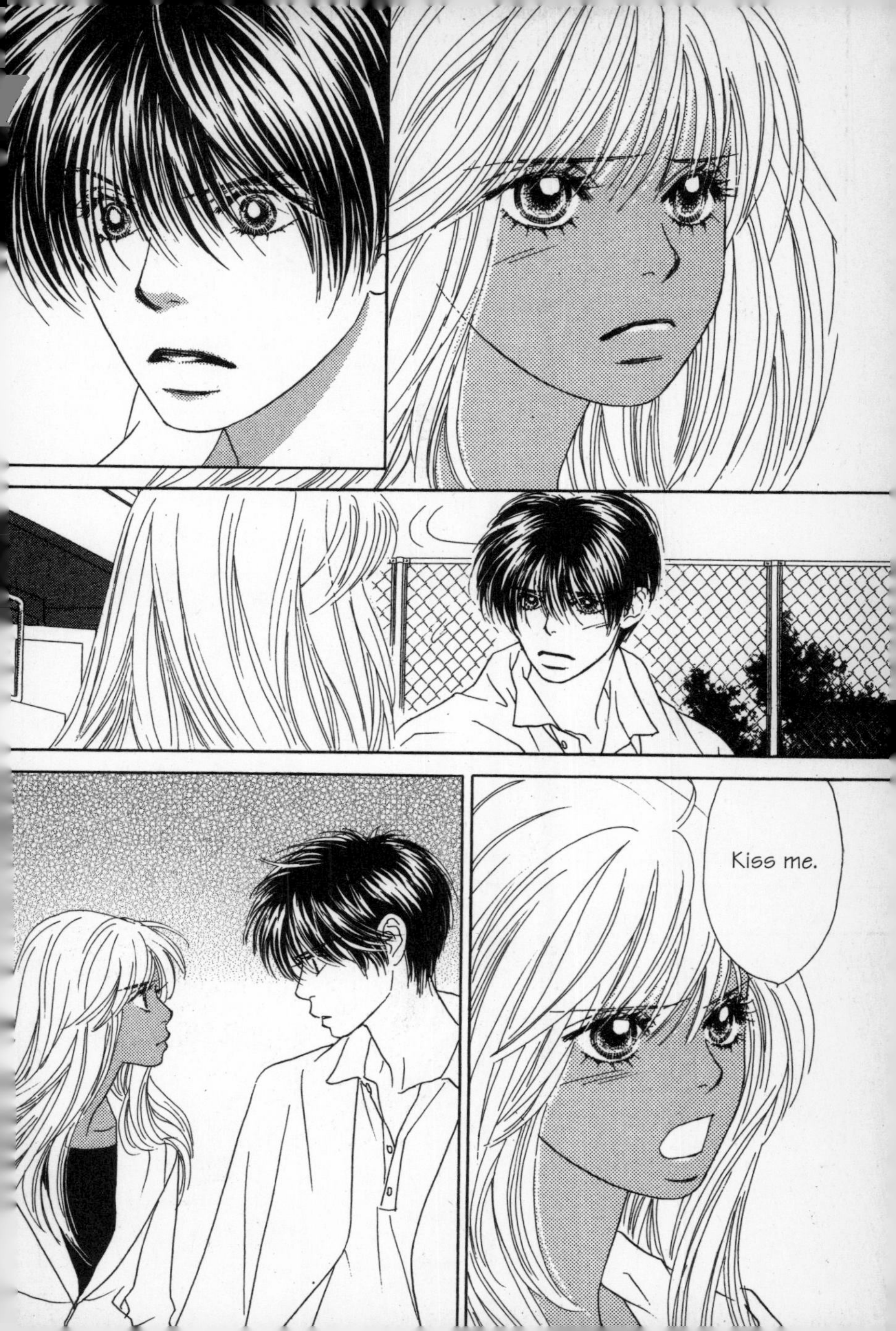
Kiss me.

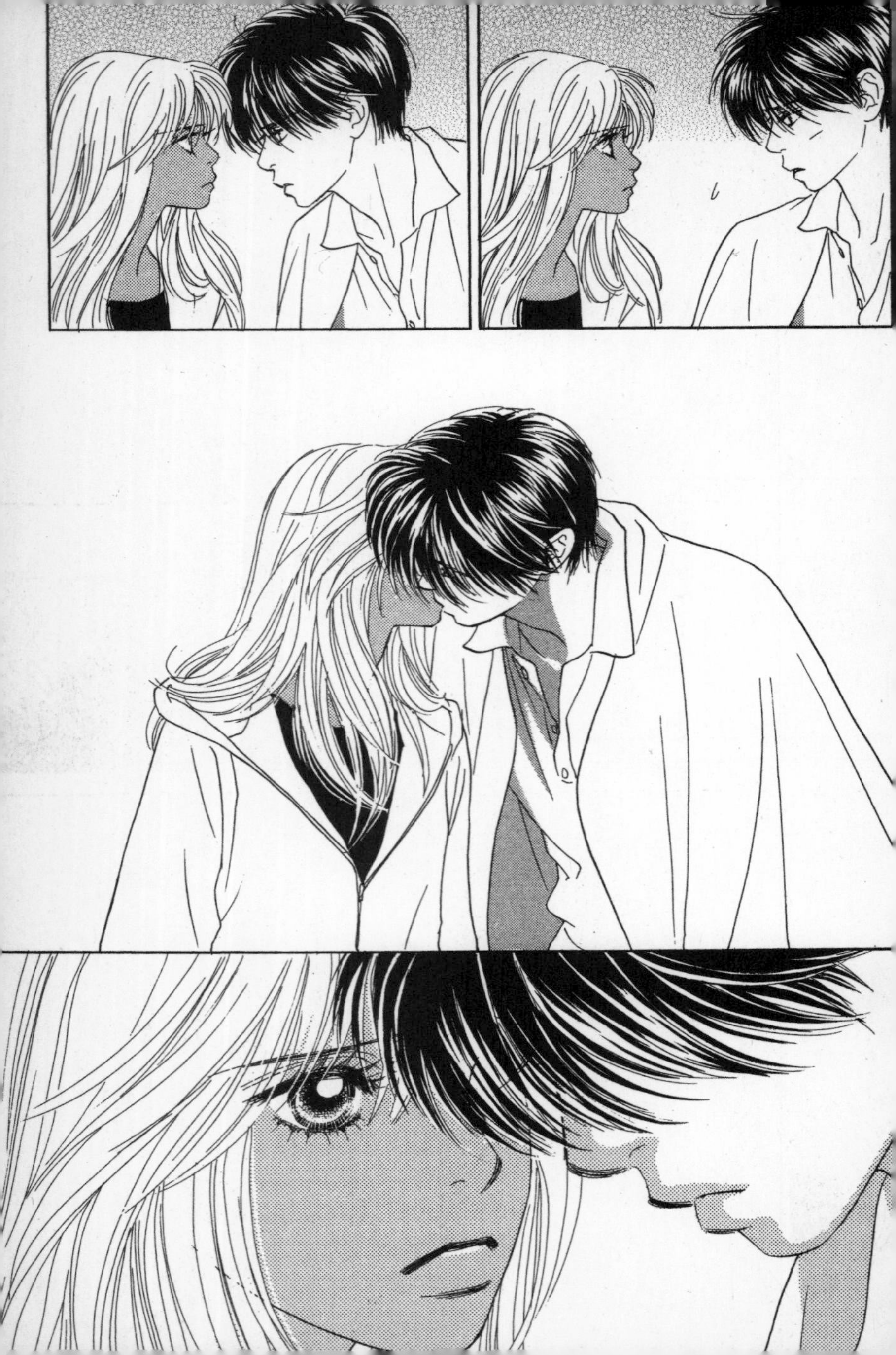

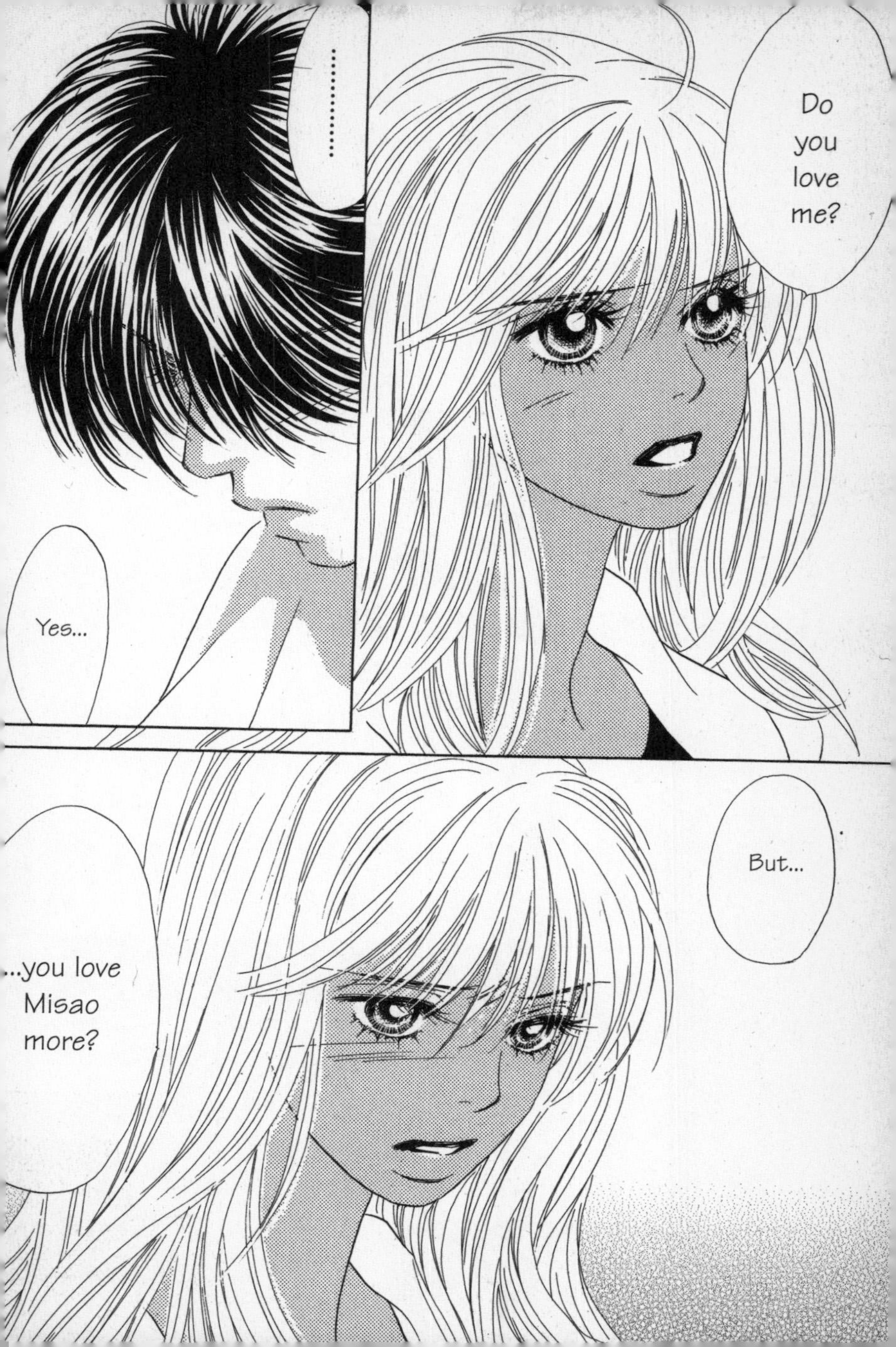
Do you love me?
......
Yes...
But...
...you love Misao more?

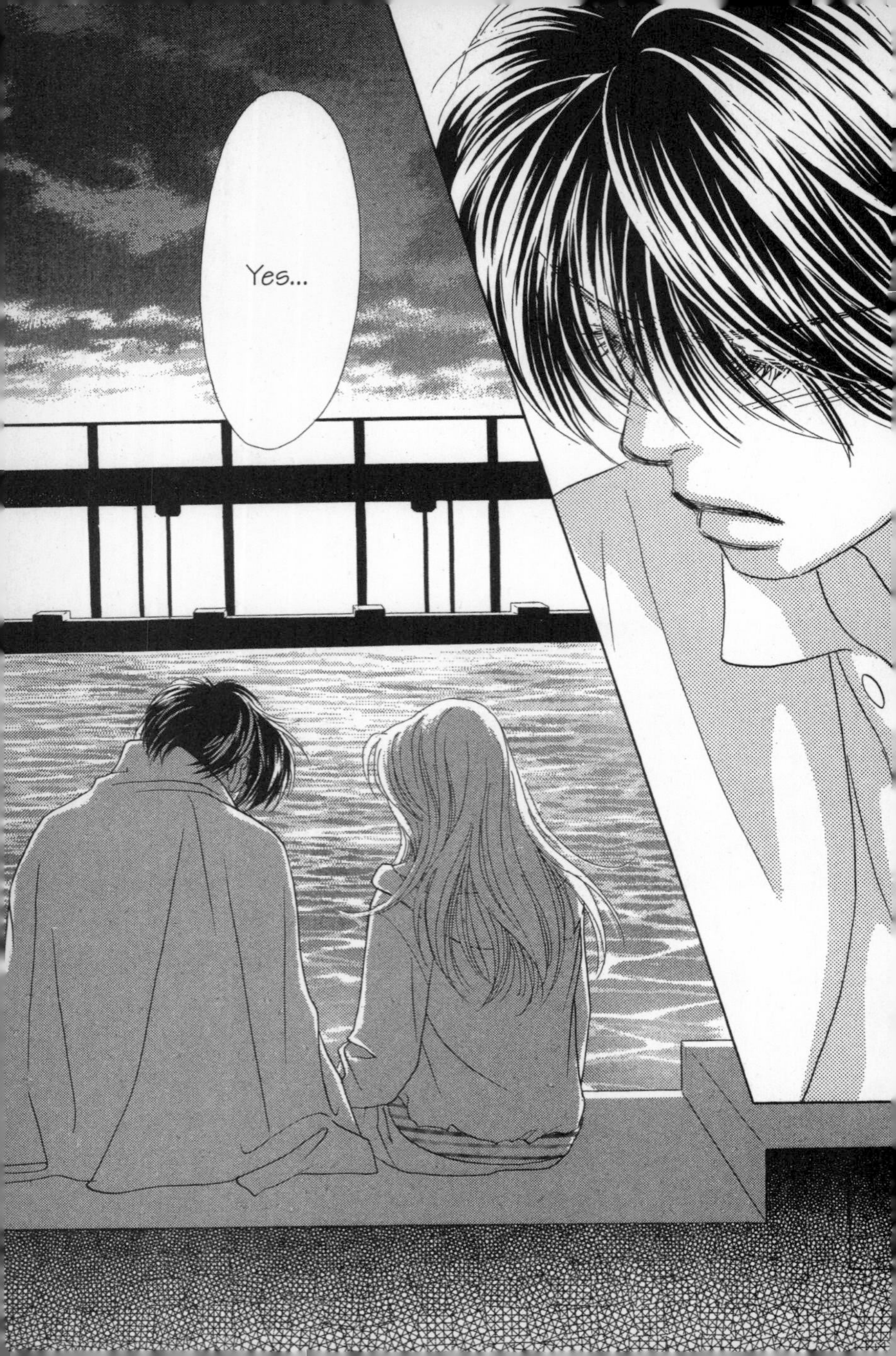
Yes...

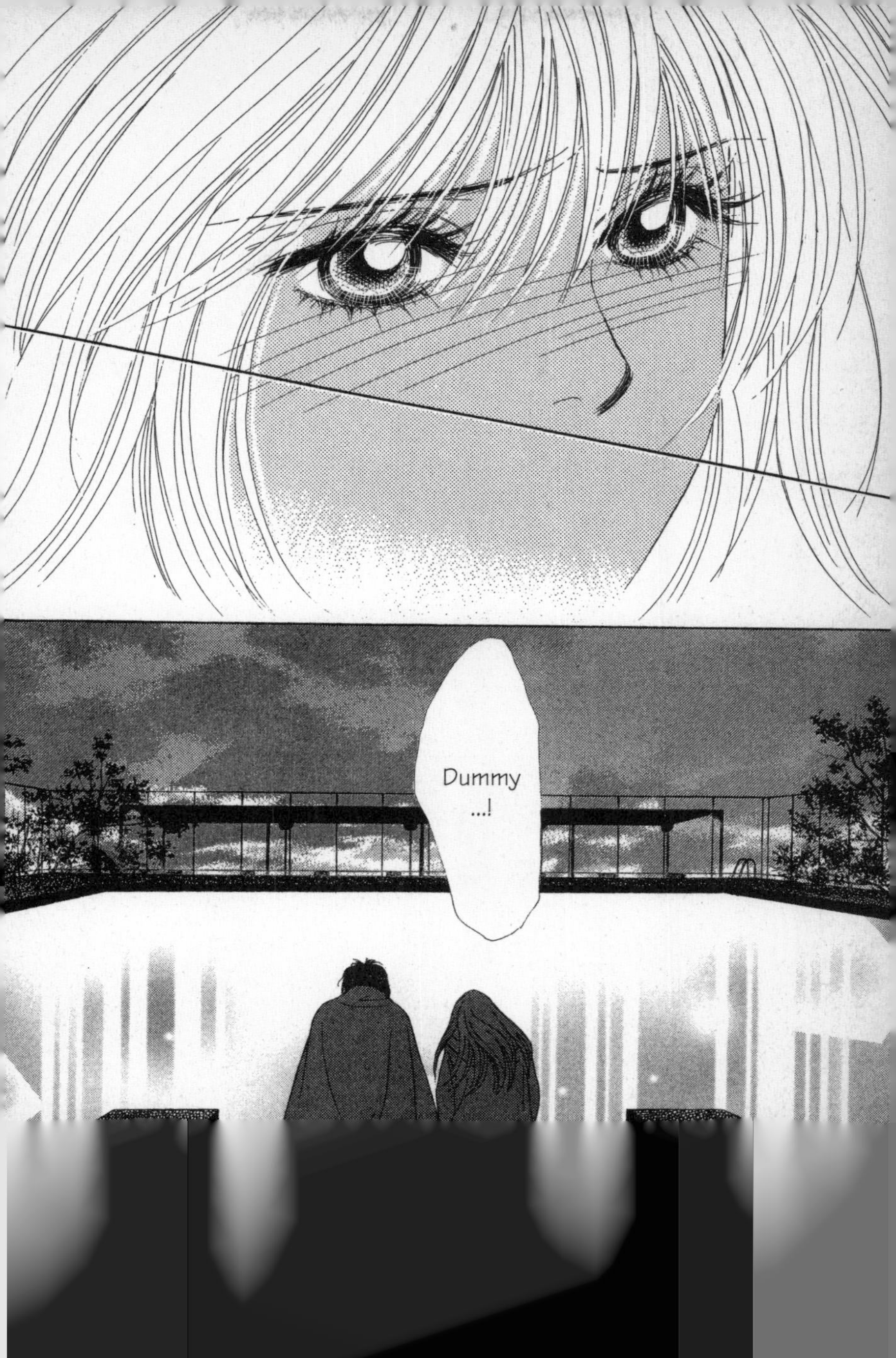
Dummy ...!

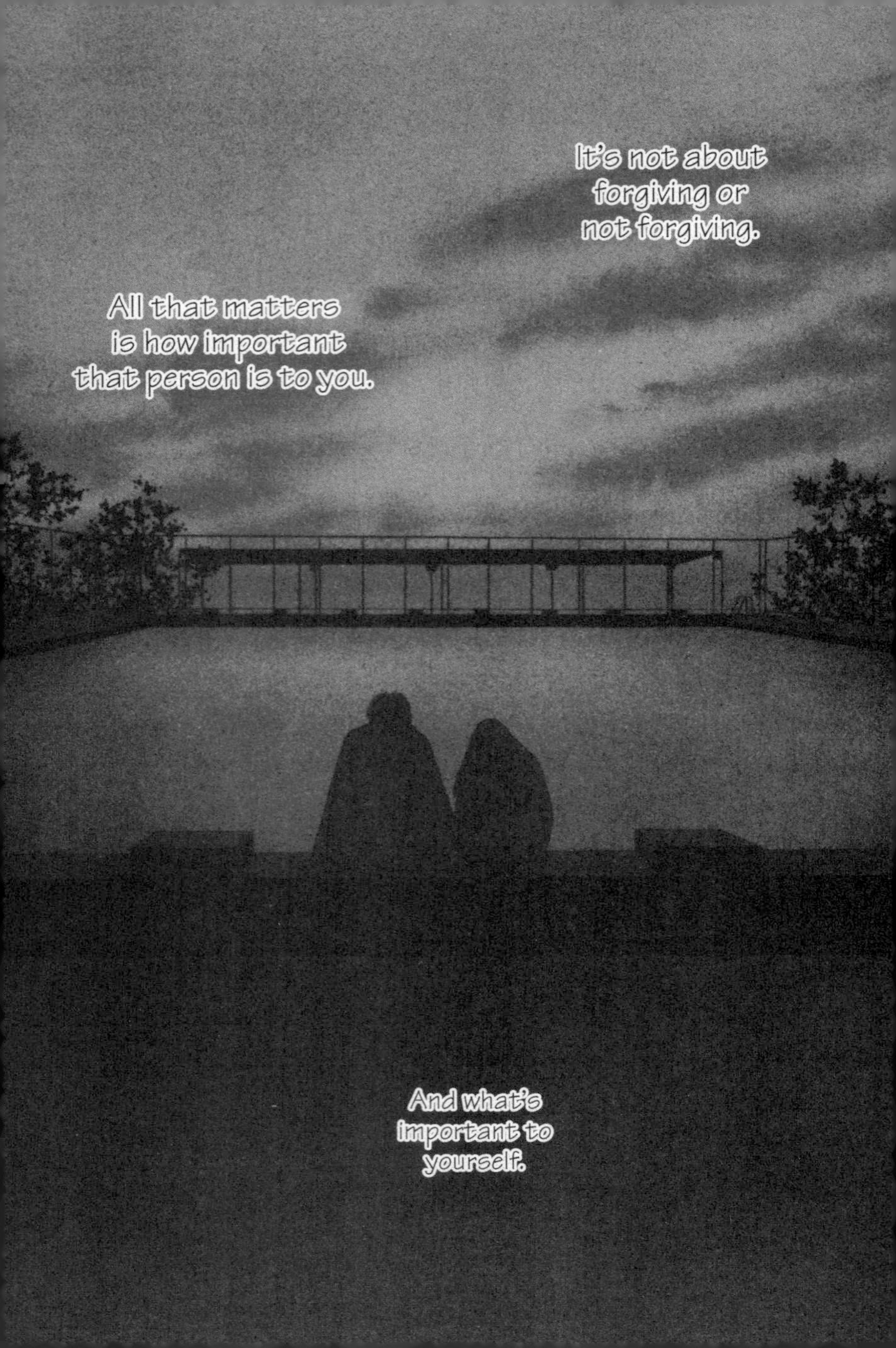
It's not about forgiving or not forgiving.
All that matters is how important that person is to you.
And what's important to yourself.

ピーチガール

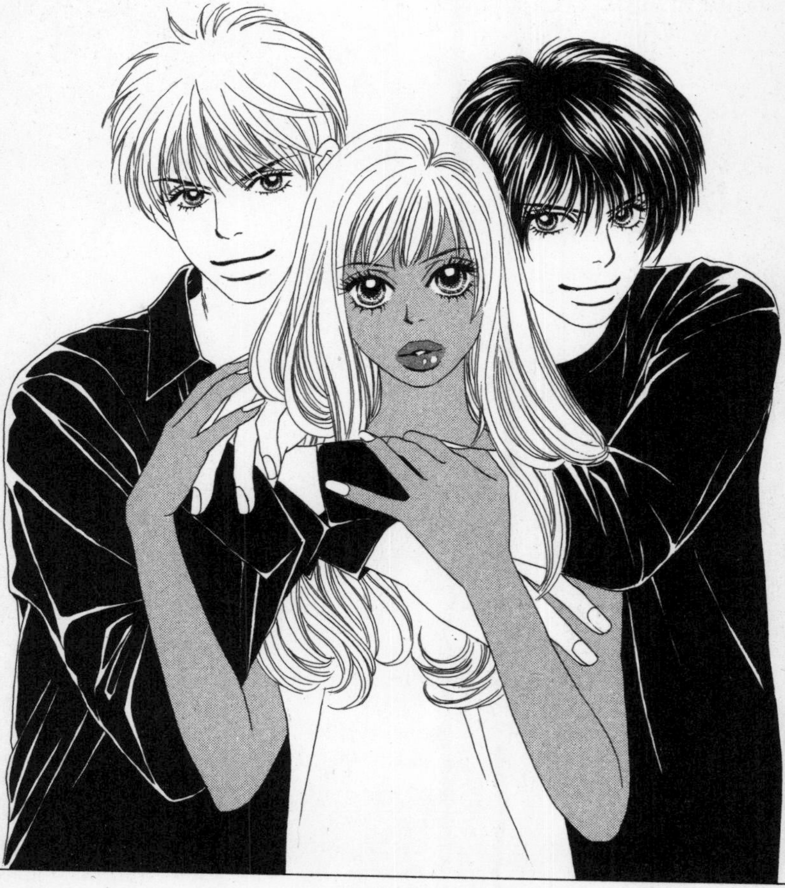

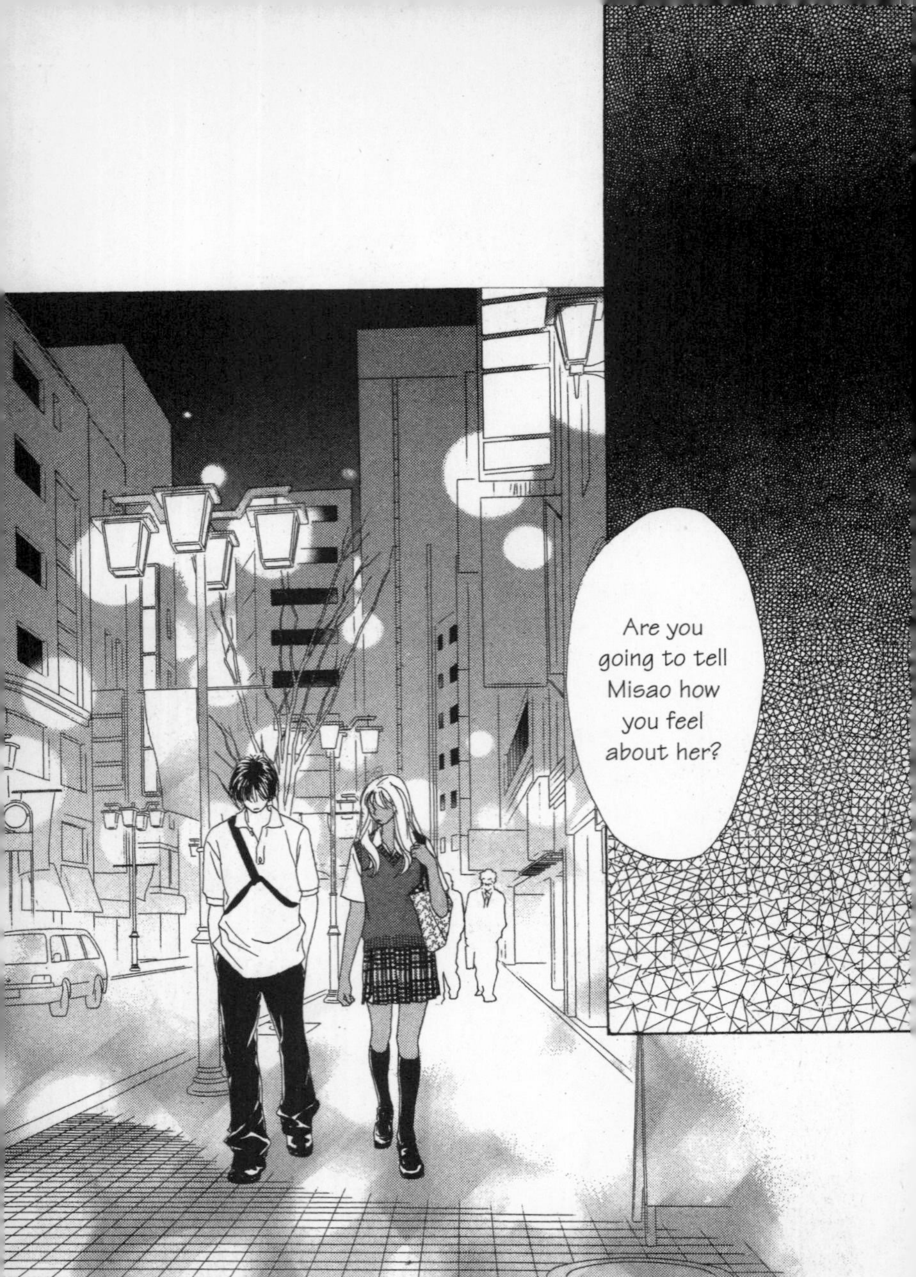
Are you going to tell Misao how you feel about her?

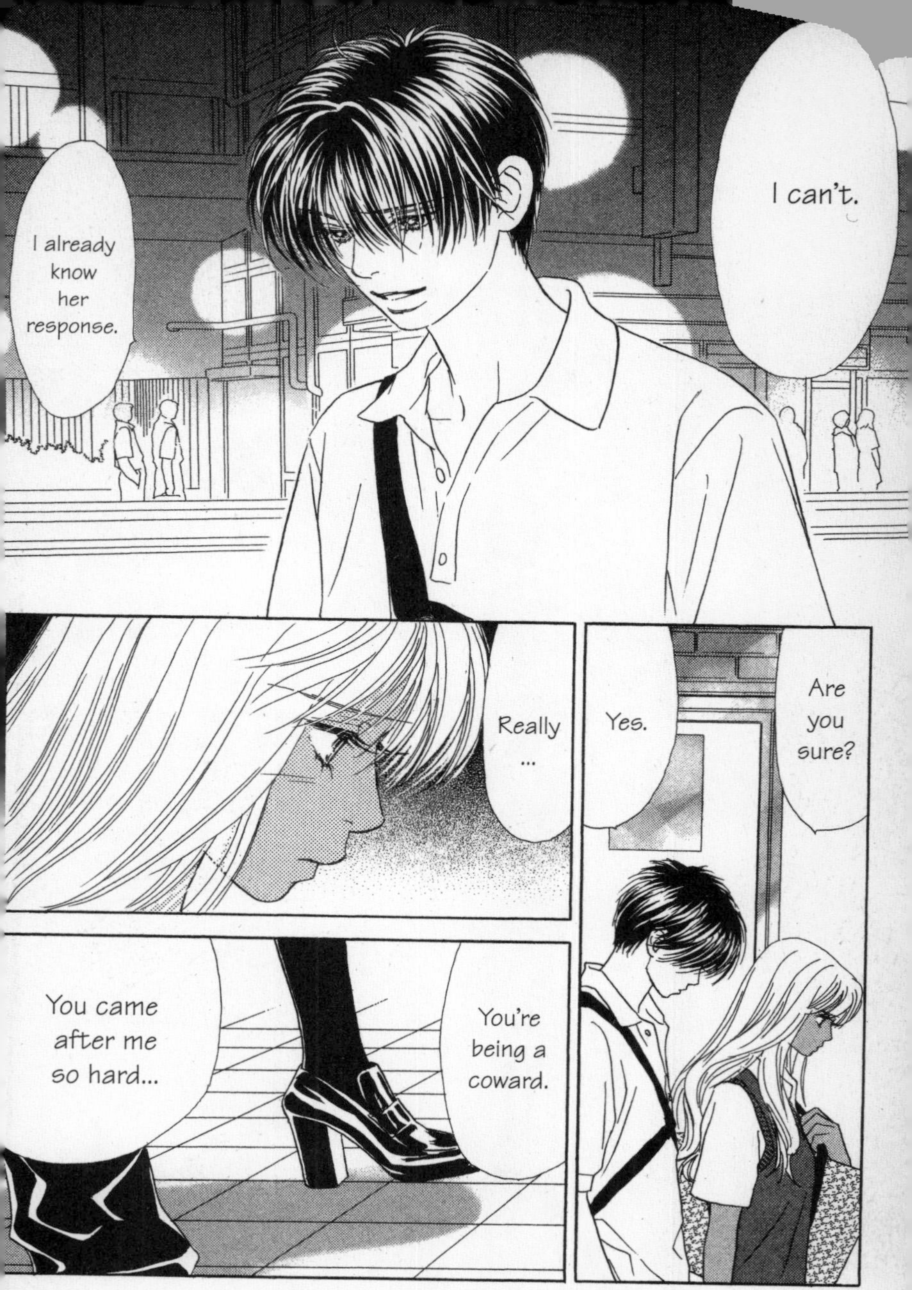
I can't.
I already know her response.
Are you sure?
Yes.
Really ...
You're being a coward.
You came after me so hard...

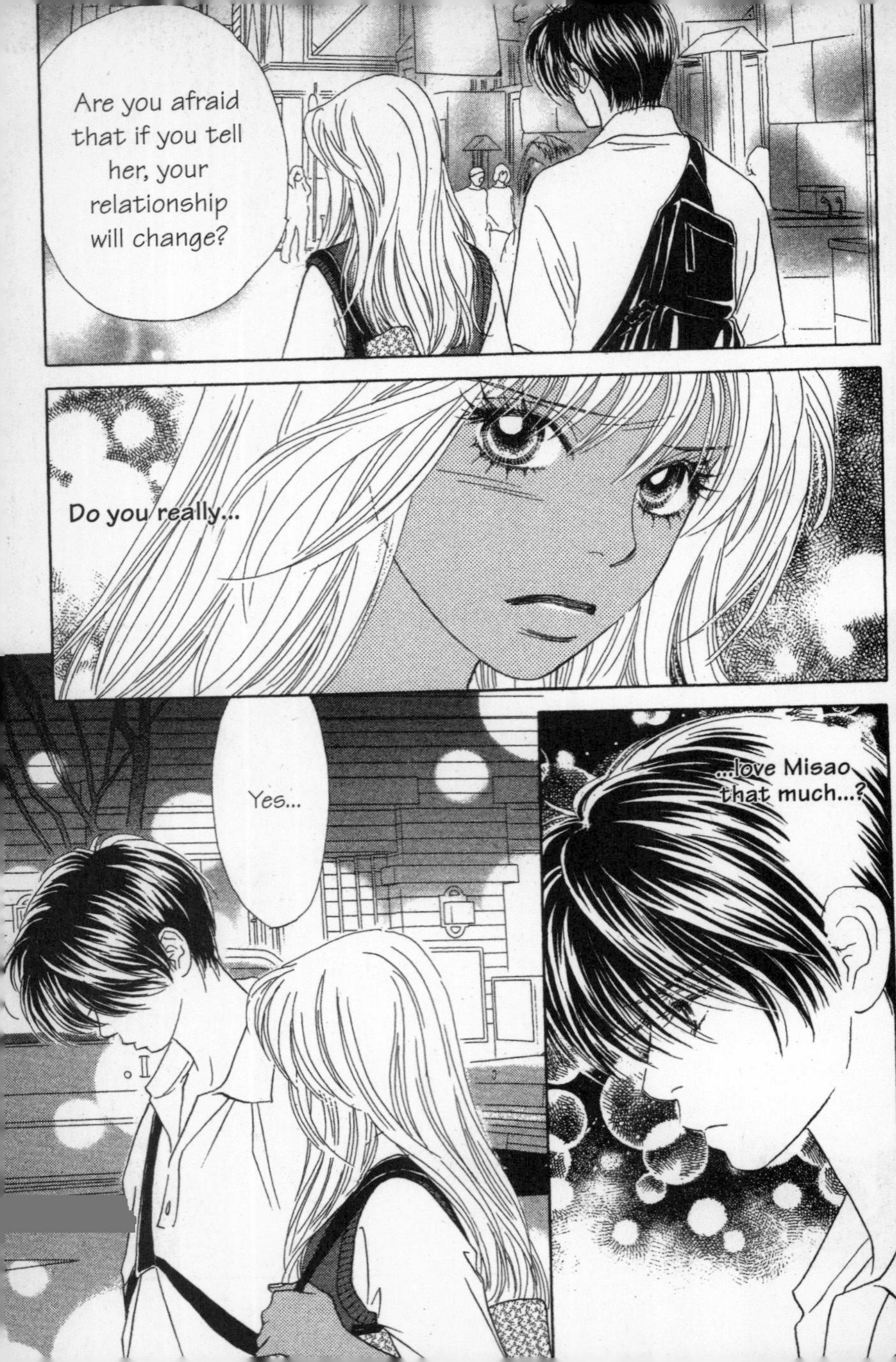
Are you afraid that if you tell her, your relationship will change?
Do you really...
...love Misao that much...?
Yes...

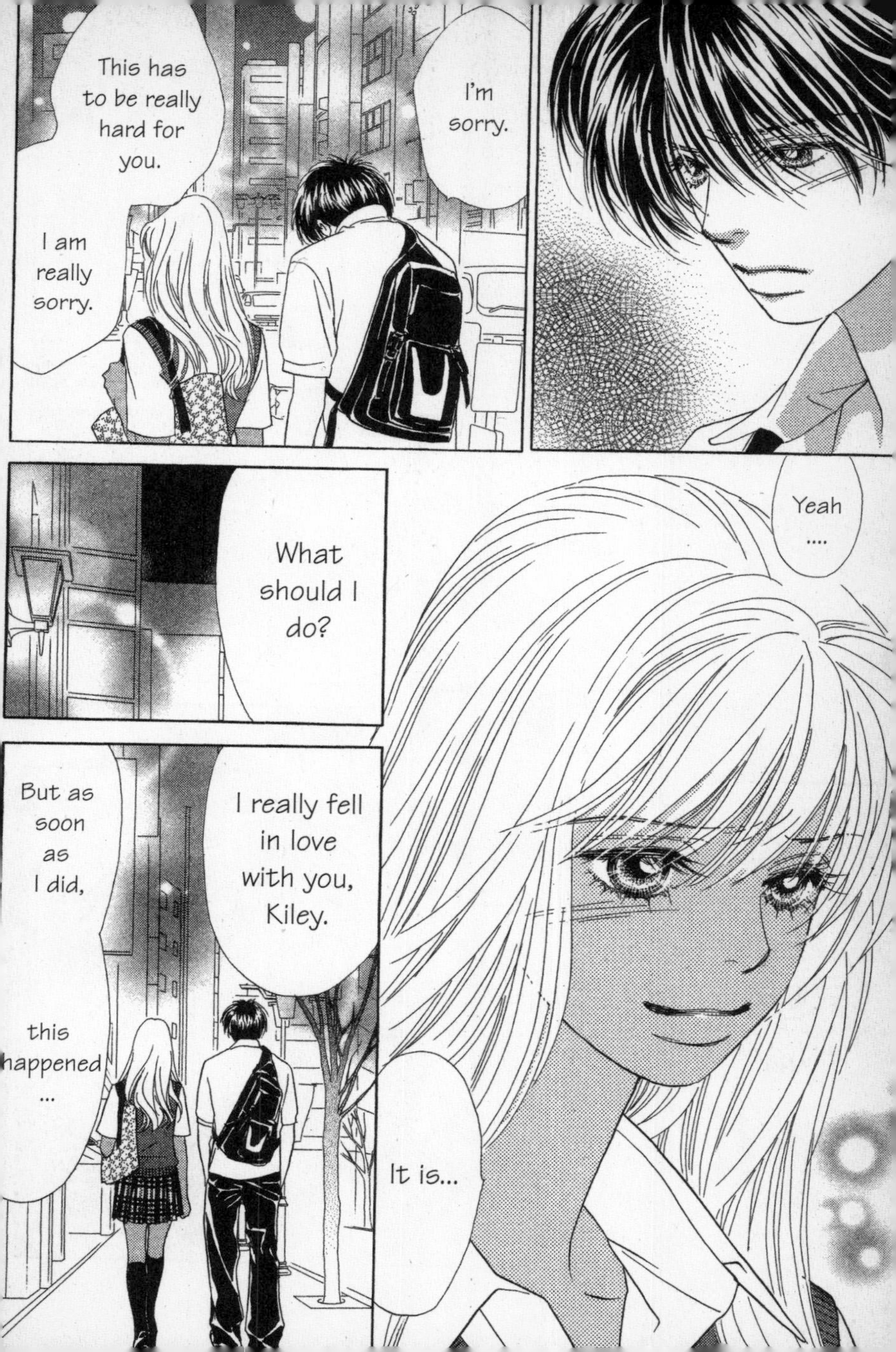
I'm sorry.
This has to be really hard for you.
I am really sorry.
Yeah ....
It is...
What should I do?
I really fell in love with you, Kiley.
But as soon as I did,
this happened ...

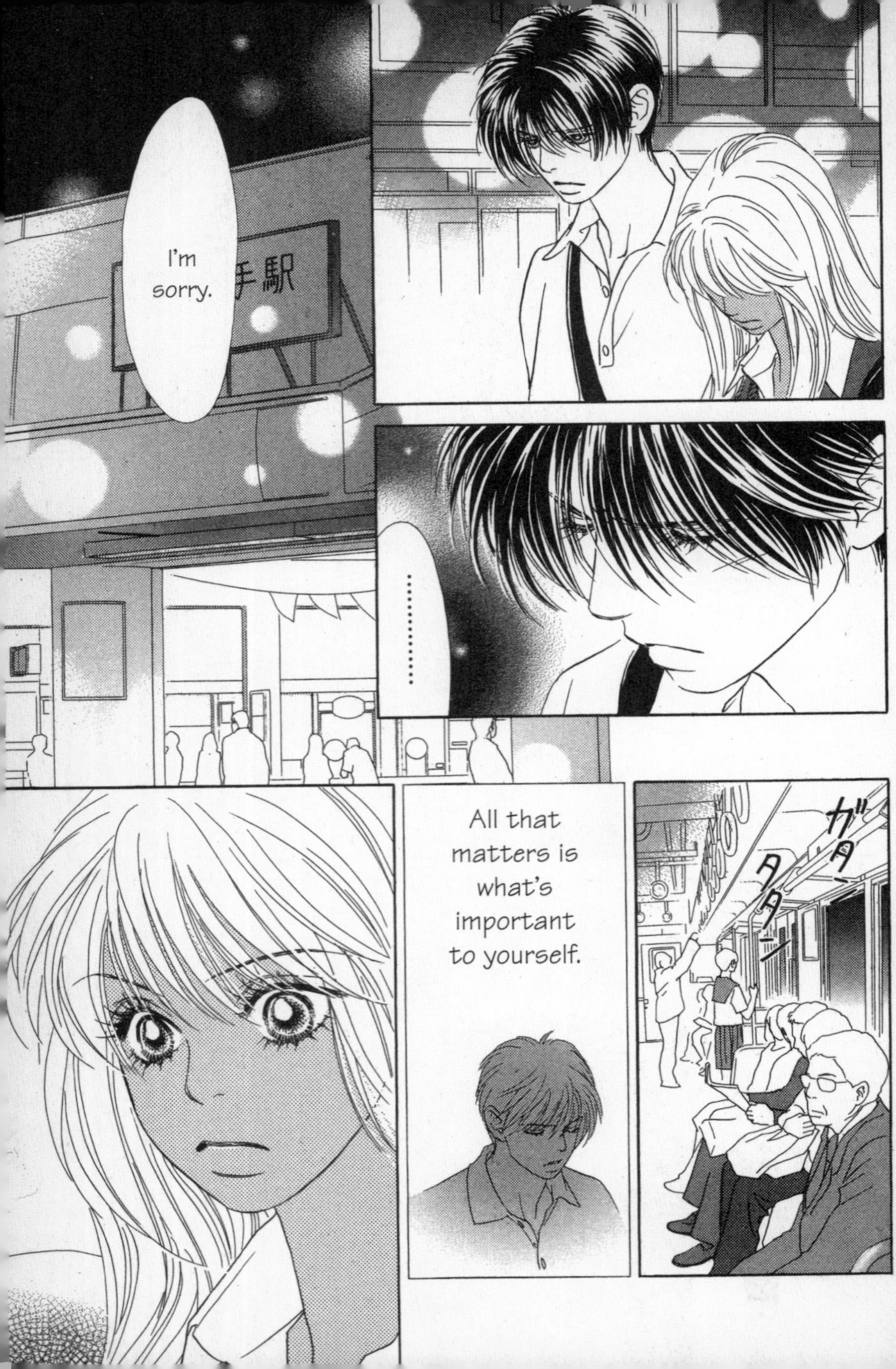
......
手駅
I'm sorry.
ガタ
タタン
All that matters is what's important to yourself.

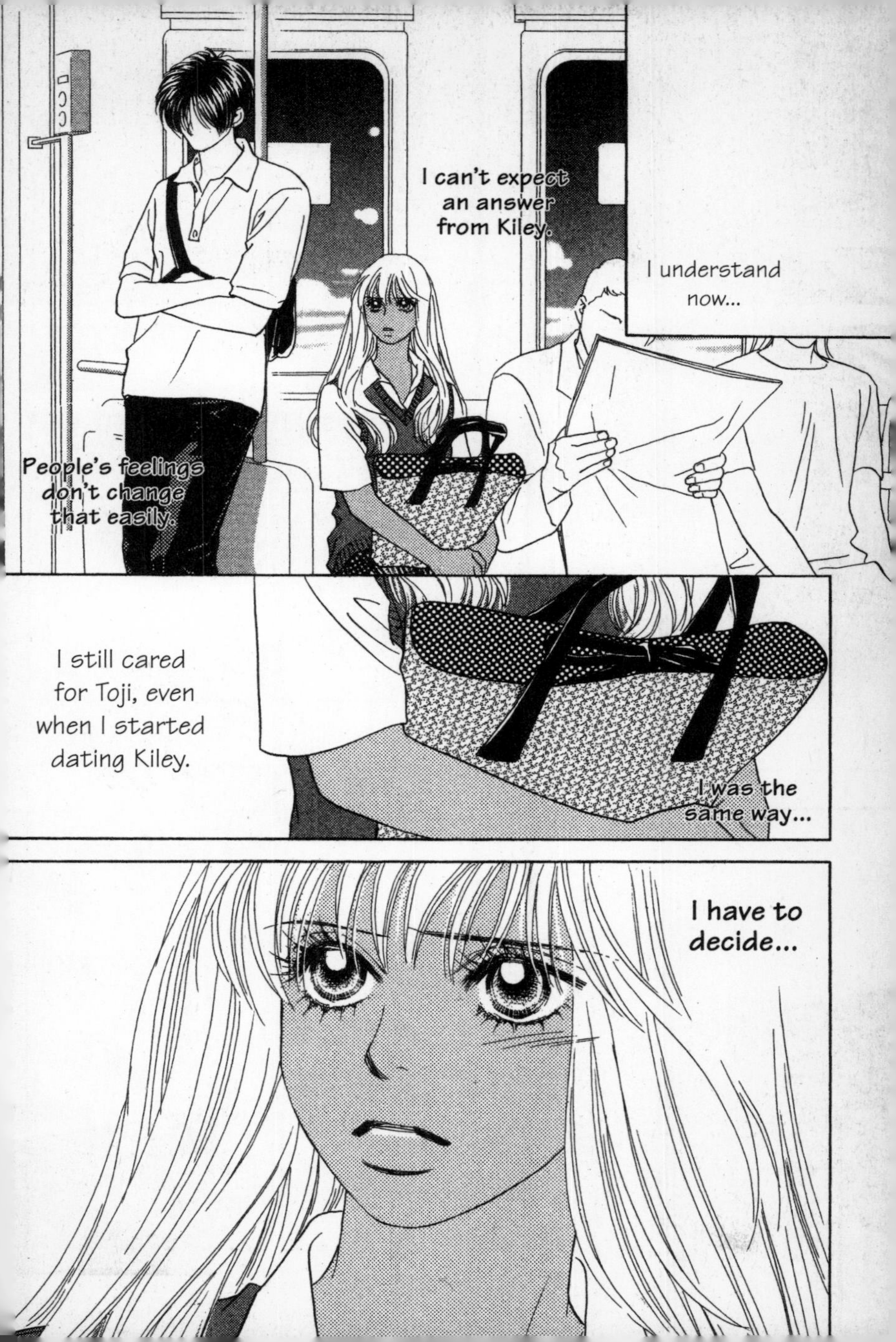
I understand now...
I can't expect an answer from Kiley.
People's feelings don't change that easily.
I was the same way...
I still cared for Toji, even when I started dating Kiley.
I have to decide...

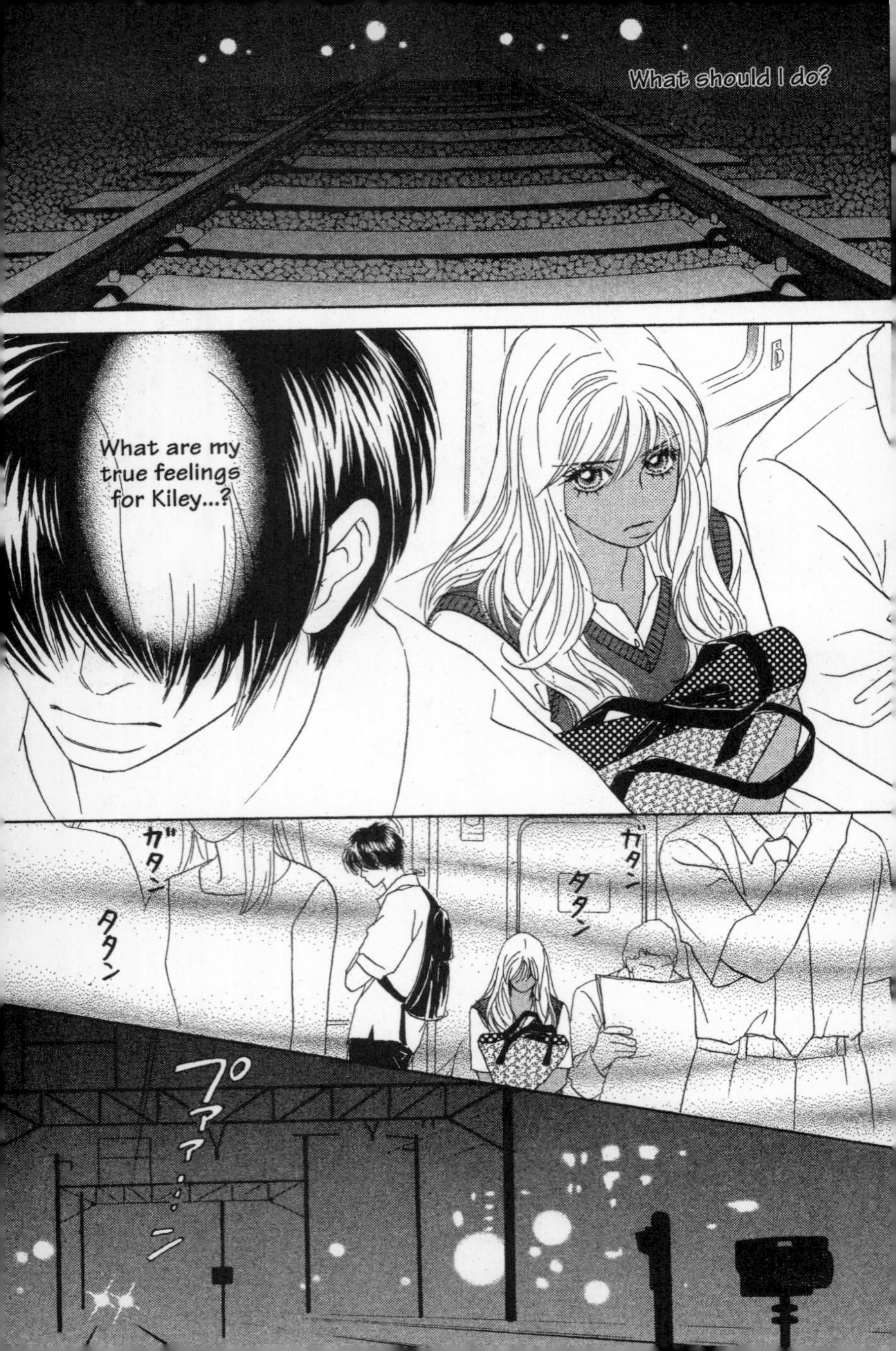
What should I do?
What are my true feelings for Kiley...?
ガタン
タタン
ガタン
タタン
プアア…ン

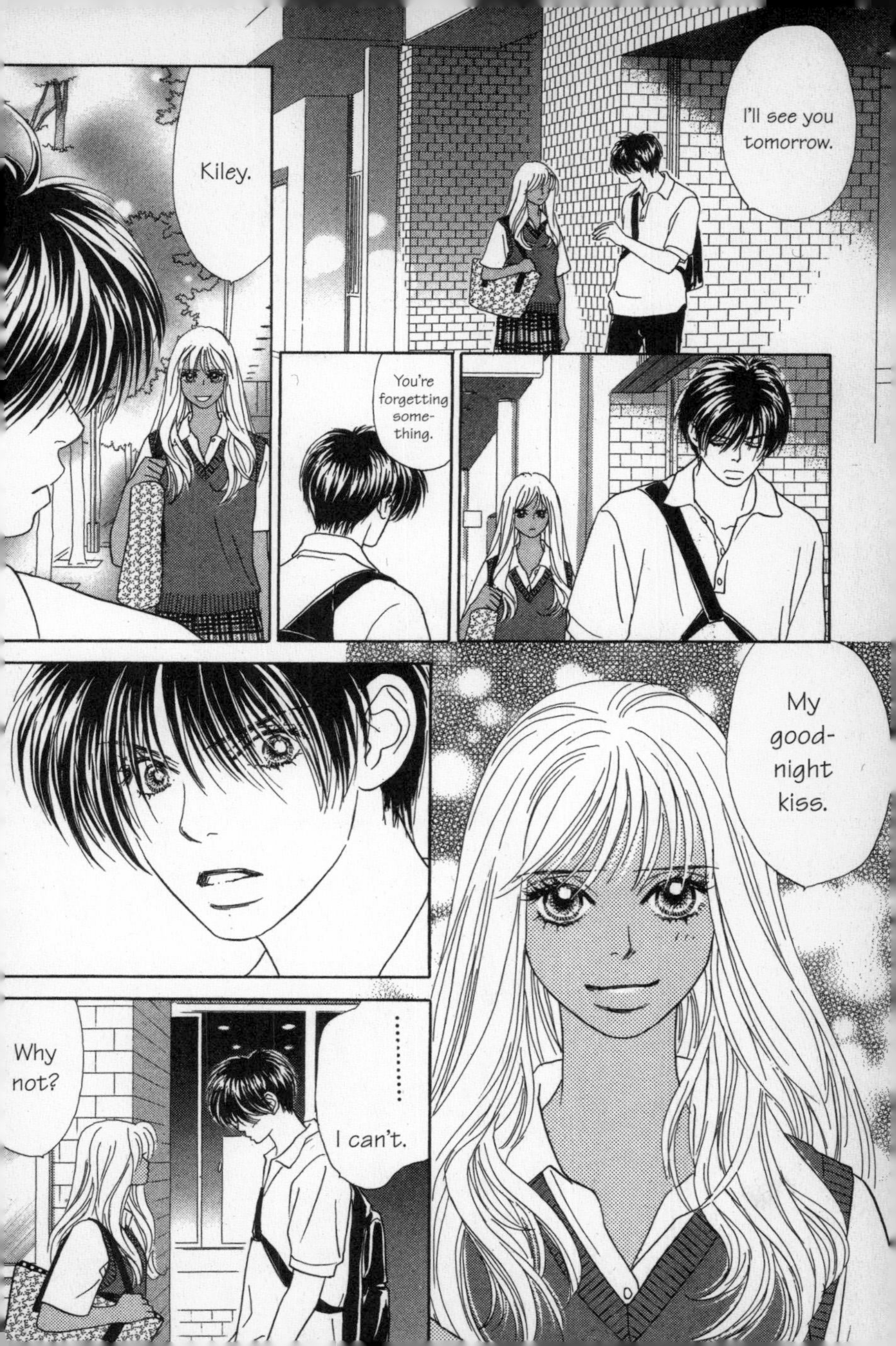
I'll see you tomorrow.
You're forgetting something.
Kiley.
My good-night kiss.
......
I can't.
Why not?

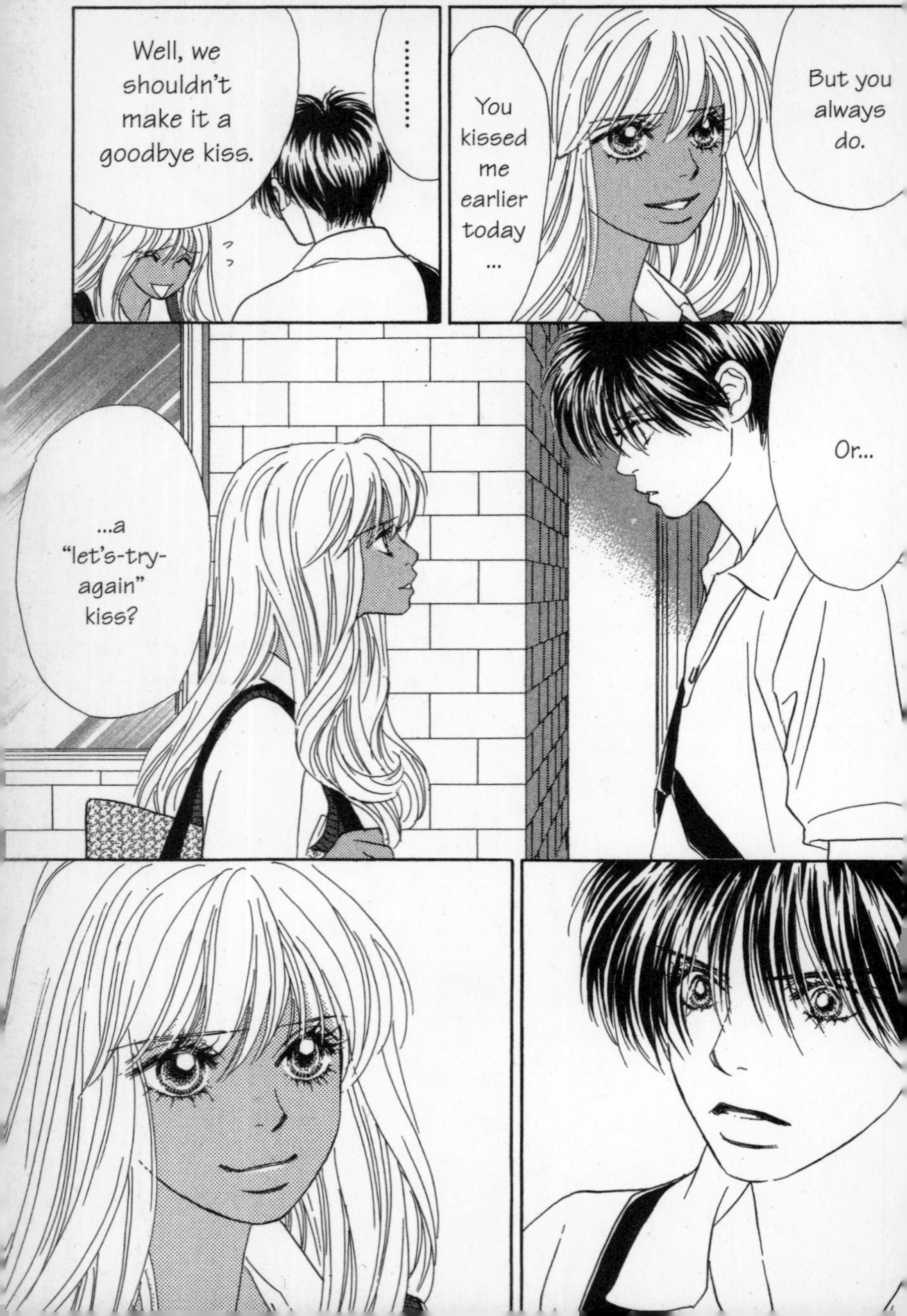
But you always do.
You kissed me earlier today ...
......
Well, we shouldn't make it a goodbye kiss.
Or...
...a "let's-try-again" kiss?

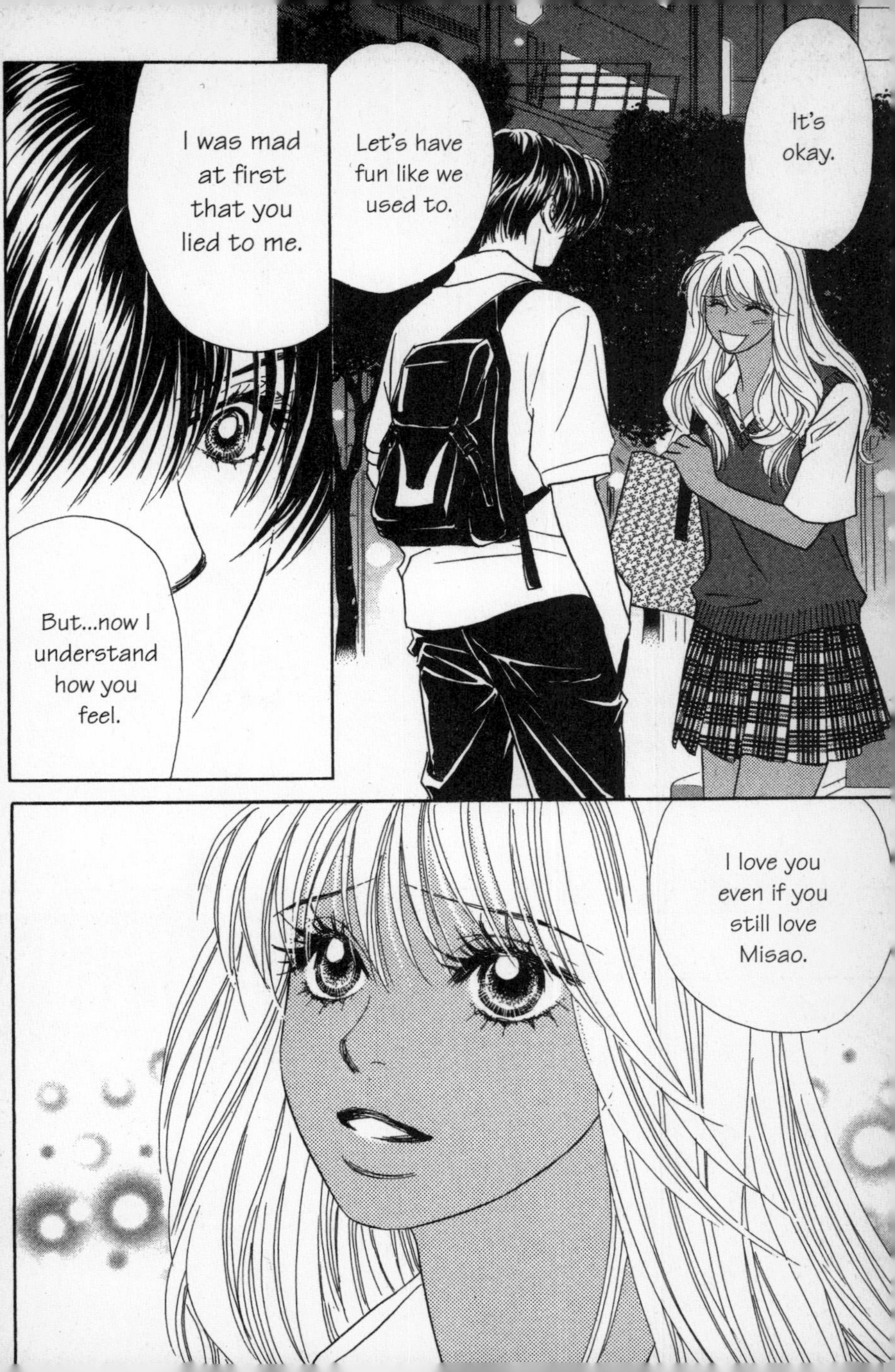
It's okay.
Let's have fun like we used to.
I was mad at first that you lied to me.
But...now I understand how you feel.
I love you even if you still love Misao.

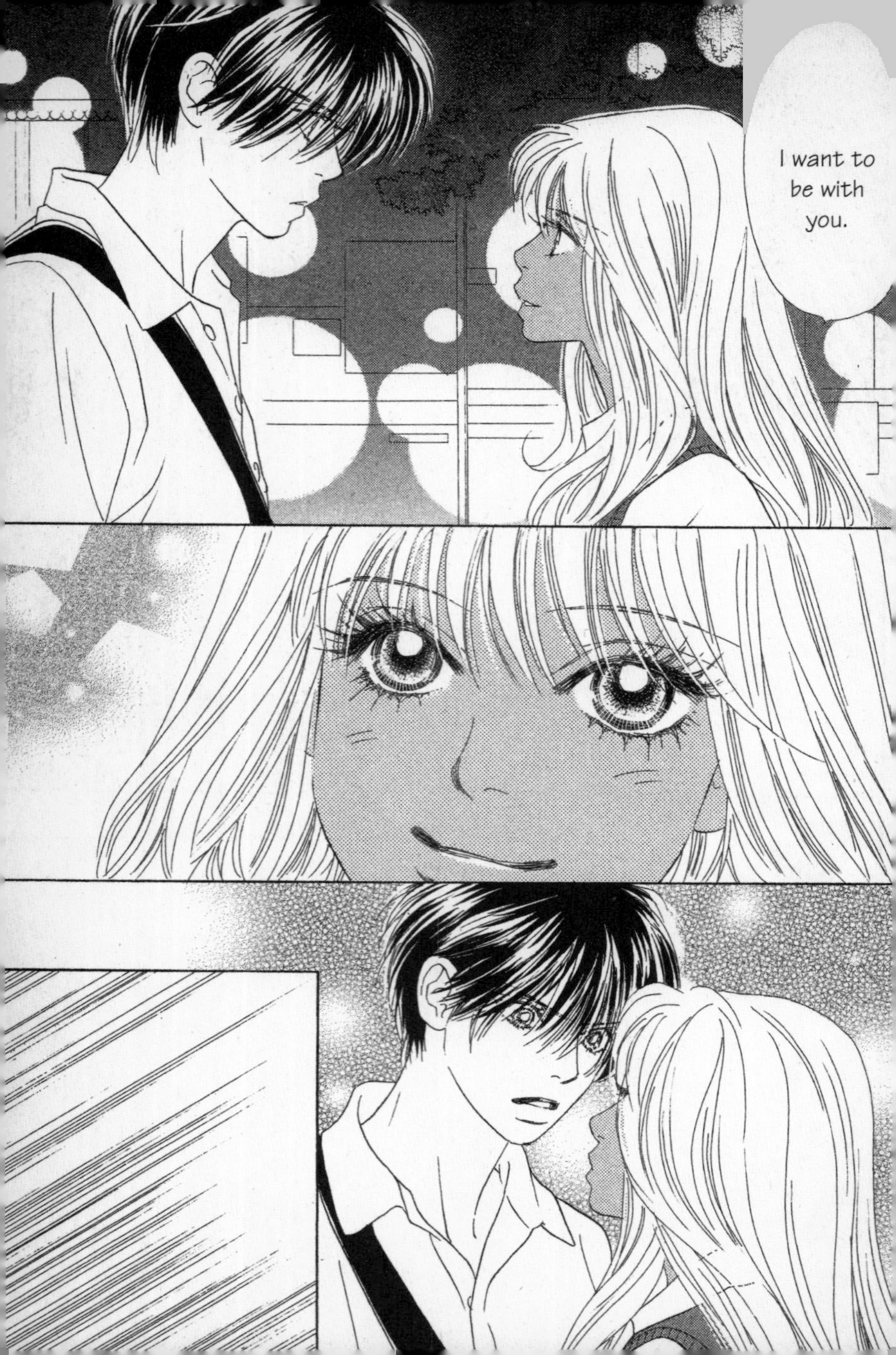
I want to be with you.

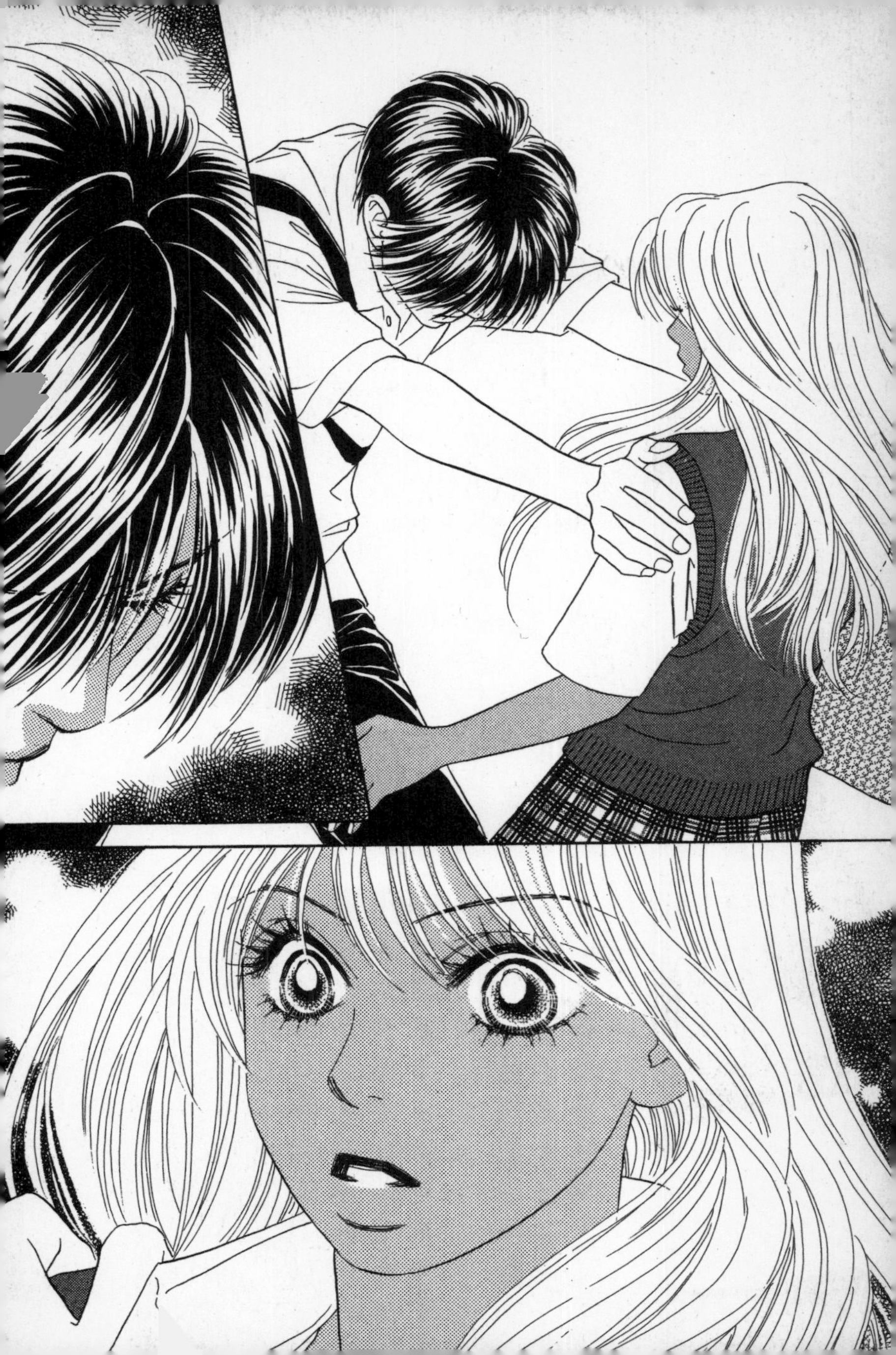

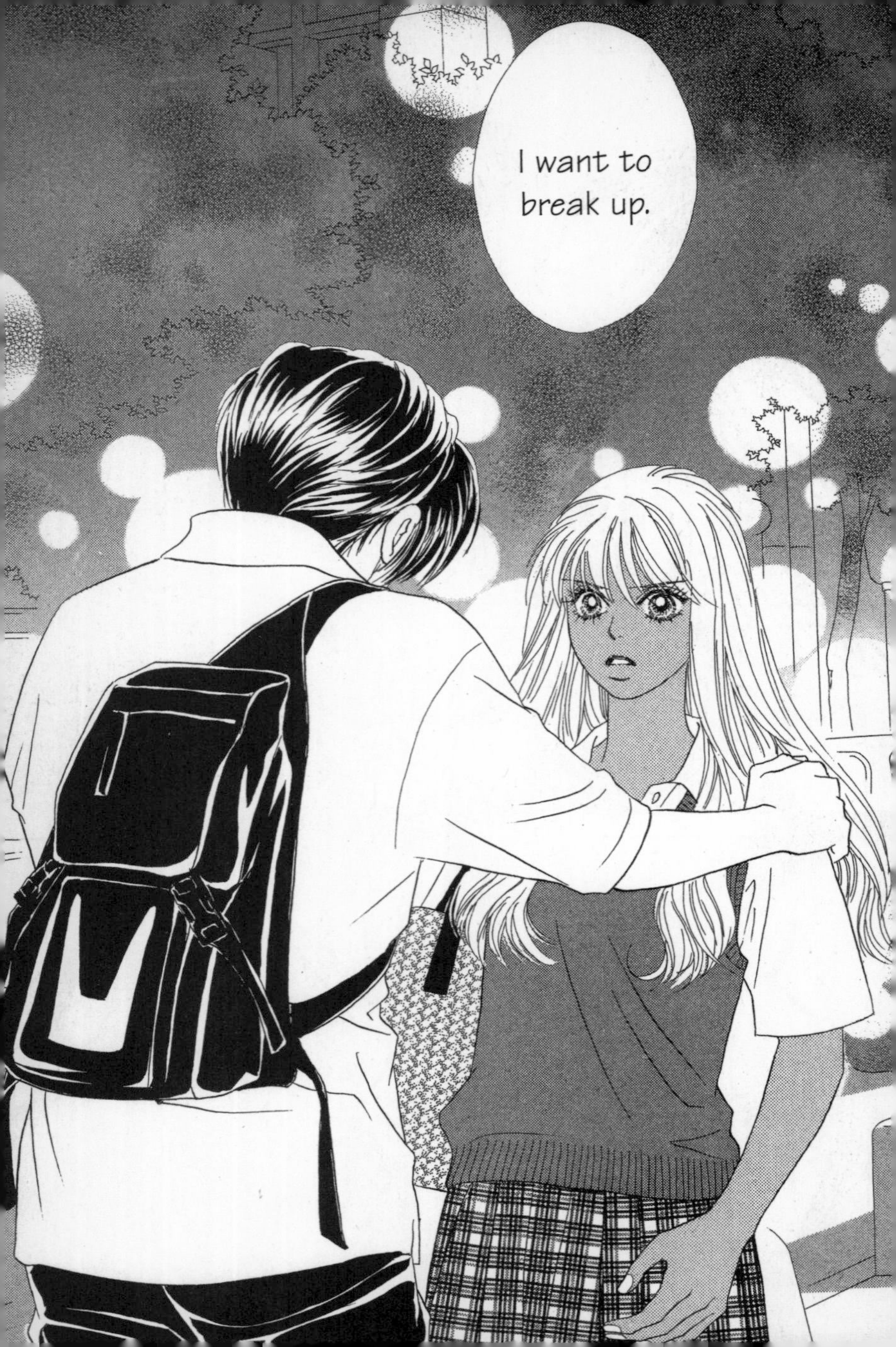
I want to break up.

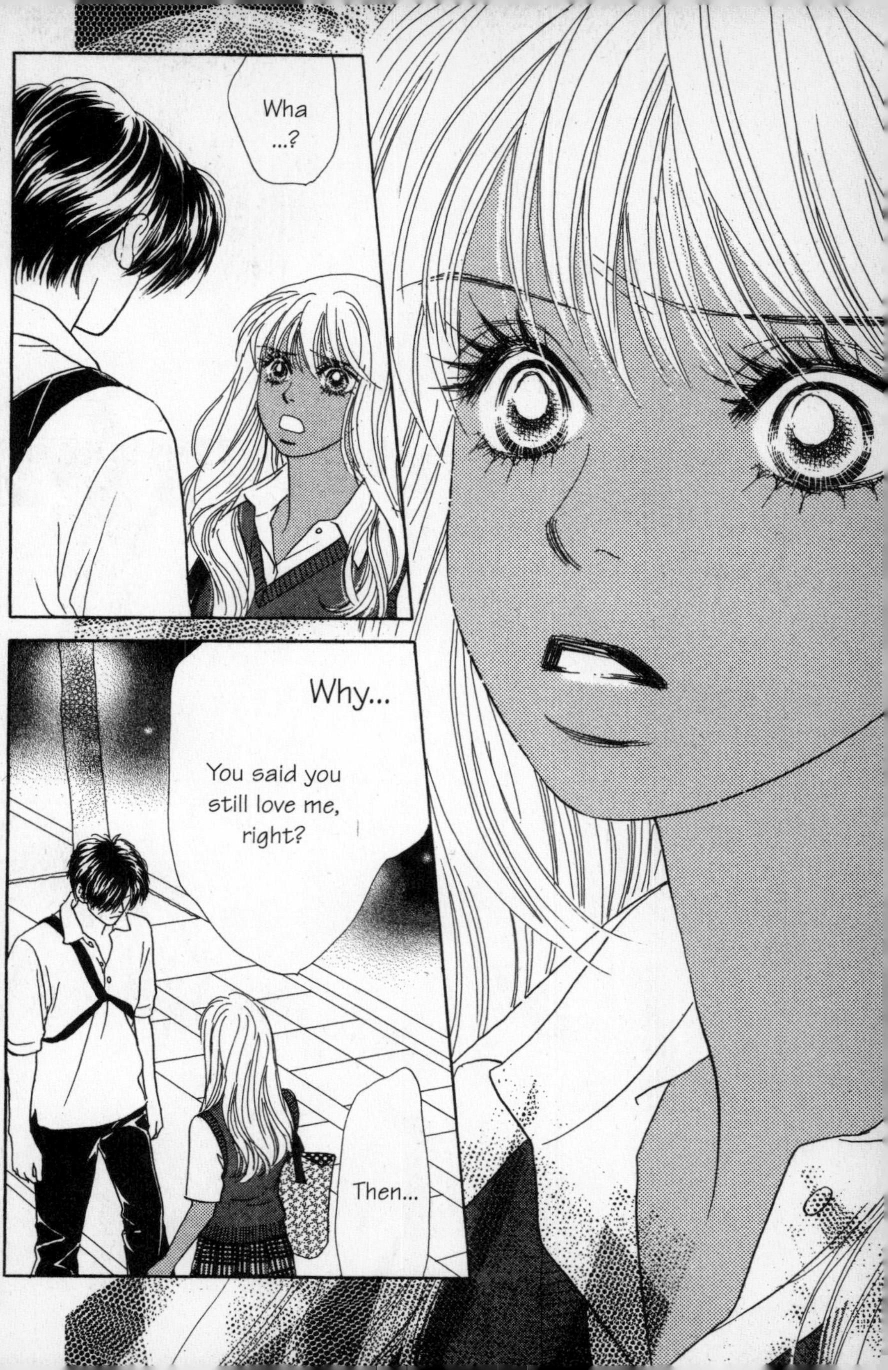
Wha ...?
Why...
You said you still love me, right?
Then...

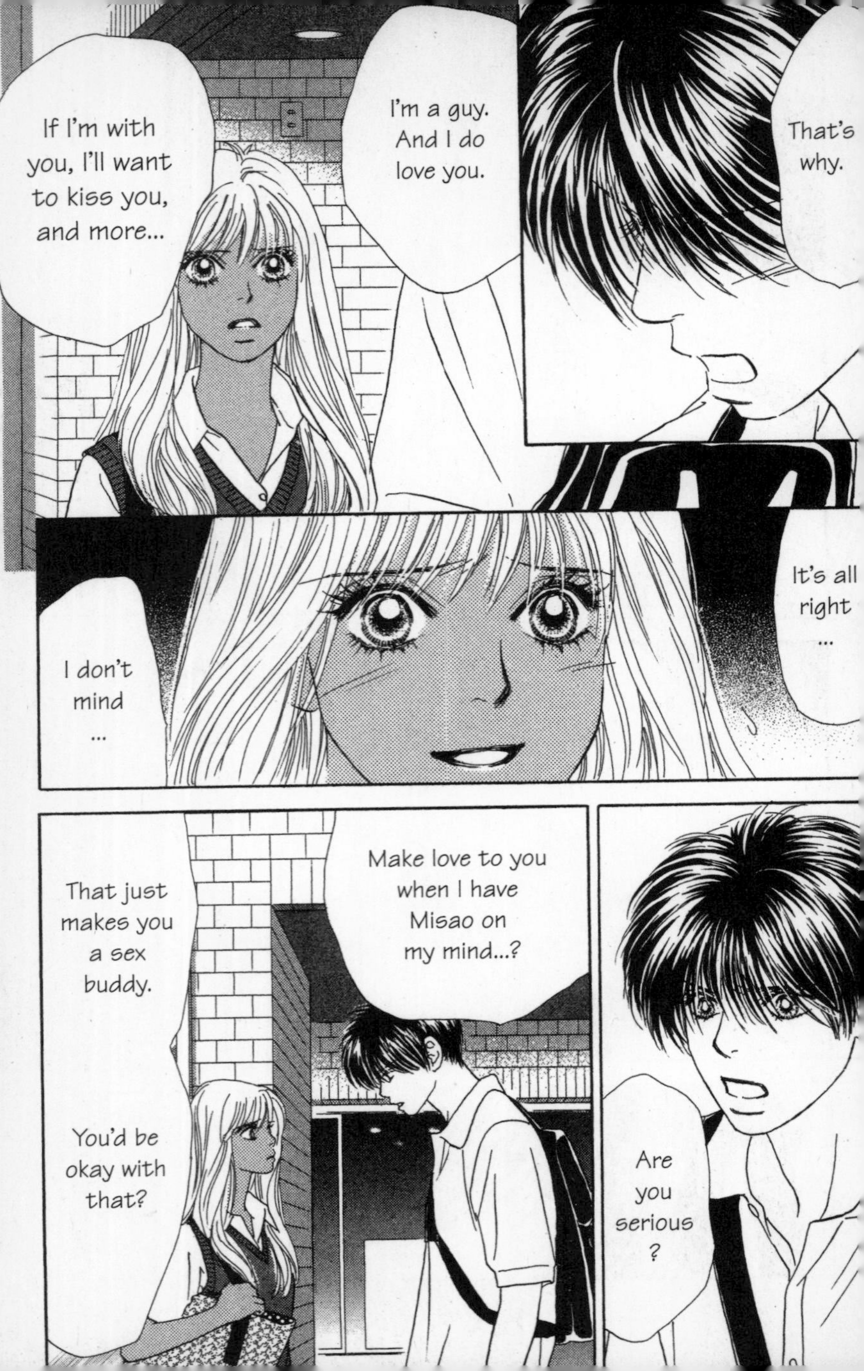
That's why.
I'm a guy. And I do love you.
If I'm with you, I'll want to kiss you, and more...
It's all right ...
I don't mind ...
Are you serious ?
Make love to you when I have Misao on my mind...?
That just makes you a sex buddy.
You'd be okay with that?

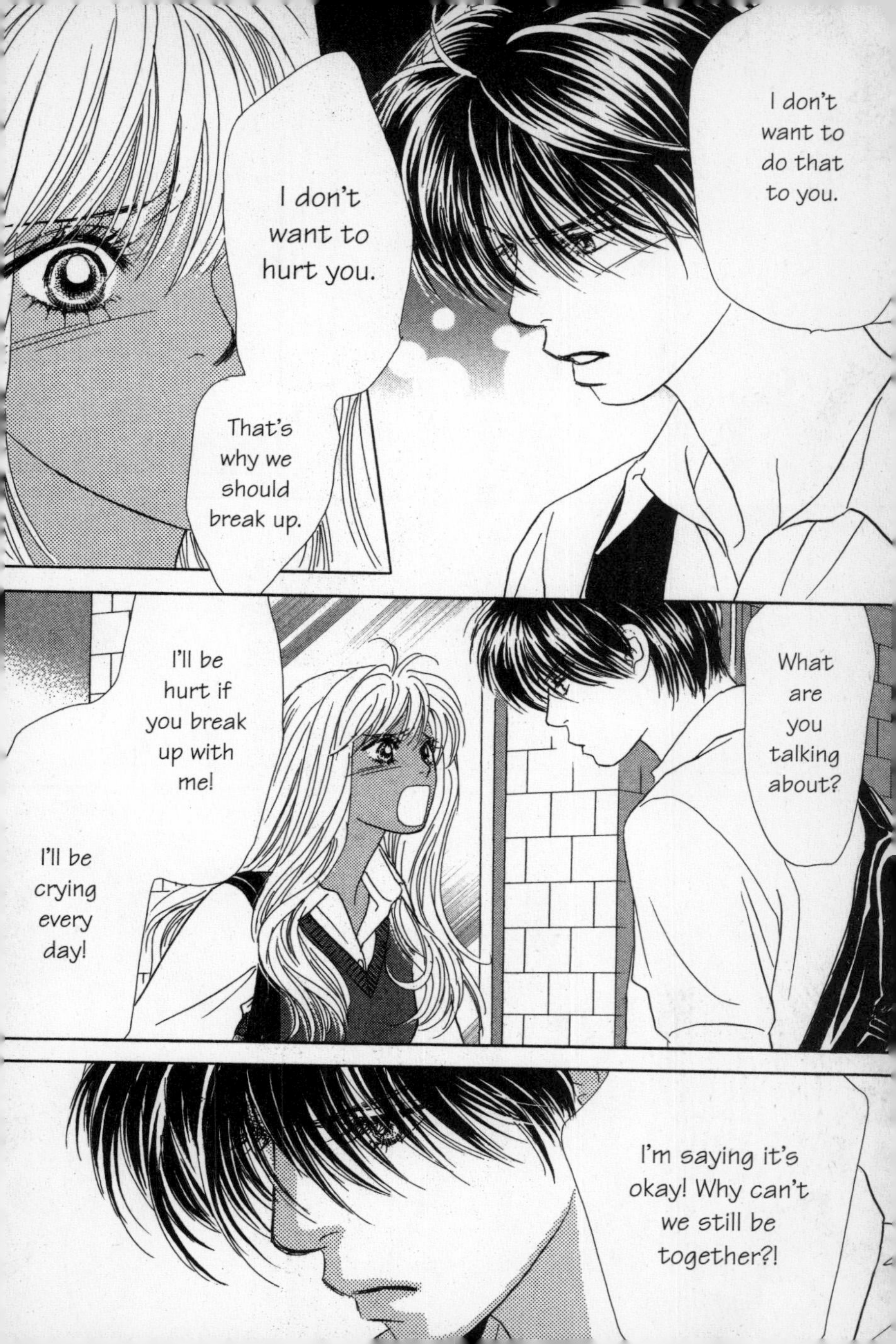
I don't want to do that to you.
I don't want to hurt you.
That's why we should break up.
What are you talking about?
I'll be hurt if you break up with me!
I'll be crying every day!
I'm saying it's okay! Why can't we still be together?!

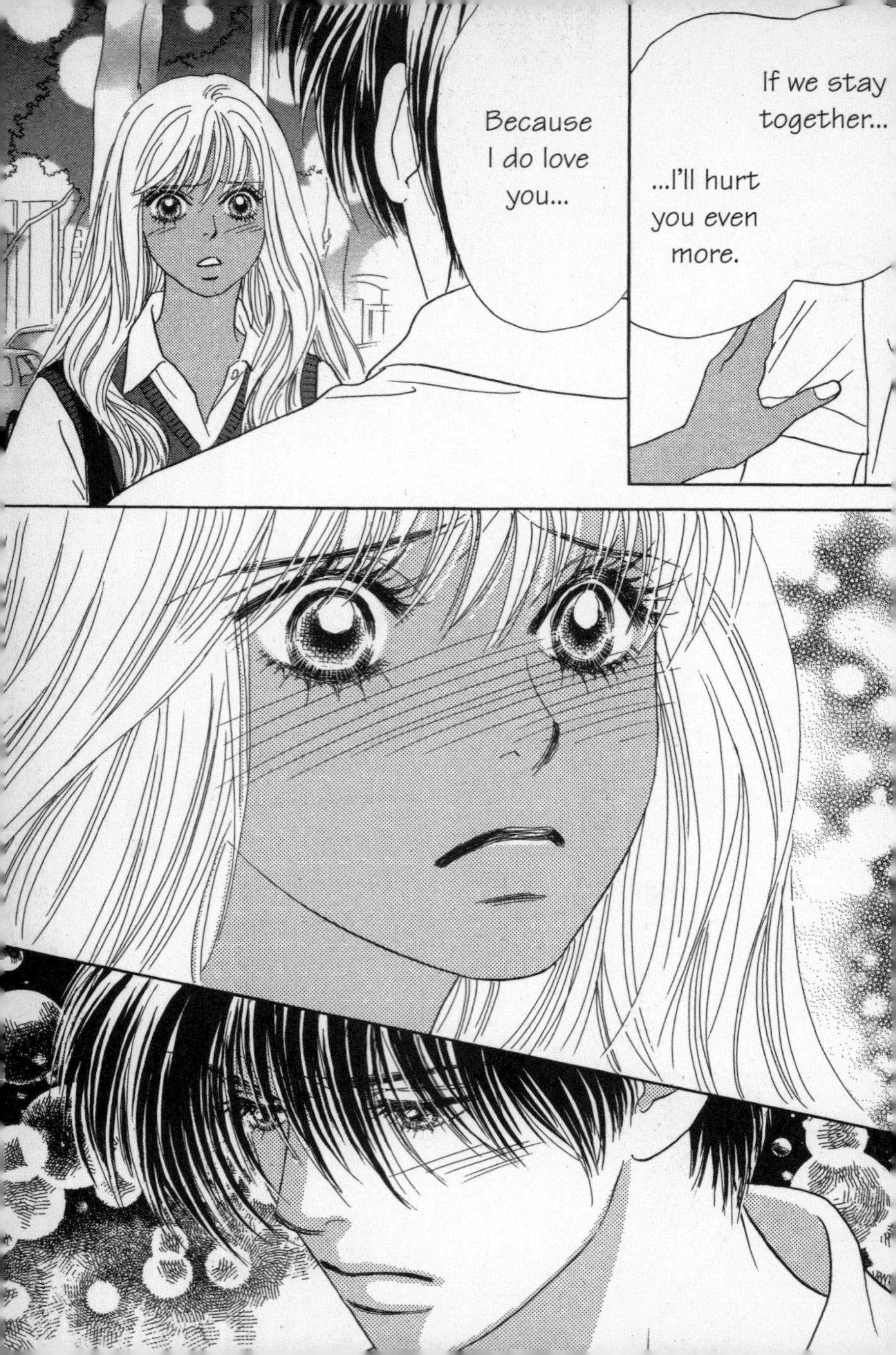
If we stay together...
...I'll hurt you even more.
Because I do love you...

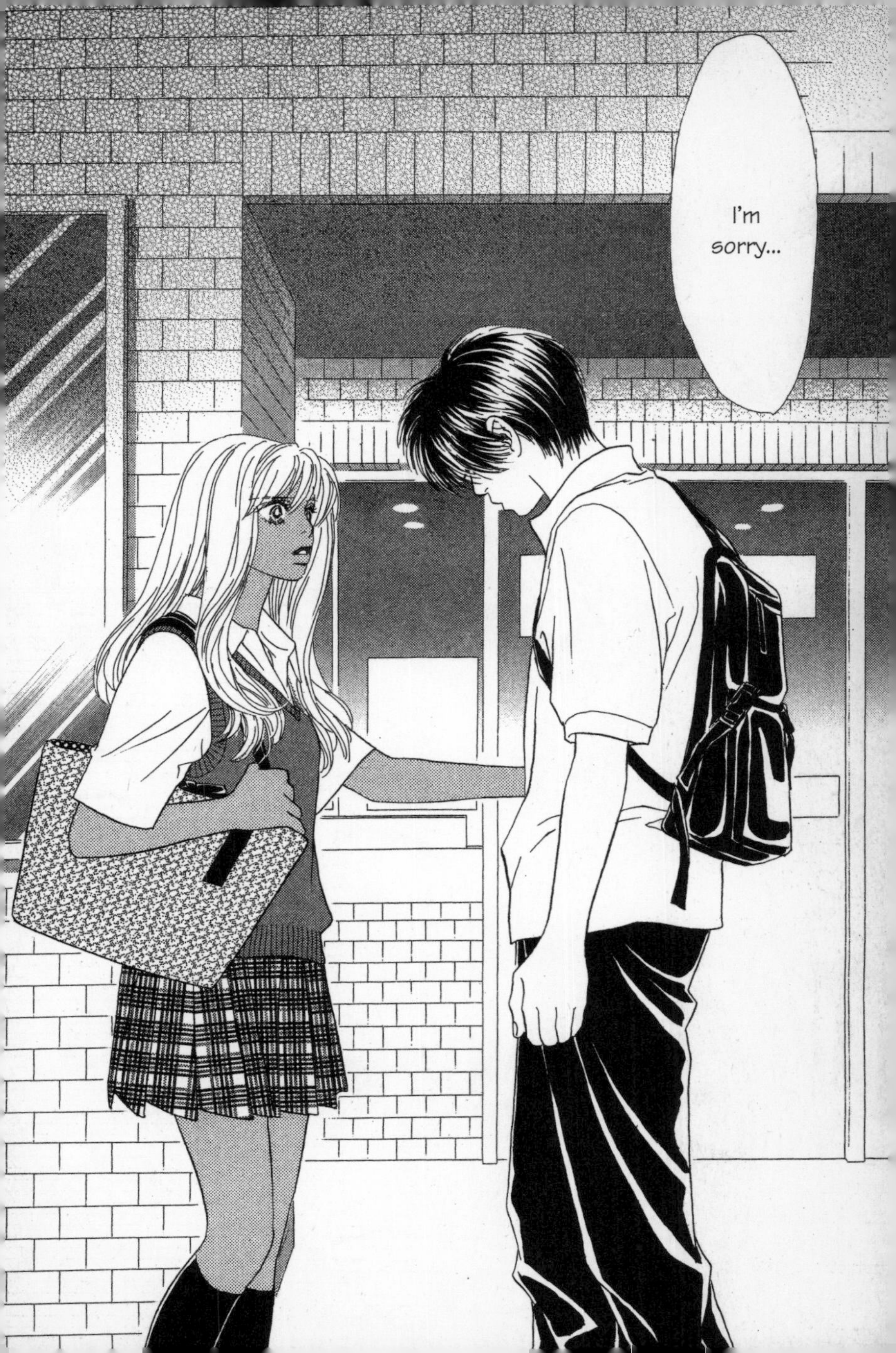
I'm sorry...

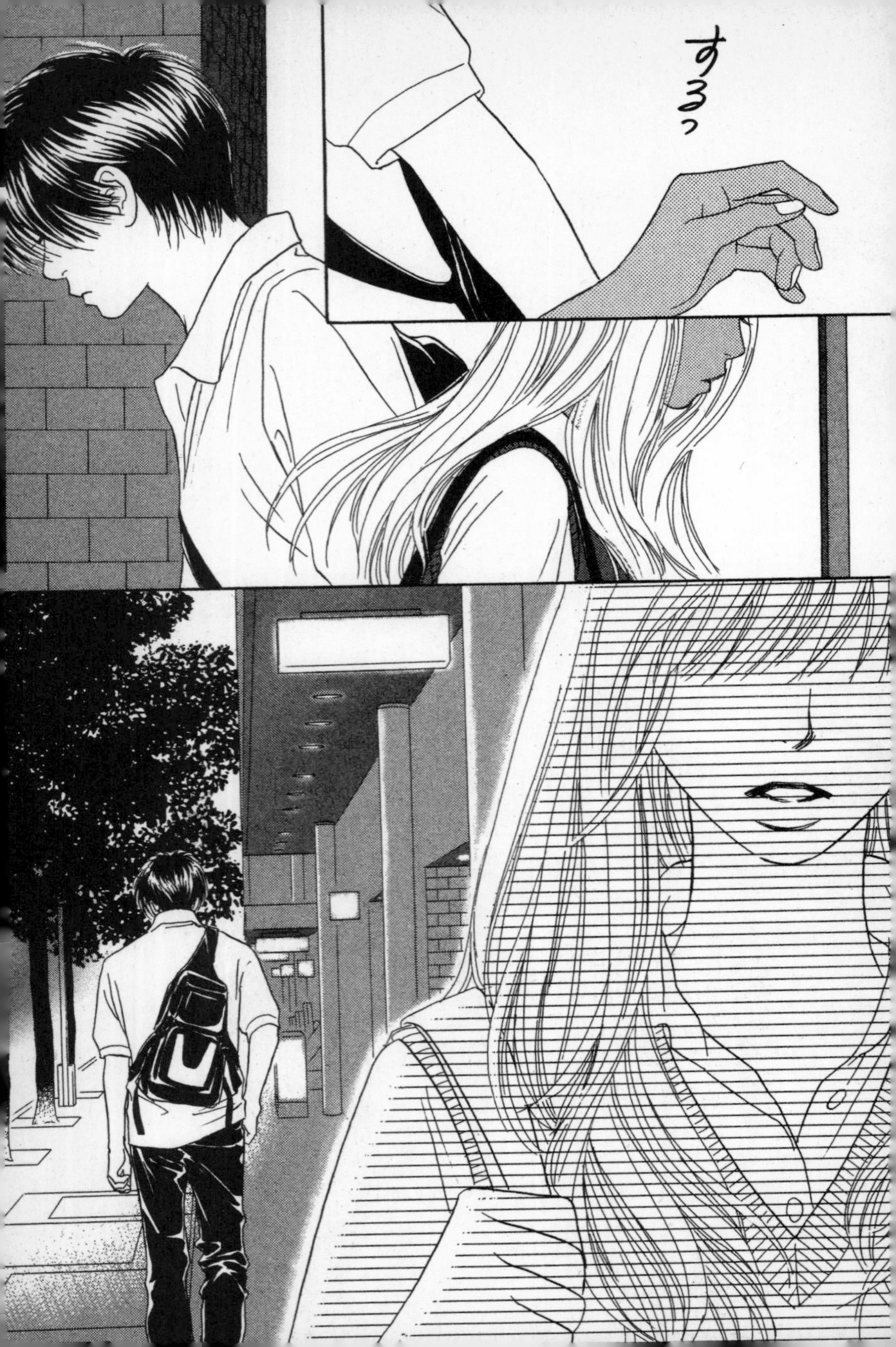
するっ

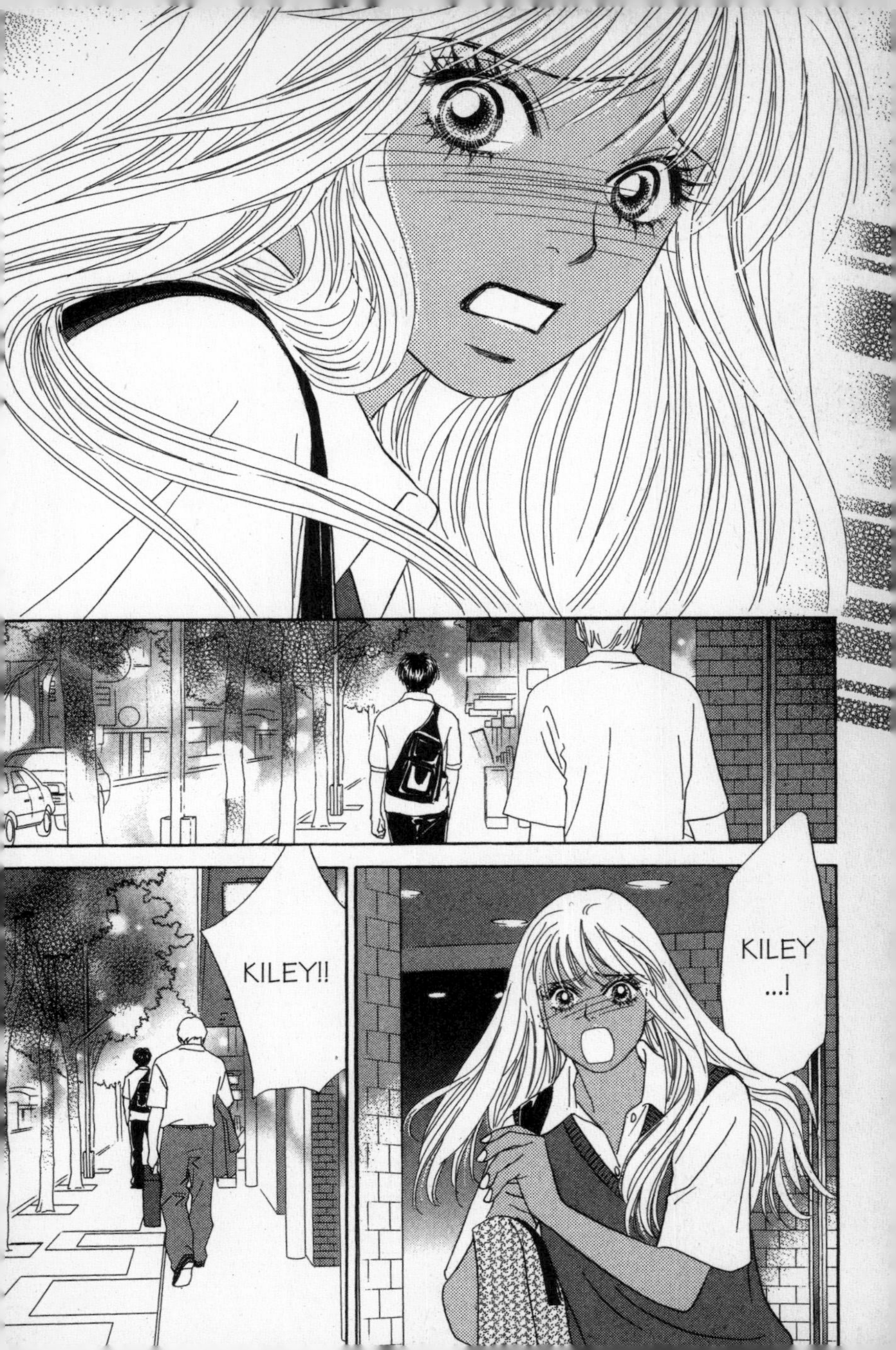
KILEY ...!
KILEY!!

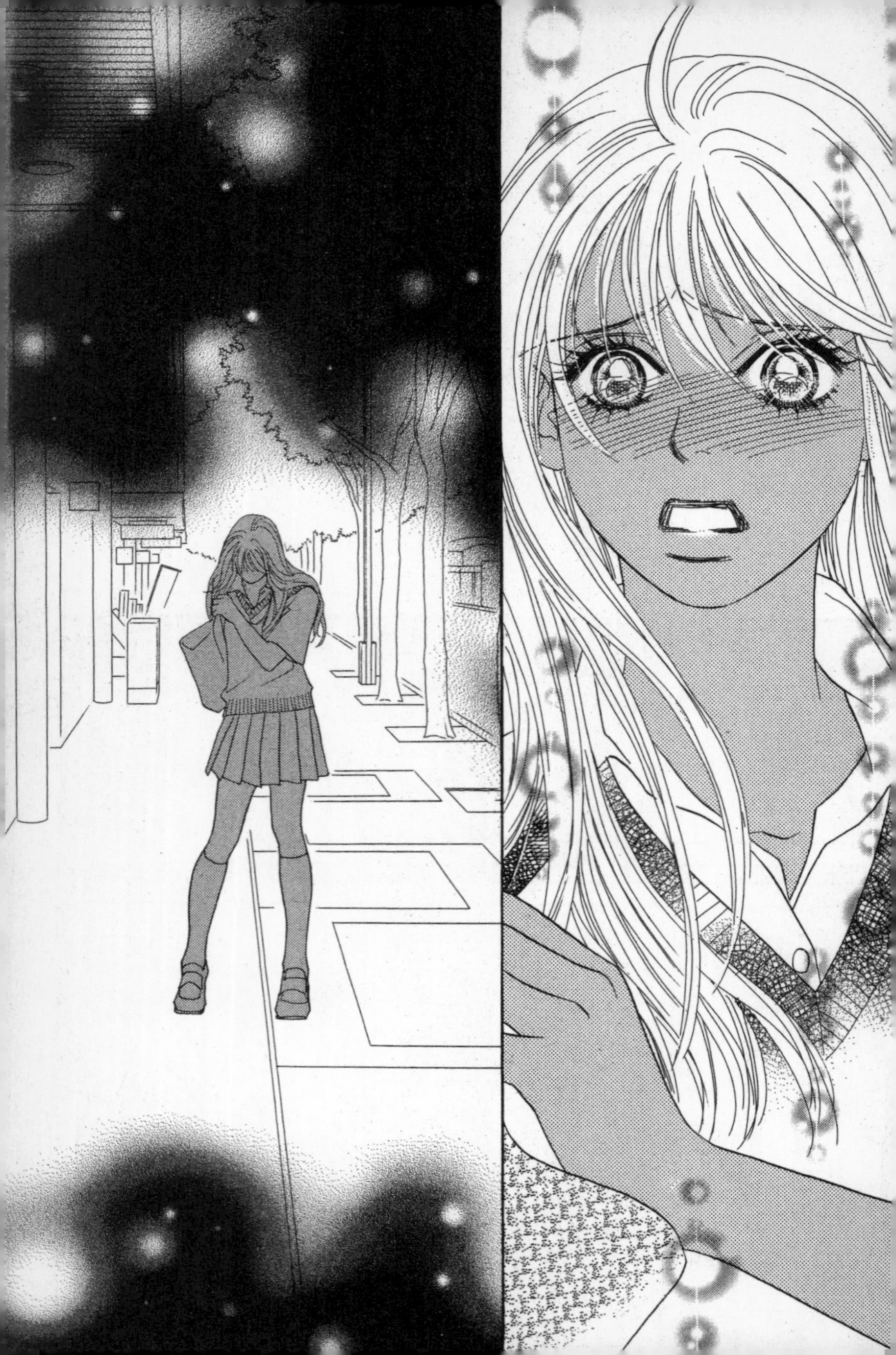

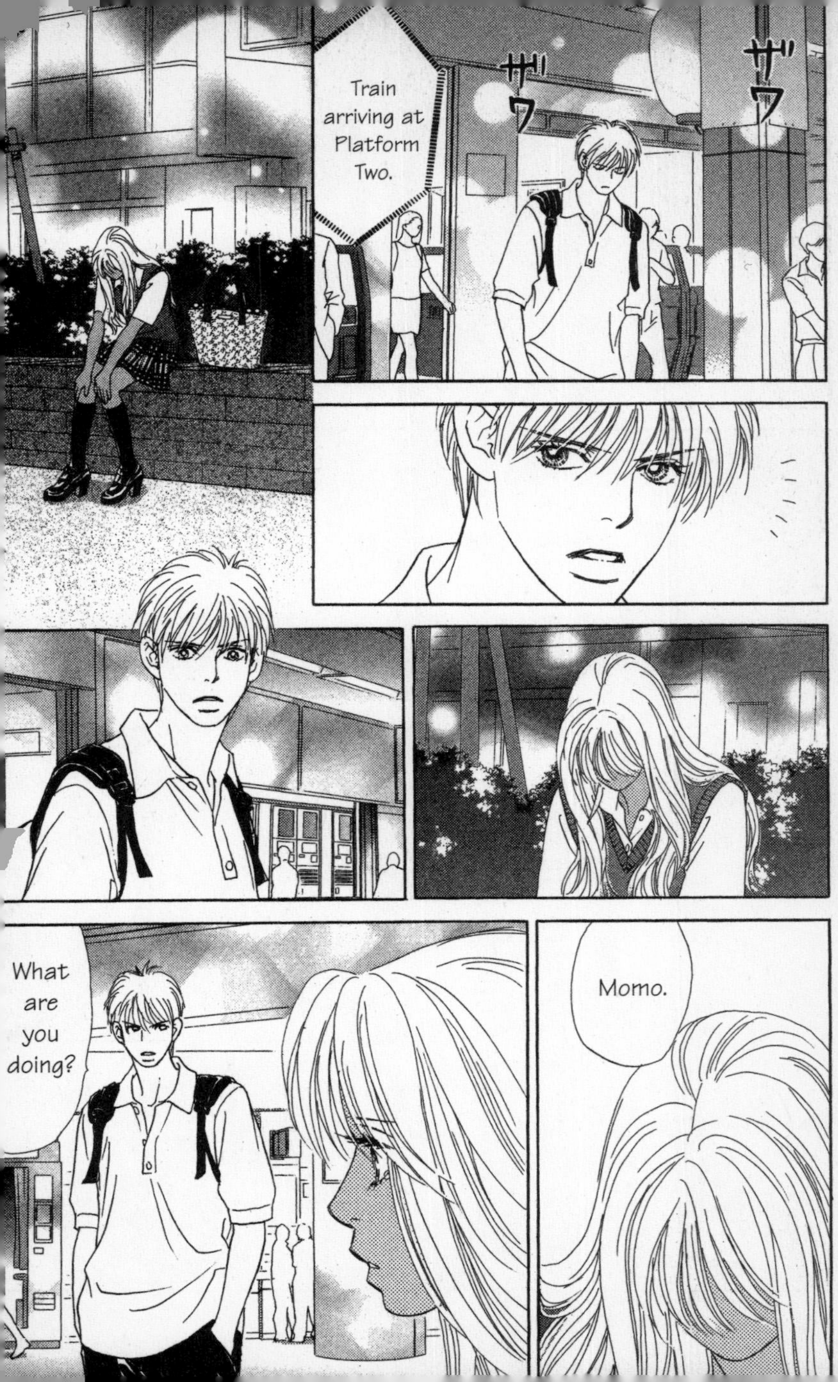
ザワ
ザワ
Train arriving at Platform Two.
Momo.
What are you doing?

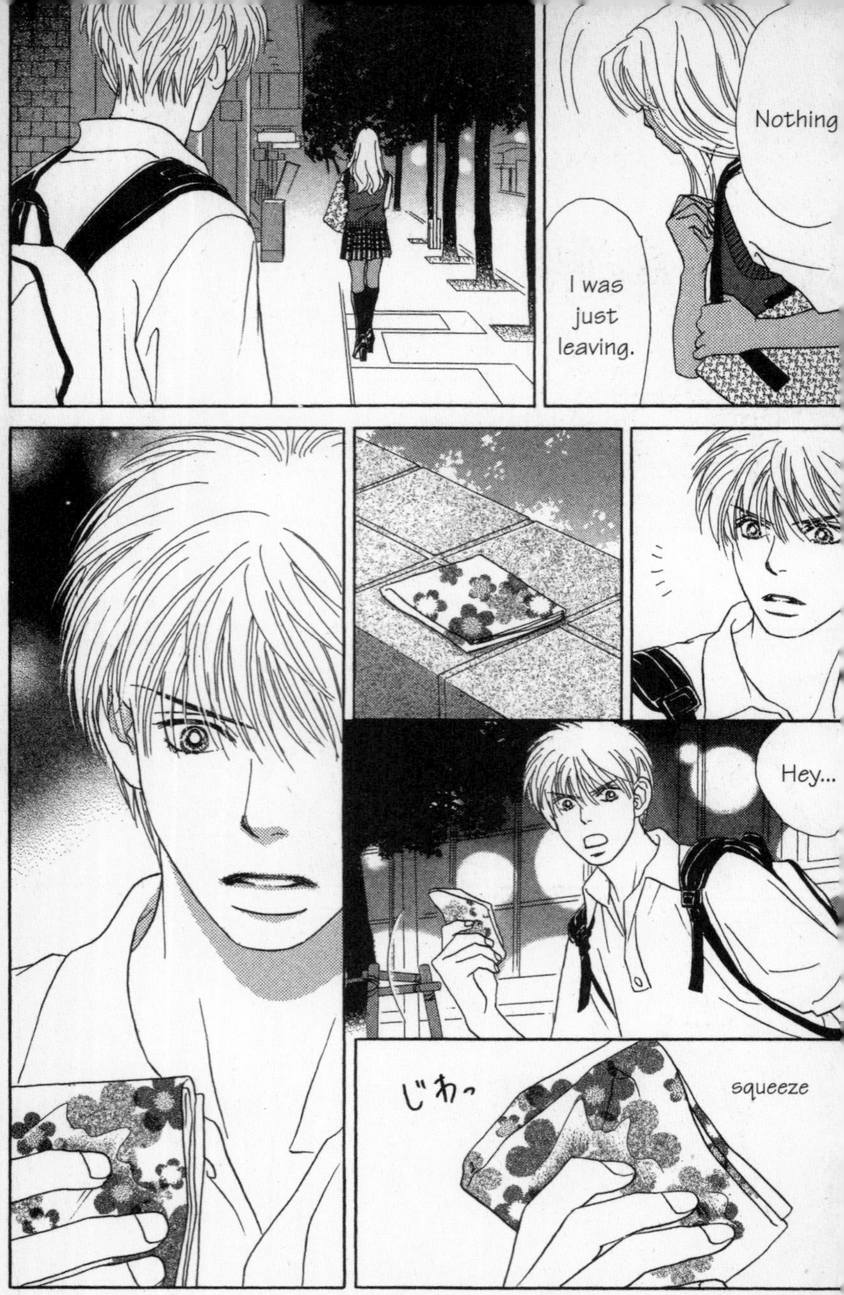
Nothing
I was just leaving.
Hey...
squeeze
じわっ

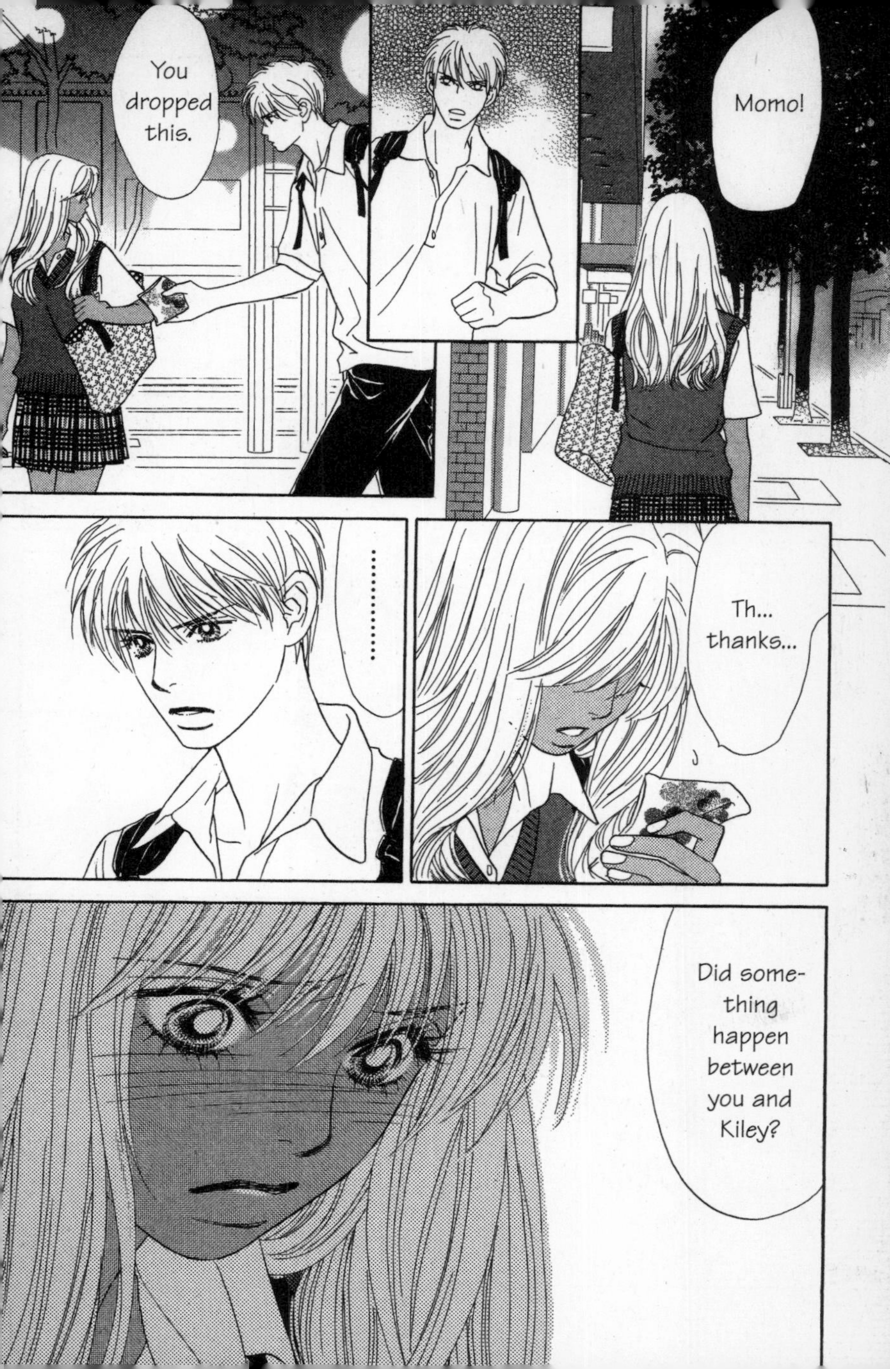
Momo!
You dropped this.
Th... thanks...
....
Did some-thing happen between you and Kiley?

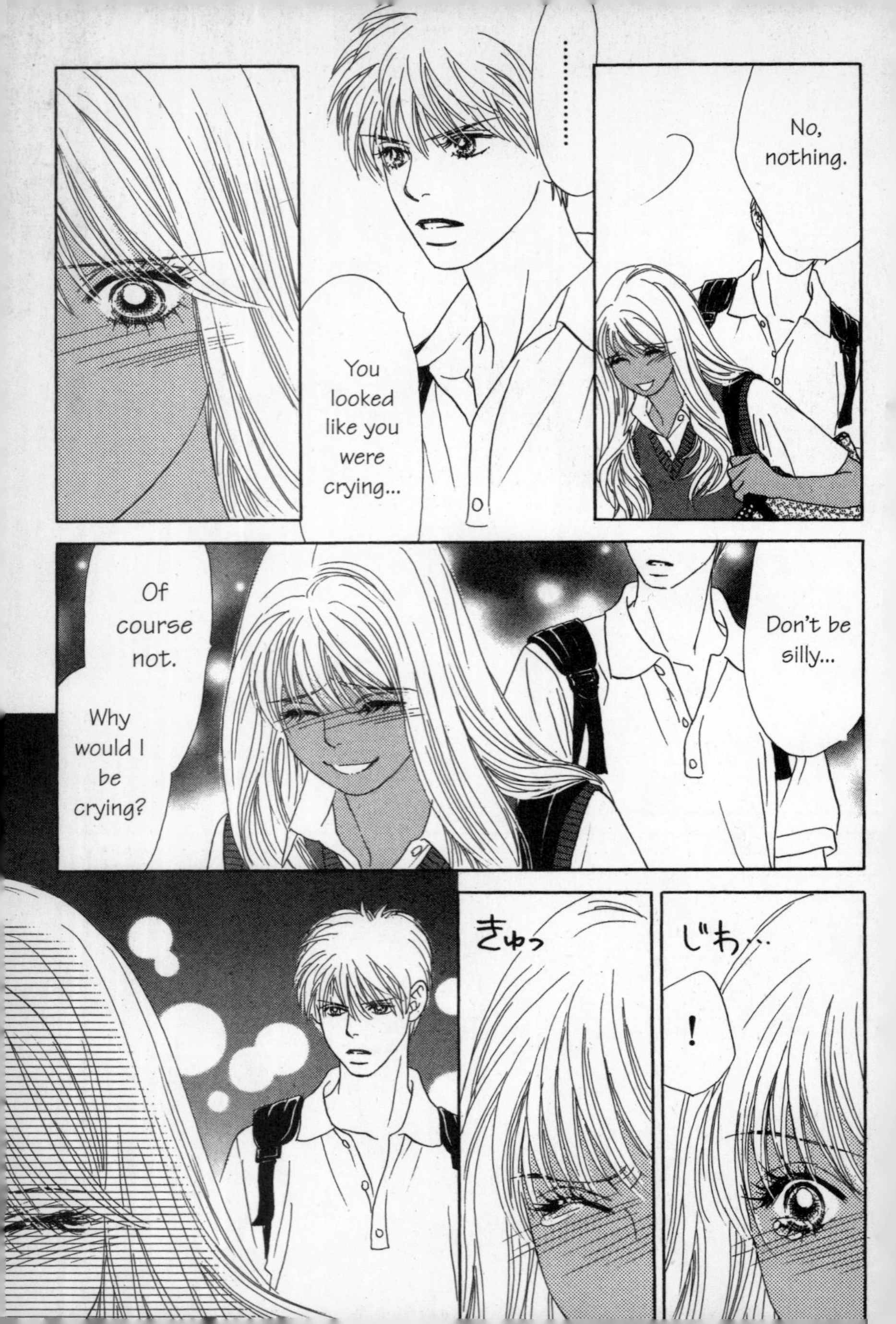

No, nothing.
......
You looked like you were crying...
Don't be silly...
Of course not.
Why would I be crying?
じわ…
!
きゅっ

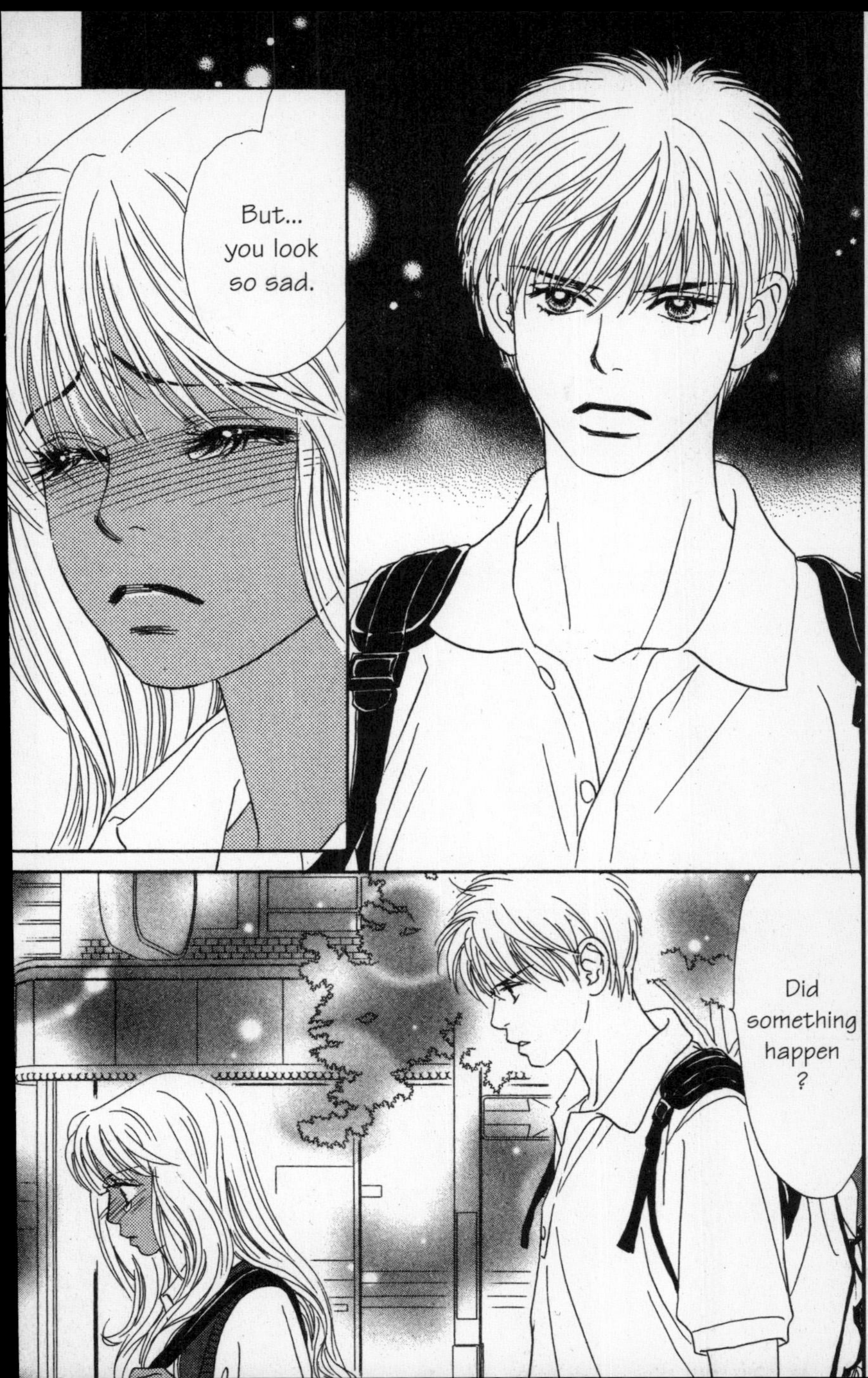
But... you look so sad.
Did something happen ?

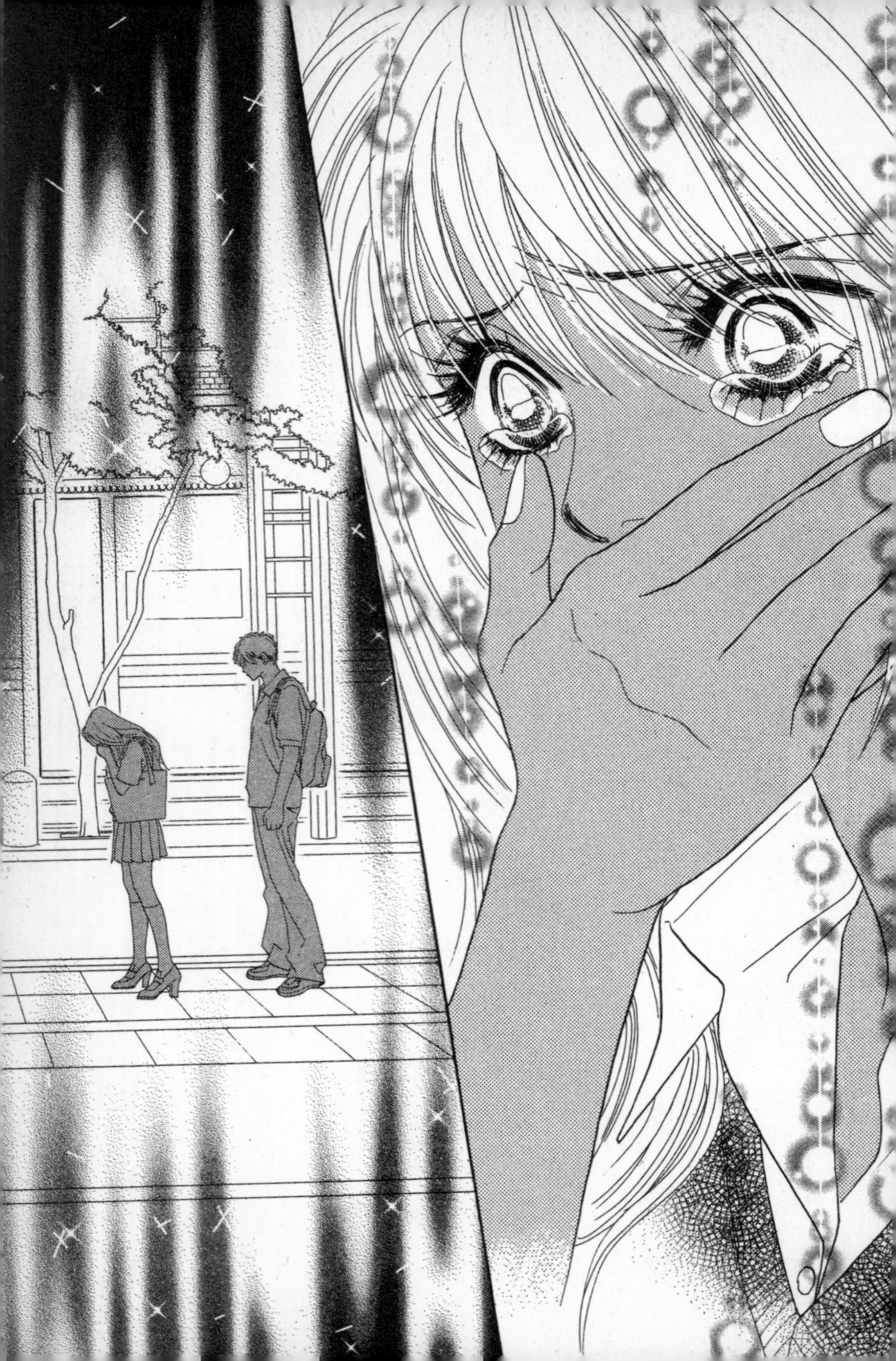

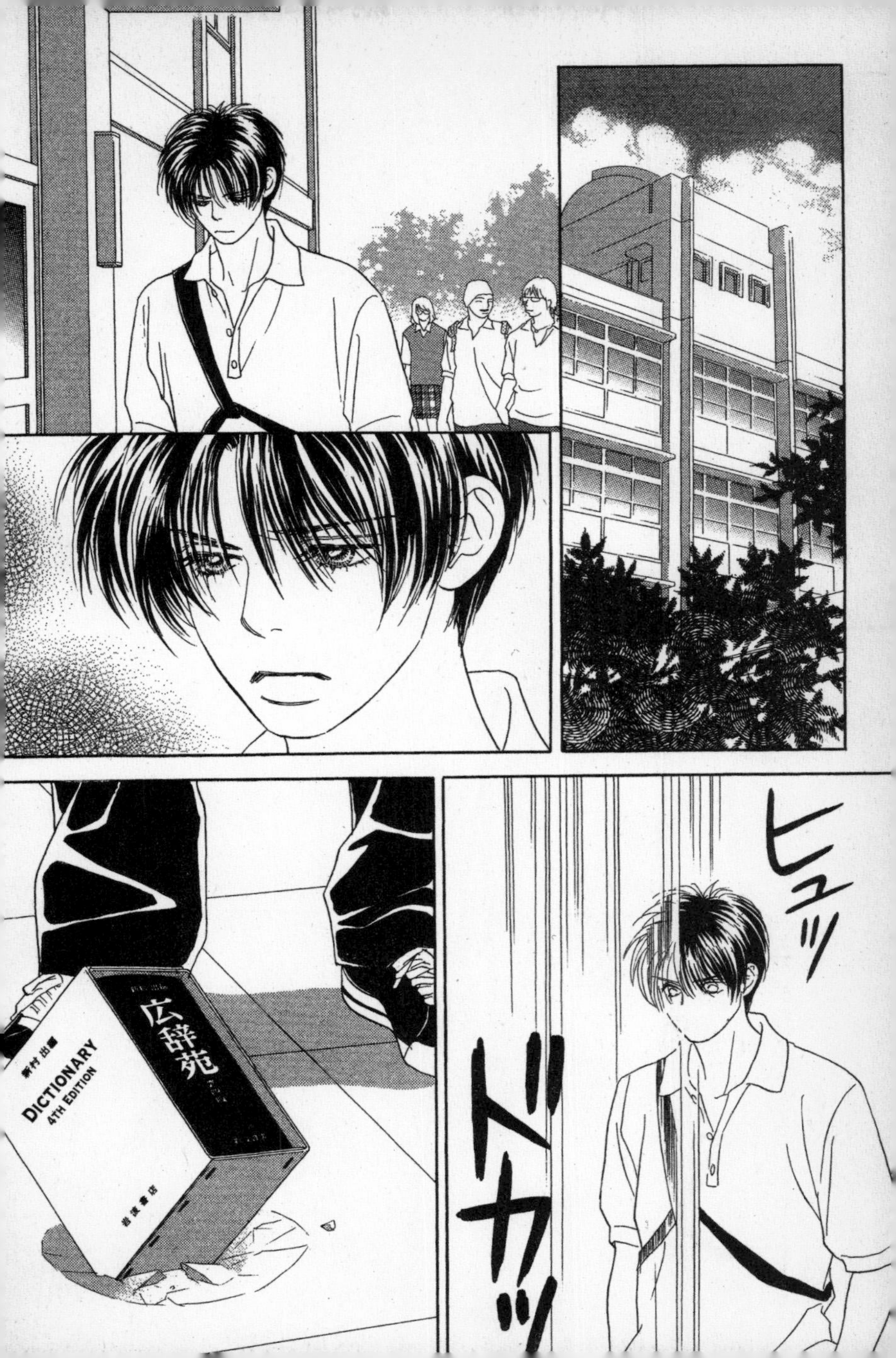
ヒュッ
ドカッ
広辞苑
新村 出 編
DICTIONARY
4TH EDITION
岩波書店

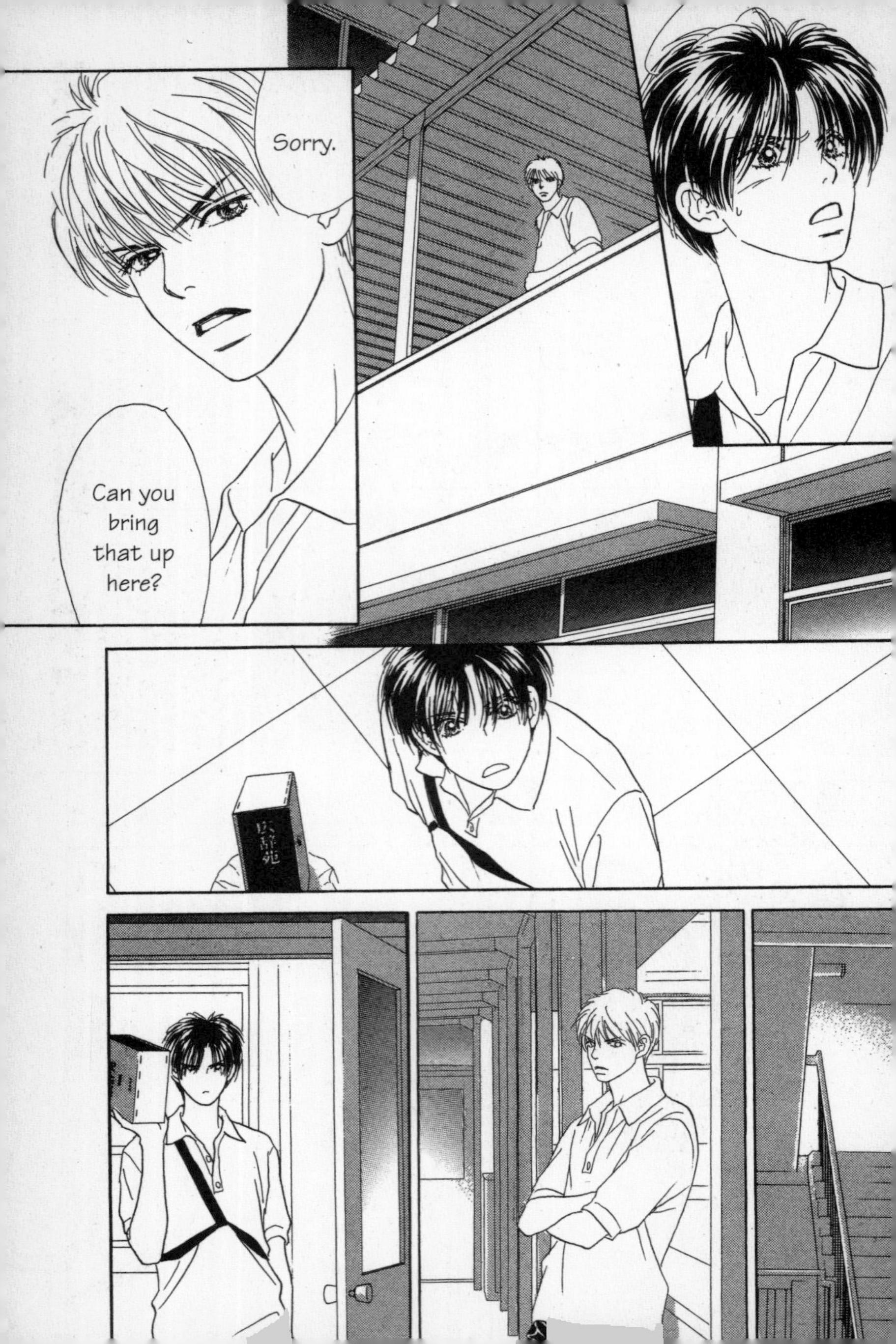
Sorry.
Can you bring that up here?

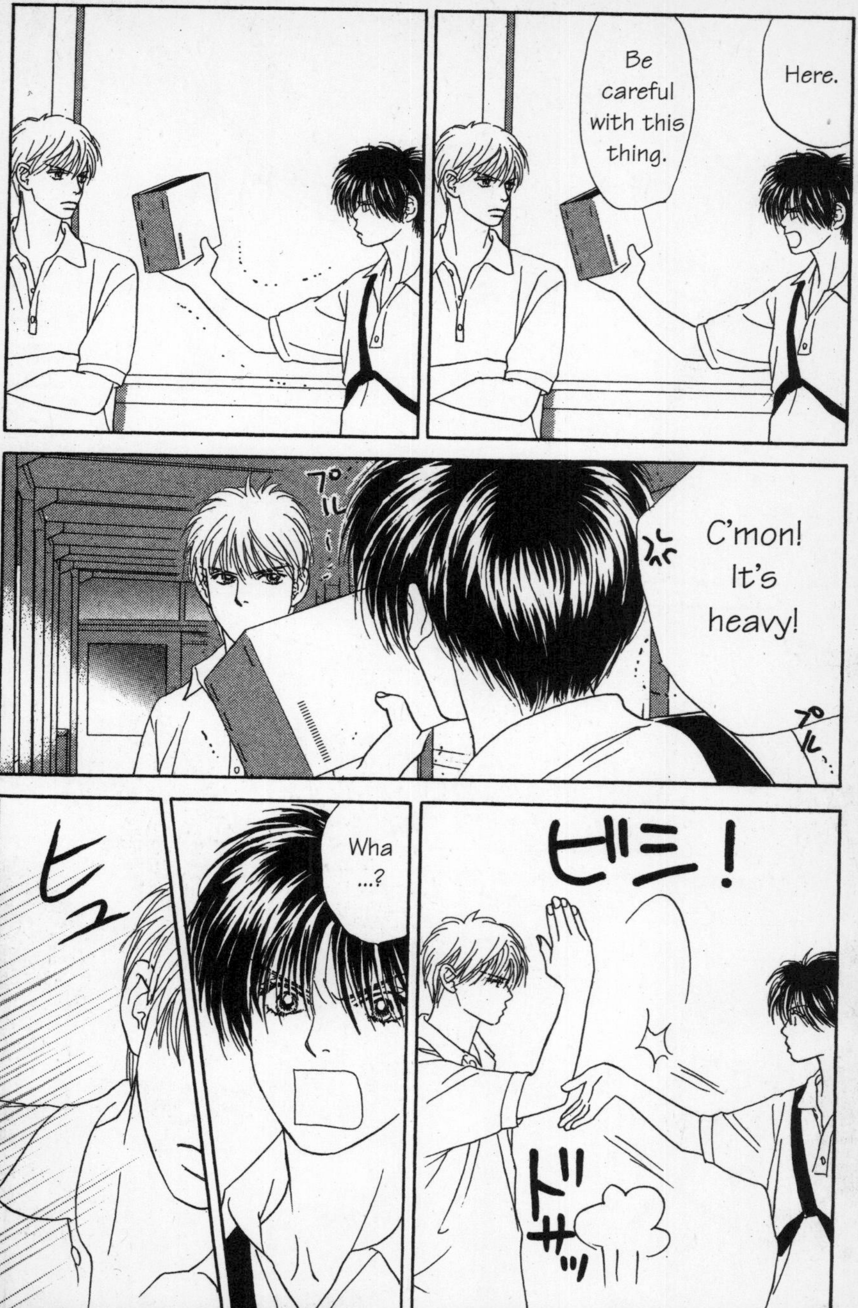
Here.
Be careful with this thing.
C'mon! It's heavy!
プル…
プル…
ビシ!
ドサッ
Wha ...?
ヒュ

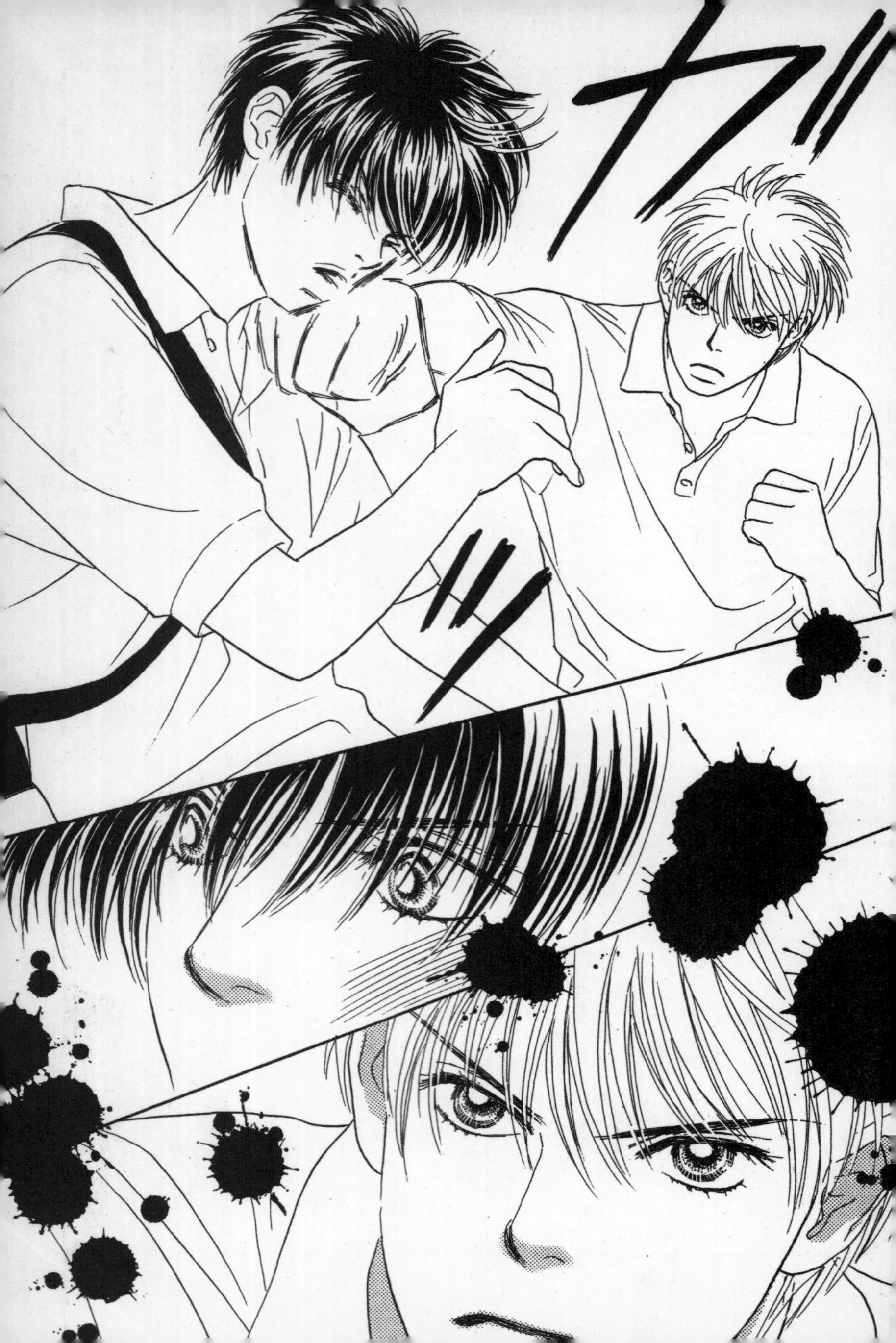
ガッ

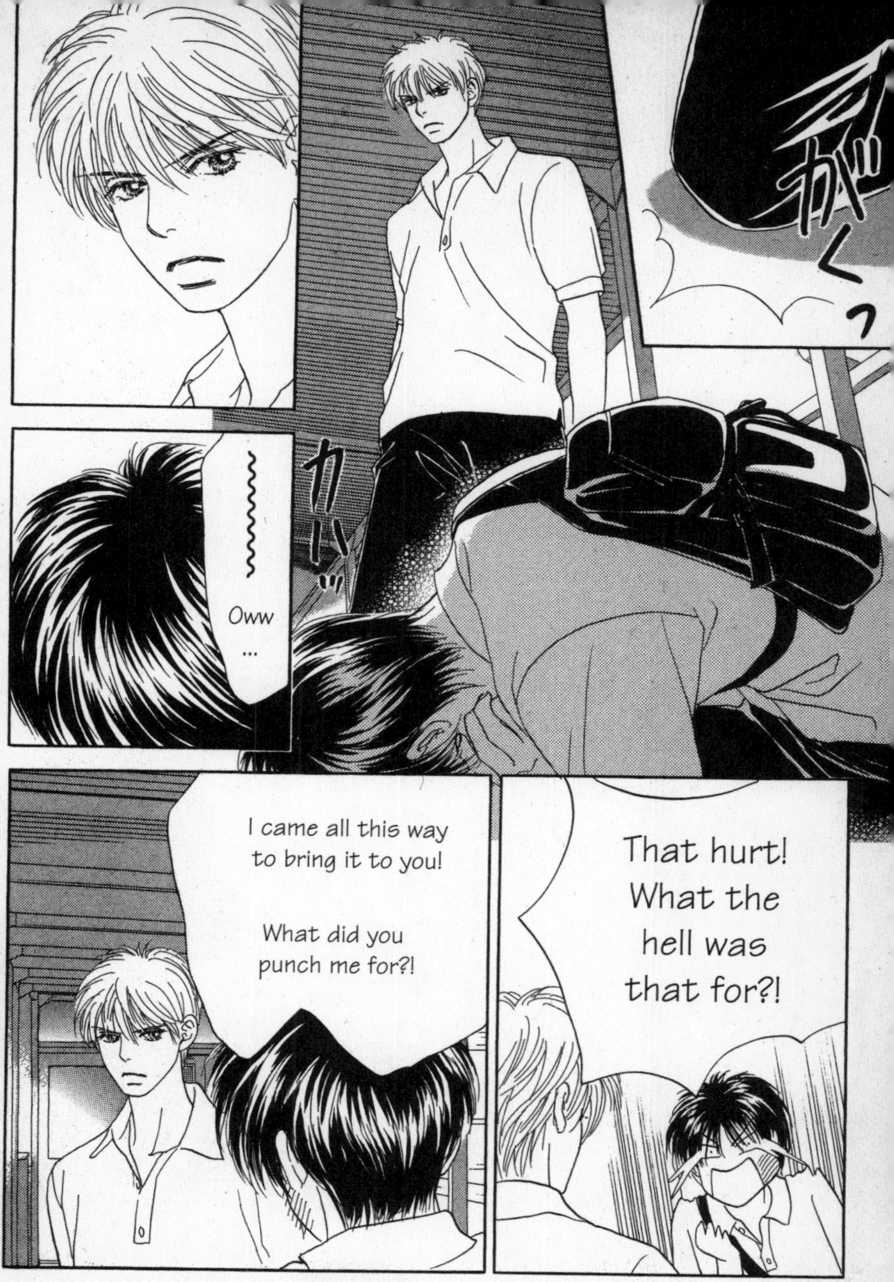

がくっ
Oww ...
That hurt! What the hell was that for?!
I came all this way to bring it to you!
What did you punch me for?!

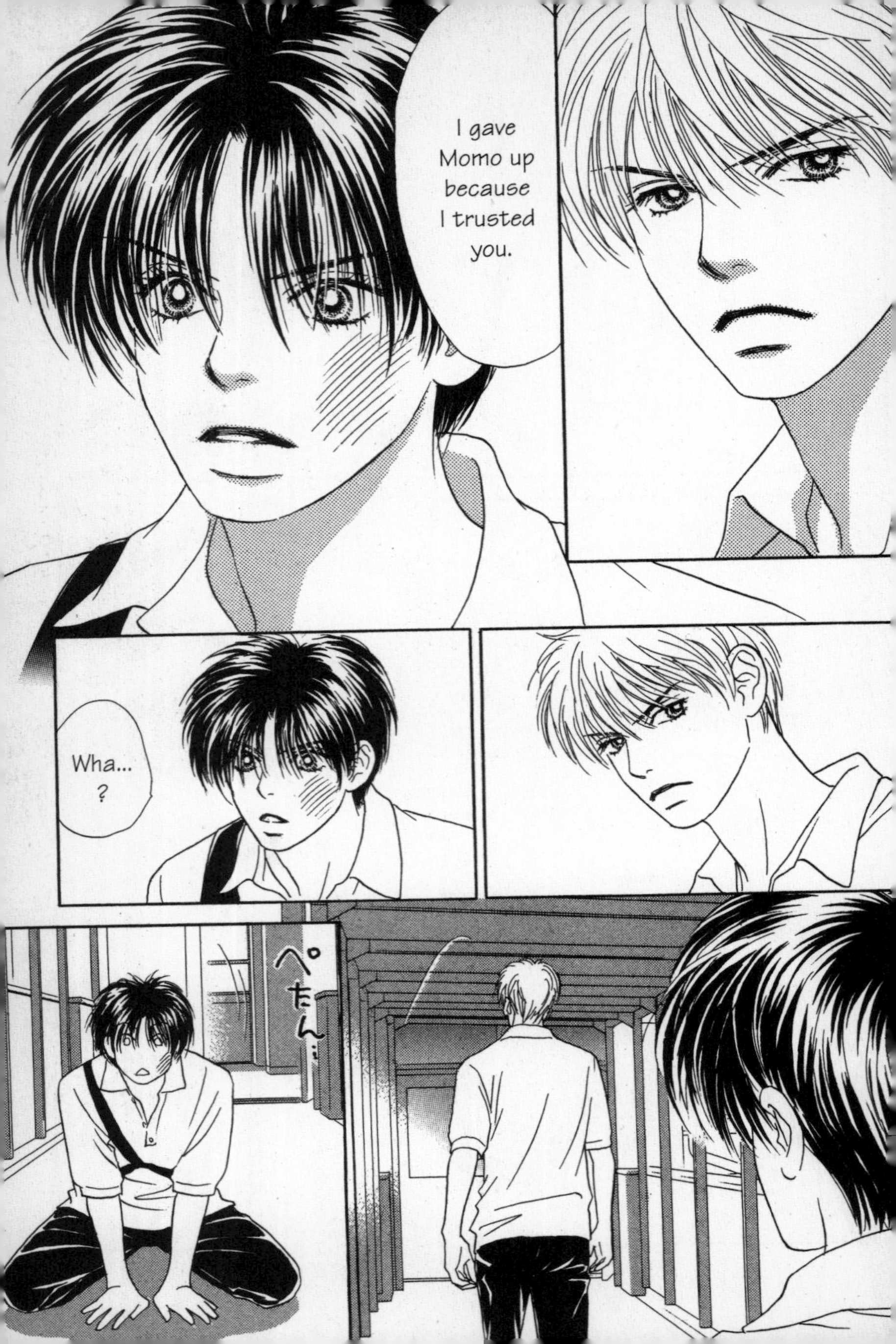

I gave Momo up because I trusted you.
Wha... ?
ぺたん...

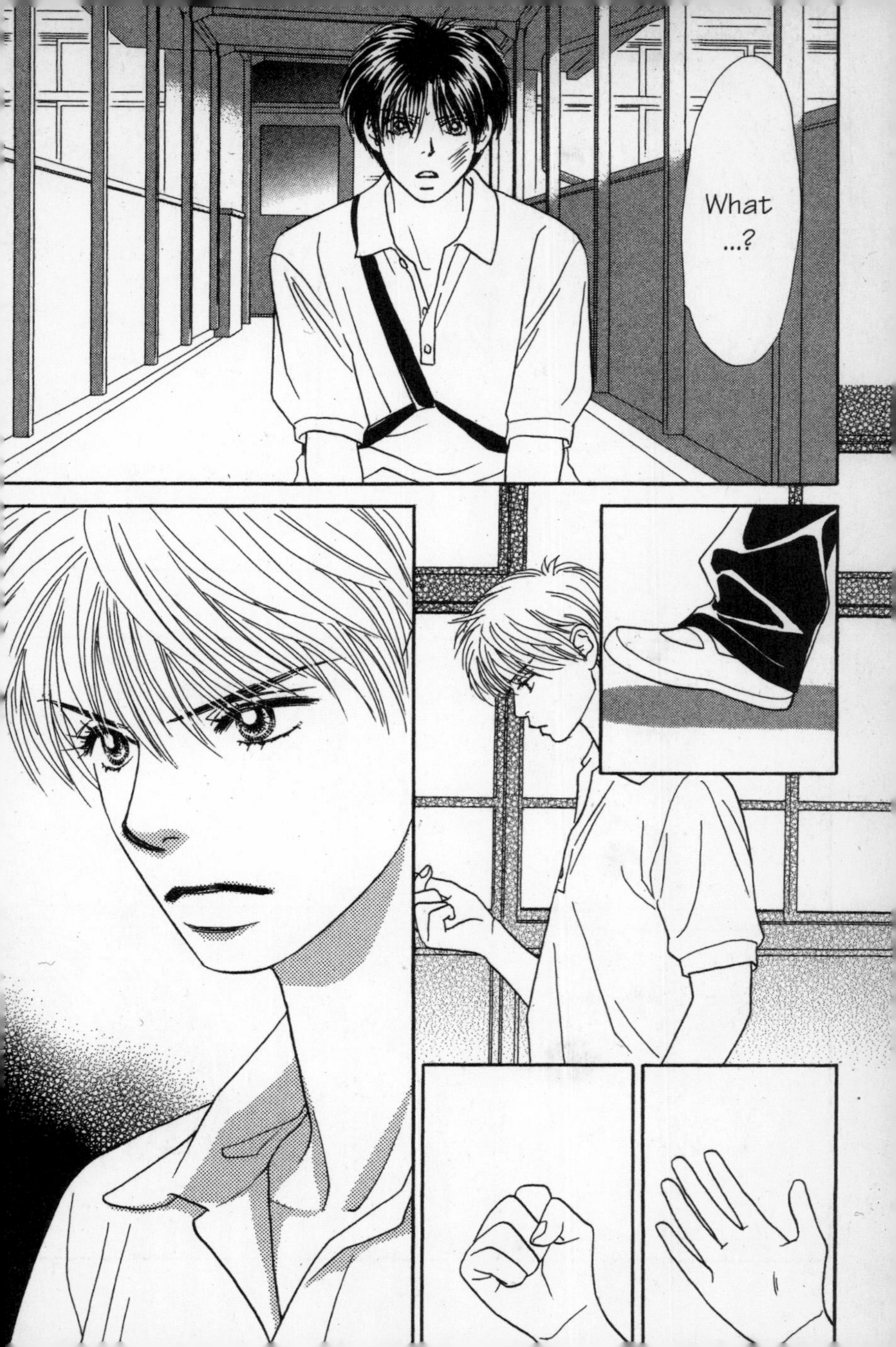
What
...?

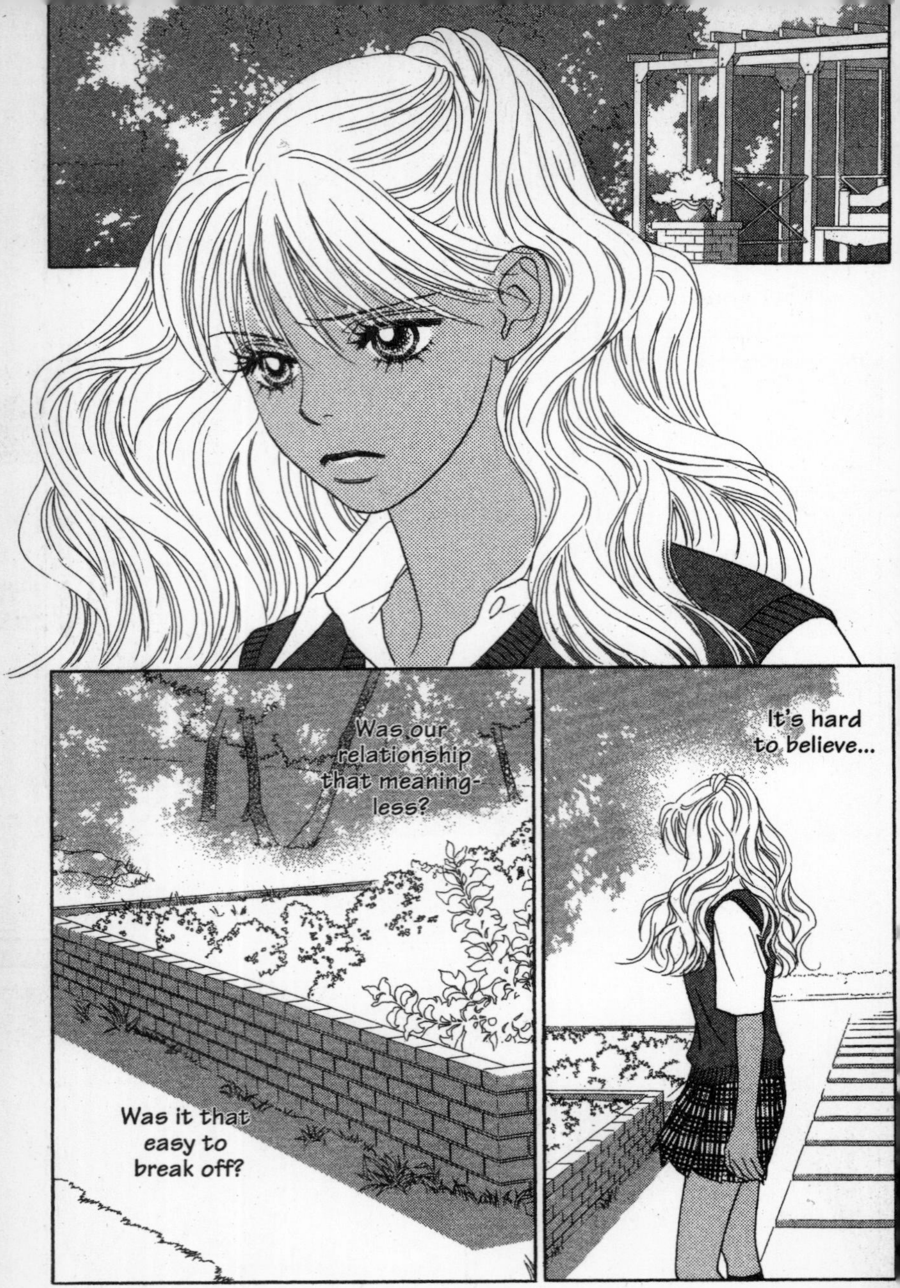
It's hard to believe...
Was our relationship that meaning-less?
Was it that easy to break off?

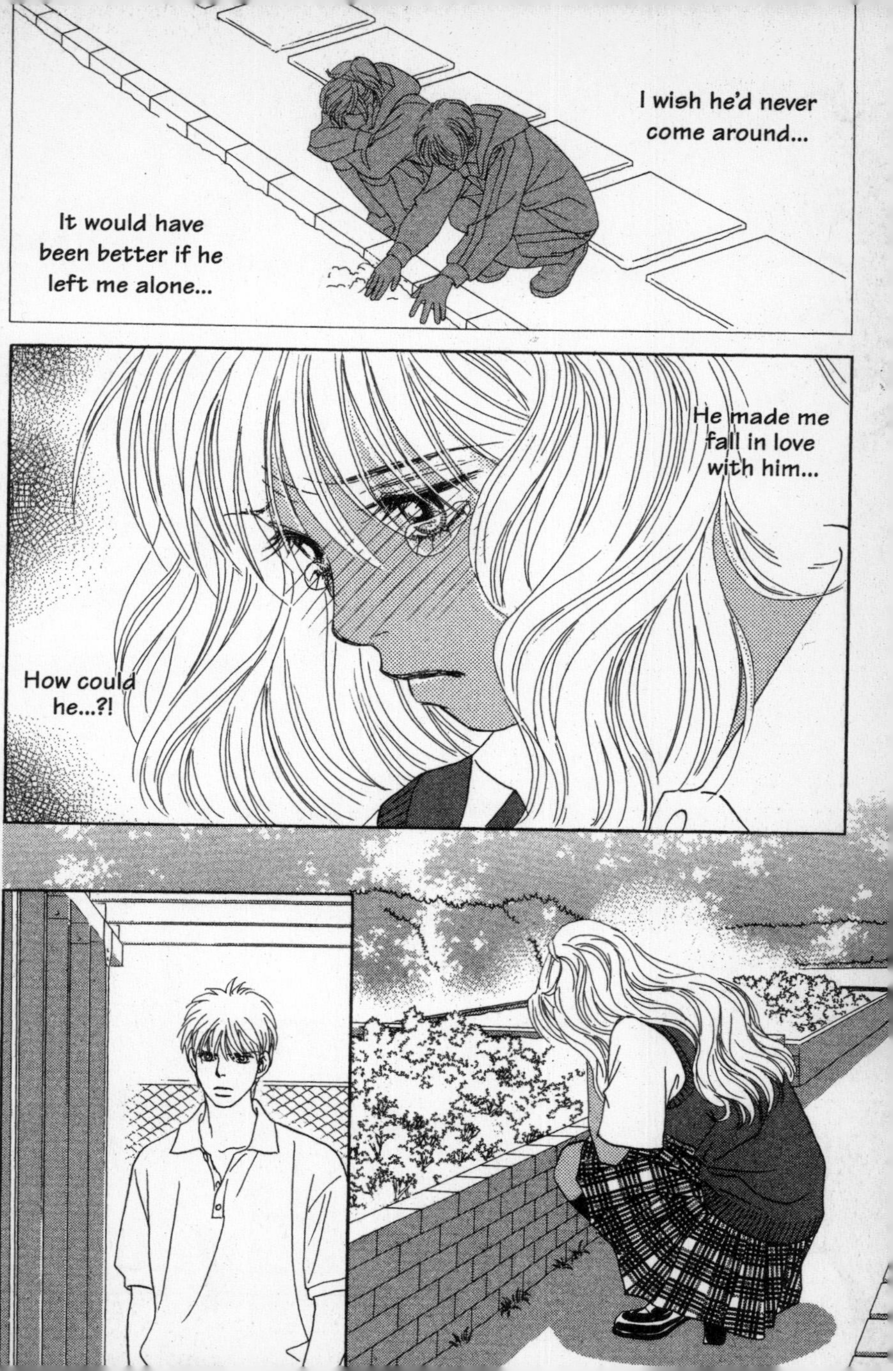
I wish he'd never come around...
It would have been better if he left me alone...
He made me fall in love with him...
How could he...?!

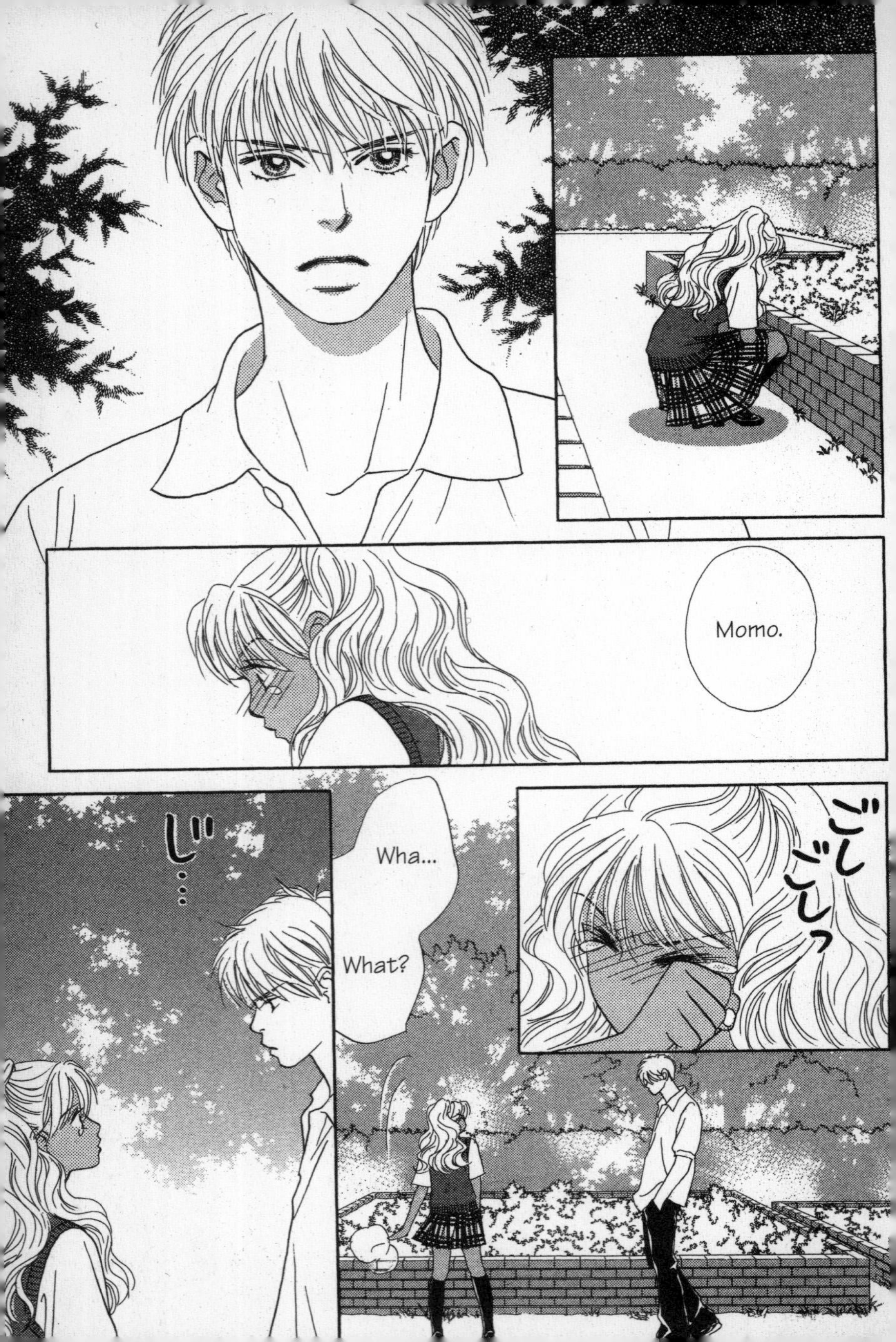
Momo.
ごしごしっ
Wha...
What?
じ…

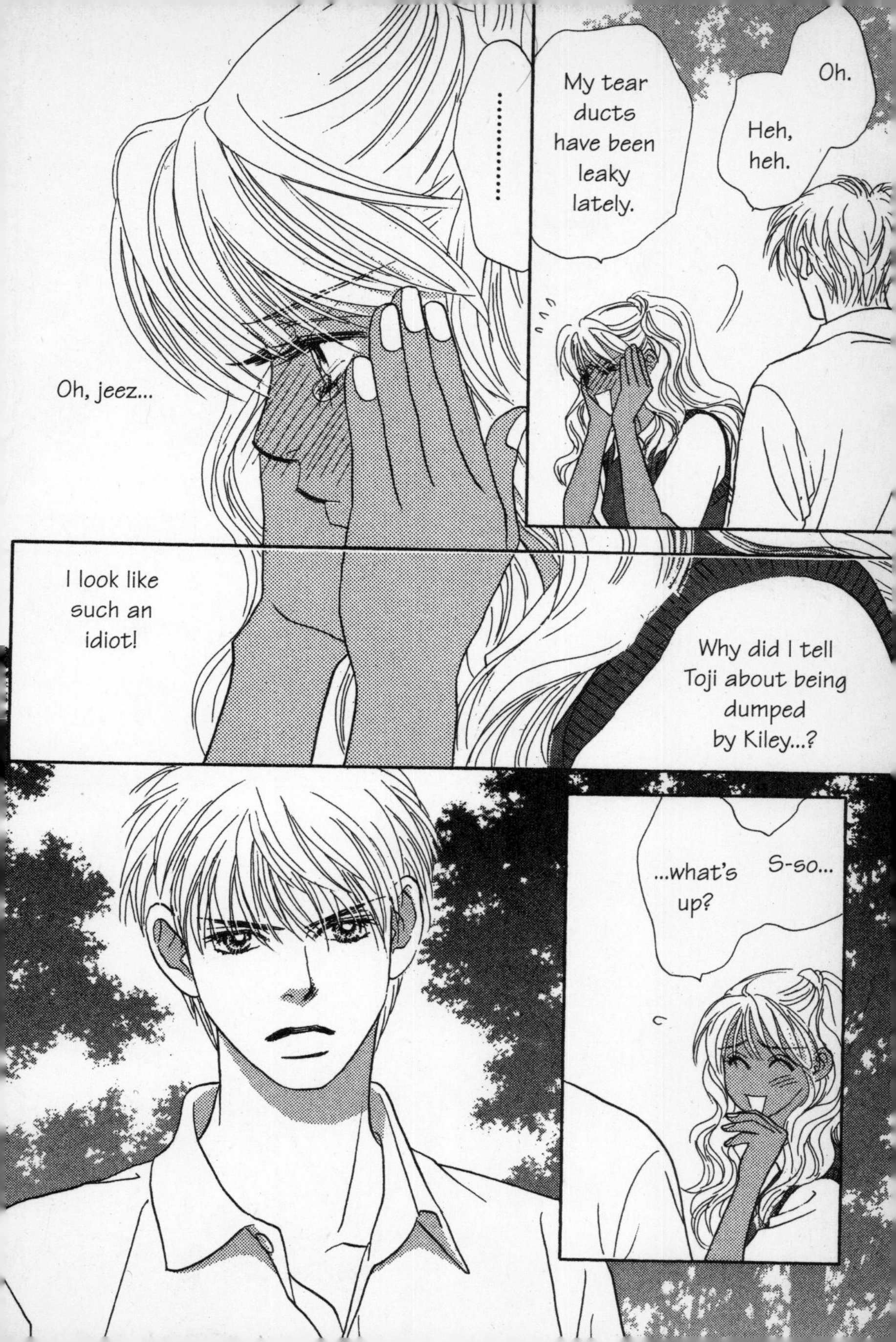

Oh.
Heh, heh.
My tear ducts have been leaky lately.
......
Oh, jeez...
Why did I tell Toji about being dumped by Kiley...?
I look like such an idiot!
S-so...
...what's up?

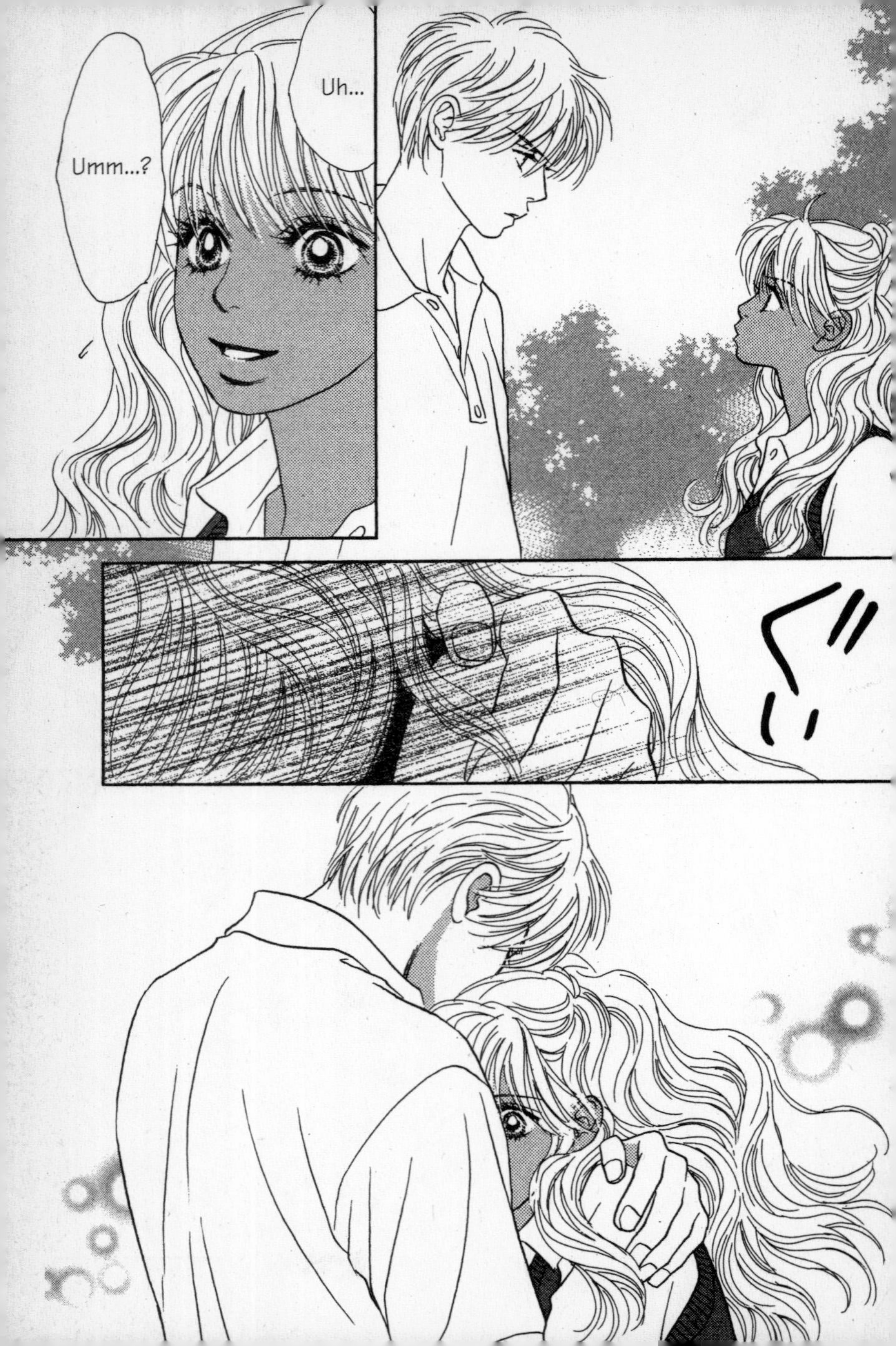
Uh...
Umm...?

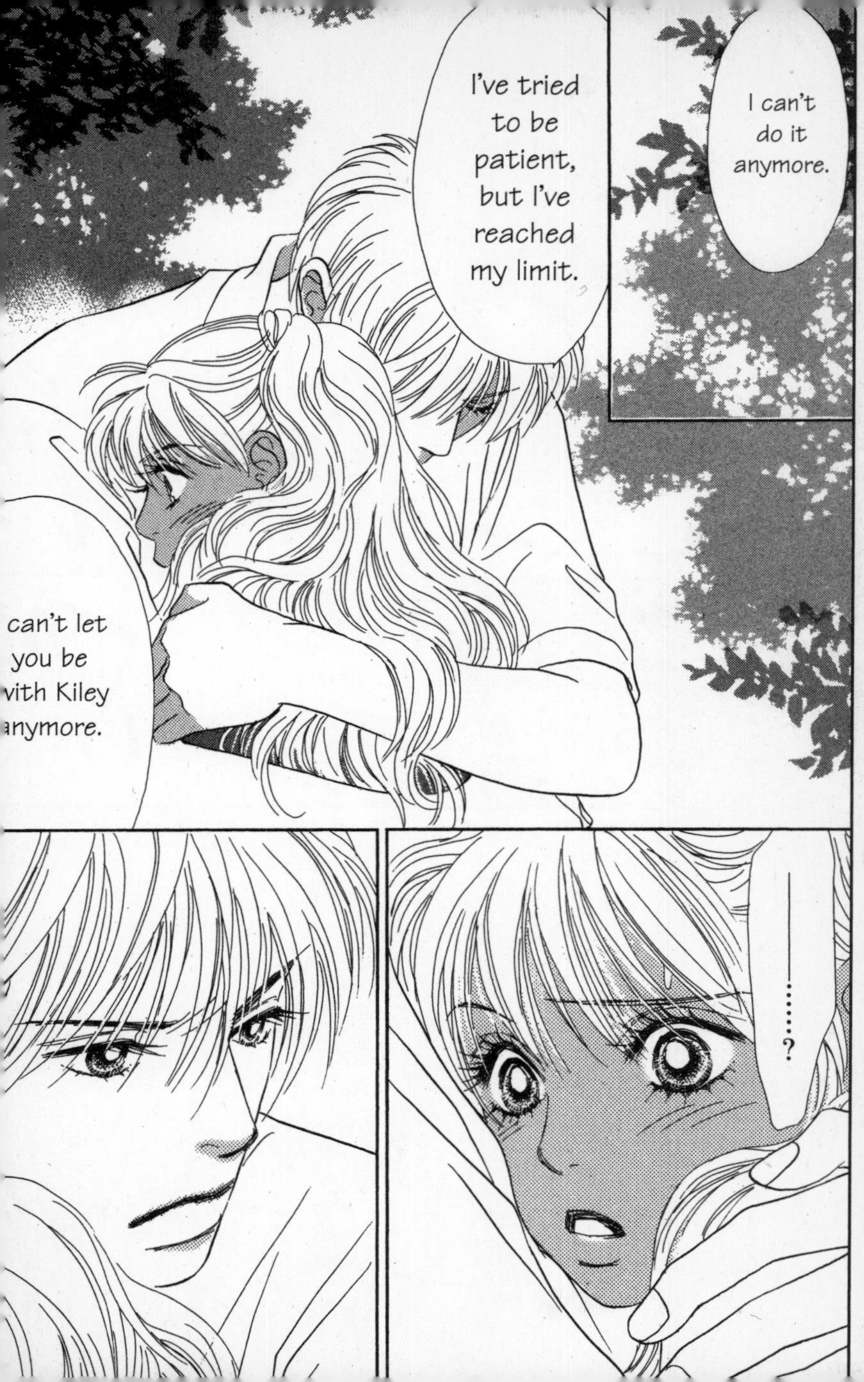

I can't do it anymore.
I've tried to be patient, but I've reached my limit.
can't let you be vith Kiley anymore.
......?

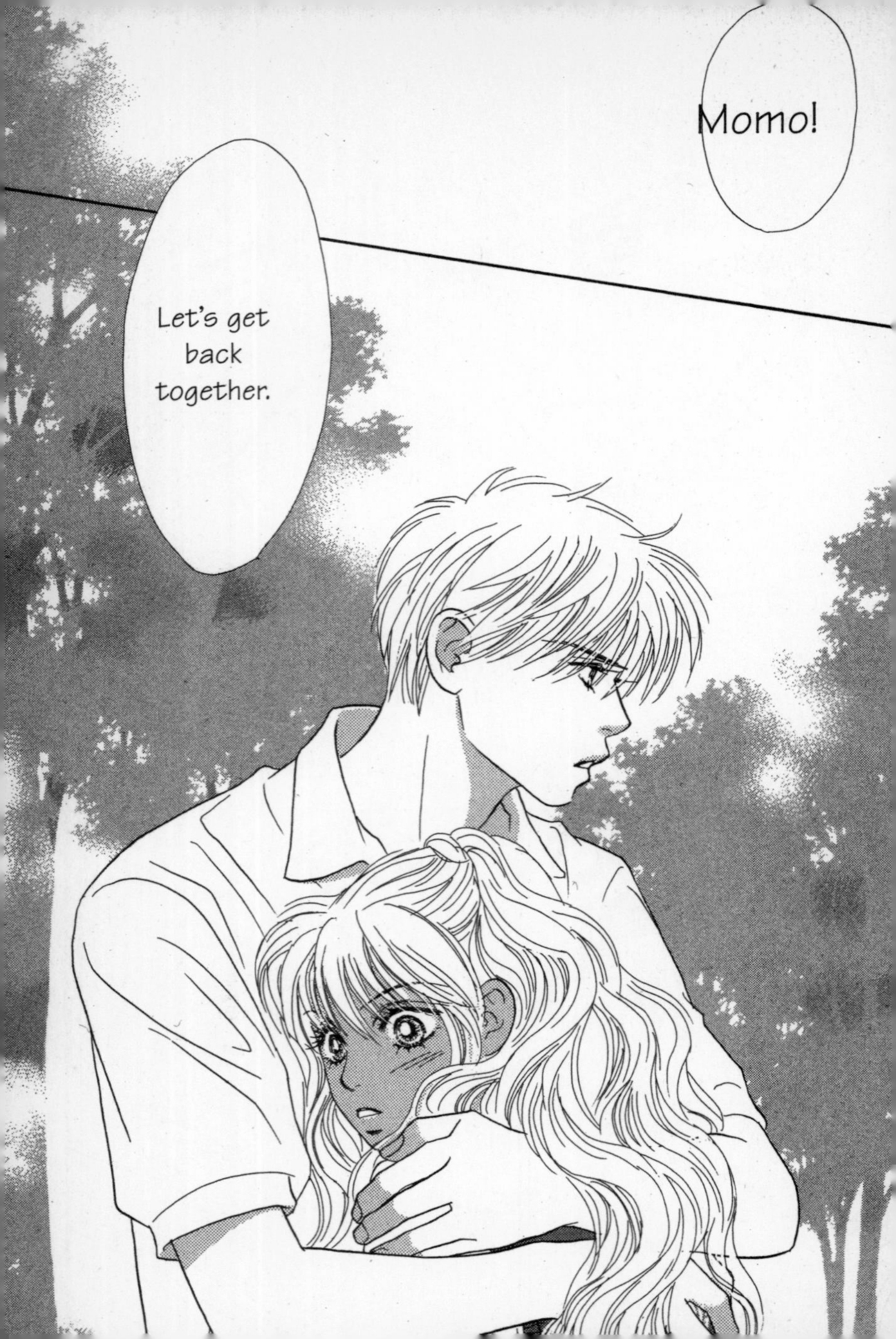
Momo!
Let's get back together.

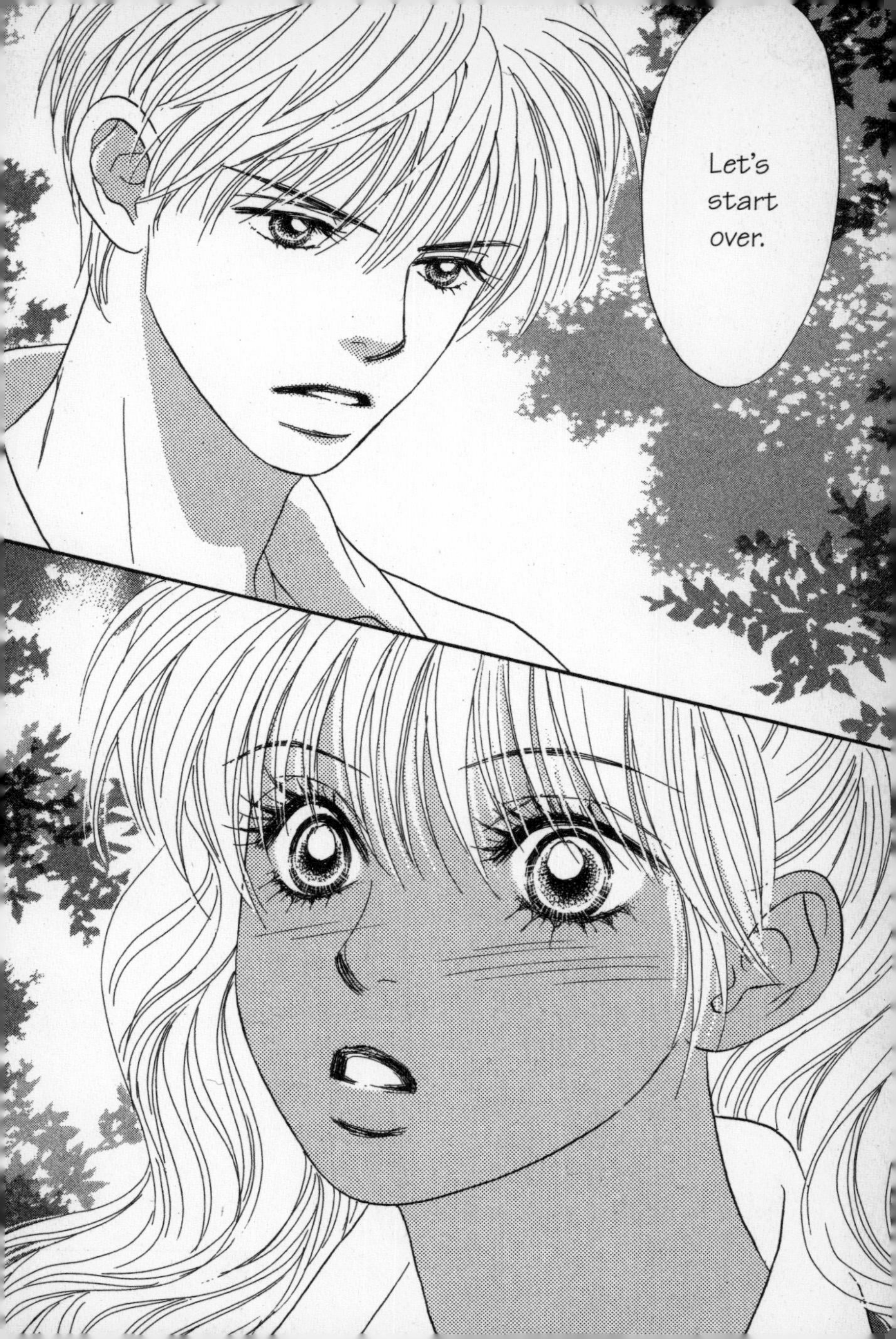
Let's start over.

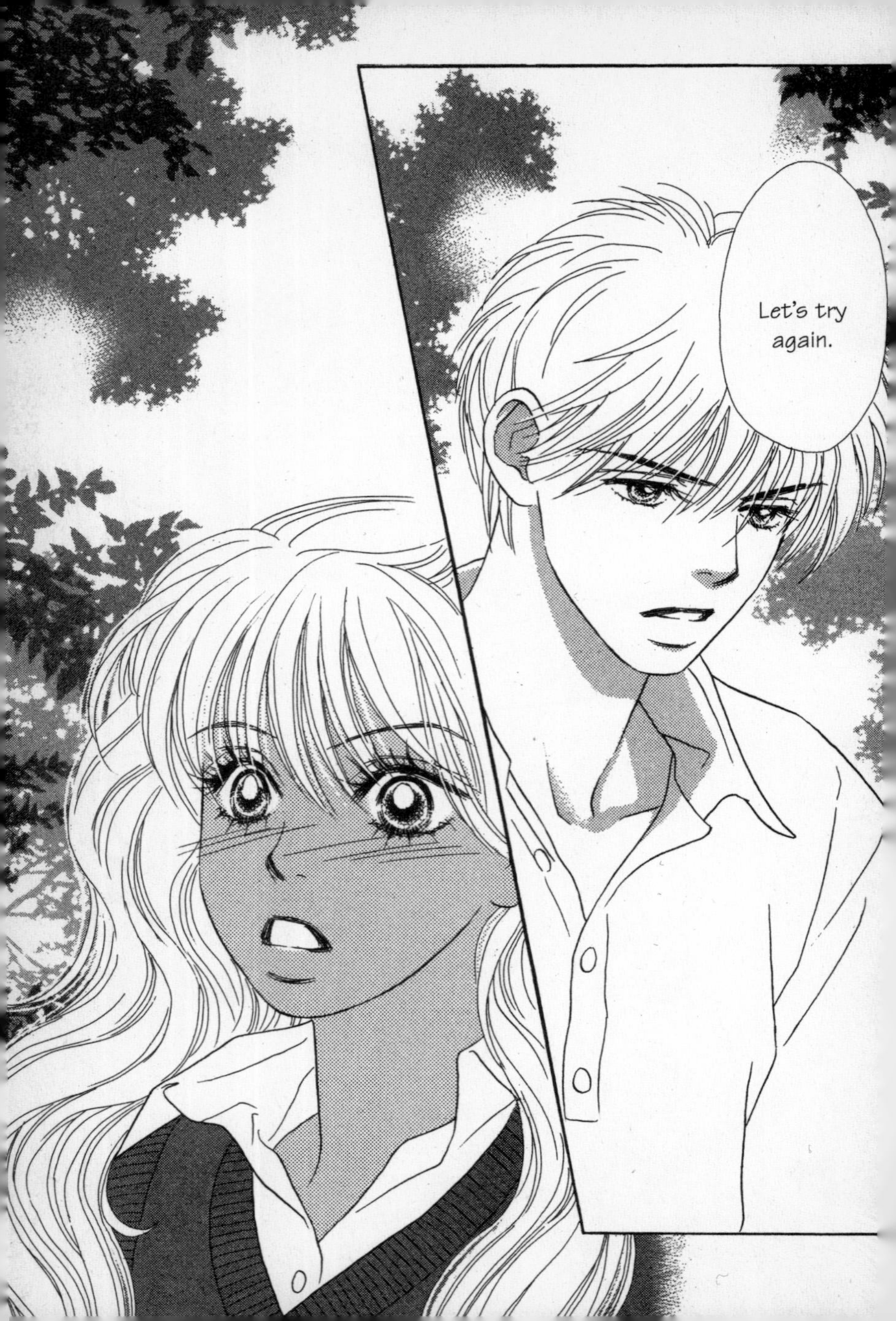
Let's try again.

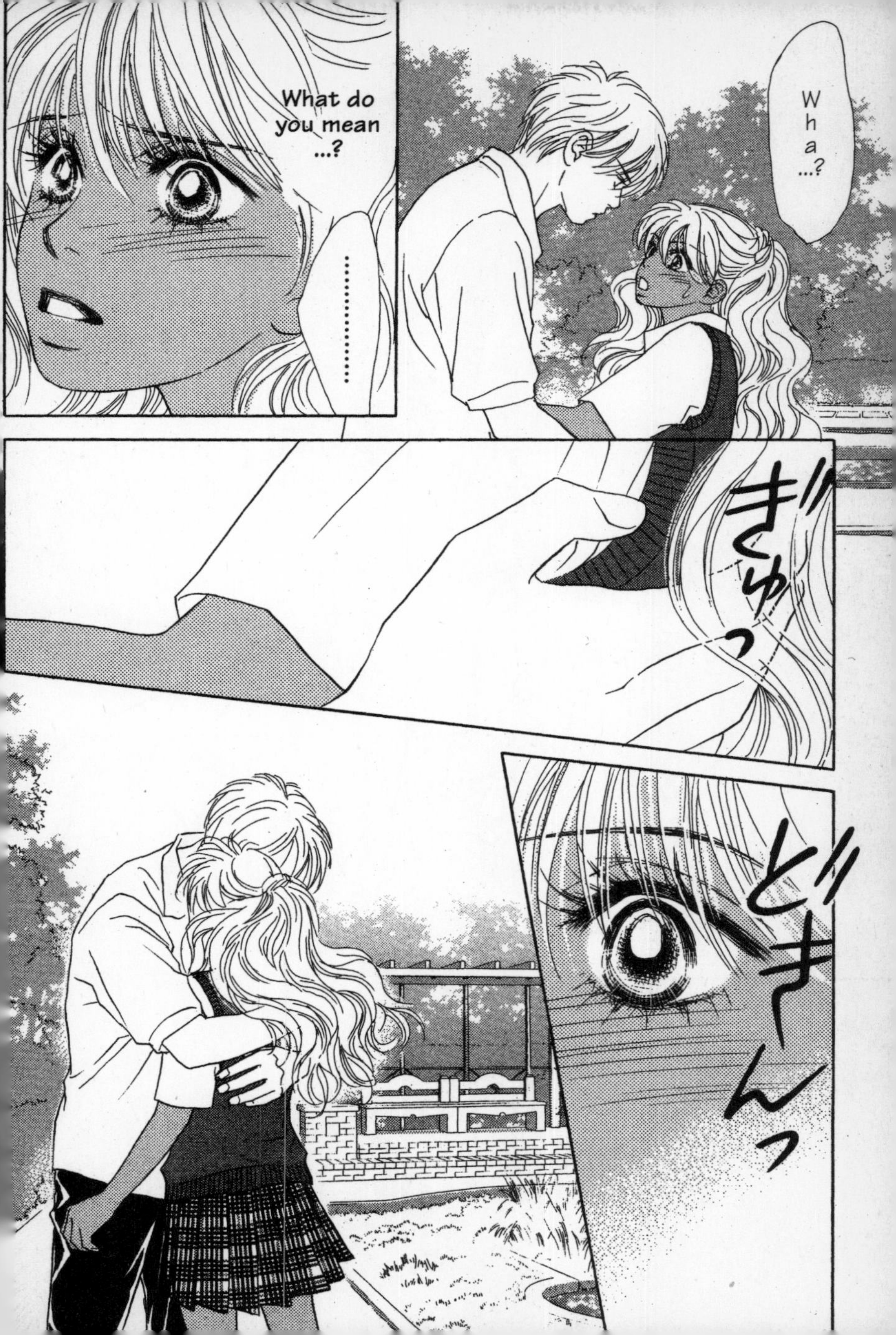
Wha...?
What do you mean ...?
......
ぎゅっ
どきんっ

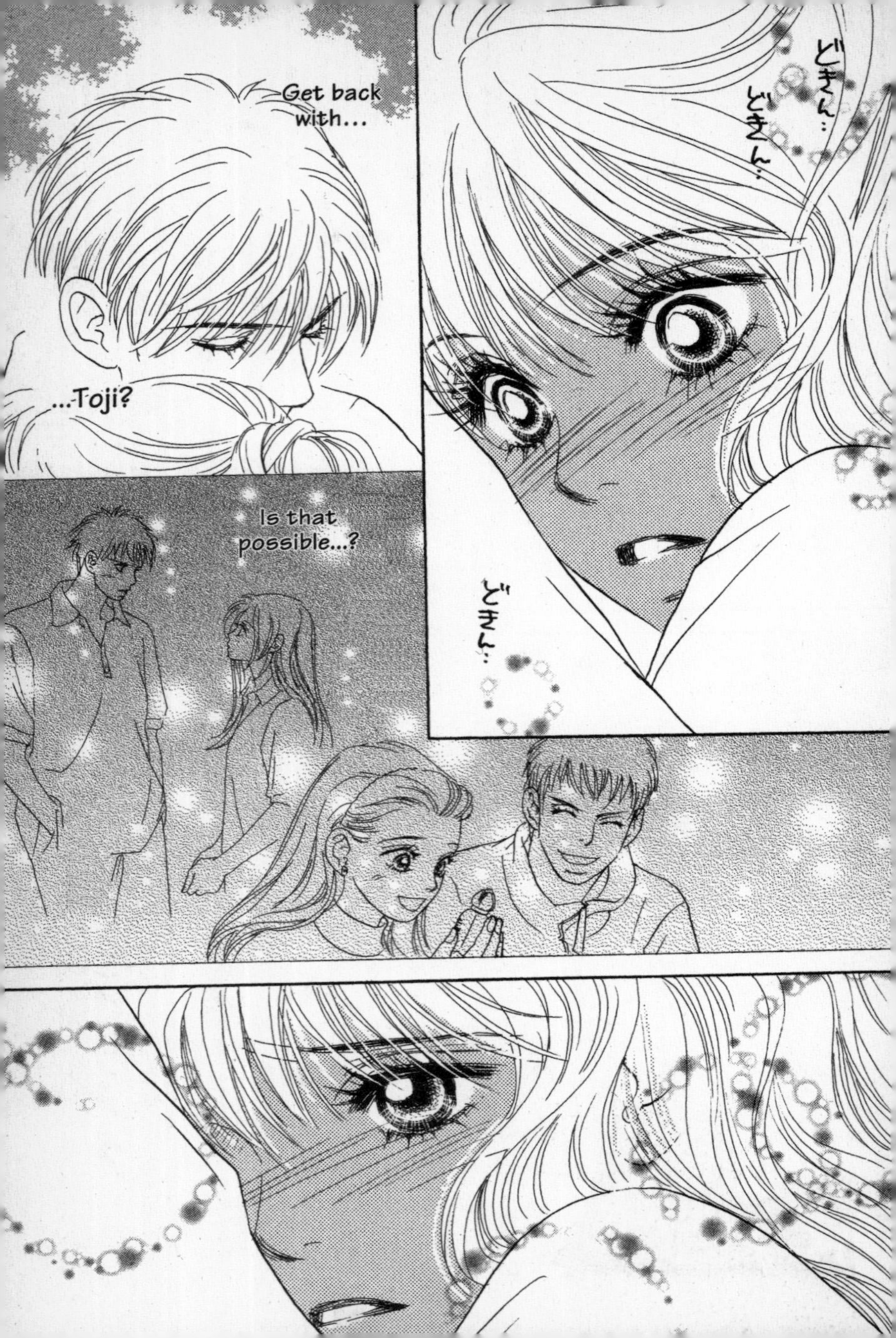
どきん…
どきん…
どきん…
Get back with…
…Toji?
Is that possible…?

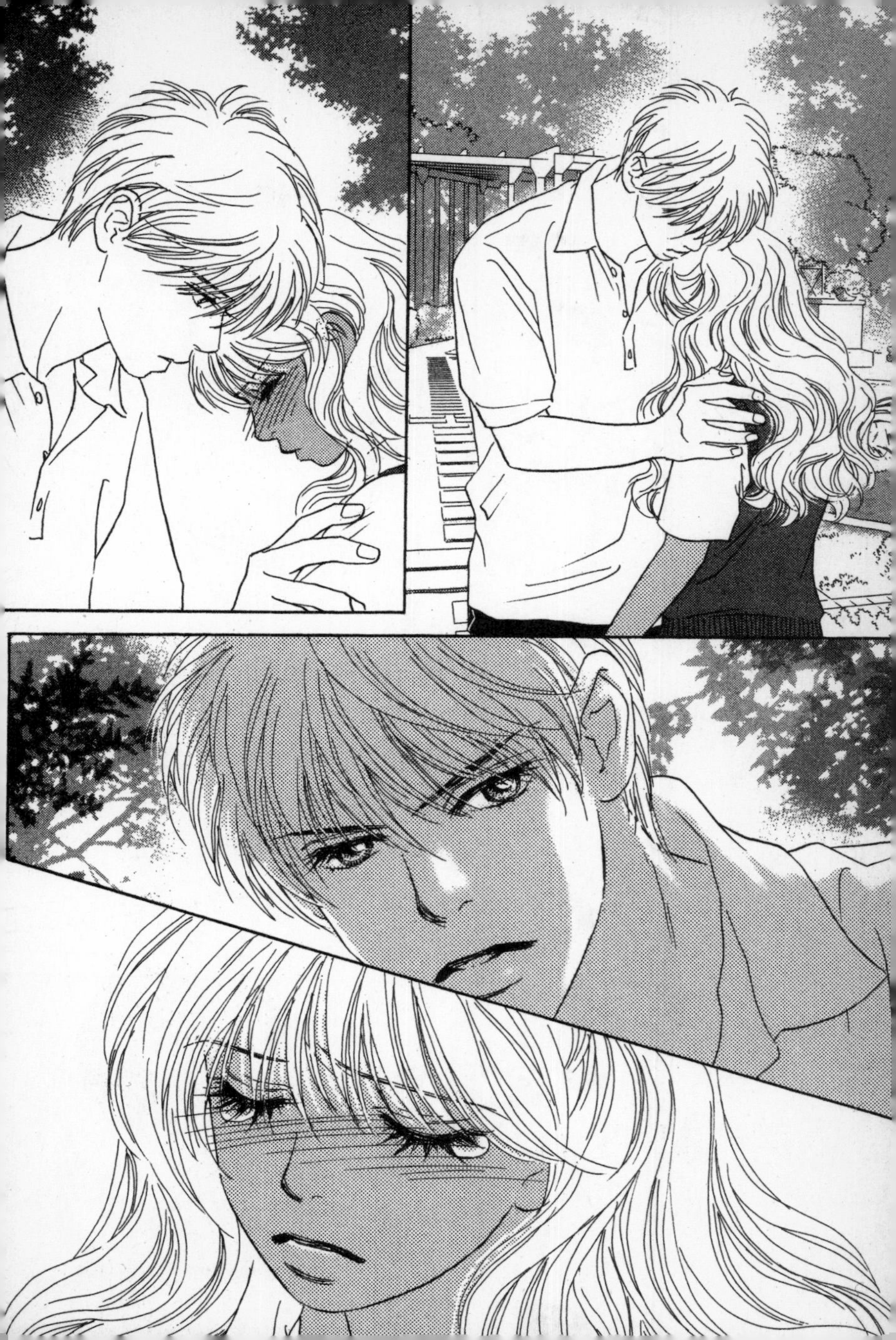

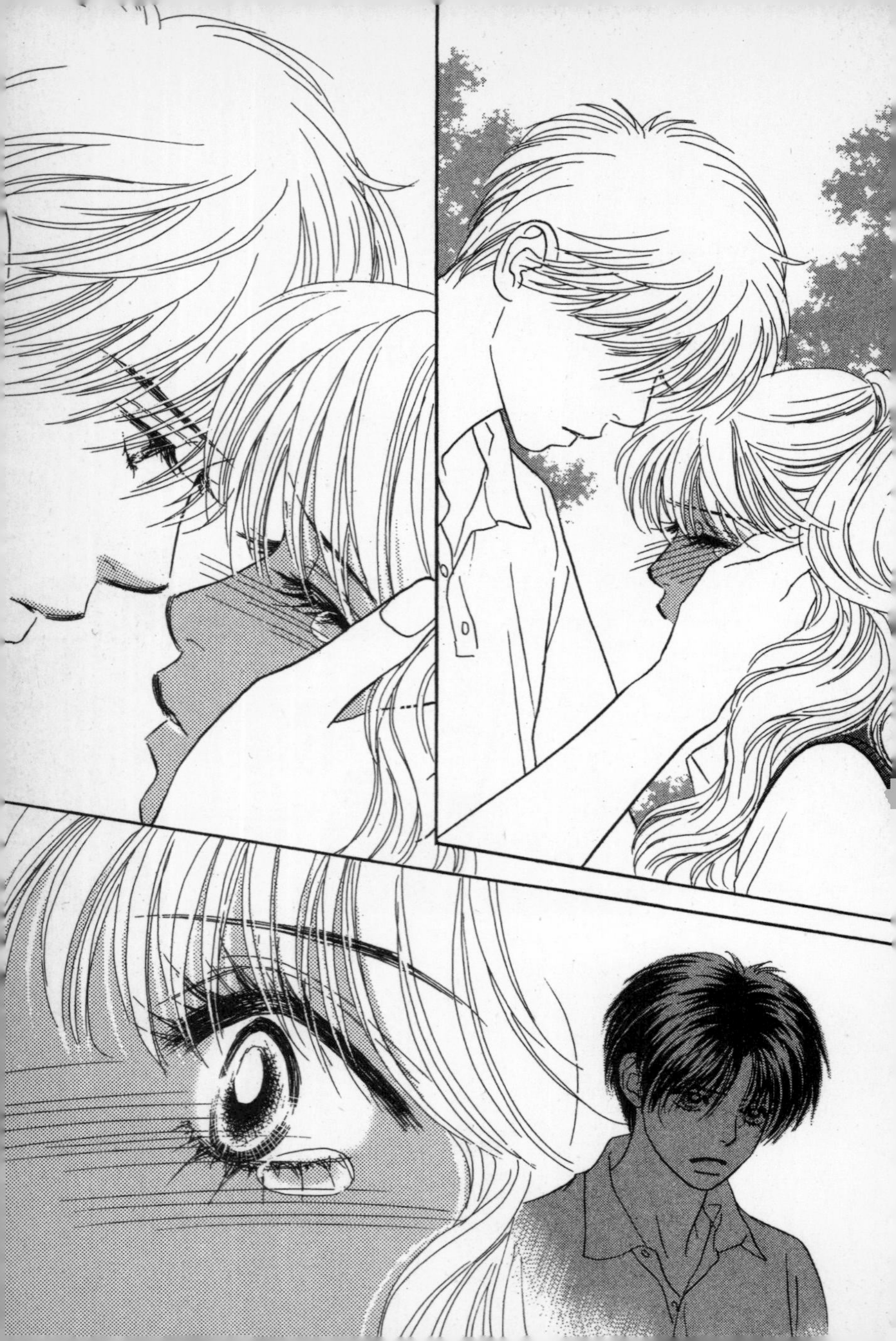

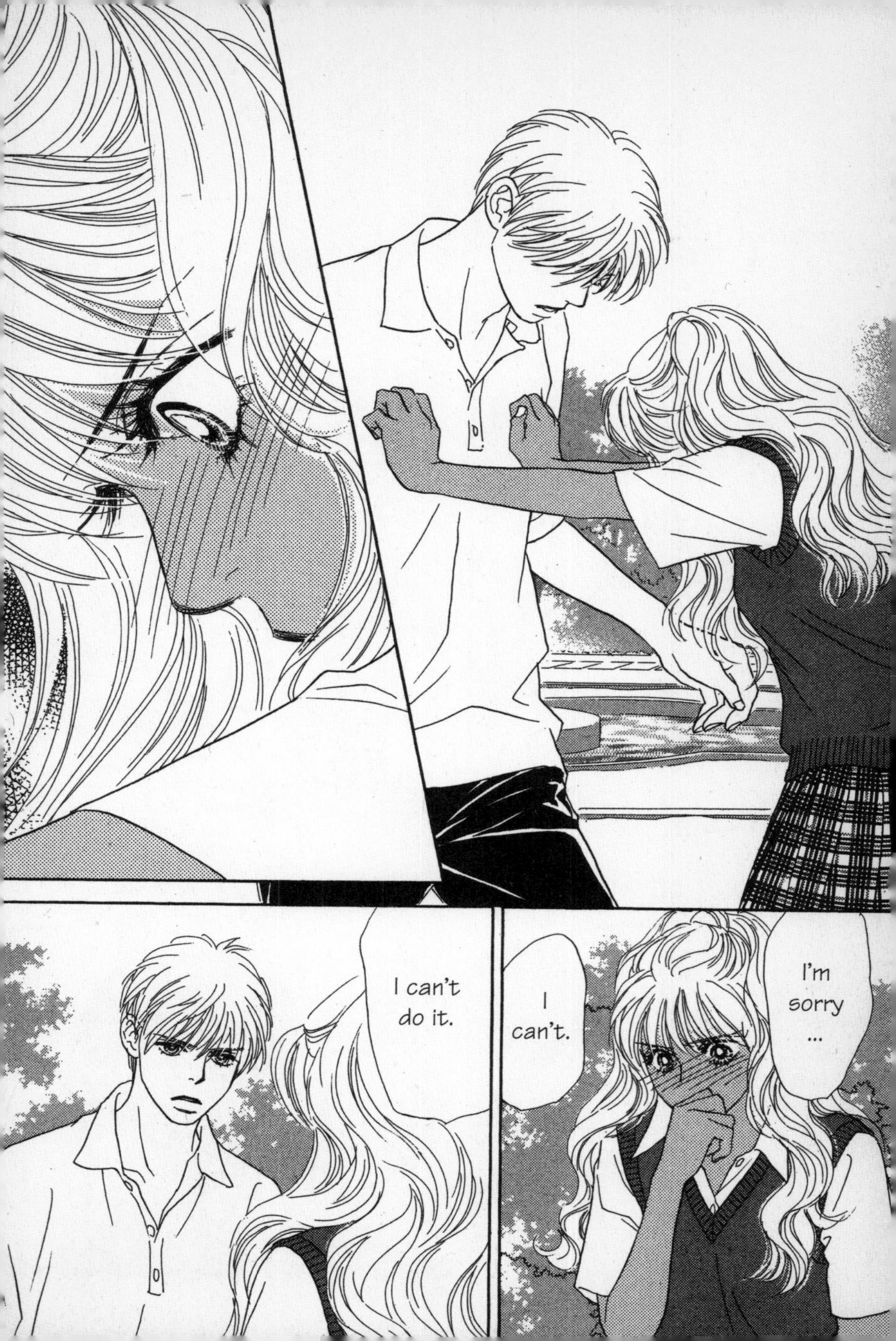
I'm sorry ...
I can't.
I can't do it.

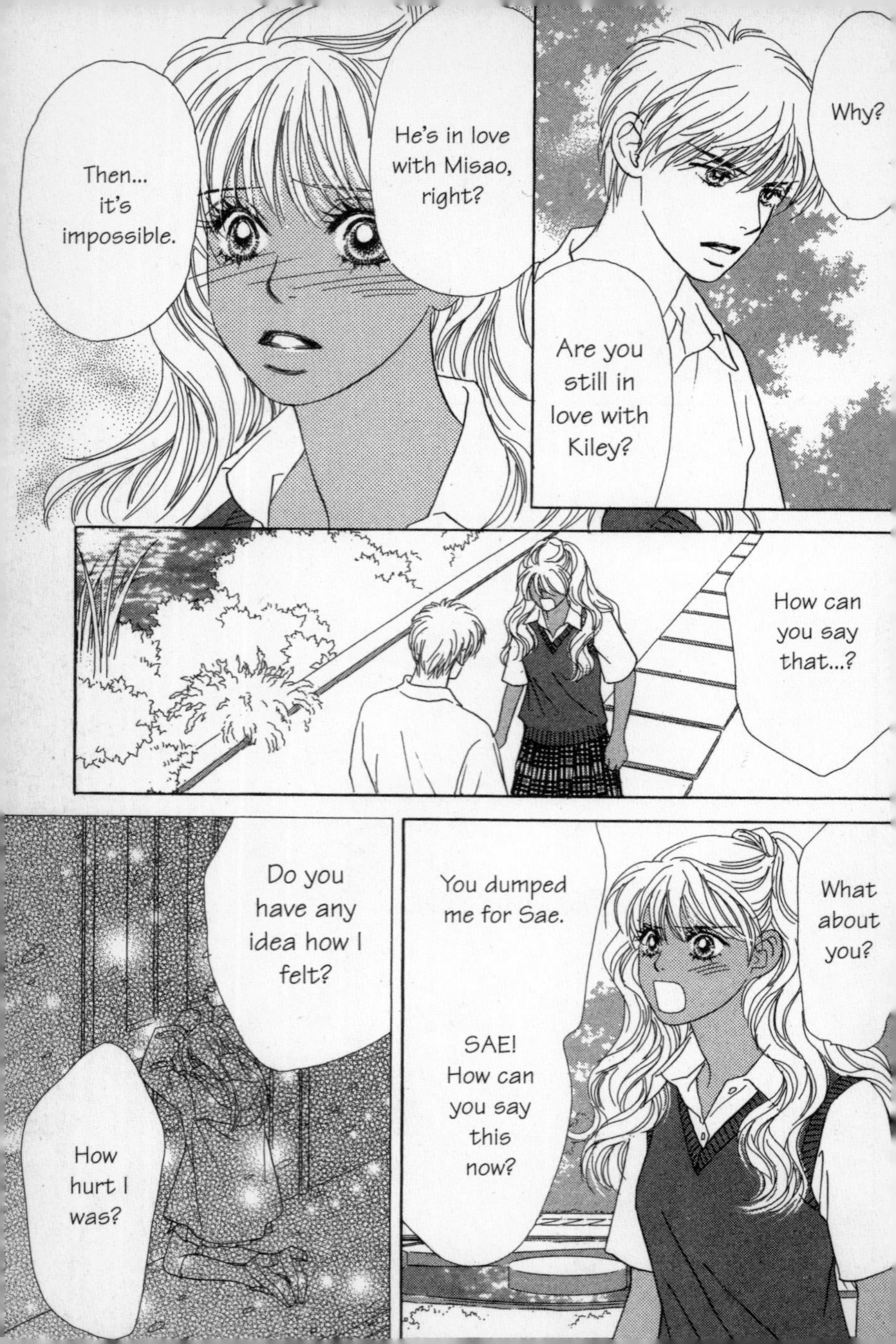
Why?
Are you still in love with Kiley?
He's in love with Misao, right?
Then... it's impossible.
How can you say that...?
What about you?
You dumped me for Sae.
SAE! How can you say this now?
Do you have any idea how I felt?
How hurt I was?

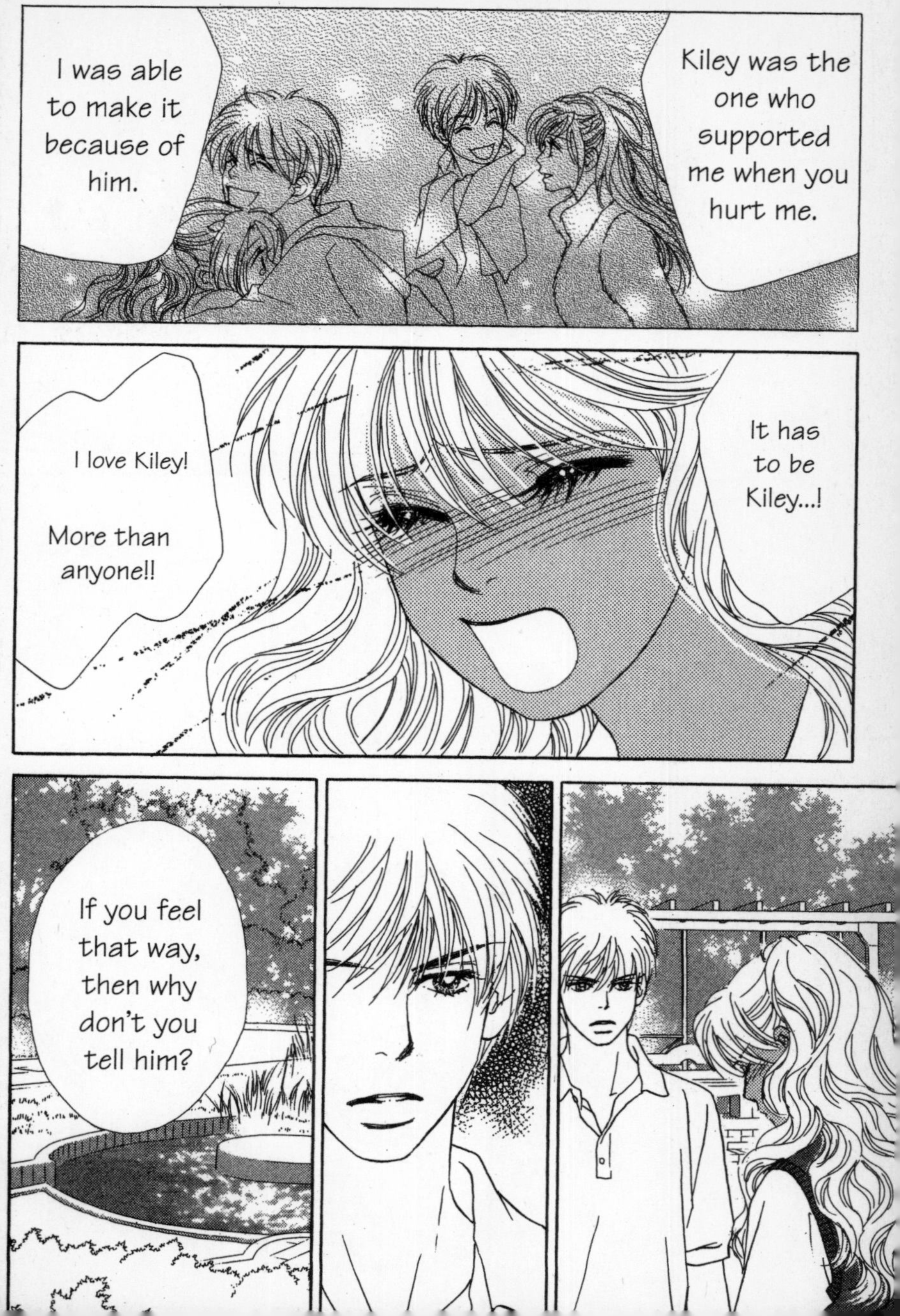
Kiley was the one who supported me when you hurt me.
I was able to make it because of him.
It has to be Kiley...!
I love Kiley!
More than anyone!!
If you feel that way, then why don't you tell him?

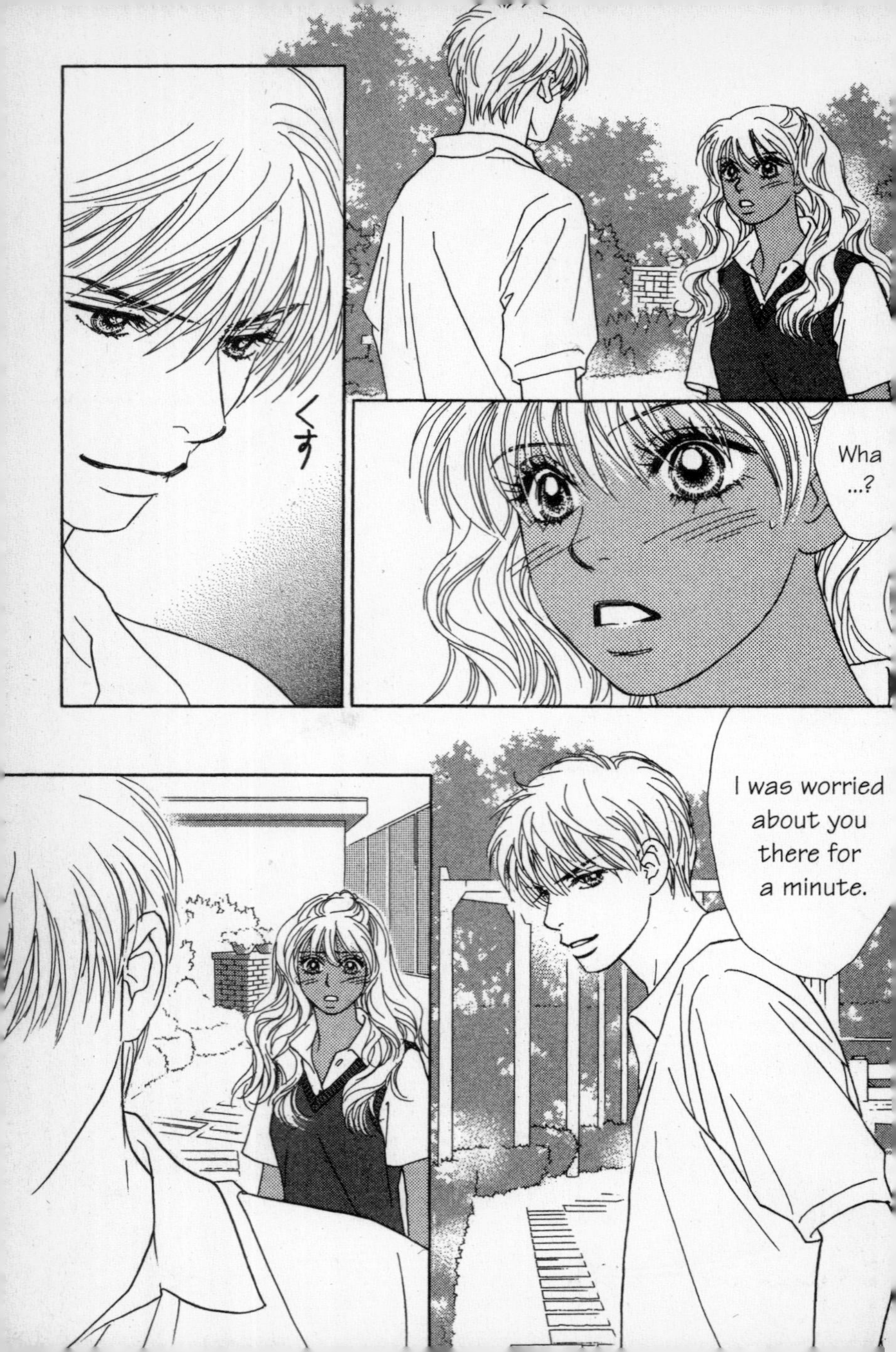
Wha ...?
くす
I was worried about you there for a minute.

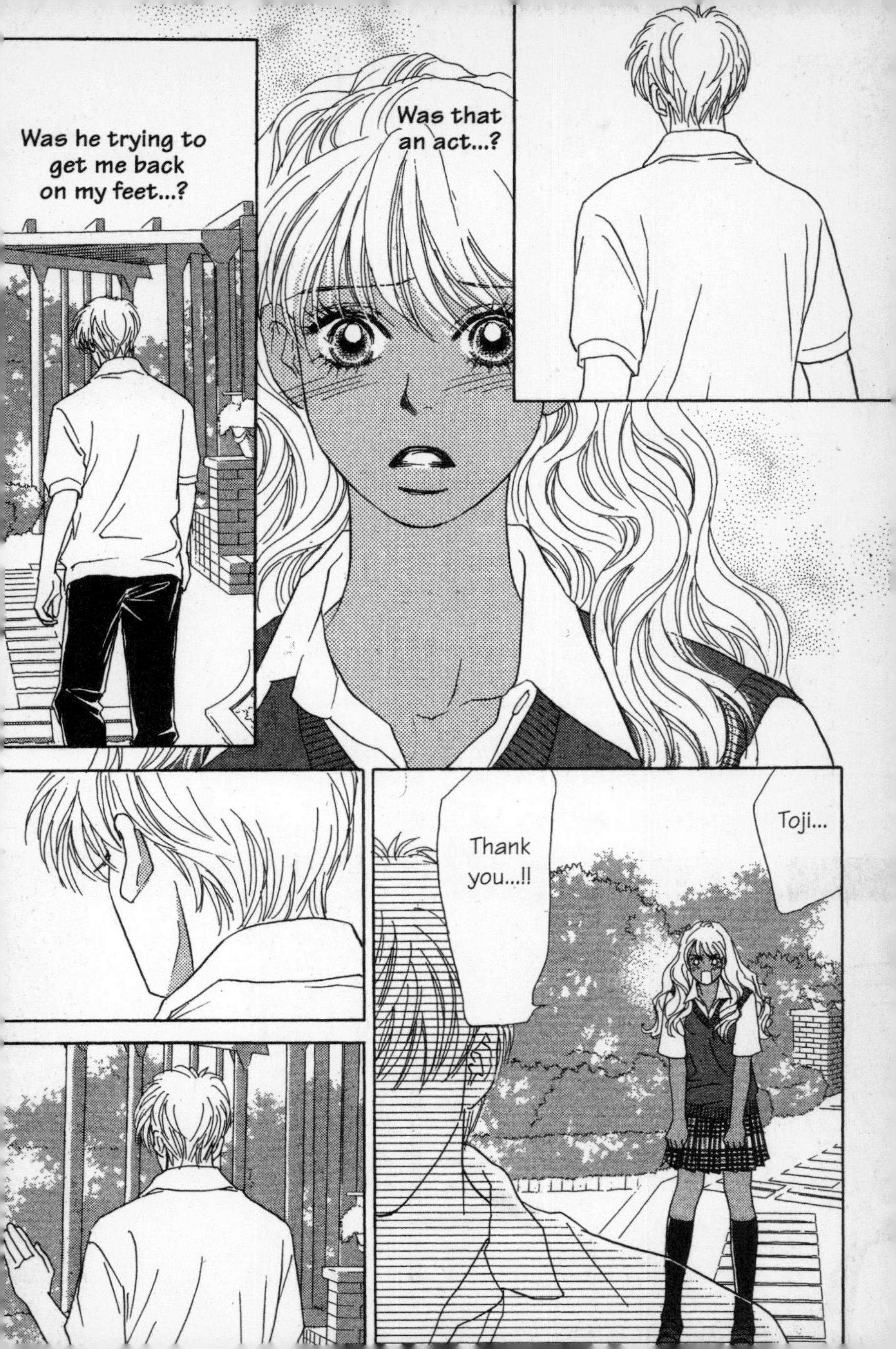
Was that an act...?
Was he trying to get me back on my feet...?
Toji...
Thank you...!!

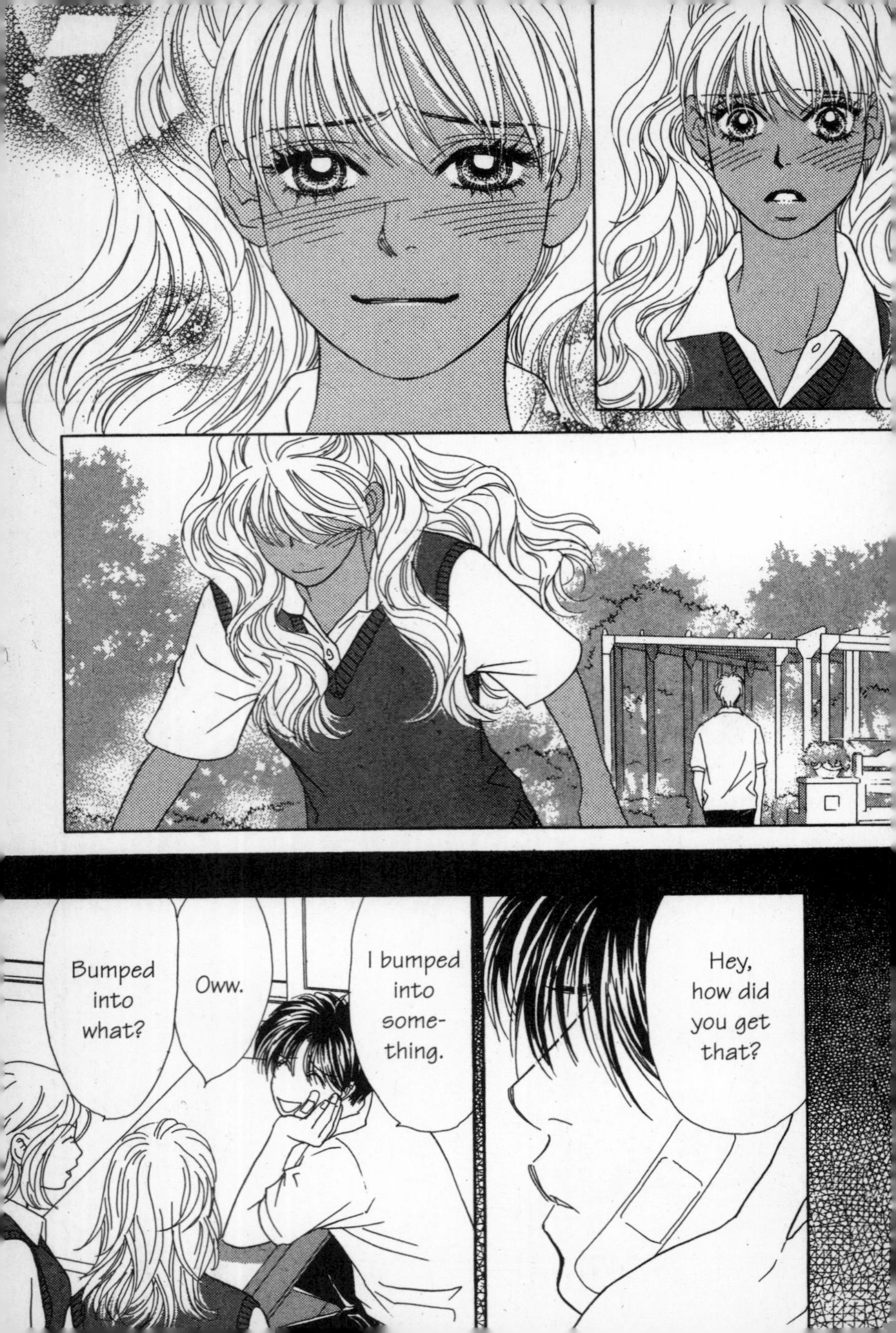
Hey, how did you get that?
I bumped into something.
Oww.
Bumped into what?

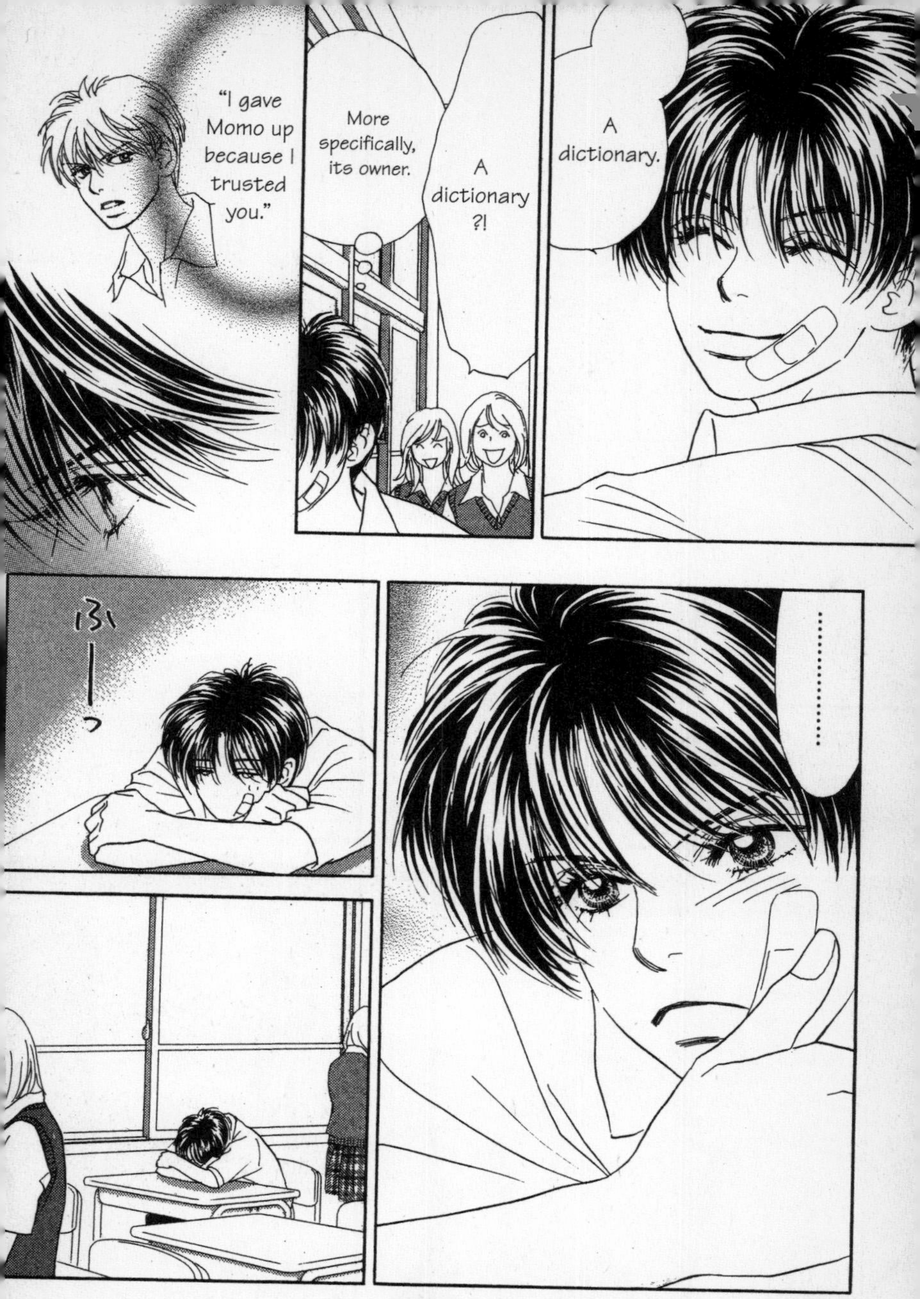

A dictionary.
A dictionary?!
More specifically, its owner.
"I gave Momo up because I trusted you."
……
ふーっ

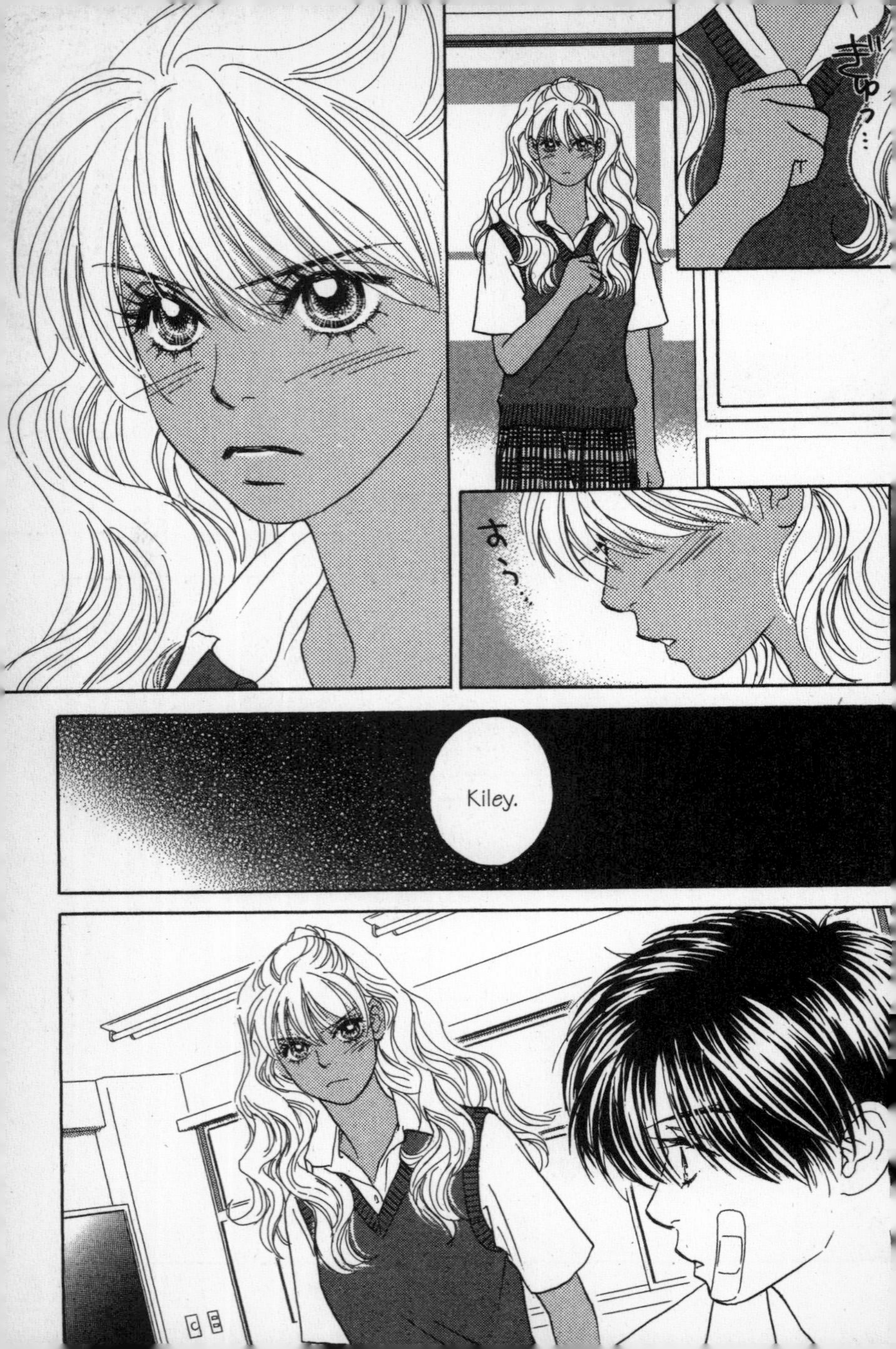
ぎゅっ…
すっ…
Kiley.

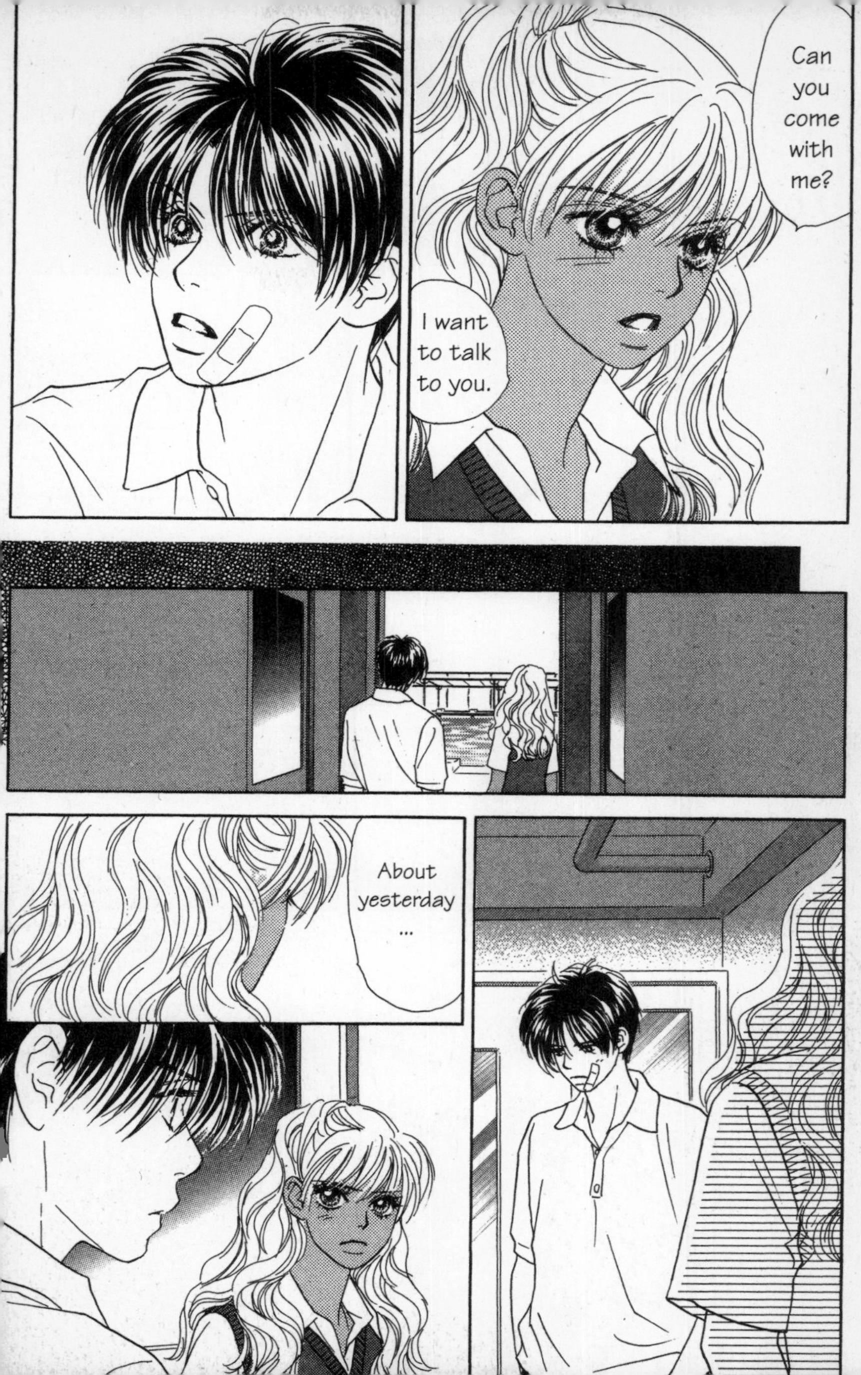
Can you come with me?
I want to talk to you.
About yesterday ...

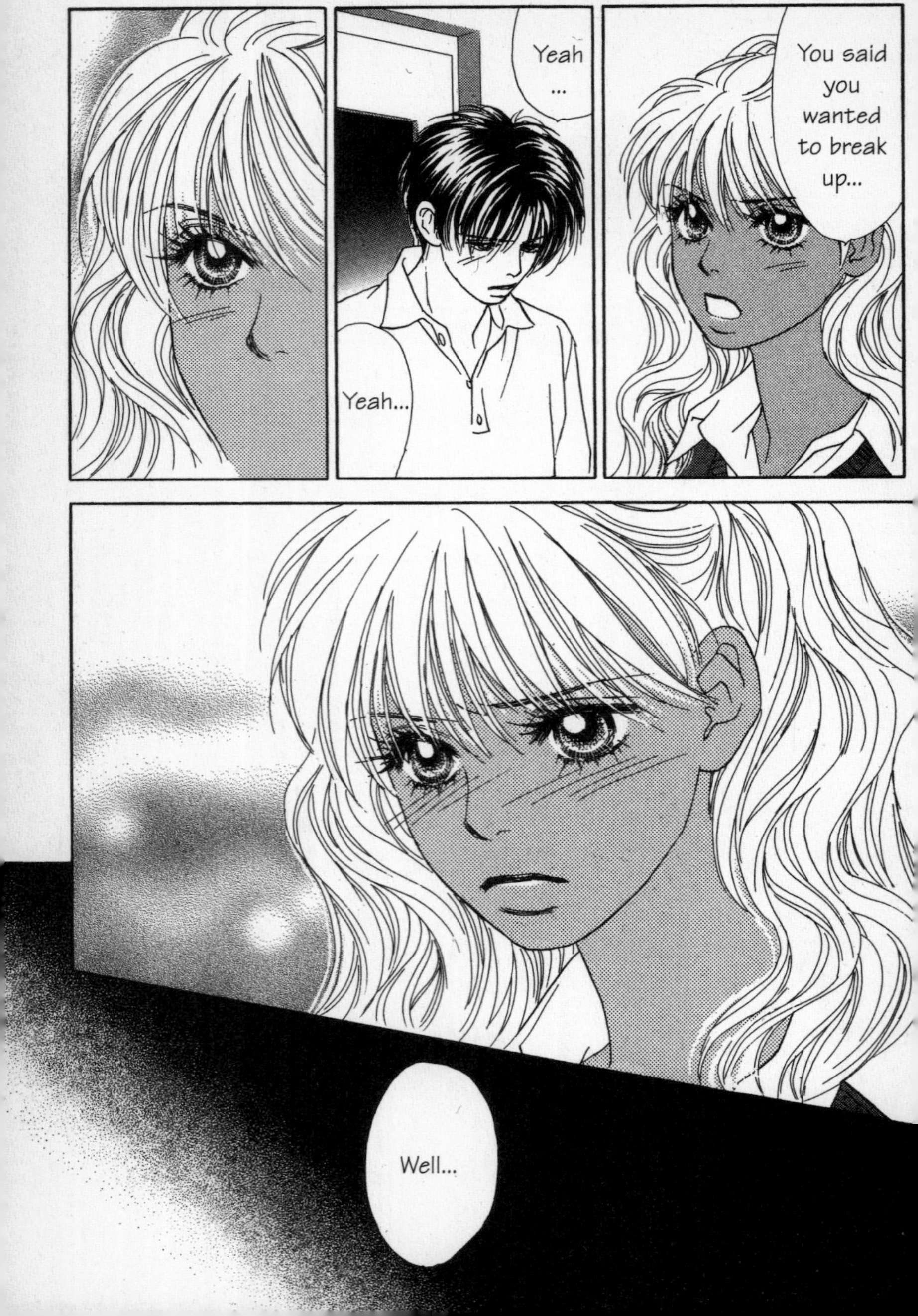
You said you wanted to break up...
Yeah ...
Yeah...
Well...

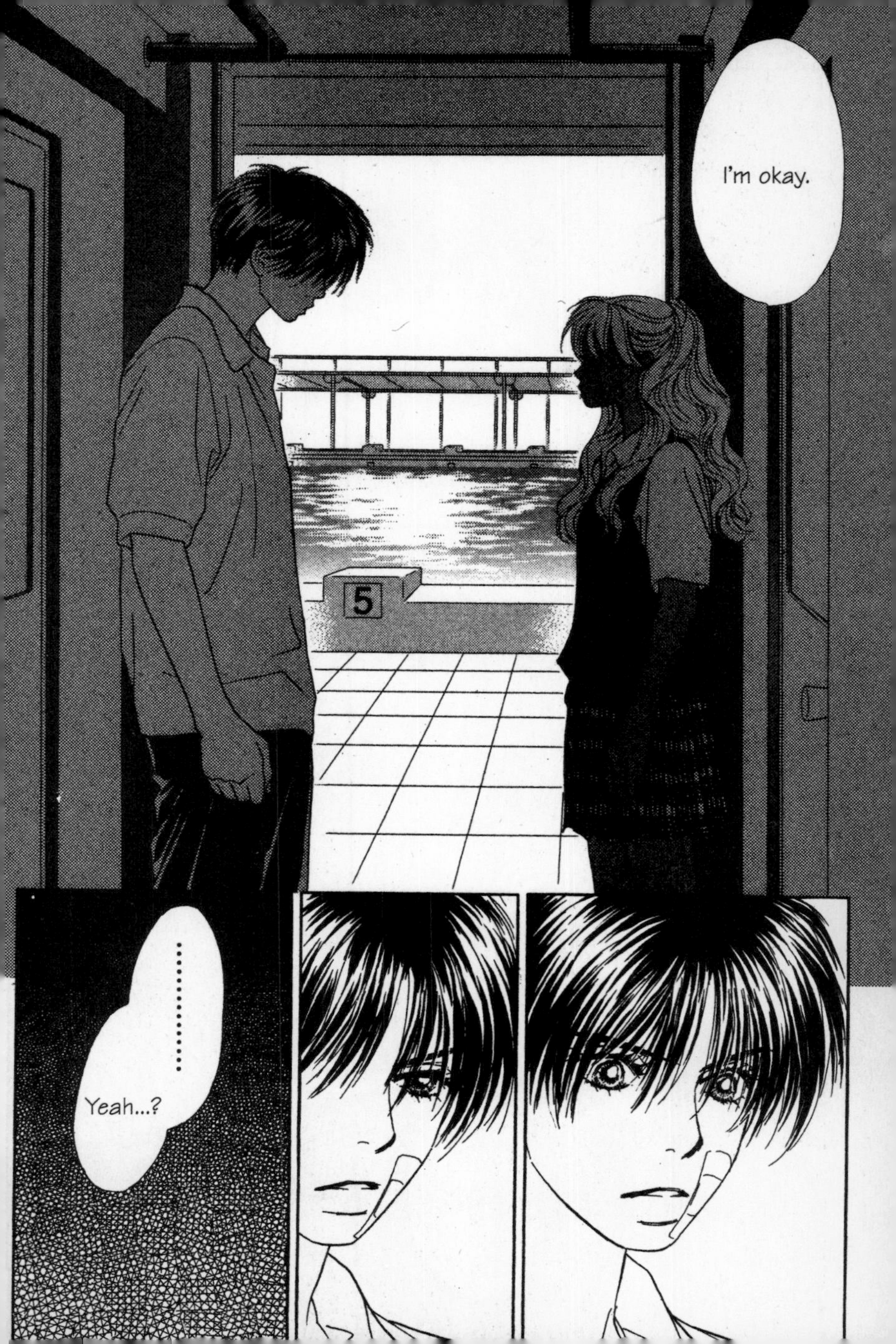
I'm okay.
.... Yeah...?

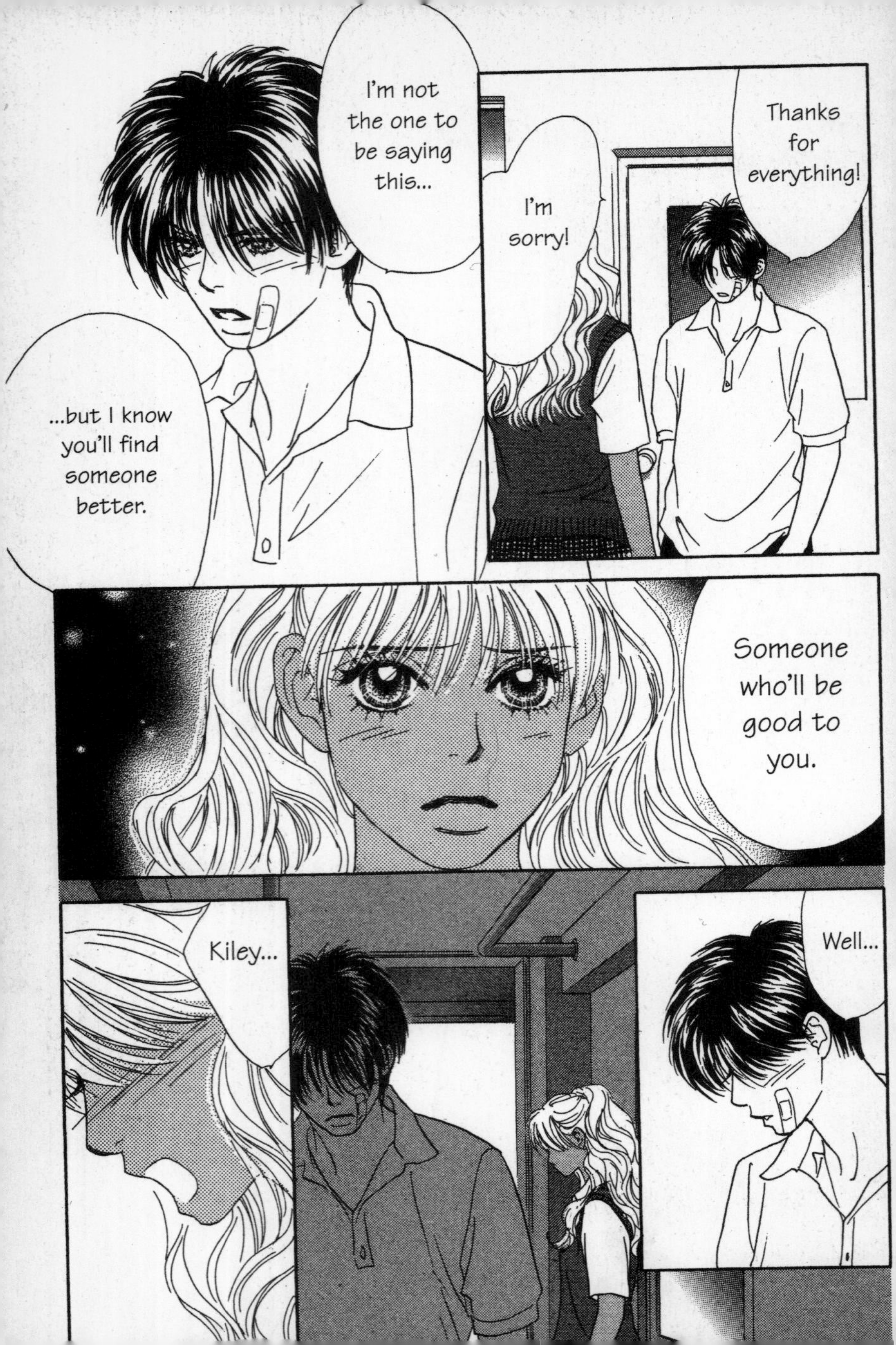
Thanks for everything!
I'm sorry!
I'm not the one to be saying this...
...but I know you'll find someone better.
Someone who'll be good to you.
Well...
Kiley...

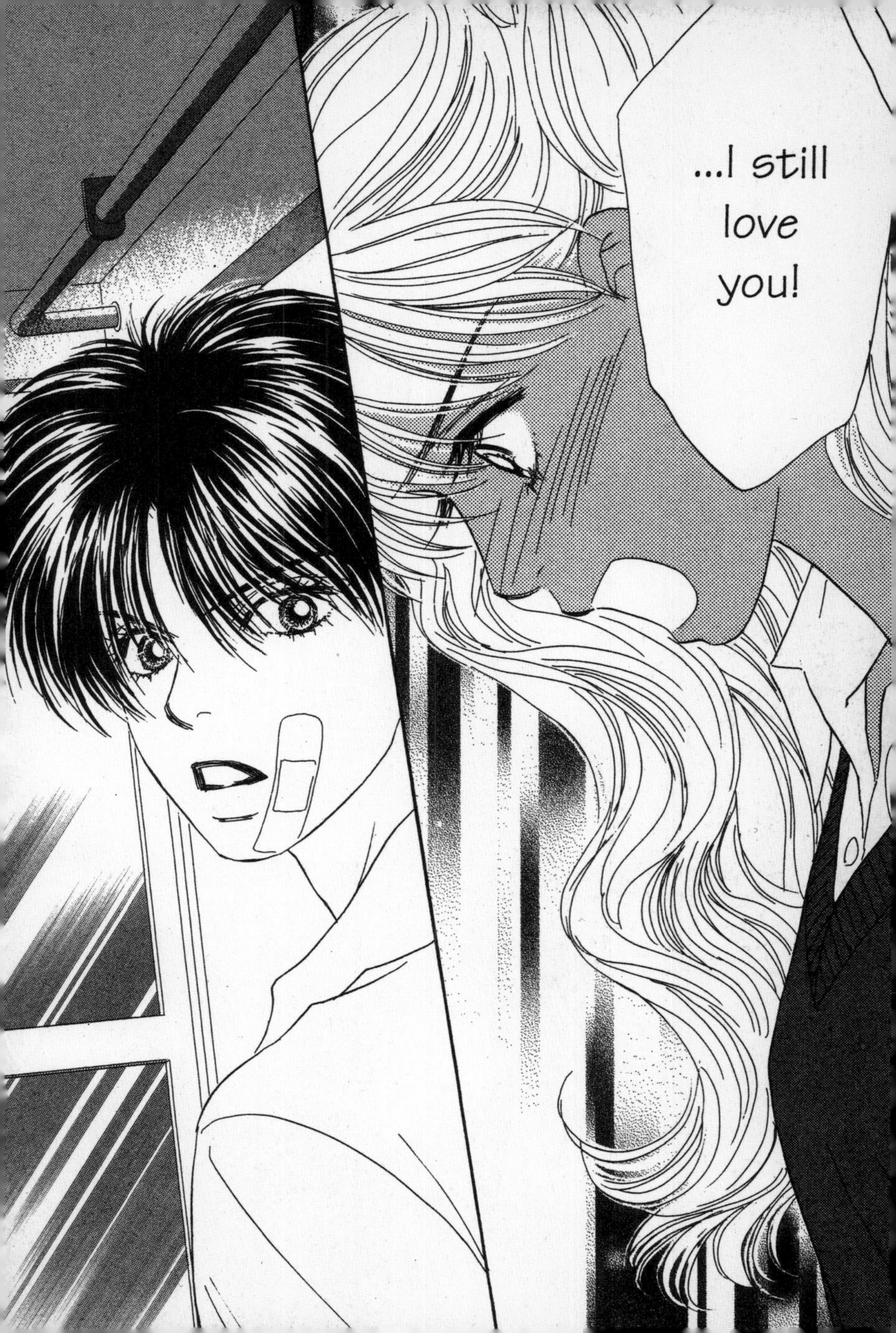
...I still love you!

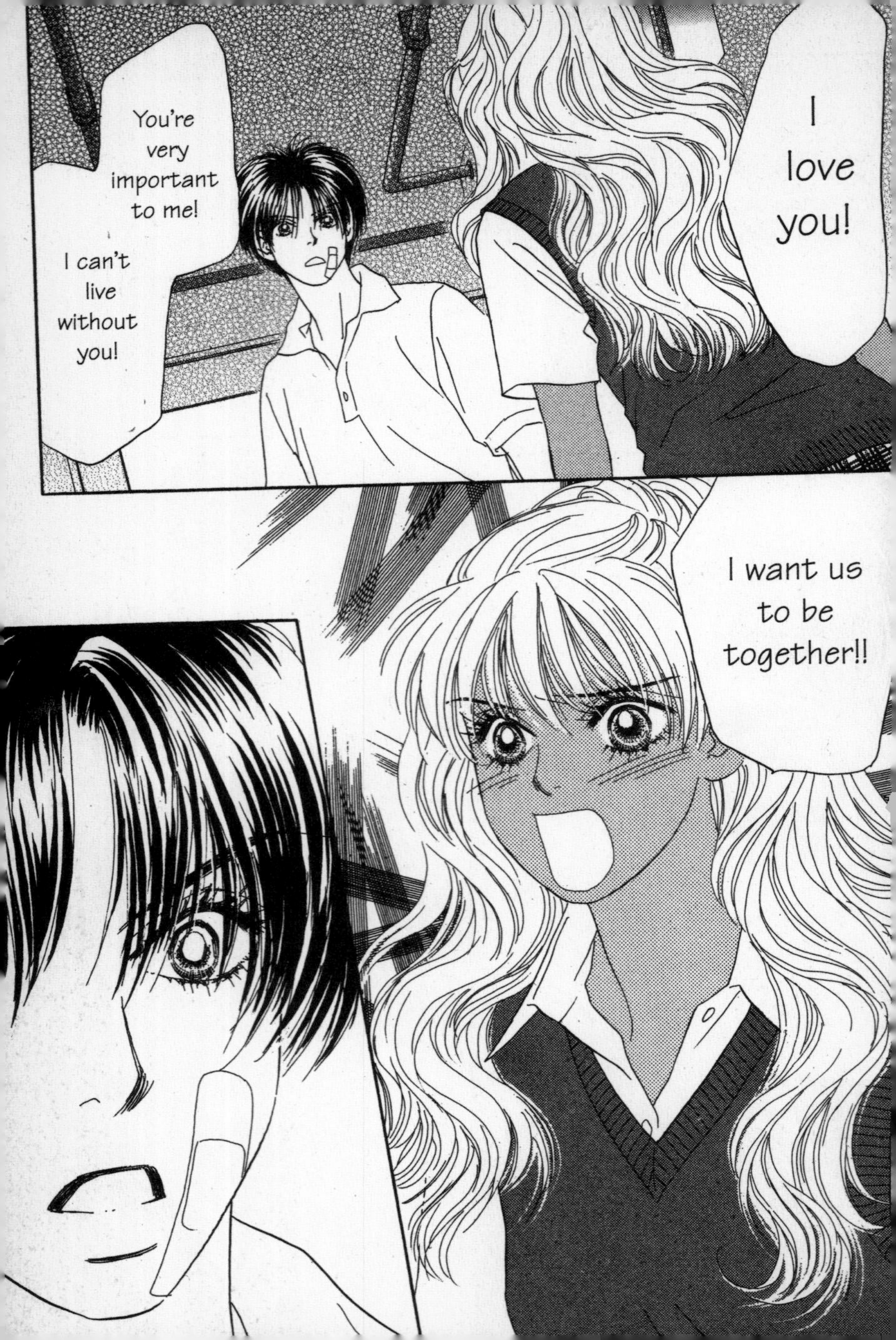
I love you!
You're very important to me!
I can't live without you!
I want us to be together!!

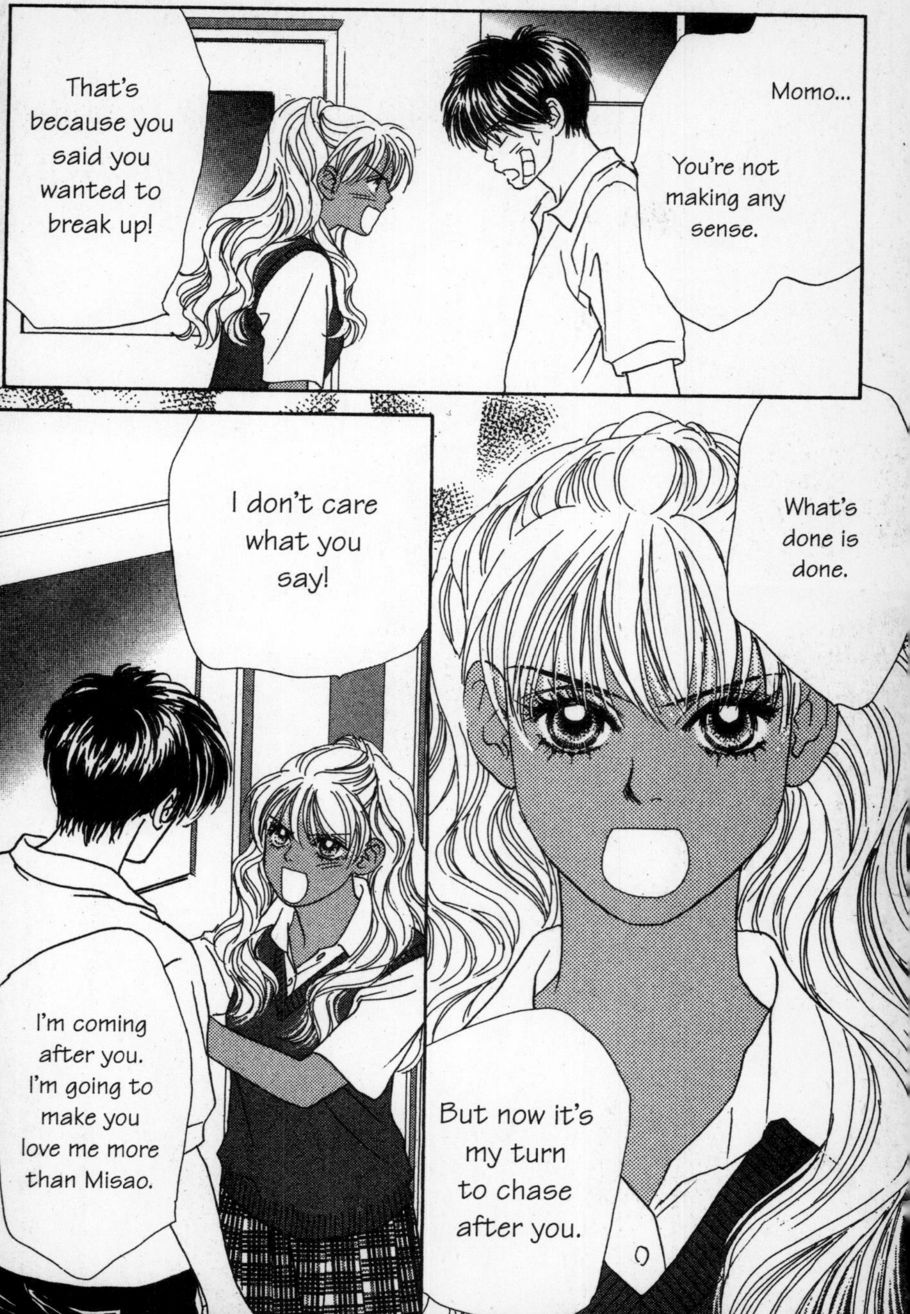
Momo...
You're not making any sense.
That's because you said you wanted to break up!
What's done is done.
But now it's my turn to chase after you.
I don't care what you say!
I'm coming after you. I'm going to make you love me more than Misao.

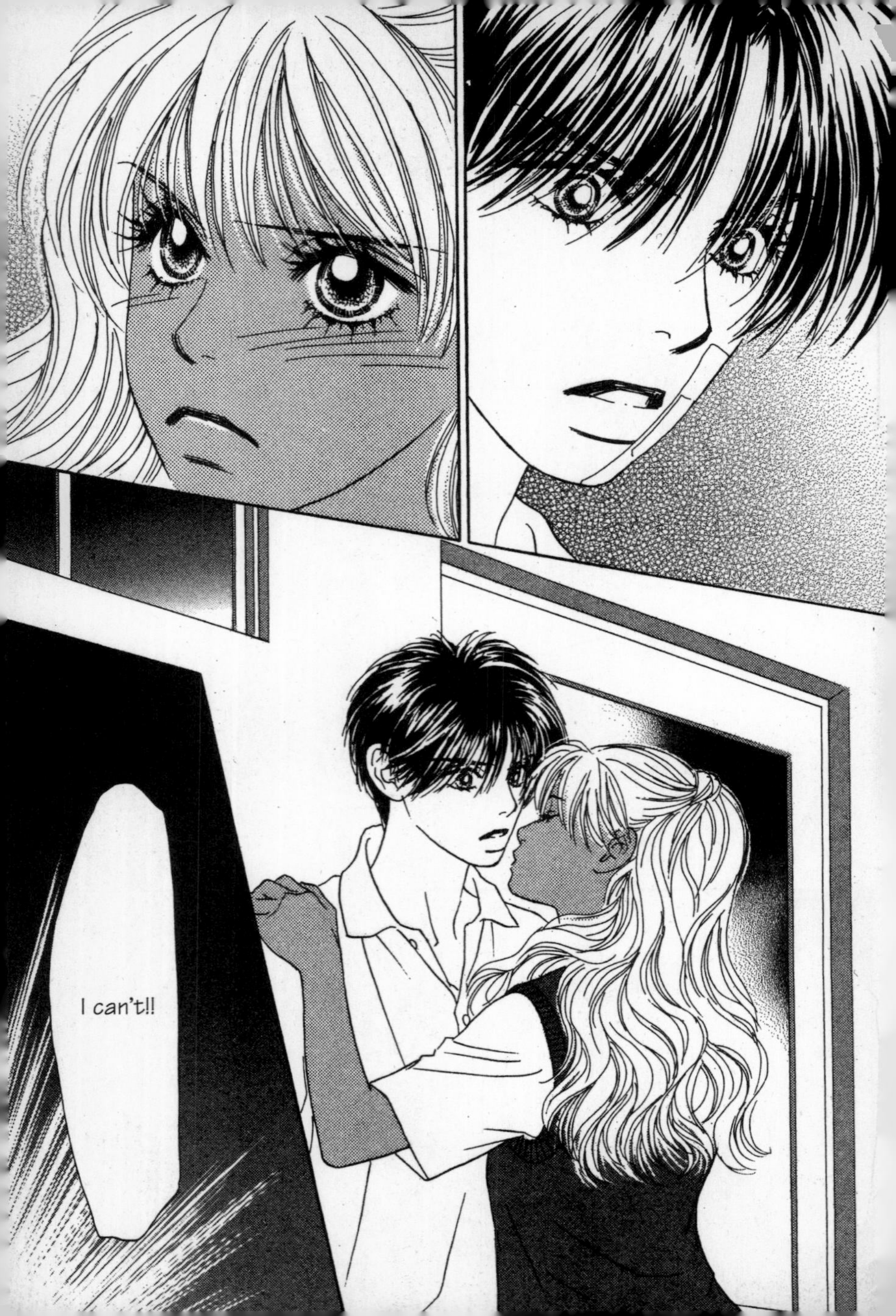
I can't!!

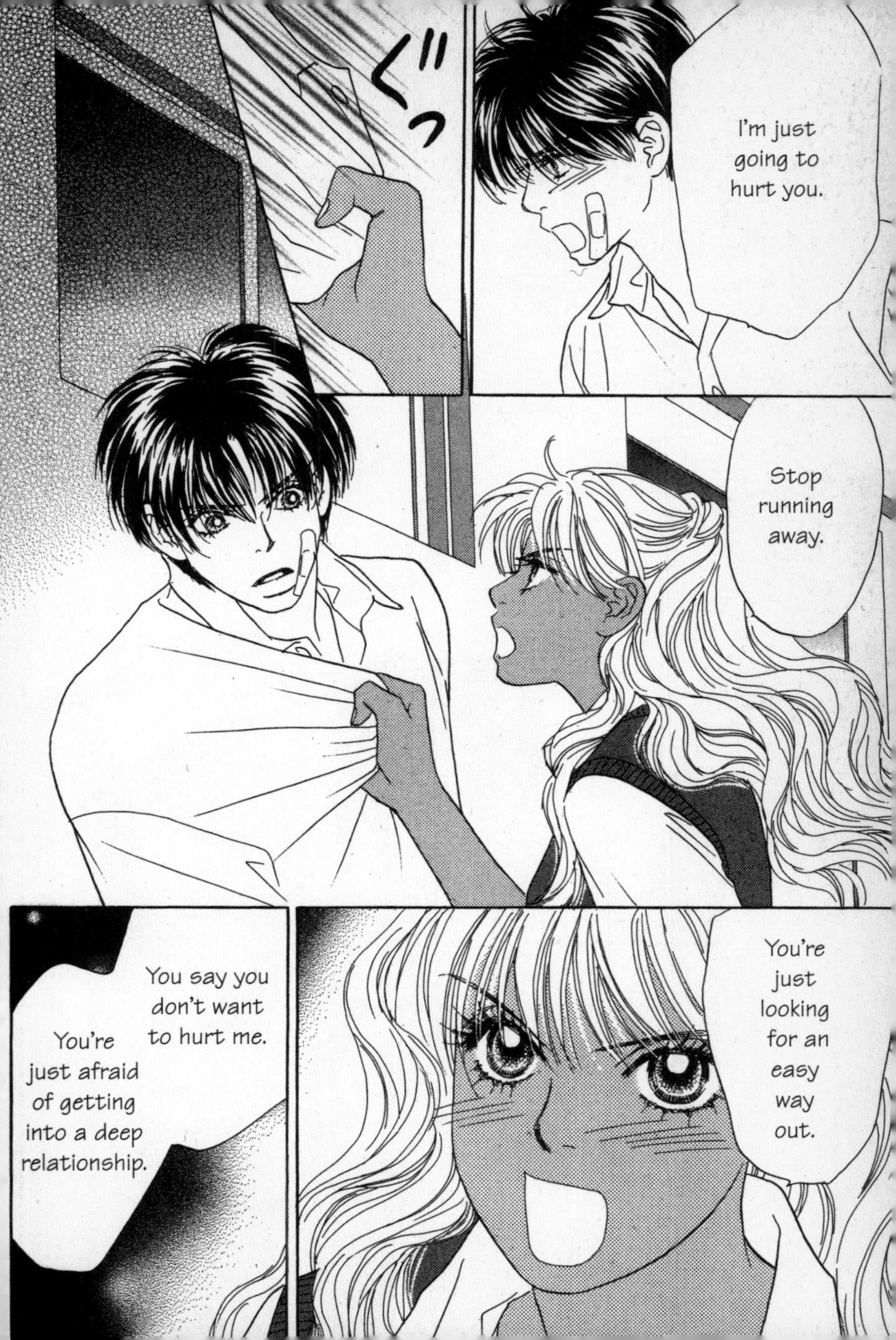
I'm just going to hurt you.
ぐっ
Stop running away.
You're just looking for an easy way out.
You say you don't want to hurt me.
You're just afraid of getting into a deep relationship.

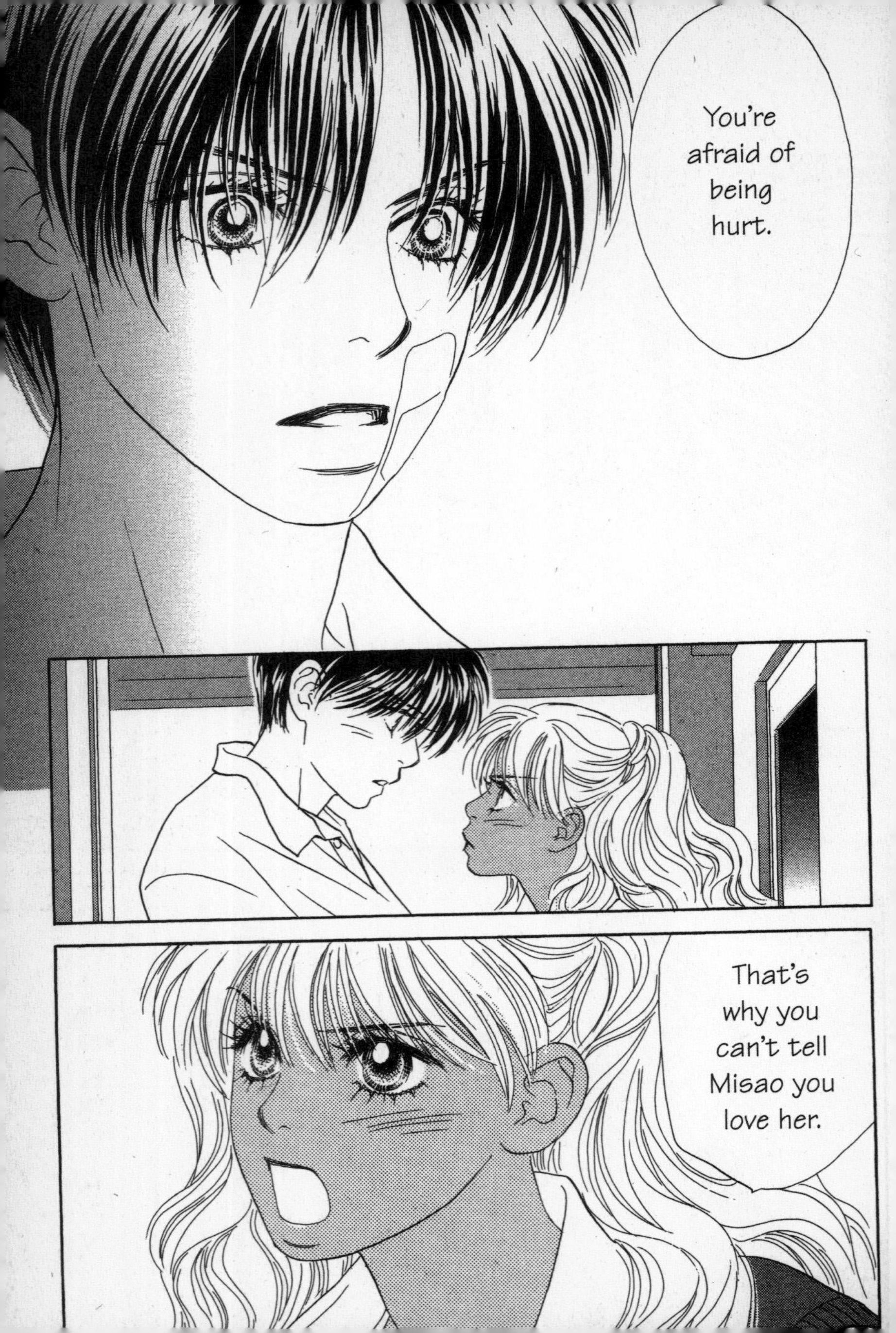
You're afraid of being hurt.
That's why you can't tell Misao you love her.

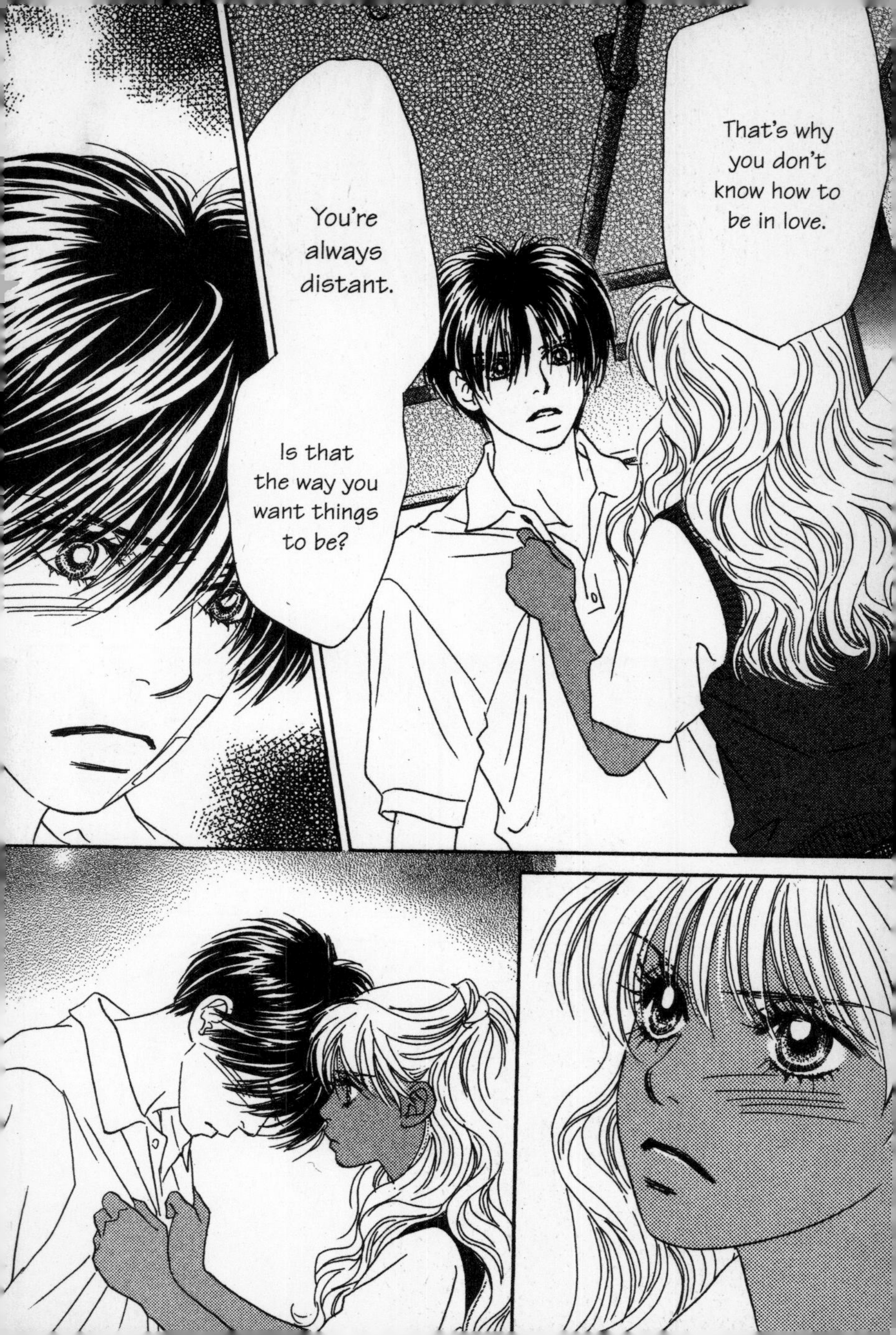
That's why you don't know how to be in love.
You're always distant.
Is that the way you want things to be?

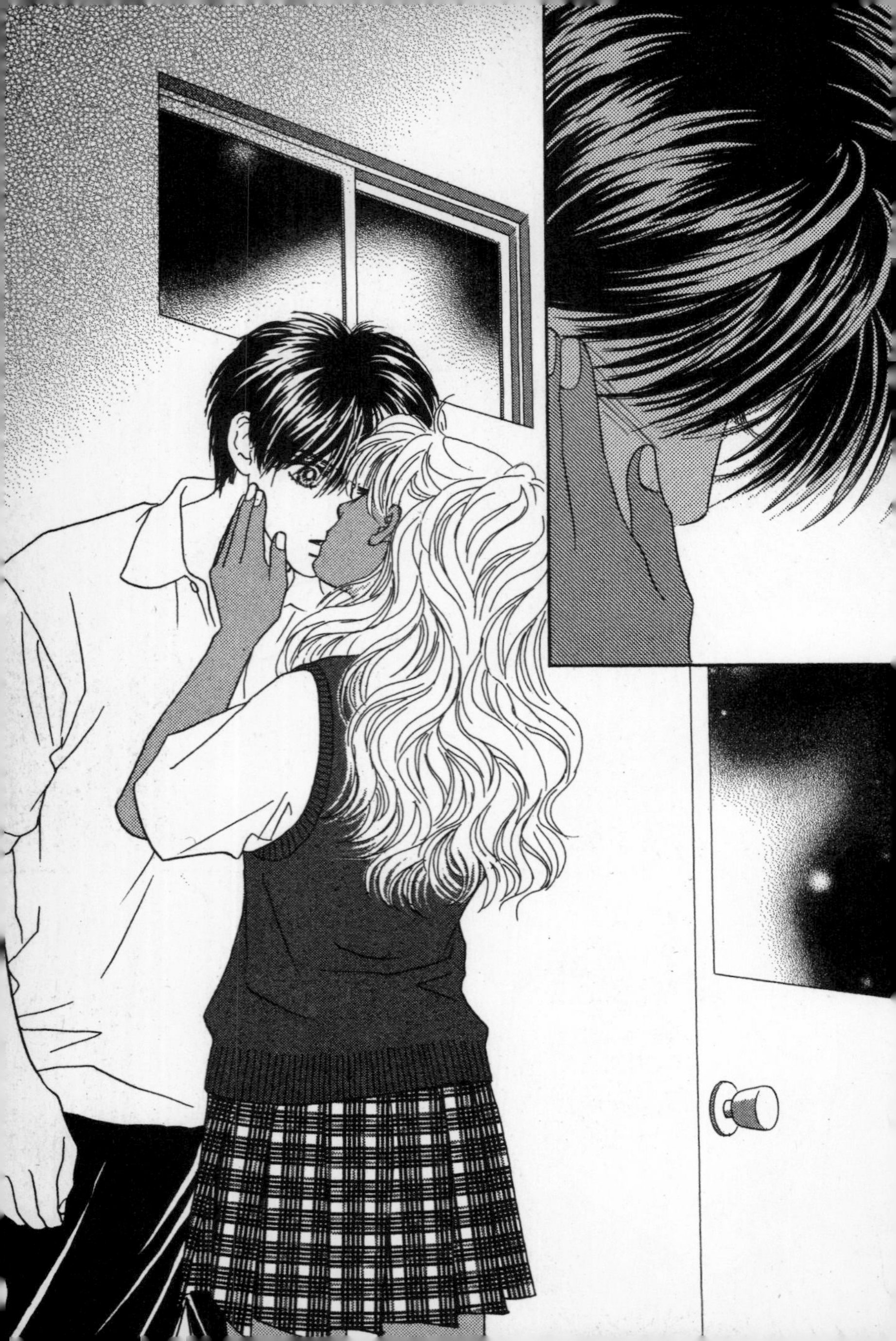

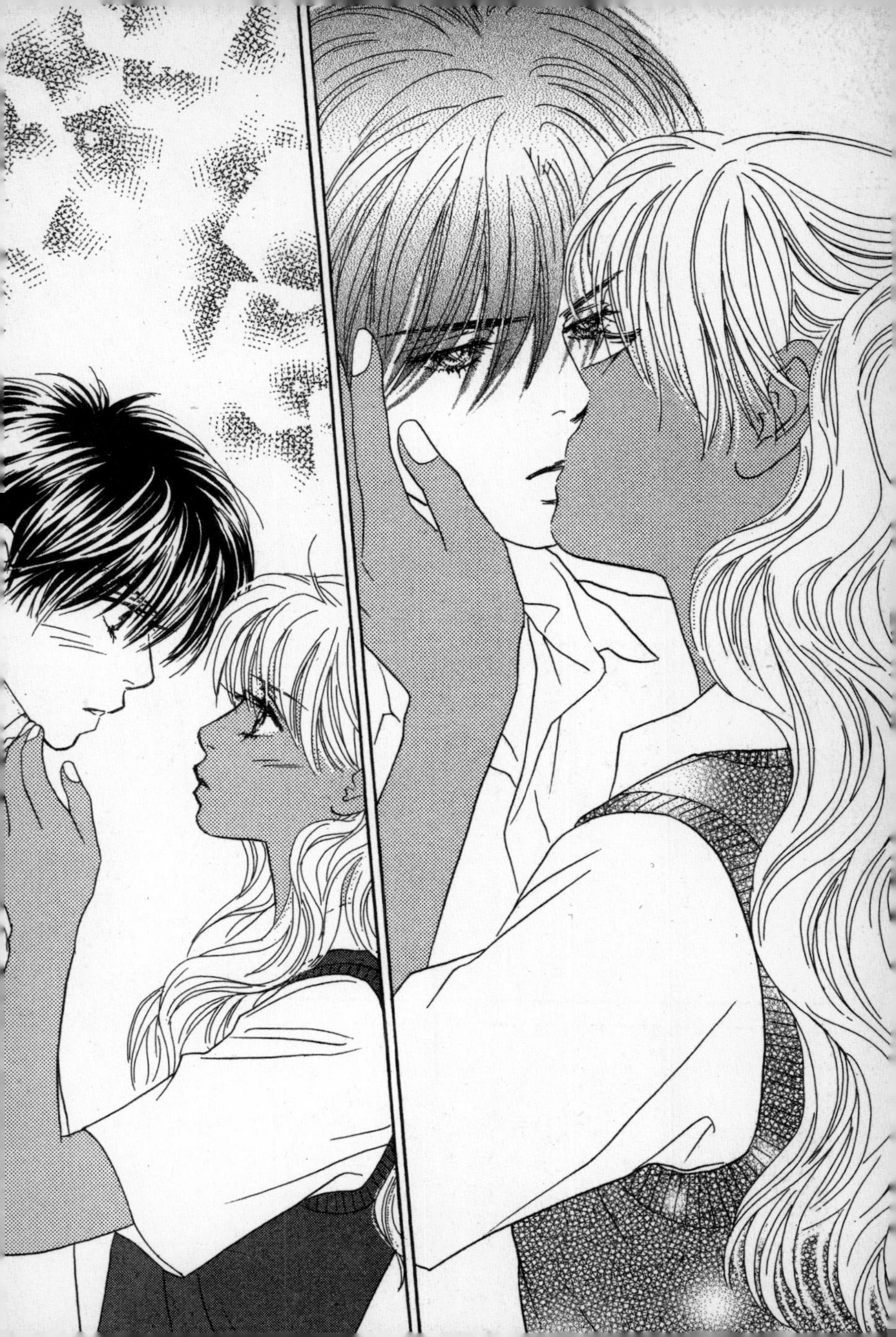

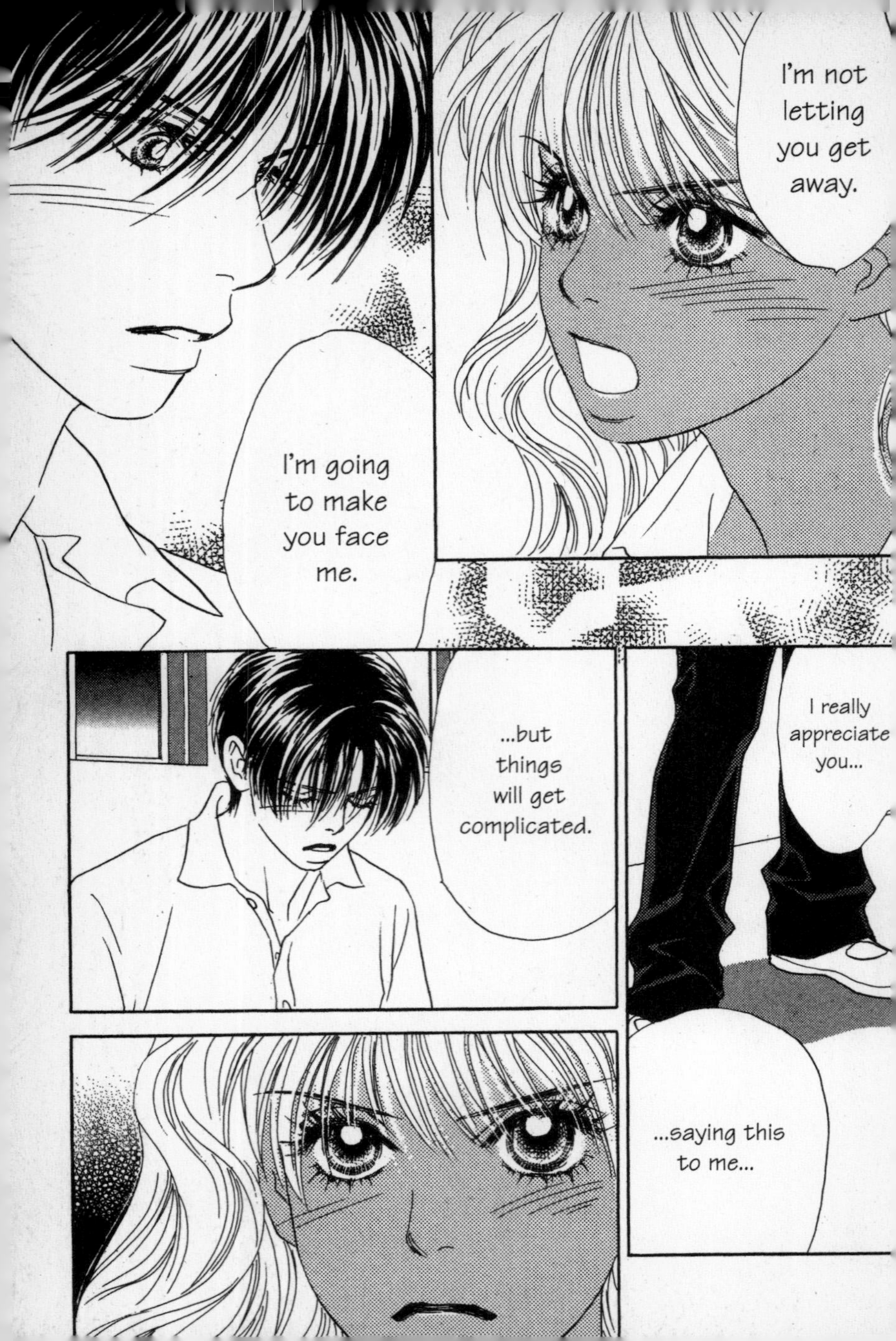
I'm not letting you get away.
I'm going to make you face me.
I really appreciate you...
...saying this to me...
...but things will get complicated.

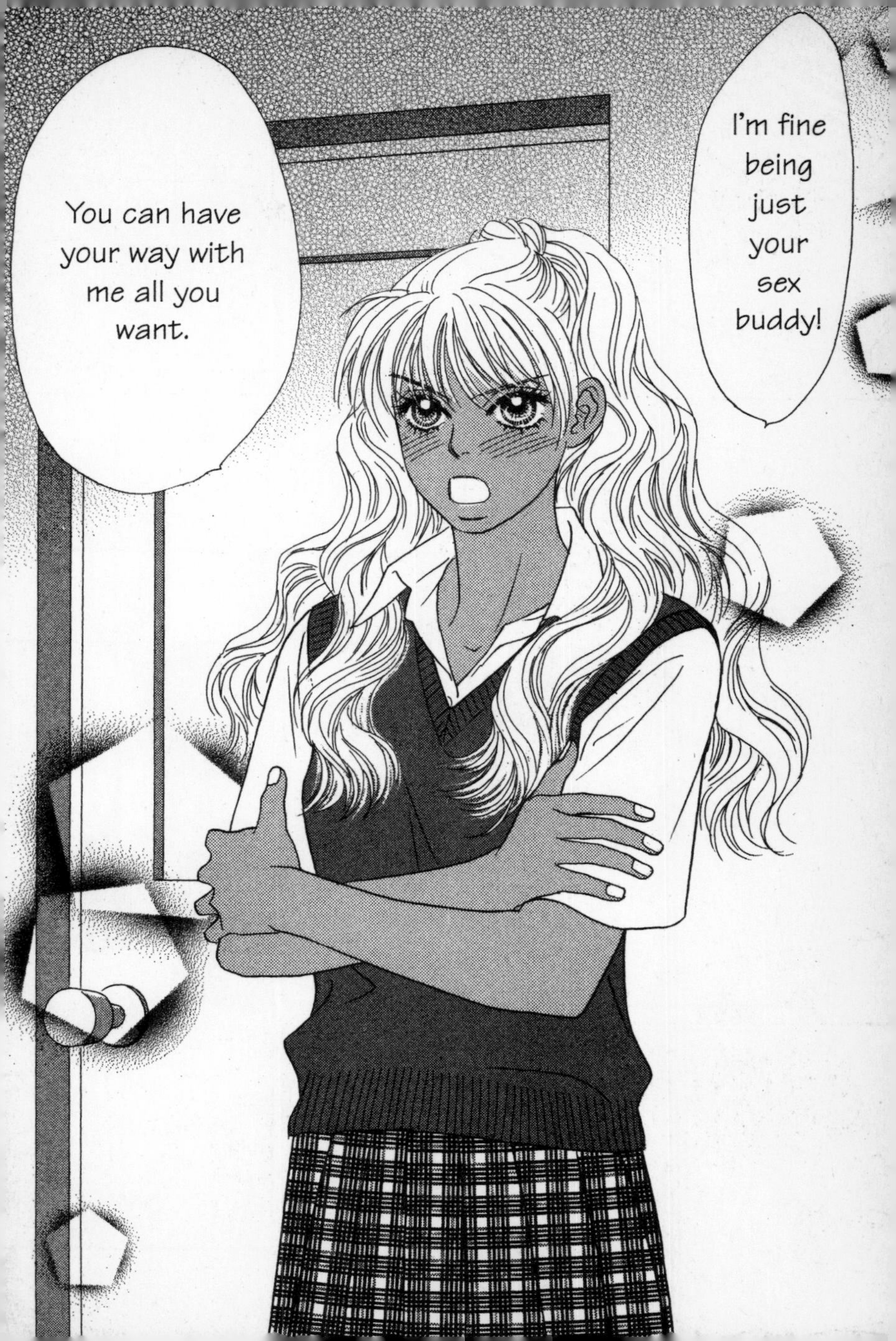
I'm fine being just your sex buddy!
You can have your way with me all you want.

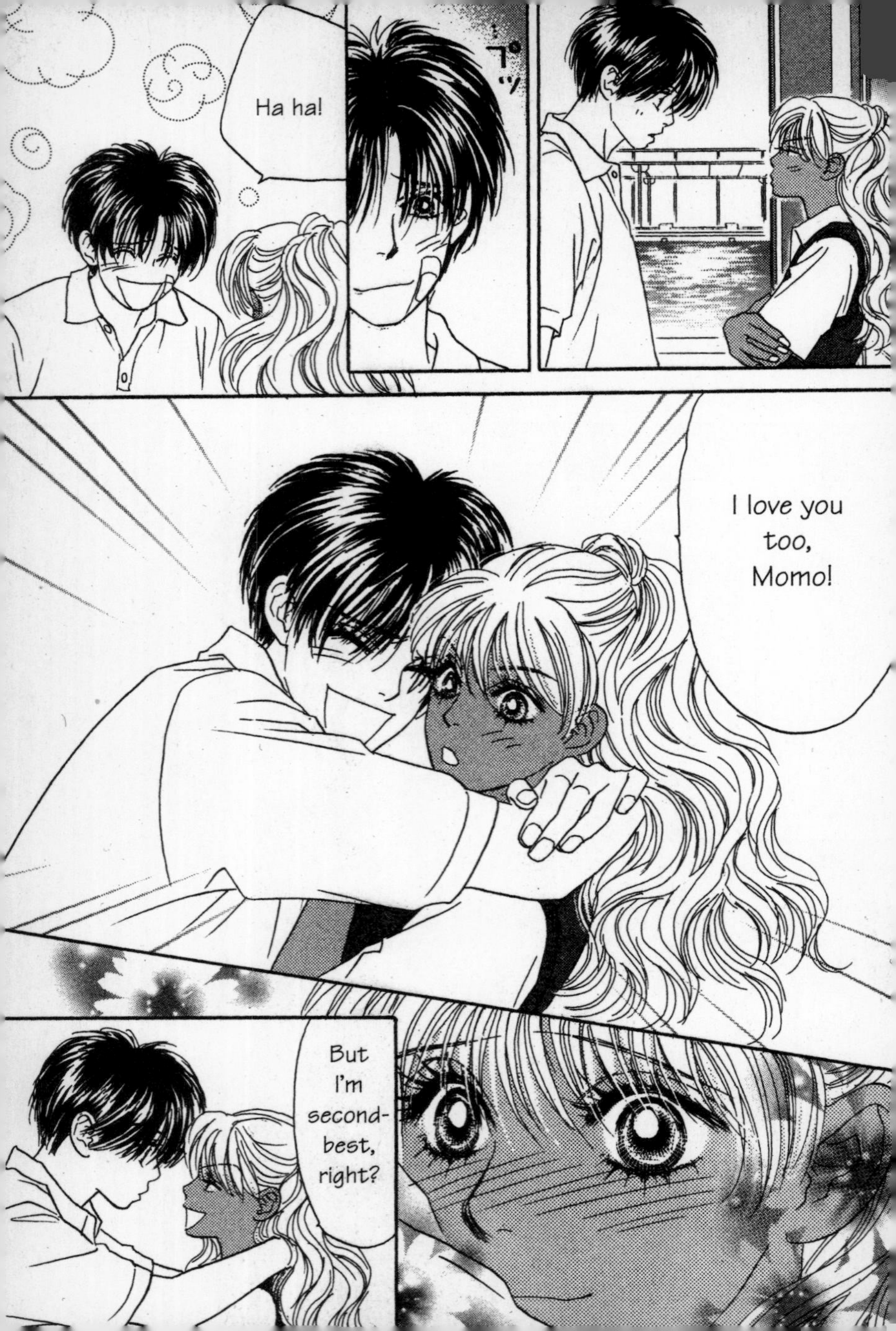
プッ
Ha ha!
I love you too, Momo!
But I'm second-best, right?

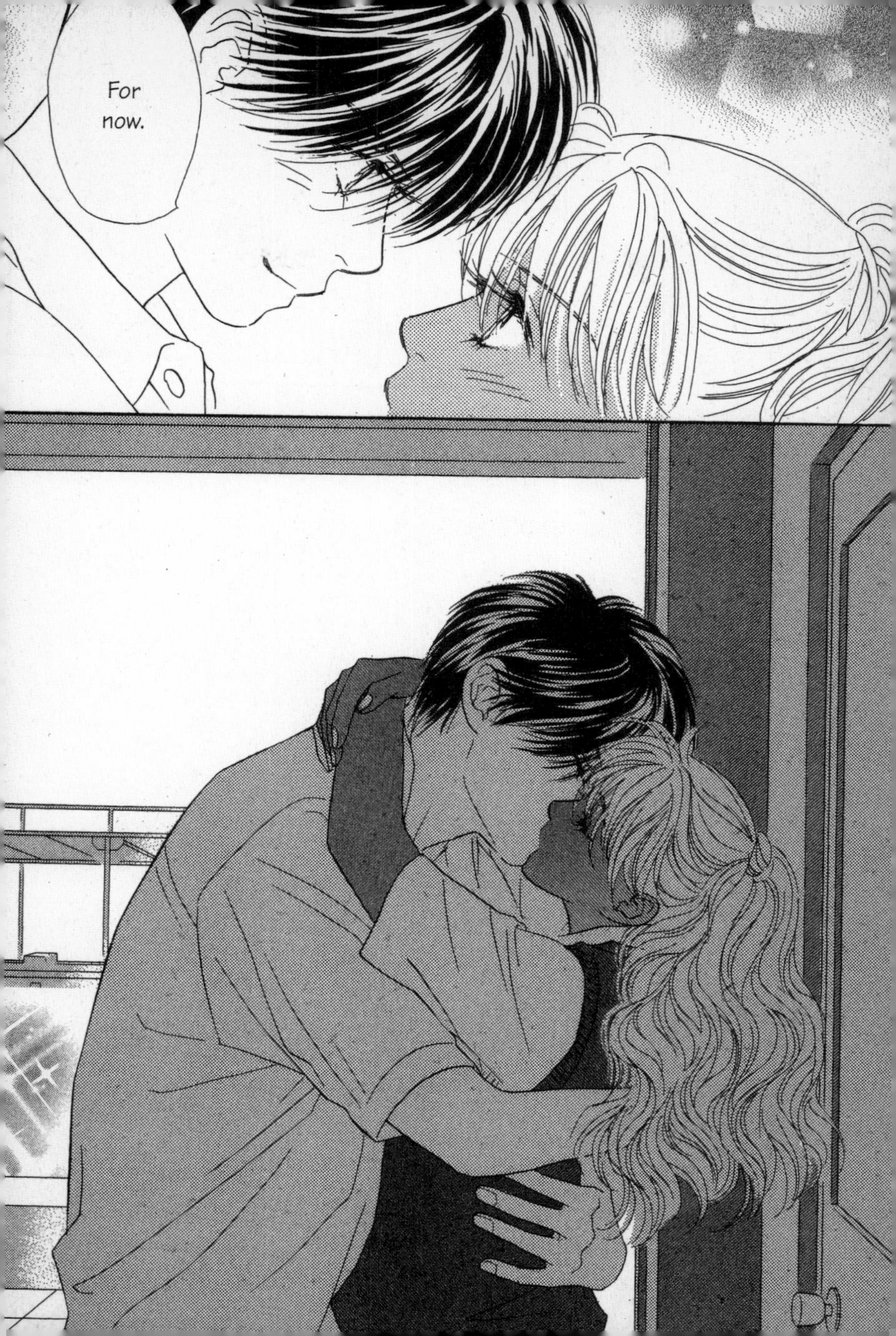
For now.

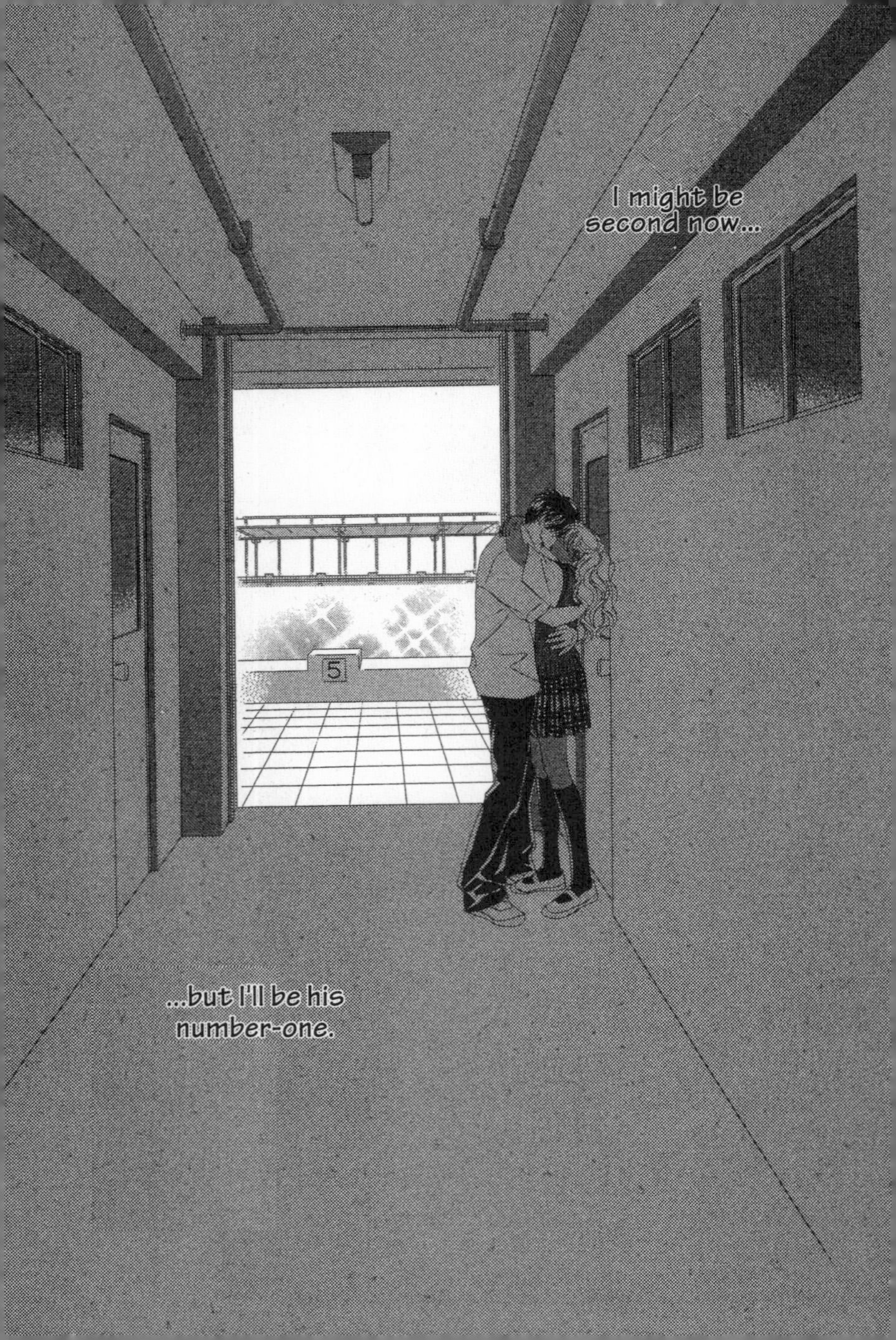
I might be second now...
...but I'll be his number-one.

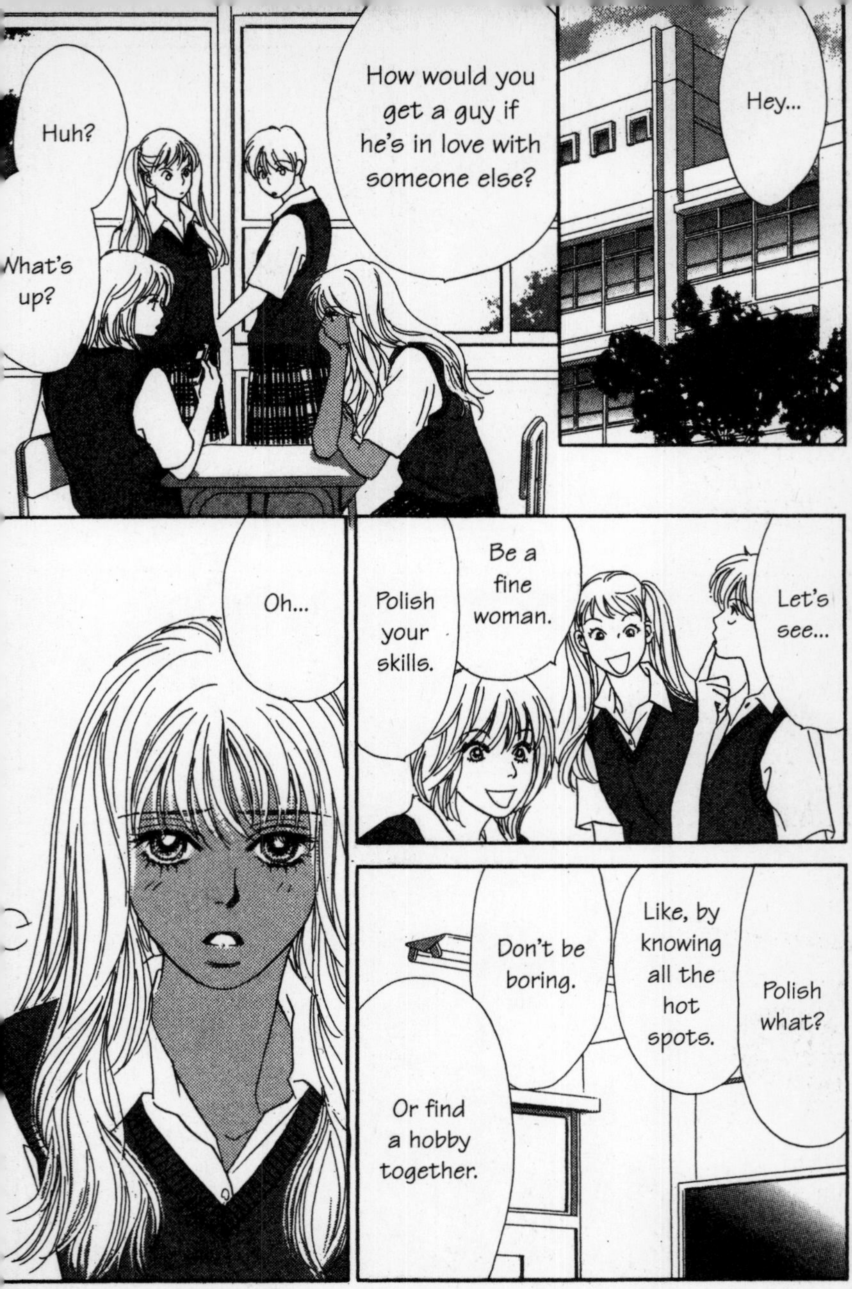
Hey...
How would you get a guy if he's in love with someone else?
Huh?
What's up?
Let's see...
Be a fine woman.
Polish your skills.
Polish what?
Like, by knowing all the hot spots.
Don't be boring.
Or find a hobby together.
Oh...

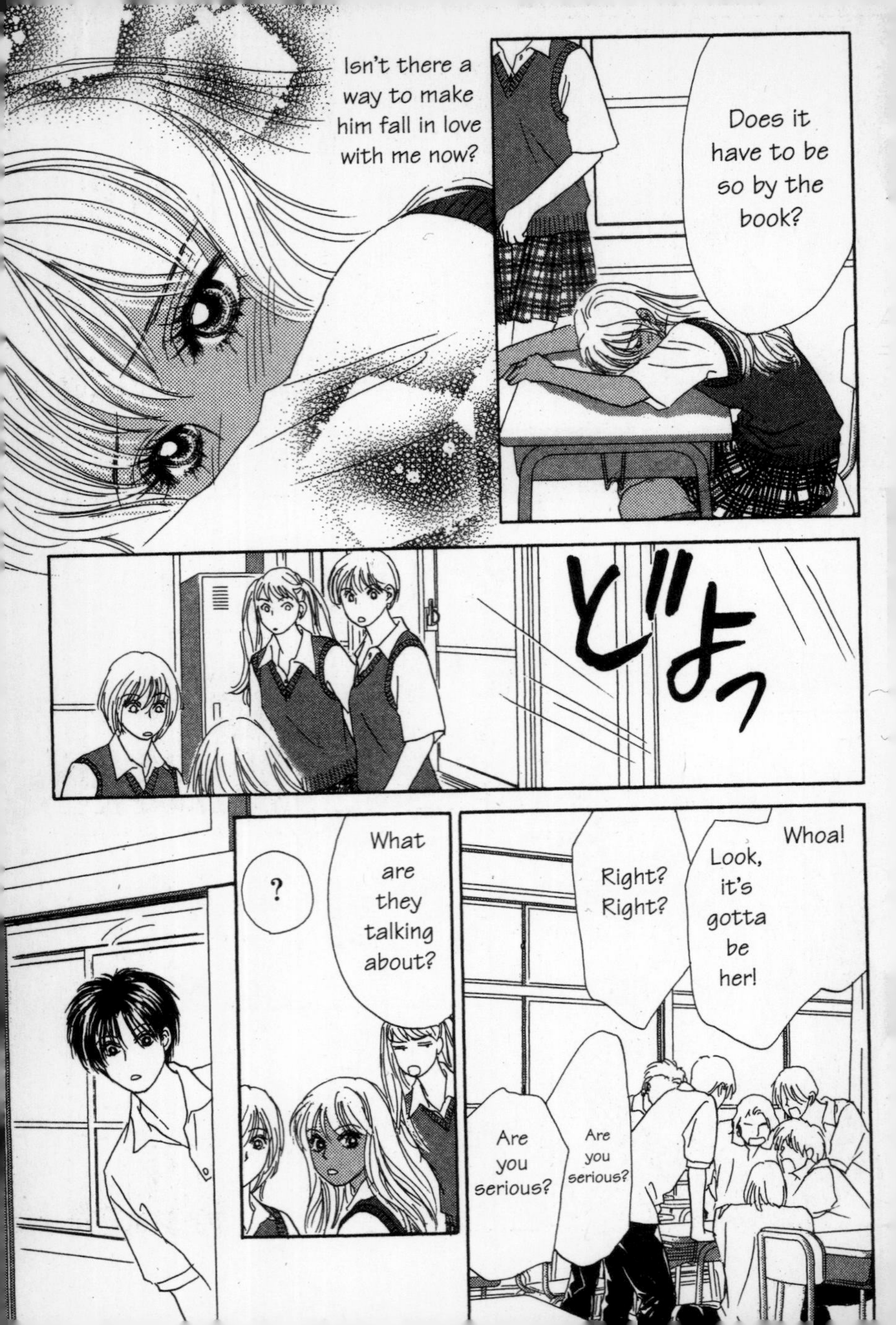
Does it have to be so by the book?
Isn't there a way to make him fall in love with me now?
どよっ
Whoa!
Look, it's gotta be her!
Right? Right?
Are you serious?
Are you serious?
What are they talking about?
?

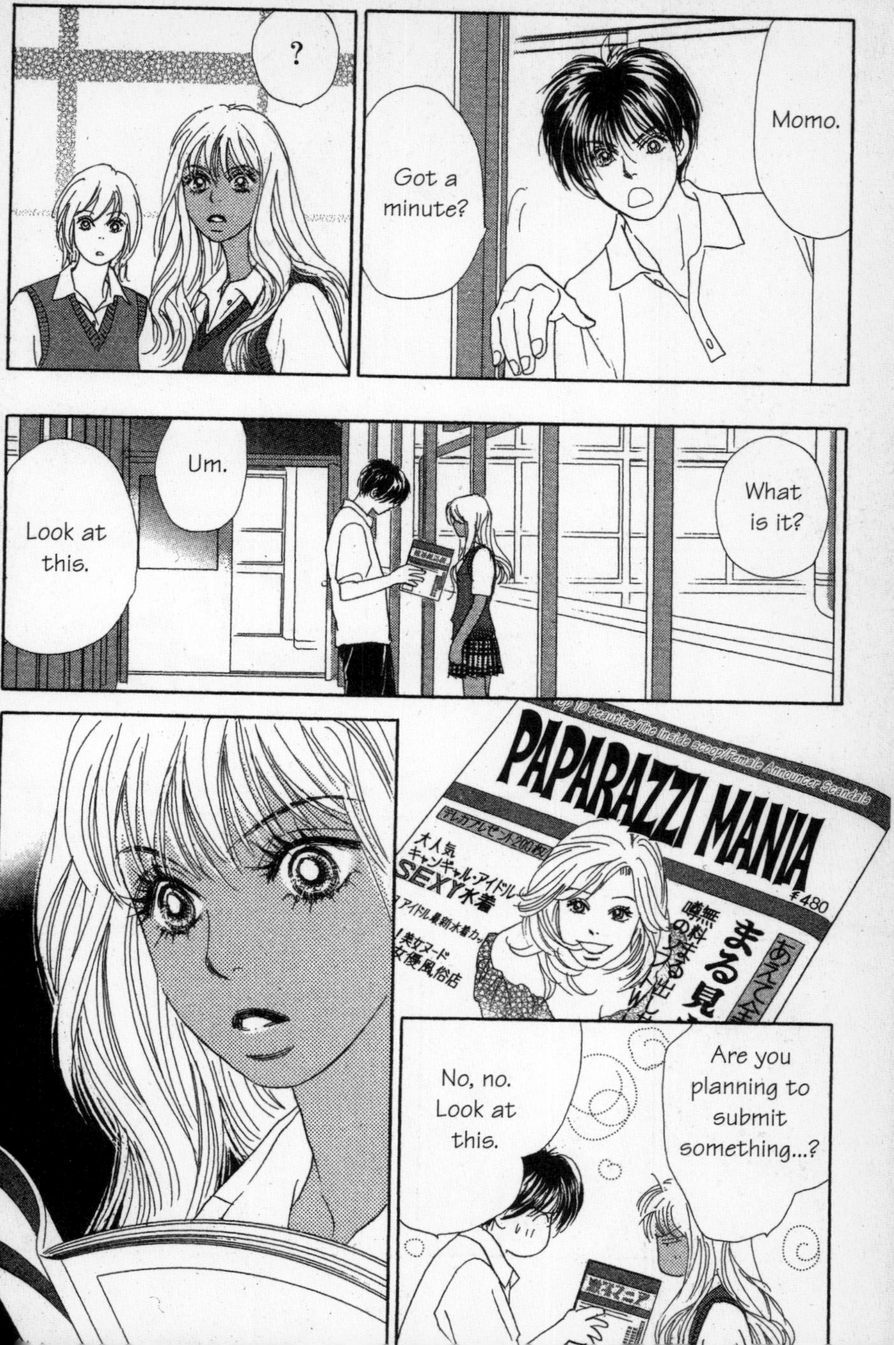

Momo.
Got a minute?
?
What is it?
Um.
Look at this.
op 10 beauties/the inside scoop/Female Announcer Scandals
PAPARAZZI MANIA
¥480
テレカプレゼント200枚
大人気
キャンギャル・アイドル
SEXY水着
アイドル最新水着カッ
美女ヌード
女優風俗店
まる見
Are you planning to submit something...?
No, no. Look at this.

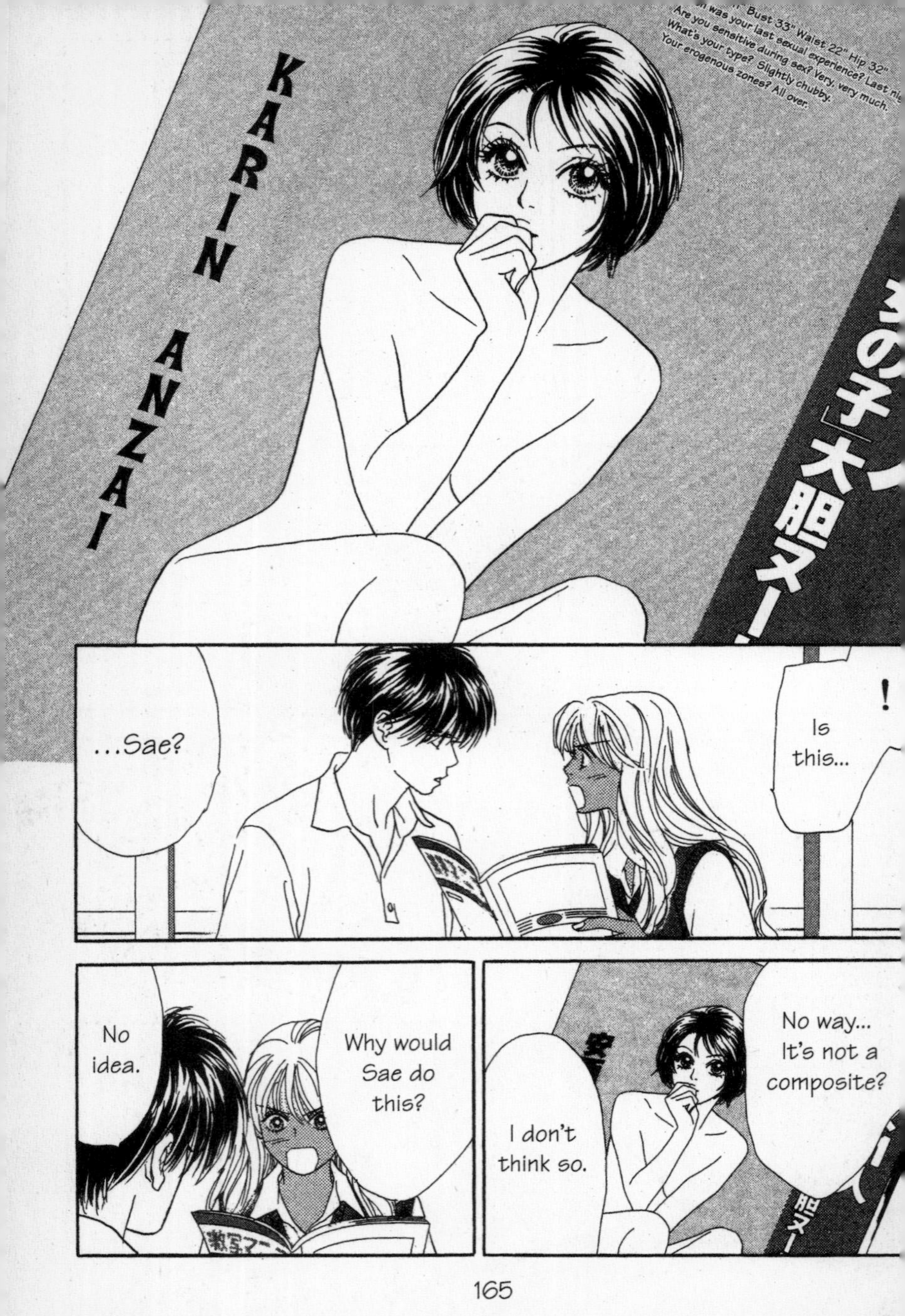
Bust 33" Waist 22" Hip 32"
was your last sexual experience? Last
Are you sensitive during sex? Very, very much.
What's your type? Slightly chubby.
Your erogenous zones? All over.
KARIN ANZAI
の子」大胆ヌー
!
Is this...
...Sae?
No way... It's not a composite?
I don't think so.
Why would Sae do this?
No idea.

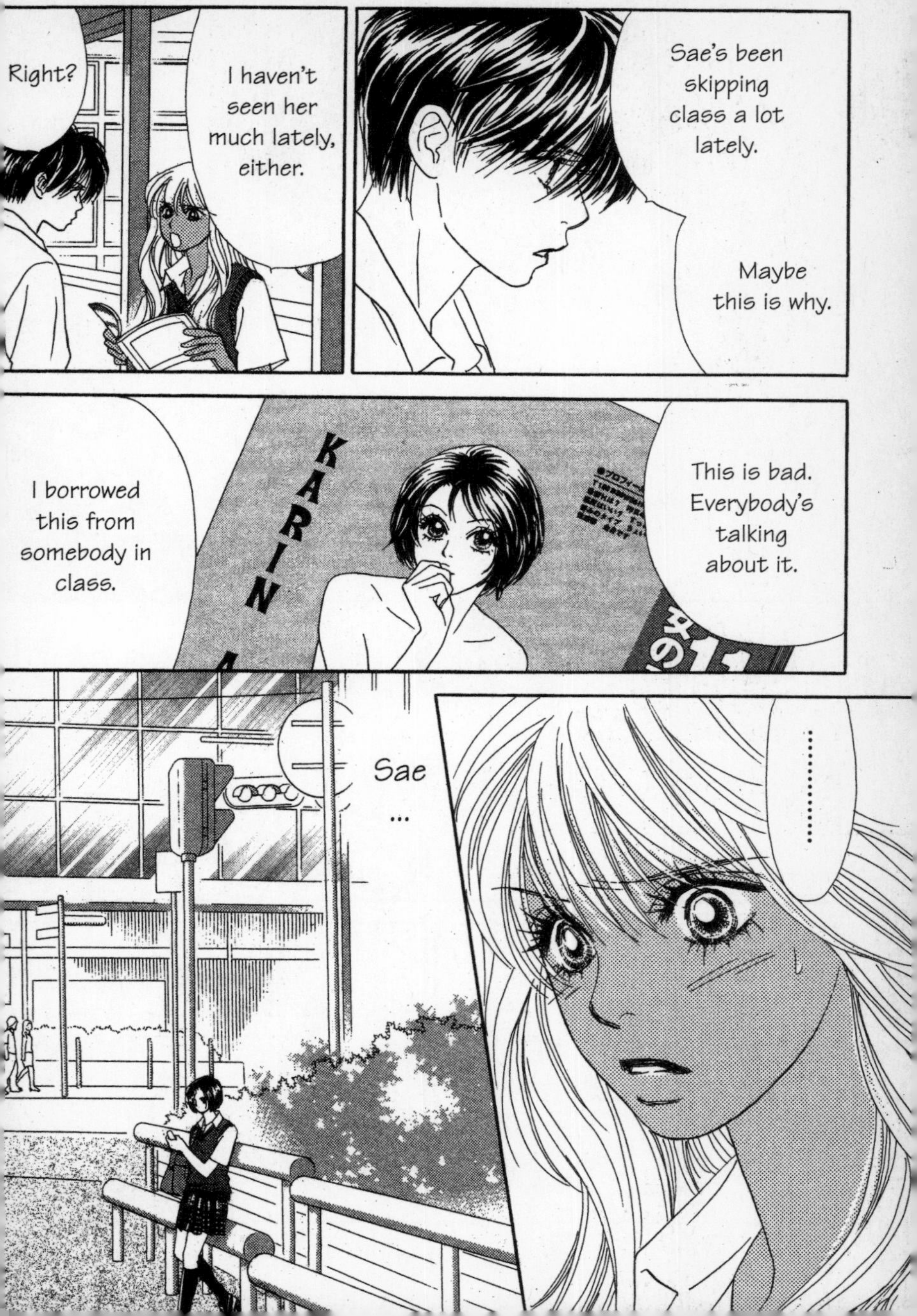
Sae's been skipping class a lot lately.
Maybe this is why.
I haven't seen her much lately, either.
Right?
This is bad. Everybody's talking about it.
KARIN
I borrowed this from somebody in class.
……
Sae ...

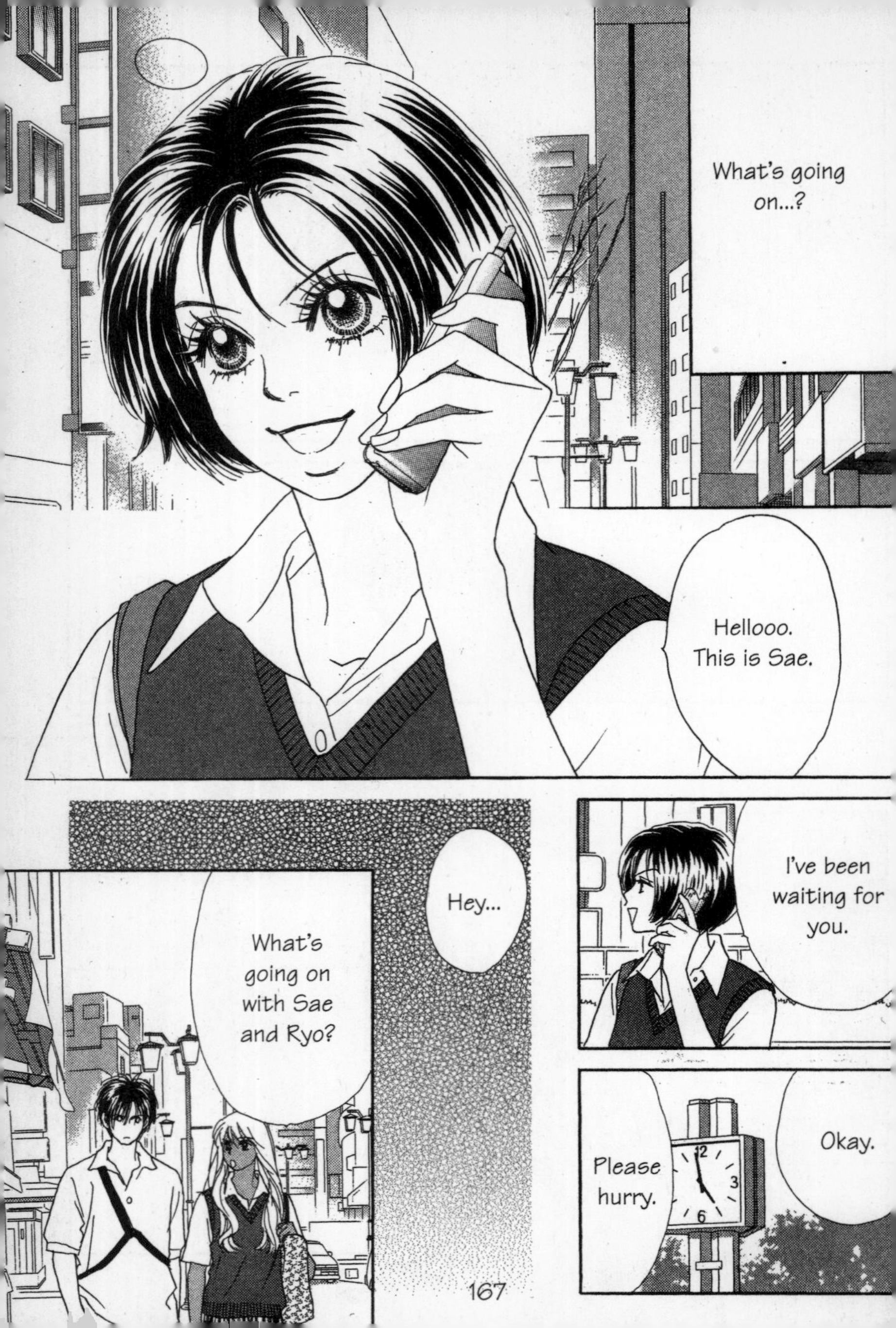
What's going on...?
Hellooo. This is Sae.
I've been waiting for you.
Okay.
Please hurry.
Hey...
What's going on with Sae and Ryo?

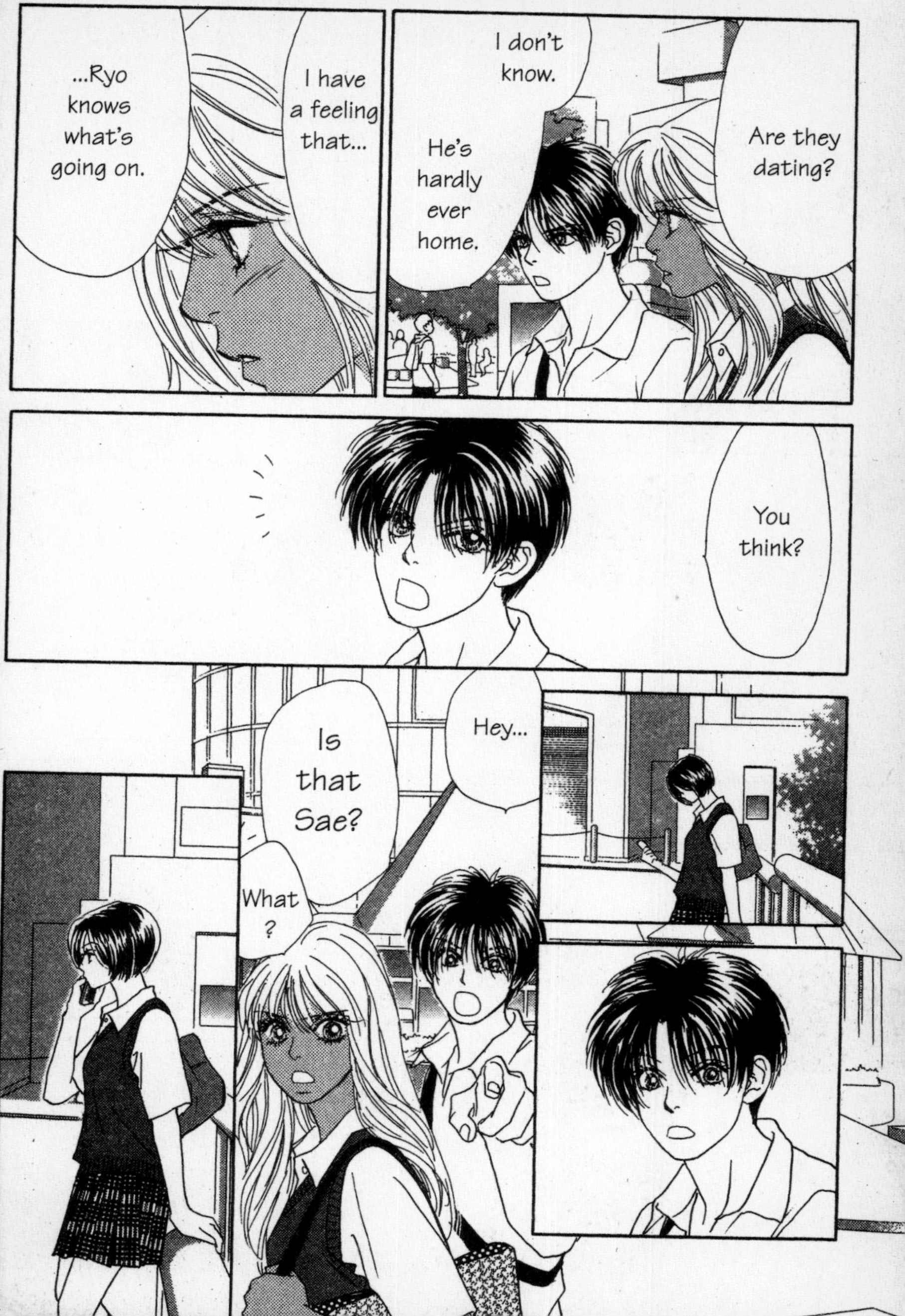
Are they dating?
I don't know.
He's hardly ever home.
I have a feeling that...
...Ryo knows what's going on.
You think?
Hey...
Is that Sae?
What ?

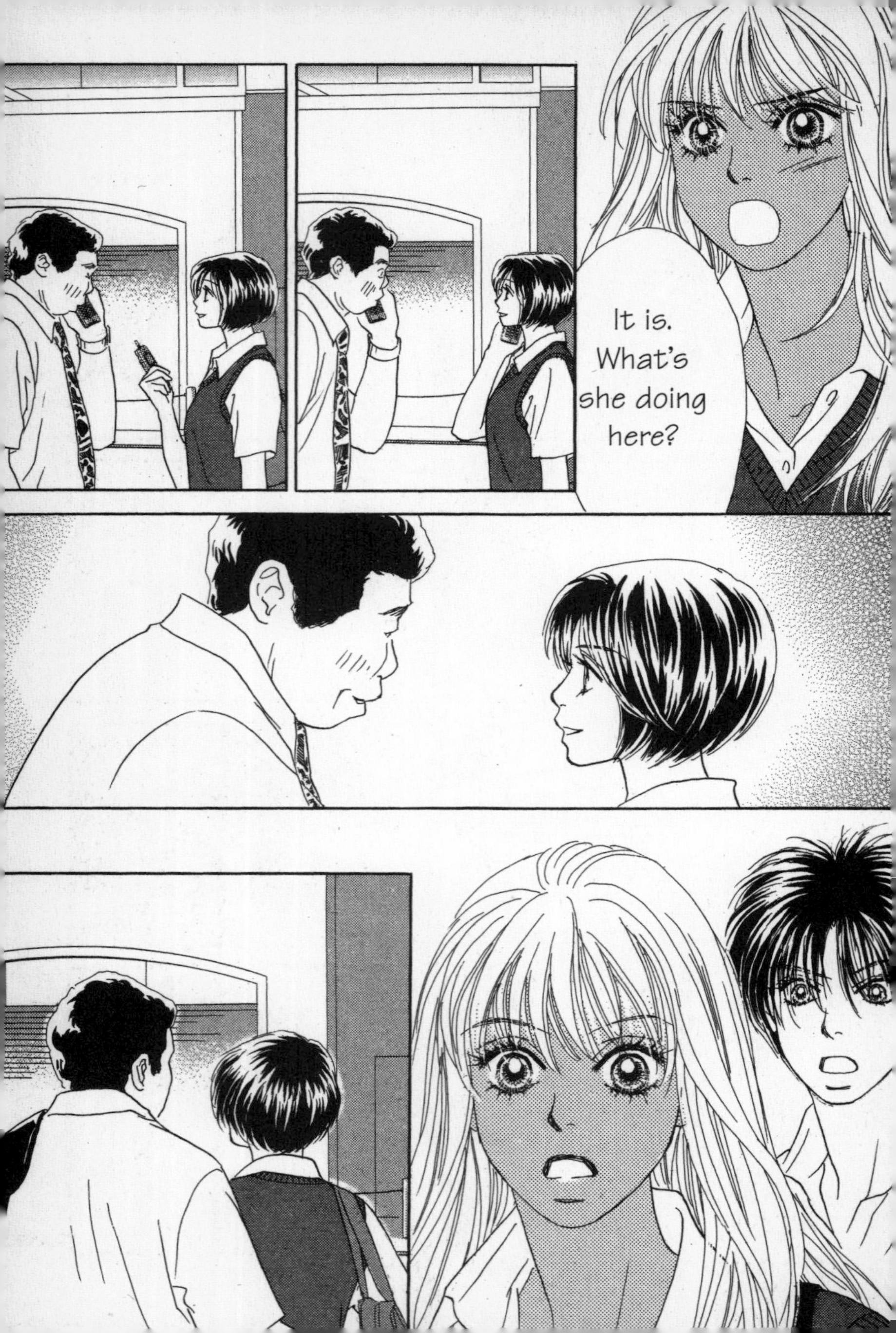
It is. What's she doing here?

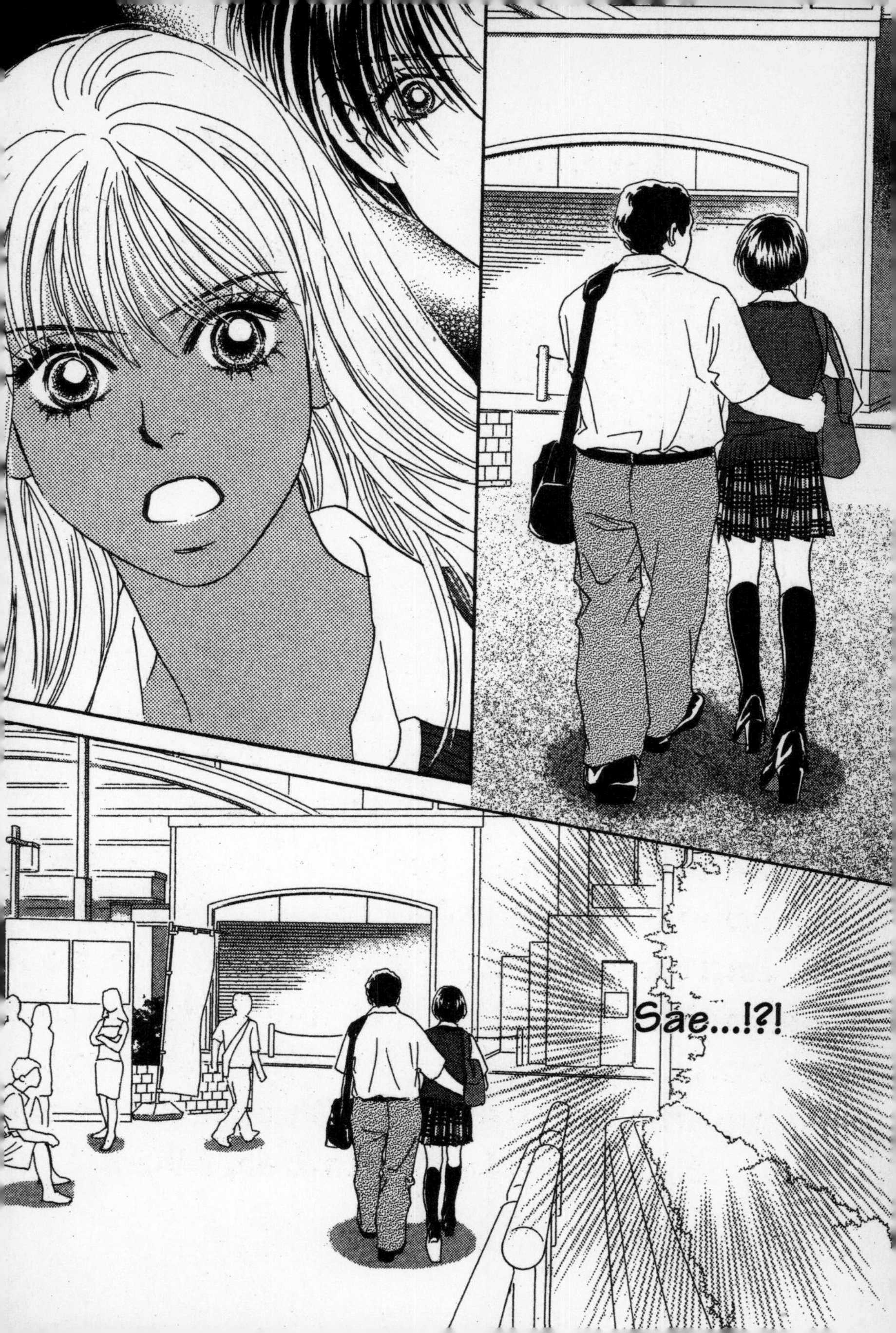
Sae...!?!

COMING SOON IN

Peach Girl
Change of Heart

Momo finally knows for sure that Kiley is in love with Misao. But Momo's plans to make Kiley love her more are put on hold when she discovers that Sae has been posing for erotic photos in some sleazy magazines. When they spy her handing money over to Kiley's skanky older brother, Ryo, they confront her and demand to know what's up. Sae confesses that she's in love...but no one can believe with who! Find out what happens in Peach Girl: Change of Heart 5, coming in November, 2003!

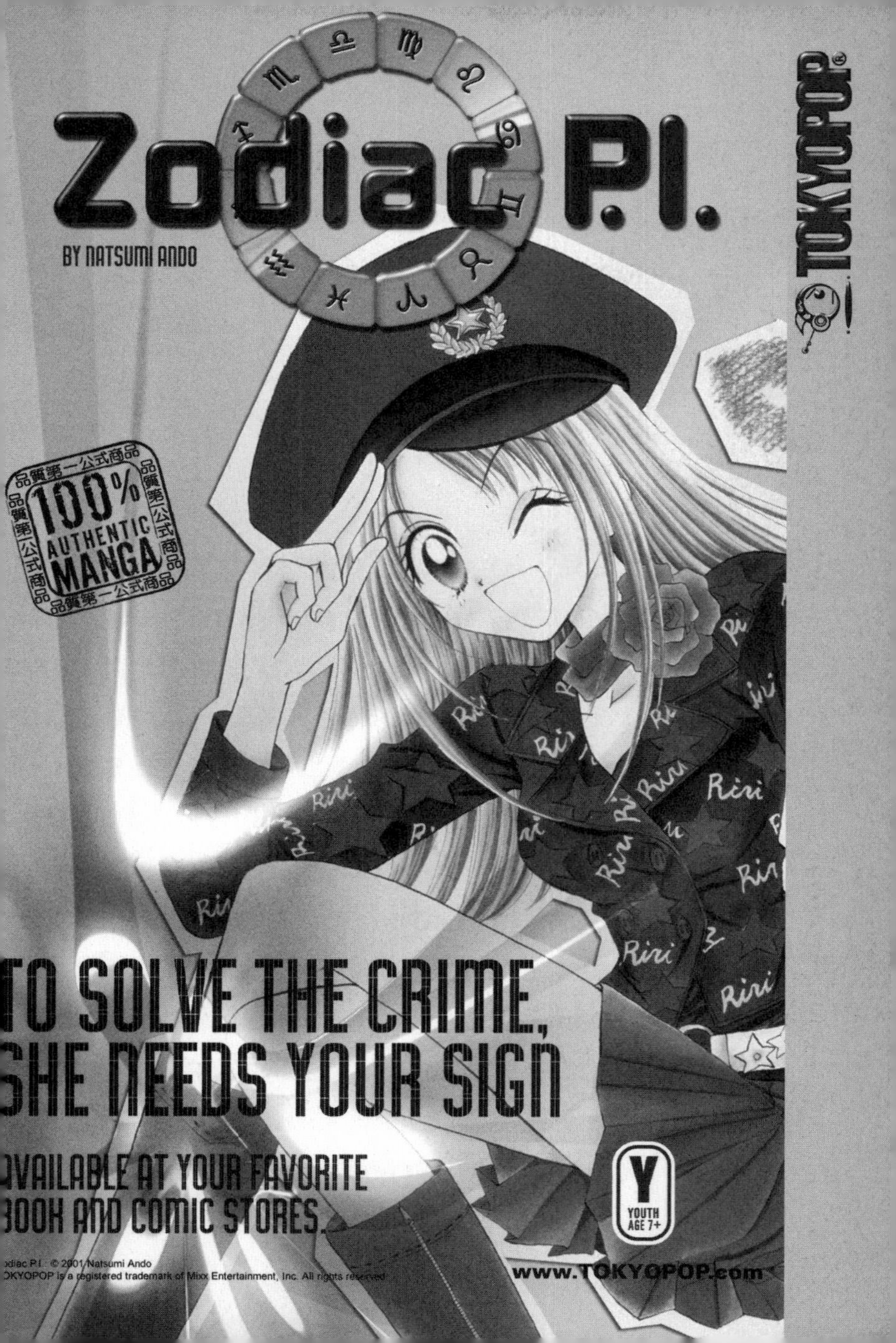
Zodiac P.I.
BY NATSUMI ANDO
TOKYOPOP®
品質第一公式商品
100% AUTHENTIC MANGA
TO SOLVE THE CRIME,
SHE NEEDS YOUR SIGN
VAILABLE AT YOUR FAVORITE
BOOK AND COMIC STORES.
Y YOUTH AGE 7+
odiac P.I. © 2001 Natsumi Ando
OKYOPOP is a registered trademark of Mixx Entertainment, Inc. All rights reserved.
www.TOKYOPOP.com

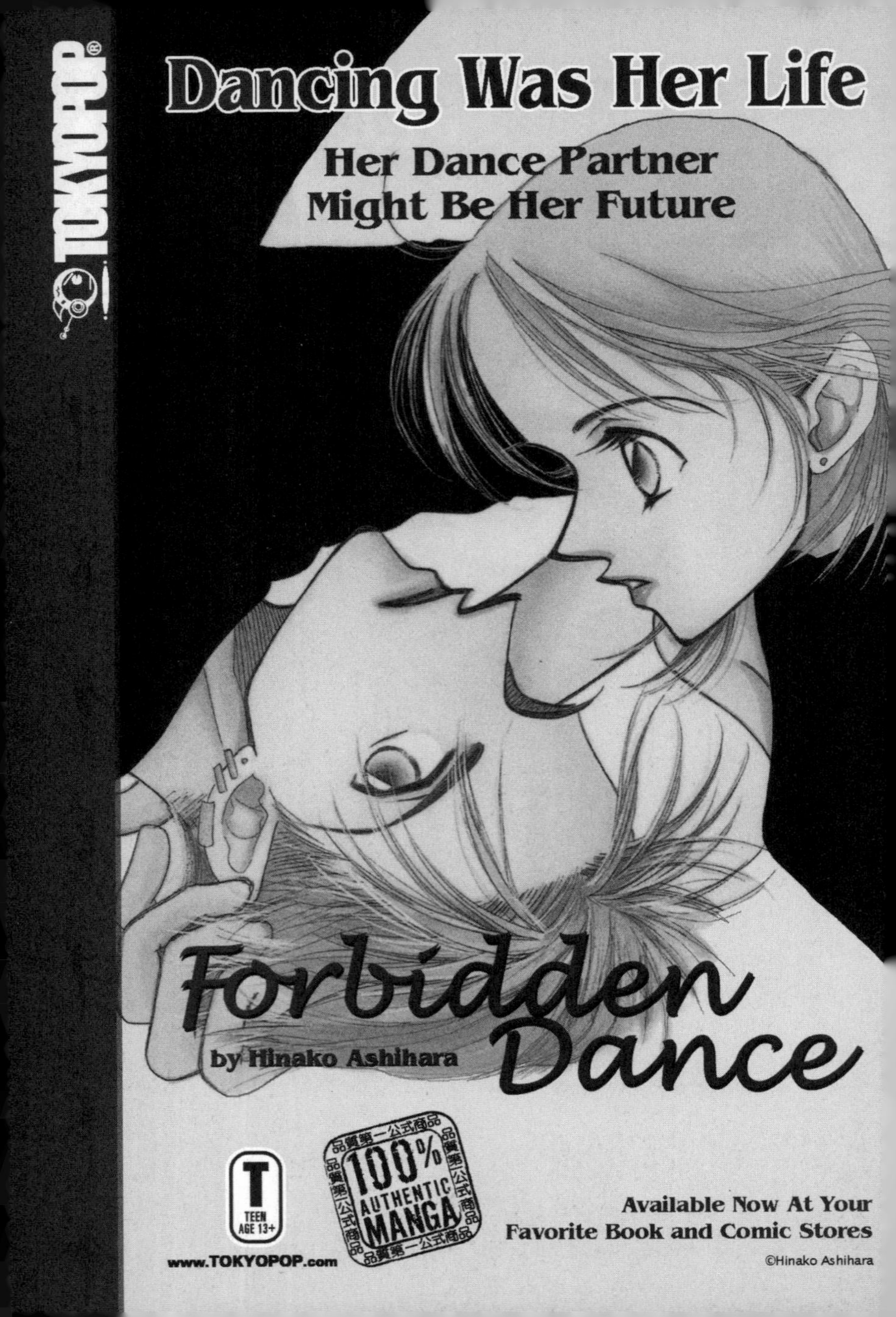
TOKYOPOP
Dancing Was Her Life
Her Dance Partner
Might Be Her Future
Forbidden
Dance
by Hinako Ashihara
T
TEEN
AGE 13+
100%
AUTHENTIC
MANGA
Available Now At Your
Favorite Book and Comic Stores
www.TOKYOPOP.com
©Hinako Ashihara

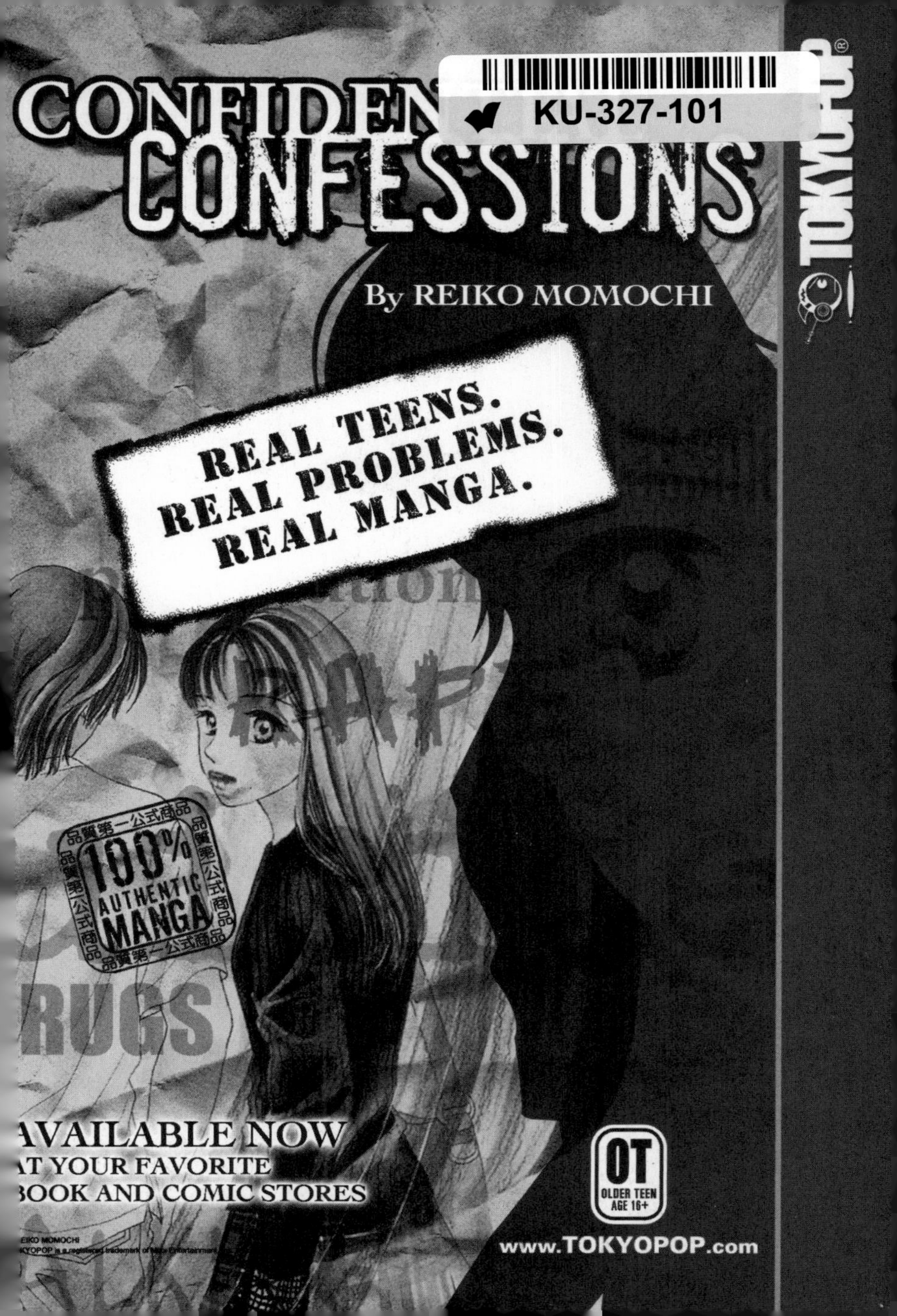
CONFIDEN
CONFESSIONS
By REIKO MOMOCHI
REAL TEENS.
REAL PROBLEMS.
REAL MANGA.
100% AUTHENTIC MANGA
品質第一公式商品
RUGS
AVAILABLE NOW
AT YOUR FAVORITE
BOOK AND COMIC STORES
OT
OLDER TEEN AGE 16+
www.TOKYOPOP.com
TOKYOPOP